The Translator and Editor

WAYNE A. REBHORN is the Mildred Hajek Vacek and John Roman Vacek Chair of English at the University of Texas at Austin, where he teaches English, Italian, and comparative literature. He is the author of *The Emperor of Men's Minds: Literature and the Renaissance Discourse of Rhetoric*, *Foxes and Lions: Machiavelli's Confidence Men*, and *Courtly Performance: Masking and Festivity in Castiglione's Book of the Courtier*. He has edited or coedited George Puttenham's *Art of English Poesy*, Thomas More's *Utopia*, and *Creative Imitation: New Essays on Renaissance Literature*. He is the translator of Boccaccio's *Decameron* and translator and editor of the Norton Critical Edition of *The Decameron*.

NORTON CRITICAL EDITIONS
RENAISSANCE

CASTIGLIONE, THE BOOK OF THE COURTIER
CERVANTES, DON QUIJOTE
DONNE, JOHN DONNE'S POETRY
ELIZABETH I AND HER AGE
ERASMUS, THE PRAISE OF FOLLY AND OTHER WRITINGS
THE GOLDEN AGE OF SPANISH DRAMA
JONSON, BEN JONSON'S PLAYS AND MASQUES
KYD, THE SPANISH TRAGEDY
LAZARILLO DE TORMES
MACHIAVELLI, THE PRINCE
MARLOWE, DOCTOR FAUSTUS
MIDDLETON & DEKKER, THE ROARING GIRL
MORE, UTOPIA
SOR JUANA INÉS DE LA CRUZ, SELECTED WORKS
SEVENTEENTH-CENTURY BRITISH POETRY, 1603–1660
SHAKESPEARE, ANTONY AND CLEOPATRA
SHAKESPEARE, AS YOU LIKE IT
SHAKESPEARE, HAMLET
SHAKESPEARE, 1 HENRY IV
SHAKESPEARE, JULIUS CAESAR
SHAKESPEARE, KING LEAR
SHAKESPEARE, MACBETH
SHAKESPEARE, MEASURE FOR MEASURE
SHAKESPEARE, THE MERCHANT OF VENICE
SHAKESPEARE, A MIDSUMMER NIGHT'S DREAM
SHAKESPEARE, OTHELLO
SHAKESPEARE, RICHARD III
SHAKESPEARE, ROMEO AND JULIET
SHAKESPEARE, THE TAMING OF THE SHREW
SHAKESPEARE, THE TEMPEST
SPENSER, EDMUND SPENSER'S POETRY
WEBSTER, THE DUCHESS OF MALFI

For a complete list of Norton Critical Editions, visit
wwnorton.com/nortoncriticals

A NORTON CRITICAL EDITION

Niccolò Machiavelli

THE PRINCE

A REVISED TRANSLATION
BACKGROUNDS
INTERPRETATIONS

THIRD EDITION

Edited and with a Revised Translation by

WAYNE A. REBHORN
UNIVERSITY OF TEXAS AT AUSTIN

W • W • NORTON & COMPANY • *New York* • *London*

W. W. Norton & Company has been independent since its founding in 1923, when William Warder Norton and Mary D. Herter Norton first published lectures delivered at the People's Institute, the adult education division of New York City's Cooper Union. The firm soon expanded its program beyond the Institute, publishing books by celebrated academics from America and abroad. By midcentury, the two major pillars of Norton's publishing program—trade books and college texts—were firmly established. In the 1950s, the Norton family transferred control of the company to its employees, and today—with a staff of five hundred and hundreds of trade, college, and professional titles published each year—W. W. Norton & Company stands as the largest and oldest publishing house owned wholly by its employees.

Printed in the United States of America

Manufacturing by Maple Press
Book design by Antonina Krass
Production manager: Stephen Sajdak

ISBN: 978-0-393-93691-9 (pbk.)

W. W. Norton & Company, Inc., 500 Fifth Avenue, New York, N.Y. 10110
www.wwnorton.com
W. W. Norton & Company Ltd., 15 Carlisle Street, London W1D 3BS

1 2 3 4 5 6 7 8 9 0

For Marlette

In Gratitude for More Than Fifty Years of Happiness

Contents

Introduction

Machiavelli and the Crisis of the Renaissance Italian City-State

Machiavelli wrote many of his best-known works—*The Prince* and the *Discourses,* in particular—between 1512 and 1520, years that coincided with the most profound political crisis of the Italian Renaissance. True, the political history of Italy in the Middle Ages and the Renaissance can be read as an endless series of political crises of every sort and at every level. The peninsula was divided into a host of states, large and small, and those states had been fighting one another for centuries before Machiavelli was born in 1469. Florence, for instance, was continually battling with Pisa, Siena, and other nearby city-states in an attempt to gain control of Tuscany. There were also continual power struggles *within* city-states: rivalries among noble families seeking political control, rivalries between the nobility and the rising class of wealthy merchants and bankers, rivalries between the major and minor guilds through which urban life was often organized. Moreover, since cities were usually subdivided into quarters or neighborhoods, the people in them also competed with one another for power and prestige. The *palio,* the annual horse race in Siena that pitted the city's *contrade,* or neighborhoods, against one another, still occurs today, serving as a more or less ritualized acting out of hostilities; in the Middle Ages and Renaissance those hostilities often had bloodier and more deadly consequences—and not just in Siena.

If a certain amount of external and internal political conflict persisted in Italy throughout the Middle Ages and the Renaissance, there was a relatively brief period when something like a balance of power was struck among the five principal states of the peninsula: Florence, Milan, Venice, the Papal States, and Naples. This peaceful interlude began in 1454 and lasted until 1494, a period coinciding with what is considered the Golden Age of Florence, when the Medici were the de facto rulers of the city. Indeed, for most of this period, from 1469 until his death in 1492, Lorenzo de' Medici—celebrated as Lorenzo the Magnificent—headed both his family and his city, and he followed his predecessors by bestowing lavish patronage on writers, scholars, philosophers, and artists. When he died, the period of peace among the Italian city-states was already coming to an end, an end that became definitive in 1494 when Charles VIII of France invaded the peninsula to seize the Kingdom of Naples.

The so-called Italian Wars, following the French invasion, engulfed practically all the states of the peninsula and involved, at different times, not just France but Spain, the Holy Roman Empire, and even England, Scotland, and the Ottoman Turks. Charles VIII did indeed capture Naples, if only for a short while, but what was most important about his invasion was what its brief success revealed—namely, the fundamental political and military weakness of the Italian city-states, which were no match for the powerful nations that would determine the political history of Europe from the sixteenth century on. The peninsula thus became the scene of an unintended proxy war, a struggle between France on the one side and Spain and the Holy Roman Empire on the other for dominance not just in Italy but in Europe more generally. All of these players fought one another inconclusively until 1519, for in that year, when Charles V, the king of Spain, was named the Holy Roman Emperor, the end was near. Neither France nor the Italian city-states could really match Charles with his two powerful kingdoms.

The crisis reached its peak in 1527. The French had been decisively defeated in 1525 and driven out of Italy, and in early 1527 Charles invaded the peninsula at the head of thirty-four-thousand-man army, which quickly seized Lombardy and Florence on its way to Rome. Although the army contained a large contingent of Spanish troops, the bulk of it was made up of Swiss mercenaries, many of whom were Lutherans, and when none of the soldiers received his pay in April, they mutinied and forced their commanders to lead them directly on to Rome, which had only a handful of soldiers for defense. And so, on May 6, 1527, the city fell, and the infamous Sack of Rome began. Charles's troops massacred the several hundred men who were defending the city; they looted churches and monasteries and the palaces of wealthy cardinals; women, including nuns, were raped; and thousands of civilians were wounded or murdered. The pope had fled to the Castel Sant'Angelo, but with hardly anyone left to defend him, he, too, surrendered. Charles, Spain, and the Empire were now in control of practically the entire Italian peninsula.

All of these developments impacted Florence and Machiavelli as well because his adult years coincided with the years of the crisis, a time when he was deeply engaged in Florentine—and hence, Italian—politics. In 1494, the Florentines threw out Piero de' Medici, the hapless son of Lorenzo the Magnificent, who had died in 1492. The charismatic priest Girolamo Savonarola won over the people, and they made republican reforms in the government at his urging.

Initially, they were taken by Savonarola's vision of Florence as an ideal Christian state, but by 1498 he had lost their support, and having been excommunicated by Pope Alexander VI the year before, he was arrested, tried, hanged, and finally burned at the stake in the Piazza della Signoria on May 23.

The Florentines set up a new republic in the same year, and Machiavelli quickly rose to a position of prominence within it. Since 1494, he had been working as a clerk in the Second Chancery, and in 1498, he was made its secretary, in essence its head, and was also appointed secretary to *The Ten of Peace and Liberty,* a committee overseeing military matters and diplomacy recently merged with the Second Chancery. Because of his political acumen, Machiavelli was repeatedly sent on important diplomatic missions both inside and outside Italy. Within the country he went to meet with Cesare Borgia in 1502, and outside it he made several trips to France, with which Florence was allied up until the fall of the Republic in 1512. He was also dispatched as Florence's emissary to the Holy Roman Empire, which took him through some of the German-speaking areas in central Europe, a trip that led him, later on, to praise the German city-states in Chapter 10 of *The Prince.*

Piero Soderini, a member of a prominent Florentine family, had played a significant role in the development of Florence's republican government after the expulsion of the Medici, and in 1502, when it became too unstable because of political factionalism, he was made the city's *Gonfaloniere a vita,* its chief executive officer or magistrate, for life. Machiavelli became one of Soderini's most trusted advisers and was thus in a position to direct, or at least to influence, both the foreign relations and the military affairs of the city. By 1506, he had convinced Soderini to establish a citizen militia, and in 1509 he led it against Pisa, capturing the city, a victory that had eluded previous mercenary armies and that thus seemed to prove Machiavelli's arguments in favor of a citizen militia. But just three years later, when a significant portion of that militia was sent to defend the nearby town of Prato from the army of Charles V, the Spanish easily routed them, prompting the Signoria to surrender the city, to send Soderini into exile, and to accept the Medici as their rulers once again.

Machiavelli himself was exiled, sent to spend what would amount to eight long years on his farm in Sant'Andrea in Percussina, with only occasional visits to his beloved Florence. Adding injury to insult, the Medici had Machiavelli arrested and imprisoned on February 12, 1513, because his name was found on a list of prominent Florentines plotting against them. Machiavelli was actually innocent, but he might have languished for months or even years in prison had not Giovanni de' Medici been elected Pope Leo X on March 11, 1513, and shortly thereafter granted amnesty to all political prisoners. Machiavelli was released—but only to be sent back once again to his farm.

The period of 1512–20 was thus the low point in Machiavelli's life. His farm provided just enough to live on, he could not return to Florence, a city he said, in a letter of 1527, he loved more than his own soul, and he could not play an active role in its government. He compensated for all of that by writing, beginning the *Discourses* some time after 1512, but then interrupting that work to write the book that would ensure his immortality as a political thinker, *The Prince,* which he had finished by the beginning of 1516 and dedicated to the Medici. According to a letter he wrote to his friend Francesco Vettori on December 10, 1513, he wanted to use his treatise as part of a "job application," showing the Medici his potential worth as a political adviser. It is not clear that they ever read *The Prince,* but if they did, it did not persuade them to offer Machiavelli the position he desired. After finishing his little treatise, he returned to writing the *Discourses,* which celebrates the republican government of Rome as a model for modern states.

When Lorenzo de' Medici died, in 1520, he was succeeded by Cardinal Giulio de' Medici as the head of the family. He admired Machiavelli as a thinker and finally allowed him back into Florence, but only as the city's official historiographer. By 1525, Machiavelli had completed his *Florentine Histories,* which he presented to his Medici patron, who had by then become Pope Clement VII. Machiavelli was never in the family's inner circle, although they respected his political acumen sufficiently to solicit a treatise from him on how to reform the government of Florence in 1520—advice they essentially ignored—and in 1526 they put him in charge of overseeing Florence's fortifications. When the Florentines, taking advantage of the disarray of Charles V's troops after the Sack of Rome in 1527, threw out the Medici again, Machiavelli expected to be given an important position in the government, but because he had been serving the Medici, the new republic did not trust him, and he died only a few months later.

The republic the Florentines created in 1527 was to be their last taste of democracy. The city was besieged by imperial troops in October 1529 and surrendered in August the following year. Alessandro de' Medici was chosen as the head of the government, and in 1533 he became a duke, thus turning his family into the hereditary rulers of Florence, which eventually morphed into the Grand Duchy of Tuscany in 1569. Essentially, then, by 1529–30 the political independence of Florence, along with that of all the other states in the peninsula except for Venice, was gone forever. All of them were now under the control, direct or indirect, of Spain and the Holy Roman Empire. The great political crisis of the Italian Renaissance, which had begun in 1494, had reached its climax, the fever had burst, and unfortunately for the city-states of Italy, the patient had died.

Machiavelli did not live long enough to see these final developments, but even in 1527, the year of his death, he must have sensed that his dream of a bright political future for Italy was over. That dream informs the *Discourses,* which presents an idealized Roman republic as a model for contemporary Italian city-states. They could return to the great days of their Roman past by forming a citizen army to protect them from the likes of Spain and France—and they might even engage in wars of expansion and re-create the empire of their ancestors. That dream is also made explicit in the last chapter of *The Prince,* in which Machiavelli urges the Medici to take his advice and create a state that would drive the "barbarians" out of Italy. But by 1529–30, that dream was as dead as the independence of almost all the city-states in the peninsula.

Machiavelli Responds to the Crisis: From The Prince *to the* Discourses

I have been speaking of the political "crisis" of the Renaissance Italian city-states, using a medical term that refers now, as it did then, to the turning point in an acute disease or fever, after which the patient either recovers or dies. That word does not appear in Machiavelli's works, although, as we will see, the notion involved may be implicit in one of the key images he uses for his prince. Instead, Machiavelli defines the political instability and personal uncertainty he and his fellow Italians were experiencing by means of another very traditional word: *fortune,* or *fortuna,* to use Machiavelli's Italian. Usually, Machiavelli identifies *fortuna* as a force or power that acts on people, that produces the situations in which they find themselves, and that forces them to deal with obstacles they must overcome. In effect, he is personifying the concept, thereby evoking the goddess *Fortuna* who had been in existence since the time of the Romans. The latter derived her name from *fors,* meaning chance or luck or hazard, and although she was imagined as a fickle deity who presided over an unstable world, the Romans saw her mostly as a benevolent figure who gave humans what we would now call their "fortunes" or put them in a fortunate position or situation. In the Middle Ages and the Renaissance, *Fortuna* lived on, but was usually seen as a more neutral or even as a malevolent figure. She could raise humans up and place them in positions of power, but she could, just as likely, do the opposite. In the Christian universe, *Fortuna* was always subordinate to God, always carrying out God's plans, but since humans were generally not privy to them, Fortune became the allegorical representation of the mysterious, unstable, unpredictable, often threatening world they lived in.

Fortune makes dozens of appearances in *The Prince* and even more in the *Discourses,* and Machiavelli devotes the entire twenty-fifth chapter, the penultimate chapter, of the former work to the subject. At the start of the chapter, he de-personifies her, identifying Fortune with raging rivers and floods. Because he had elsewhere identified her with the "winds" (p. 56), the storms and flooding rivers they produce function as a "natural" allegory of the way Fortune damages the human world. Though usually presented as a threat, Fortune sometimes seems to be the prince's ally or even his benefactor, since Fortune may offer the possibility of triumph by providing the prince with the *opportunity* to overcome obstacles and thus achieve fame and glory—and political success—in the world. One example of this "benevolent" Fortune can be found in Chapter 20:

> princes become great by overcoming the difficulties and obstacles placed in their way, and therefore, especially when Fortune wants to enhance the reputation of a new prince, . . . she creates enemies for him and has them undertake campaigns against him, so that he may have reason to overcome them and to climb up higher on the ladder which his enemies have brought him. (pp. 67–68)

Fortune thus seems the prince's helpmeet, but, as we can see in the quotation above, that is only because she supplies him with the *opportunity* to display his skills. Moreover, that opportunity takes the form of "difficulties and obstacles," so that although Fortune seems benevolent by providing princes with the opportunity to achieve greatness, she is still challenging them to overcome her. Whether good or bad, Fortune is always the enemy.

As Machiavelli indicates in Chapter 7 of *The Prince,* he really does not want the prince to depend on Fortune at all, but rather on himself for what he accomplishes in the world. This vision of an independent prince who acquires and maintains his state with no real help from anyone or anything else defines in political terms one of the most enduring myths of the Renaissance—namely, the myth of what would much later be called "the self-made man," or as we should put it nowadays, "the self-made individual." I call it a myth because it is truly impossible for anyone to discount the role that culture plays in a person's development, even if a great deal of his or her success is due to individual intelligence, hard work, and determination. In part, Machiavelli may simply be reacting to the fact that the general prosperity of Italian city-states in the late Middle Ages and Renaissance afforded individuals a chance to improve their fortunes and rise up the social hierarchy, just as the political instability of those same states offered opportunities for aggressive mercenary leaders to replace the masters they served. In

Chapter 6 of *The Prince,* which is about those who rose to power by means of their own arms and skills, Machiavelli's chief examples are Moses, Cyrus, Romulus, and Theseus, all of whom were the founders or re-founders of states and who, if not mythical, often seem so in the accounts of them that Machiavelli would have read. In each case, he specifies that Fortune provided them with only the opportunities they needed, and that they essentially relied on their own abilities; on their cunning, persistence, and ruthlessness; and on "their own arms"—that is, on the military forces they created for themselves. This is singularly important for Machiavelli's prince, because "people are by nature fickle," and although they can be easily persuaded to do something, it is hard to keep them persuaded. Consequently, the prince must "arrange things so that when they no longer believed, they can be compelled to believe by force." This vision of a well-armed ruler informs one of Machiavelli's most famous judgments—namely, that "all the armed prophets are victorious and the unarmed ones come to ruin" (p. 19). His example of such an "unarmed prophet" is Savonarola, whose short-lived attempt to make Florence into a Christian republic ended tragically when he was burned alive in 1498.

To achieve independence and overcome the obstacles that Fortune places in his way, the prince, says Machiavelli, must rely on only himself and his ability. This last term is one possible rendering of Machiavelli's *virtù,* a polysemous word that seems almost beyond translation both because it has so many meanings and because more than one may be involved any time it is used. At one extreme, the word identifies what it does today: some admirable moral quality. Quite frequently, it can be translated in a more neutral fashion as "ability," "skill," or "talent." However, since, in using his *virtù,* the prince often does so by setting conventional morality aside, the word could often be more accurately rendered as "cunning," "resourcefulness," or "duplicity." These meanings point to the prince's mental agility and craftiness: he is the fox of Chapter 18, who not only recognizes the traps that are set for him but knows "how to do a good job of coloring over this character, and to be a great pretender and dissembler" (p. 56), someone who will break his word when that is necessary. Finally, *virtù,* like the Latin *virtus* from which it comes, can mean "energy," "vigor," "(martial) prowess," "force," or "violence." The Latin *virtus,* harkening back to its root *vir* (man), meant "manliness," but a manliness identified with the attributes of the warrior and ruler. *Virtù* signifies such manliness as well. Perhaps this key word has so many meanings simply because the prince's enemy, Fortune, is so protean a figure; she appears in myriad guises because she represents all the contingencies of the historical world, and *virtù* must be equally multifaceted to deal with her.

If a prince has *virtù*, that seems to mean—more often than not—that he is capable of *seeing* what other men cannot. Sight involves the ability to penetrate and manipulate appearances, thus allowing the prince, for instance, to convince others that he has various virtues he may not actually possess simply by making a show of them. But "to see" is another way of saying "to understand": for the prince, *sight* and *insight* are thus synonymous.

Insight is also what Machiavelli feels he himself possesses and aims to offer his readers in his works, as he attempts to formulate rules and strategies and to model various ways of analyzing the world. Sometimes he does this quite directly, as when he presents relatively simple, straightforward taxonomies of the different sorts of states at the start of *The Prince*. Later on in that text, when he is grappling with situations and events so complex that it is virtually impossible to reduce them to a single rule, he still invites us to follow his reasoning process as he goes from a generalization to some cold hard fact that qualifies it and from there to a new generalization, after which the entire process may be repeated again. At times, Machiavelli admits the importance of specificities rather than generalizations, such as when he is discussing whether a prince should build fortresses, but even so, he still wants to formulate rules. As he puts it: "although one cannot provide a definitive judgment about [building fortresses] without going into the particular circumstances of those states in which some similar deliberation had to be made, nevertheless I will speak in as general a way as the subject matter itself will allow" (p. 66). Later, in the same chapter, Machiavelli begins a paragraph by saying that a prince will find more loyalty in those who were considered suspect at the start of his reign than in those he trusted, but after a single example, Machiavelli seems to give up trying to formulate rules: "on this matter one cannot speak in generalities, because it varies according to the case involved." And yet, the very next sentence opens with "I will only say this" (p. 68), and he then goes on to provide an analysis, using generalizations to explain why princes can place more trust in those who began as their enemies than in those they trusted from the start.

Machiavelli never really gives up on rational analysis and the formulation of rules, even when the process seems to self-destruct. That problem is most dramatically revealed in Chapter 19, which has a specifically pedagogical purpose: teaching princes how to avoid hatred and contempt. What Machiavelli says there, for example, about the assassination of the Roman emperor Marcus Aurelius Antoninus Caracalla shows how hard he must struggle to "explain" that assassination so the reader can avoid something similar. Machiavelli offers an initial explanatory generalization for what happened (Antoninus was so cruel and killed so many people that he was universally hated), but he follows it immediately with a qualification (nevertheless, only a man possessing an "obstinate spirit" [p. 63] will really be a threat, and such men are rare). This then leads to yet another generalization (do not keep a man you injured in your service), followed by yet another qualification (do not threaten that man every day while keeping him around you), which leads to Machiavelli's "conclusion" about Antoninus's failure: "This was a rash thing to do, and as it happened, one that led to his ruin" (p. 64). The problem here is that there are so many qualifications and additional generalizations that the final "rule" winds up seeming to apply to only this one particular case, which means it cannot really function as a rule at all. Still, that failure does not lead Machiavelli ever to abandon rational analysis.

To put the matter differently, the insights Machiavelli offers us are a matter of demystifying the workings of politics, a process almost always followed by a prescription for behavior to be applied in the future. His interest in demystification explains why he frequently expresses his opposition to what he considers dubious conventional wisdom, such as that contained in "that trite proverb, that 'he who builds on the people builds on mud'" (p. 33). Machiavelli also expresses his hostility to the conventional thinking of his contemporaries by mocking them for failing to explain things, labeling them, instead, "marvelous" or "miraculous," terms he always treats with withering scorn. For instance, in Chapter 17 of *The Prince,* which is devoted to the question of whether it is better to be loved or feared, Machiavelli specifically recommends that the prince needs to inspire fear in his role as a military leader. Not only must he *do* horrifyingly cruel things at times but he must also have a *reputation* for cruelty if he is to control his army. People, he writes, think that because Hannibal kept his army unified and obedient, despite his soldiers' diverse origins and the ups and downs of their fortunes in battle, his success should be considered "marvelous"—in other words, a complete mystery. Machiavelli, as usual, has a rational explanation:

> This [success] could not have arisen from anything other than that inhuman cruelty of his, which, together with his numberless talents [*virtù*], always made him a figure of awe and terror in the sight of his soldiers, and without that, his other talents [*virtù*] would not have sufficed. (pp. 53–54)

If Machiavelli's Fortune operates in a seemingly whimsical universe, one in which divine control is either absent or irrelevant, human behavior and historical events can and must be explained by reason, not by appealing to marvels and miracles.

The prince must not just possess superior sight and insight, however; he must also have foresight, the ability to generalize from what he knows and to make predictions about what Fortune will throw at him in the future. The need for foresight is implicit in *The Prince,* just as it is in the *Discourses,* for it provides a rationale, indeed *the* rationale, for the "instruction" Machiavelli is imparting. Foresight, however, is made explicit and dramatized in one of the key images he uses for the prince: that of the doctor. In Chapter 3 of *The Prince,* when Machiavelli praises the Romans' methods for dealing with newly acquired territory, he argues that they "did what all wise princes ought to do: they have to keep an eye not only on present troubles but on future ones, and make every effort to oppose them." He then shifts from the metaphor of sight to that of medicine:

> if troubles are seen from afar, they can easily be remedied, but if you wait until they are on top of you, there is no time to use medicine, since the malady has become incurable. (p. 9)

Words involving some idea of remedy or cure appear over a dozen times in *The Prince,* and every time such words occur, they inevitably conjure up the image of the prince-as-doctor who not only must cure the ills with which Fortune afflicts the state but must seek to identify them ahead of time in order to prevent them from becoming potentially lethal—that is, from becoming the kind of *crisis* that the city-states of Renaissance Italy were going through during Machiavelli's lifetime. The problem here is that Fortune is always changing her tactics, so that the prince—or the Roman state, or any political entity—can never really avoid having to deal with crises. In short, if the prince is a doctor, then the doctor must always be "in."

There are, of course, many *different* diseases the state has to face, and that points to another way to conceptualize what Machiavelli means by *virtù.* As was noted earlier, because Fortune is constantly changing, the prince must be able to change constantly as well. In other words, he must be able to vary the roles he plays, depending on how the winds of Fortune are blowing. The notion that the prince must play many parts is the essence of the advice Machiavelli offers in Chapters 15 through 19 of *The Prince.* Those chapters are devoted to virtues—mercy, faithfulness, integrity, humanity, religion—that countless medieval and Renaissance books of advice for princes, books belonging to the tradition of the *Speculum principis,* or Mirror for Princes, identified as the core values every ruler had to possess. Machiavelli is opposed to this tradition on pragmatic grounds: one cannot always do the *right* thing in politics. It is important to note, however, what he is *not* saying here: he is *not* endorsing the wholesale abandonment of traditional virtues. On the contrary, he insists that the prince should strive to be good, but—and this *but* is crucial—only if that does not threaten his survival. Machiavelli's final word on the subject is simple: "a prince who wants to preserve himself must learn how not to be good, and to use this knowledge and not use it as necessity requires" (p. 49).

Furthermore, Machiavelli actually wants the prince to play the role of benevolent ruler. Functioning as a kind of impresario, he should stage impressive spectacles for his subjects designed to enhance their positive view of him. "A prince," writes Machiavelli, "must . . . show himself a lover of virtue [*virtù*], give recognition to virtuous men [*uomini virtuosi*], and honor those who excel in any particular art" (p. 73). He should encourage people to work at their trades in peace and security, confident that their gains will not be taken from them. He must even "prepare prizes" for such industrious citizens, and "at appropriate times during the year," he should "keep the people occupied with festivals and spectacles." In producing such spectacles, he is really focused on his own interests, for he is acting the role of benevolent ruler by showing people "his humanity and magnificence, while always firmly maintaining the majesty of his position" (p. 73).

These examples of the positive things the prince should do are all clustered at the end of Chapter 21 in *The Prince*. For most of the work, however, Machiavelli is more concerned with the negative things the prince should do that involve his playing less attractive roles, such as those of the savage warrior, the relentless punisher of recalcitrant subjects, the ruthless leader who does not hesitate to inflict the harshest discipline on his troops. Perhaps the most dramatic example of the prince's staging a show that enhances his image by instilling fear in his subjects is Cesare Borgia's treatment of his lieutenant Remirro de Orco. Remirro had been sent to pacify the Romagna, a province Cesare had recently conquered, and when that task had been completed, Cesare began to worry that people might hate him because of his lieutenant's harsh methods. So he had the hapless Remirro tried and convicted, after which, "one morning he had him put in the piazza at Cesena in two pieces, with a piece of wood and a bloody knife beside him" (p. 24). Cesare is quite the showman here and comes across to his subjects as a ruler both terrifying and benevolent, for, as Machiavelli puts it, the "ferocity of *such a spectacle* left those people feeling at one and the same time both *stunned* and *satisfied*" (p. 24, my emphasis).

When Machiavelli insists in the opening of Chapter 25 of *The Prince* that the prince can deal successfully at least half the time with Fortune's raging rivers by building dikes and embankments, he seems to be offering a relatively upbeat assessment of princely success in the perennial struggle between *virtù* and *Fortuna*. He seems to support this view again at the end of the chapter when he speaks—or seems to speak—once more with confidence about how one can control Fortune. But these two passages bookend the much less optimistic view contained in the middle section of the chapter. He begins this section by emphasizing the flexibility and adaptability the prince needs to have in order to deal successfully with the endlessly changing, unpredictable world of Fortune. He reduces this to a rule: "the man who adapts his mode of proceeding to the nature of the times will be happy, and similarly, . . . the man whose mode of proceeding is not in accord with the times will be unhappy" (p. 79). What seemed like a simple recipe for success—namely, relying on one's own *virtù*—thus turns out to be much more complicated. Using a series of binaries, Machiavelli goes on to say that in affairs involving glory and riches—the affairs that princes typically care most about—men will "proceed in different ways: one with caution, the other with impetuosity; one by means of violence, the other with stealth; one through patience, the other with its contrary" (p. 79). He then reduces this series of binaries to a single one, caution and impetuosity, and notes how sometimes, if two men act with caution, one will succeed and the other will not, and also how one man will succeed by being cautious and another, by being impetuous. Working with something like mathematical precision, Machiavelli solves the problem involved in these contradictory formulations, for it "arises from nothing other than the nature of the times, which are, or are not, in conformity with the way" (p. 79) men proceed.

In itself, this generalization does not seem particularly pessimistic. Machiavelli, however, goes on to stress the limits of human adaptability: there is no man, he says, who is "so prudent that he knows how to adapt himself to this [i.e., the infinite variability of the times], both because he cannot deviate from that to which he is inclined by nature, and also because, when he has always prospered by walking down one path, he cannot be persuaded to depart from it" (p. 79). In other words, no matter how much insight human beings possess, no matter how many roles they play, underneath it all they simply cannot change their characters. Thus, although people may enjoy success for a while, they will inevitably fail when they cannot adapt to the changing times. This recognition is as troubling for Machiavelli's enterprise in writing *The Prince* as the difficulty he has, particularly in the second half of the work, when trying to produce clear, simple rules or generalizations to deal with all the complications involved in real-world events. For if Machiavelli cannot produce such rules, and if no man can be truly adaptable enough to beat Fortune all the time, then what is the point of writing a book that is supposed to guide princes to success? This is a question that does not, I believe, ever get fully answered in *The Prince.*

The unresolved conflict between Machiavelli's desire to produce a how-to manual for princes and his pessimism both about human adaptability and about his own ability to explain human experience by means of rules leads to the strange turn that Chapter 25 takes, a turn that occurs just after Machiavelli has reached the conclusion that no one is adaptable enough to win every battle with Fortune. He then decides to offer empirical evidence to "prove" that this conclusion is valid by looking at a specific example—namely, the career of the infamous warrior-pope Julius II. Since Julius, he says, always acted impetuously, one might expect Machiavelli to point to an example of a time when caution was called for and the impetuous Julius failed. And yet, Machiavelli does no such thing. Instead, he observes that Julius "found the times and circumstances so in conformity with that mode of proceeding of his, that he always achieved felicitous results" (p. 79). After recounting a few examples of the specific successes Julius achieved, Machiavelli is reduced to making a desperate maneuver to save his generalization that our limited adaptability will inevitably lead to failure: "the shortness of his [i.e., Julius's] life prevented him from having the opposite experience [i.e., failure], for if times had come in which it was necessary to proceed with caution, he would have been ruined, for he never would have deviated from these methods to which his nature inclined him" (p. 80). Essentially, Machiavelli invents a future for Julius II, a future he did not live to have, and since that future is purely imaginary, it cannot serve as "proof" for Machiavelli's generalization.

One may well ask at this point: Why does Machiavelli choose such a terrible example to validate his general rule? I believe the explanation involves one aspect of princely *virtù* to which I have paid relatively little attention so far. To speak of *virtù* as though it were primarily a matter of sight, insight, rational calculation, and role-playing is to treat it as though it were all about being a fox rather than a lion. In Chapter 18, when Machiavelli tells princes that they must make use of the animal parts of their nature if they wish to succeed, he goes on to recommend those two animals in particular: "for the lion cannot defend himself from traps, and the fox cannot defend himself from wolves. It is therefore necessary to be a fox to recognize traps and a lion to frighten off the wolves" (p. 55). Although Machiavelli seems to be giving equal play here to both animals, he seems to favor the fox throughout much of his treatise. Indeed, in the very next sentence following those cited above, Machiavelli says that princes "who base their behavior simply on the lion do not understand" (p. 55) the importance of being a clever fox. Ironically, despite the fact that Machiavelli emphasizes the need for the prince to be, first and foremost, a warrior, his book is not an exercise manual for soldiers; it is an attempt to train his readers how to *think*, how to *see*, like (Machiavellian) princes.

The lion nevertheless turns out to be really just as important as the fox in Machiavelli's thought, and nowhere more so than in Chapter 25, in which the chief example showing how a prince will inevitably fail because he is insufficiently adaptable is Julius II, whose impetuosity involves force, not cunning. The chapter, however, does begin, as we have noted, by emphasizing the prince's ability to make rational calculations. Indeed, he is imagined there as a builder or even an architect, someone who uses his brains, his foresight, to erect dikes and embankments to control the floods unleashed by Fortune. But by the time Machiavelli gets to the end of the chapter, after having insisted that even the best prince will fail sooner or later because he cannot always adapt to the times, he seems to realize—perhaps without being aware he has reached this point?—that the prince's inability to adapt to Fortune's changes really amounts to an acknowledgment that using his brains is not enough. Consequently, if the prince will fail by relying primarily on the fox when dealing with Fortune, there is a case to be made for using the lion, for relying on brute force and impetuosity rather than cunning and fraud. But to rely on force: Is that not precisely what Julius II always did? And was he not always successful, at least in the real world rather than in the fictional future Machiavelli imagines for him?

So, there may actually be a curious "logic" at work in Machiavelli's strange choice of Julius II as his chief example in this chapter: if the ability to adapt, which depends on the perception and cunning of the fox, is doomed to fail, then perhaps the only alternative the prince has is to abandon the fox and rely instead on the irrational force symbolized by the lion. And that is precisely what Machiavelli is advocating in the very last paragraph of the chapter when he states this simple conclusion: "it is better to be impetuous than cautious" (p. 80). At this point it is clear that he has moved far away from where he started in the chapter, from his belief that a shrewd prince could cope with Fortune by engaging in flood control. Consequently, here at the end, he replaces the image of Fortune as a raging river with a very different one, the traditional image of Fortune as a woman, whom the prince will conquer by means of brute force. The fox may dominate large swaths of *The Prince,* but at this moment, as Machiavelli desperately seeks to preserve the hope that princely *virtù* can overcome *Fortuna,* reason and cunning yield to impetuosity and irrational force, to a snap judgment to use the power of the man, the *vir,* at the etymological heart of *virtù.* As the chapter ends, the lion comes forward and occupies center stage, roaring out Machiavelli's last word on the subject of the contest between *virtù* and *Fortuna:* the prince will win, but only if he literally and figuratively beats Fortune into becoming either his lover or his prey—or perhaps both at the same time.

Since impetuosity essentially means an irrational, impulsive judgment, involving the use of force, Machiavelli can *recommend* it, but he cannot really *teach* it. The conclusion of Chapter 25 thus reveals just how seriously the pedagogical function of *The Prince* has been compromised. Moreover, as was said before, that pedagogical function had already been rendered problematic by the difficulty Machiavelli had in formulating clear, simple rules to explain complicated historical events, such as assassinations, thereby providing rules for future action. These problems compromising Machiavelli's pedagogical program in *The Prince* are not the only ones that have troubled critics over the years. There is, for example, the question of how Machiavelli can criticize certain princes in Chapter 8 for committing crimes that lead him to condemn them as evil and unworthy of glory but that do not seem very different from the deeds other princes are praised for elsewhere in the work. One of the other problems for Machiavelli's pedagogy in *The Prince* is the double judgment he makes of Cesare Borgia, his supposedly ideal prince, in Chapter 7, because he failed, after the death of his father, Pope Alexander VI, to prevent the election of Julius II. Initially, Machiavelli excuses Cesare by declaring that "the fault was not his but resulted from the extraordinary and extreme malice of Fortune" (p. 21), but later, Machiavelli retries the case and reaches a different verdict: Cesare can "be blamed for making Julius pope, where he made a bad choice, because, as I said, if he could not make a pope to his liking, he could have kept someone else from the office" (p. 26).

Thus, despite the elevated rhetoric of the last chapter of *The Prince,* in which Machiavelli urges the Medici to use the advice he offers them to create an all-powerful autocratic state that will drive the "barbarians" out of Italy and thus end the political crisis that began with the devastating descent of the French into the peninsula in 1494, one might wonder: Does *The Prince,* for all its brilliant political insight, offer a successful way to deal with that crisis? Perhaps; though Machiavelli has supplied another answer that might seem more likely to succeed: the *Discourses on the First Ten Books of Titus Livy.*

Dedicated to his like-minded friends rather than to Medici autocrats, the *Discourses* reveals that for Machiavelli, the Roman Republic was the true model, thanks to its social, political, and military institutions, for contemporary Italian city-states to follow if they wish not merely to drive out the "barbarians" but possibly even to conquer their enemies and create an empire for themselves. And Machiavelli reinforces this praise of Rome with repeated arguments about the fundamental ways in which republics in general are superior to princely states and the people are superior to princes.

In the *Discourses,* Machiavelli lauds many Roman institutions, starting with its mixed constitution that combined the three major forms of government: the princely rule of the consuls, the aristocratic rule of the senate, and the popular rule of the plebeians through the tribunes who represented them. He sees these groups as constituting something like a "system of checks and balances" insofar as each one kept "watch over the other" (p. 111). But because republican government can be slow and deliberate—something that is also to its credit, many heads usually being better than one—Machiavelli praises the Roman institution of the *dictator,* a magistrate who could rule in times of crisis with something like absolute power. But lest this *dictator* be confused with an autocratic Renaissance prince—let alone a modern dictator—Machiavelli stresses that he "was appointed for a limited term, not in perpetuity, and only in order to deal with the issues because of which he was chosen," nor could he take "away the authority of the senate or the people," let alone change any of the fundamental institutions of the city (p. 134). Finally, Machiavelli devotes most of Book 3 of the *Discourses* to Rome's success in curing the disease produced by people's endless desires and conflicting ambitions, a disease that periodically threatened to corrupt the republic by turning it into an autocracy and that finally destroyed it, in Machiavelli's view, with the rise of Julius Caesar and the creation of the empire under Augustus. The cure in question was the ability the Romans had to lead their state back to its healthy republican origins, something that was due to its institutions and, more important, to "the virtue [*virtù*] of a citizen" (p. 154) who would provide the necessary support for those institutions or would "have such a reputation and be so exemplary that good men will desire to imitate him and bad ones will be ashamed to lead lives contrary to his" (p. 155).

Of the many Roman institutions Machiavelli praises, perhaps the most important is religion. This might seem ironic, since Machiavelli was famous in his own time, as he is today, for his irreverence and hostility to religion. But that hostility is really directed at Christianity, which Machiavelli faults for being morally corrupt, for preventing the Italian city-states from uniting together to resist the "barbarians," and for being a religion of weaklings, not of warriors. By contrast, he admires Roman religion precisely because it taught the people civic and military virtue, primarily by inspiring them with a fear of the gods, a fear the leaders of the state could rely on in their pursuit of Rome's political and military ends. As a result, Machiavelli argues that Numa Pompilius, the king who succeeded Romulus, deserves more credit for the founding of Rome than his predecessor, because he made religion its key institution. When he saw that the Romans were "a very savage people," writes Machiavelli, Numa

> turned to religion as an institution, necessary beyond all others, for the maintenance of a civil society, and he established it in such a way that for many centuries nowhere was

> there such fear of God as in that republic, which facilitated whatever enterprise the senate or the great men of Rome decided to undertake. (p. 120)

Machiavelli's vision of Roman religion supports one of his most important arguments for the superiority of republican government. He does admit that a princely state can be successful, since it can "be held together by the fear of a prince which will compensate for the lack of religion," but then he makes his crucial argument: "because the lives of princes are short, that state will, of necessity, fail quickly," since the prince's *virtù* will die along with him and will rarely be "revived by his successor" (p. 121). Thus Machiavelli concludes that republics, at least republics on the Roman model, are better than principalities because the people's behavior will be determined by the basic institutions, such as religion, enshrined in the constitution of the state.

But Machiavelli does not think republics are superior to princely states just because of their institutions. He also thinks so because he believes the people, admittedly a well-trained people like the ancient Romans, are superior to princes. The title of Chapter 58 of Book 1 of the *Discourses* says it all: "The Masses Are Wiser and More Constant Than a Prince" (p. 139). In making this claim Machiavelli is actively disagreeing not just with contemporary opinion, but with Livy himself, who condemned the masses for their vanity and inconsistency as well as with "all the [ancient] writers [who] attack" (p. 140) them on similar grounds. The people, argues Machiavelli, "are more prudent and more stable, and have better judgment than a prince," and he praises them because of their ability to "foresee the evil and the good that may befall them" and because they rarely fail to choose the right side when they are listening to "two orators of equal talent [*virtù*] advocating different alternatives" (p. 142). In the course of this chapter, Machiavelli alludes to the popular saying *vox populi, vox Dei* (the voice of the people is the voice of God), suggesting that if Machiavelli really was religious, then his religion might well have been a faith in republican government and the civic virtues of its people.

This evaluation of the people in the *Discourses* may seem at odds with Machiavelli's sometimes disparaging remarks about the people and his apparent commitment to the rule of autocrats in *The Prince*. It must be remembered, however, that even in that work, he argues vehemently for the superiority of a popular militia to mercenary armies, heaping scorn, as we have noted, on the "trite proverb, that 'he who builds on the people builds on mud'" (p. 33). His celebration of the people here is not identical to the one in the *Discourses*, to be sure, for in *The Prince* the people are superior because they have been well managed by the ideal prince, a man who "knows how to command and is a man of courage, . . . and who keeps up the spirits of the entire people by means of his courage and his orders." Such a man, says Machiavelli, "will never find himself deceived" (p. 33) by the people. The difference between *The Prince* and the *Discourses* in this case is that in the former, the people require the constant, active intervention by a prince whose successors cannot be assured of their loyalty, whereas in the latter, Rome's religion and its other institutions ensure that the people will not turn out to be "mud." Instead, they will have the solidity of stone, so that anyone who "builds" on them will find that they are indeed the soundest foundation a state can have.

Despite the upbeat ending of *The Prince,* in which Machiavelli urges the Medici to put his advice to good use and save Italy from the "barbarians," there is a fundamental pessimism haunting the work, a pessimism revealed by his model prince, Cesare Borgia, who wound up a failure; by the irresolvable contradictions he cannot seem to avoid in his arguments; and by his attempt at the end of Chapter 25 to "prove" that princely *virtù* will triumph over Fortuna. By contrast, the *Discourses* seems relatively optimistic. Machiavelli ends his chapter on Numa and Roman religion by stating what must be understood as his fundamental motive for writing this work: his belief that what Rome did in the past can still be done in the present. After all, he remarks, with malicious irony, countless people believed in Savonarola "without having seen anything extraordinary to make them" (p. 122) believe in him, so why should they not believe in something much better? For Machiavelli, too, is a believer, one who believes, or wants to believe—and wants his countrymen to believe—that a new Numa might actually be somewhere in Italy, waiting for his cue, his nod from Fortune, to come forward and teach the people how to remake Christianity in the image of Roman religion, create a republic on the Roman model, and then unify Italy and drive out the "barbarians."

The "Real" Machiavelli?

The preceding discussion would seem to suggest that the "real" Machiavelli is the republican of the *Discourses,* not the theorist of autocratic rule in *The Prince.* That may be so, but it is also important to recognize that Machiavelli adopts different authorial positions and strategies in his works, depending on the goals he aims at and the audience he is addressing. In *The Prince,* he offers the Medici serious, though not, as we have seen, unproblematic, advice on how to be successful autocrats. It would be a mistake to consider his treatise a satire or an exposé of tyranny, as some scholars have proposed: The letter he wrote to Francesco Vettori on December 10, 1513, makes it clear that he was composing *The Prince* because he wanted to impress the Medici with his political acumen in order to facilitate his return to Florence and to play the role of deferential political adviser with them that he is already doing in *The Prince* itself. By contrast, in the *Discourses* he serves as the mentor of like-minded friends who shared his republican sympathies. In *The Legation to Cesare Borgia,* he is the diplomat, sending reports filled with valuable insights and observations back to his superiors in Florence. In those reports he is consistently deferential: The Ten, to whom they are addressed, are always "Your Lordships" (*Vostre Signorie*), and Machiavelli typically closes each one by commending himself to The Ten as their "servant" (*servitor*). By contrast, when he writes personal letters to Francesco Vettori and Francesco Guicciardini, he comes off as a sincere friend and something like an equal. He may address them deferentially, especially at the start of a letter and in other places where he is asking for their advice and assistance, but what he says in those letters is familiar and frank, and he can even be wryly ironic at his friends' expense, as when he begins the letter he sent to Guicciardini from Carpi with a series of elevated titles in Latin for his friend, but then opens the letter proper with "I was seated on the crapper when your messenger arrived" (p. 173). In short, the various documents included in this book may share many of Machiavelli's common themes and aspirations, but they also reveal a number of different Machiavellis.

Machiavelli was adept at role-playing—just as his prince was expected to be. Indeed, in the well-known letter he wrote to Vettori, when he describes his daily routine, he reveals how he plays a host of different roles from morning to evening. At the beginning, he is the serious, sometimes frustrated, though often witty, satirical, and even self-satirical estate manager. After that he becomes the lover who goes off by himself to reflect on his own amatory experiences and to read the love poetry of Dante and Petrarch, Ovid and Tibullus. He then turns into the keen observer of "the diverse tastes and the different fancies of men" (p. 170), whom he encounters and talks with as he goes down the road, until he reaches his house and is soon playing a new role, that of the family man, and eating dinner there. Soon he is off again, this time to amuse himself during the afternoon by playing cards with some local yokels at the nearby inn, becoming one himself and describing all of them in comic terms as shouting at one another so loudly that they can be heard as far away as San Casciano—"and most of the time we are fighting over a penny" (p. 170). Changing his persona in the very next sentence, however, he distances himself from the other cardplayers and speaks of them disparagingly, assuring Vettori that what he is really doing at the inn is getting rid of his frustration at being forced to live in Sant'Andrea: "Cooped up this way among these lice, I wipe off the mold from my brain and vent my feelings about the malice of my fate" (p. 170). Finally, Machiavelli returns home in the evening to play one final role, the role that he insists is truly his own. He becomes the astute interpreter of the classics, who, after changing out of his dirty "everyday clothes" and putting on "regal and courtly garments," goes into his study and loses any consciousness of the passage of time as he reads the books of the ancients and converses with them, feeding himself "on that food which is mine alone and for which I was born" (p. 171).

Still, despite all his role-playing, Machiavelli does reflect his prince in that he, too, cannot escape his "nature." Moreover, just as he believes that no prince can ever succeed in adapting to all the changes in the world of history, ruled over by the capricious goddess *Fortuna,* neither could Machiavelli himself, as the history of his life reveals, with all its vicissitudes, its triumphs—usually temporary and limited—and its resounding failures and humiliations. If Machiavelli's prince can never be sufficiently adaptable to defeat Fortune at every turn "because he cannot deviate from that to which he is inclined by nature" (p. 79), neither can Machiavelli. One example of Machiavelli's inability to transcend his "nature" is his irrepressible impulse to formulate rules to explain human behavior in rational terms even when that seems impossible. A more serious example of his failure to transcend his "nature" involves his profound republican sympathies. Even though he attempts to teach the Medici how to be successful autocrats in *The Prince,* those sympathies are certainly the reason why he praises the people over princes in the *Discourses* and why he wants the Medici to place their trust in a citizen militia in *The Prince.* At an even deeper level, Machiavelli's republicanism may be the explanation for the contradictions in his presentation of Cesare Borgia: he both wants to endorse Cesare as a model for the Medici, and to criticize him for his failure, since, as he says quite clearly in the *Discourses,* republics are always superior to princely rule because they do not cease to exist when their ruler dies.

There are yet other ways in which Machiavelli's "nature" cannot be repressed. The first involves the ambiguous character of the role of adviser he plays in *The Prince.* That role would seem to place him in a socially appropriate inferior position to the men he advises. But does it? Machiavelli is certainly aware that there is a potential problem here, for in Chapter 22 of that work, "On the Secretaries of Princes," he expresses his concern about the intellectual relationship, which is also a power relationship, between the prince and his adviser (or minister, or secretary). He begins by saying that it is important for a prince to have good advisers because they enhance their master's reputation, and he offers as an example the case of a ruler of Siena and his chief minister. Things then get complicated, however, for Machiavelli, following Livy and other ancient writers, says there are three kinds of brains: those that understand things on their own, those that do so thanks to what others understand, and those that cannot understand things at all. He then says that if the ruler of Siena was not in the first group, he was at least in the second, so that he was able to "recognize the good deeds as well as the sorry ones of his minister" (p. 74). Machiavelli proceeds to discuss the way a good ruler can tell a good minister from a bad one, but if the ruler of Siena is in the *second* group—possessing a brain that understands things only when shown them by others—then who will show him how to distinguish a good minister from a bad one? The answer is: the minister himself, of course. Indeed, as the chapter goes on to explain how to make distinctions between good and bad ministers or advisers, it is clear that these words were not written by a prince, but by a would-be adviser to princes—namely, Machiavelli himself. Thus, as he tells the Medici how to choose their advisers, he is, essentially, telling them: "Pick me!"

Perhaps it would be better to say that what Machiavelli's "nature" makes him do in *The Prince* reveals that he is not just a would-be adviser to princes, but a would-be prince himself. After all, that is what he appears to have wanted to be during the days of the Republic when, as the secretary running the Second Chancery and the secretary to The Ten, he was effectively directing—or trying to direct—Florence's foreign policy and military affairs while technically being the "servant" of The Ten and ultimately of the Signoria. It seems that the writer of *The Prince* simply cannot help himself—and thus he cannot prevent an astute reader from seeing what he really wants to be. It is not clear if the Medici ever bothered to read Machiavelli's treatise, but if they did, then Machiavelli's desire to rule may be one reason he was not invited to return to Florence until 1520 and, even then, was never really allowed into the inner circle of the government. Or perhaps it was simply that this "secretary," this "keeper of secrets," as the name indicates, lets the cat out of the bag in *The Prince,* in which case the Medici knew better than to trust *their* secrets to such a man.

The *Discourses,* like *The Prince,* was not published in Machiavelli's lifetime. It was intended for like-minded friends and reveals his greatest hope, the hope that Florence could be transformed into a republic on the Roman model, a republic that would include some version of consuls and senators and tribunes; that would instill a deep religiosity in its people, not to save their souls so much as to ensure their loyalty to the state; and that could, with the help of great leaders, periodically revitalize itself by returning to its healthy republican roots; drive the "barbarians" out of Italy; and become a great empire like Rome. In the Preface to the first book of the *Discourses* Machiavelli declares that his purpose in writing is to show his contemporaries how to read ancient history so as to obtain "a true understanding" (p. 107) of it. But that "true understanding" is not really the understanding of the historian who wants to make sense of what happened in the past; it is that of the man of politics, the *politico* as Machiavelli and his contemporaries would have called him, who wants to understand the past in order to make use of it in the present—or, rather, in the future. For Machiavelli was profoundly concerned about the future of Florence—and Italy—a future in which his dream of the creation of a powerful, independent, secular republic would become a reality. Unlike the hereditary monarchies of the time, which derived their authority from God and considered their institutions divinely authorized, Machiavelli's republic would be a man-made entity, something created by and for its inhabitants. It would be generally modeled on Rome and would be related to, though not identical with, the Florentine Republic, which had been destroyed by the forces of Charles V and Pope Leo X.

To Machiavelli's great disappointment, this new republic did not come into being during his lifetime any more than did some idealized form of the state he imagined in *The Prince.* But that fact does not make Machiavelli's place in history any the less important, for his importance is not about what his political thought created in Renaissance Italy but about the impact his thought had on later political, and especially republican, theorists, from John Harrington, Hobbes, and Locke in the seventeenth century, through Spinoza, Rousseau, and Montesquieu in the Enlightenment, down to the Founding Fathers of the American republic, and John Adams in particular. In a sense, by looking backward toward Rome, Machiavelli was profoundly shaping the future, a future he could not have imagined, of course, and doing so by developing a vision of the republic as the best form of government, a vision that would ultimately be realized, in different ways, in England, France, the United States, and even in Machiavelli's own Italy. In essence, his political works, *The Prince* and the *Discourses,* are classics for many reasons, but one of the most important is clearly that they invented, or helped in significant ways to invent, the republics of our modern world.

A Note on My Translations

My revised translation of *The Prince* and new translations of supporting materials in this volume are based on Machiavelli's works in Italian but also, to some degree, on the very readable versions of some of those texts translated by Robert M. Adams for previous versions of this Norton Critical Edition. I have also consulted other translations as I worked on my own. My general goal has been to produce a modern English version of Machiavelli that is readable and completely idiomatic, while being as true as possible to his thought, his particular political vocabulary, and, when possible, even his syntax. Like Adams, I have chosen to put Machiavelli's polyvalent word *virtù* (and its adjectival form *virtuoso*) in square brackets every time it appears in his texts. I have also chosen to capitalize "Fortune" because Machiavelli's *fortuna* is given so much agency that it almost always feels like a personification and thus an implicit reference to the goddess *Fortuna;* on some occasions, I have even used this Latin form. There are certain words Machiavelli employs repeatedly, and because many have English cognates, I have tried to use those cognates throughout, including such words and phrases as *to come to ruin, foundations, cure, remedy,* and *happy* (for *felice,* even though this word often implies something like "prosperous"). Likewise, I have been scrupulous in retaining the shifts Machiavelli makes from the third person to the second person throughout *The Prince* and the *Discourses,* because those shifts—often quite unexpected—speak to the dual nature of those texts: they have both the abstract, impersonal character of treatises written for a distant, invisible set of readers and, at the same time, the personal, rhetorical, emotional, and oral character of dialogues in which Machiavelli engages his readers as though they constituted a live audience. I also elected to translate the Latin titles of the chapters of *The Prince* into English, and to do the same thing with the occasional Latin word (e.g., *tamen,* meaning "nevertheless") in his Italian sentences—probably a reflection of Machiavelli's immersion in the world of the quasi-bilingual Second Chancery. Finally, I have annotated a number of words and phrases when I felt that my translation might seem strange or could be misleading for the reader. My translation cannot be the equivalent of Machiavelli's actual words, but I have tried to make it come as close as possible despite knowing it could never really reach that goal.

Acknowledgments

Anyone working on a project like this one incurs numerous debts over the years. I would like to thank the hundreds of students, both graduate and undergraduate, who have studied Machiavelli with me, for helping me sharpen my thinking and often offering me extremely important insights. I also owe John Najemy a huge debt for helping me deal with the enormous bibliography on Machiavelli as well as steering me right on a number of historical matters. He is a brilliant scholar, and I wish I could have printed more of his work in this book. Several items by John are in the Bibliography, and I especially recommend that readers consider seeking out his article "Machiavelli and Cesare Borgia" for a subtle argument against seeing Cesare as Machiavelli's model prince.

I would like to thank the College of Liberal Arts for awarding me a College Research Fellowship during the fall of 2017, which allowed me to bring much of the work on this book to completion. My department chair, Elizabeth Cullingford, played a key role in making that happen, and I cannot begin to express my gratitude to her for the award as well as for her support and friendship over many years.

I deeply appreciate all the help I have had from Carol Bemis, the General Editor of the Norton Critical Edition series, who first invited me to revise the second edition of Machiavelli's *The Prince* many years ago. I do not know how to thank her for her patience and support through an overly long but ultimately satisfying experience as a translator, an editor, and a scholar. Her feedback and guidance have always been just what I have needed at various stages of this project. I also thank Thea Goodrich, Associate Editor at Norton, who has put so much effort into making this project possible that I really do not know what I would have done without her. I admire her negotiating skills with publishers, her editorial abilities, and the dependability and competence of her responses to my questions and needs.

My dear friend and colleague Douglas Biow deserves a special place in the circle of Paradise reserved for friends and scholars. He has helped me out on numerous occasions with translation issues, scholarly judgments, and my critical approach to Machiavelli. I really do not know how I can thank him enough.

Finally, there is my wife, Marlette, who has been something of a "Machiavelli widow" for quite some time now. She has been enormously supportive of my work both intellectually and emotionally. Plus, being married to a historian for over fifty years has helped me keep my feet on the ground and my mind focused on what is essential. I have dedicated this book to her for her love, her support, and her patience.

The Text of THE PRINCE

Niccolò Machiavelli to the Magnificent Lorenzo de' Medici[1]

It is a frequent custom for those who seek the favor of a prince to make him presents of those things they value most highly or which they know are most pleasing to him. Hence one often sees gifts consisting of horses, arms, cloth of gold, precious stones, and similar ornaments suitable for men of such nobility. I, too, would like to commend myself to Your Magnificence with some token of my readiness to serve you, but I have not found among my belongings anything I prize so much or value so highly as my knowledge of the actions of great men, acquired through long experience of contemporary affairs and continual reading of the ancients. For a long time I have thought carefully about these matters and examined them minutely; now I have condensed my thoughts in one little volume and am sending it to Your Magnificence. Although I know it is unworthy to enter your presence, still, I trust that you, in your humanity, will accept this work, since I could give you no greater gift than this, which will enable you to grasp in short order everything I have learned over many years through many trials and tribulations. My book is not stuffed with lengthy periods or bombastic, high-sounding words, nor is it decorated with any form of extrinsic rhetorical ornamentation, such as many writers use to present and embellish their materials. For I wanted my book to be absolutely plain, or at least distinguished only by the variety of the examples and the importance of the subject.

I hope it will not be thought presumptuous if a man of low and humble social station should dare to discuss the governing of princes and to set down instructions for them. When artists want to paint landscapes, they stand on low ground to contemplate the mountains and hills; they climb to the tops of the mountains to view the valleys. Similarly, to know the people well, one must be a prince, and to know princes well, one must be one of the people.

Will Your Magnificence, then, deign to accept this little gift in the same spirit that I send it? If you will read it over and study it

1. This translation is based on Niccolò Machiavelli, *Il principe,* in *Opere,* edited by Niccolò Conti, vol. 4: 270–372 (Firenze: N. Conti, 1820). When he first wrote it, Machiavelli dedicated his book to Giuliano de' Medici, the duke of Nemours (1479–1516), the third son of Lorenzo the Magnificent. After Giuliano's death on March 17, 1516, Machiavelli rededicated it to Lorenzo, the duke of Urbino (1492–1519), one of the original Lorenzo's grandsons, here called "magnificent," but not to be confused with his grandfather. From Machiavelli's letter to Francesco Vettori of December 10, 1513 (p. 171), in which he mentions writing a little book called *de principatibus* (*On Principalities*), he had completed at least the first, more taxonomic part of *The Prince* by then. The work must have been completed before, probably well before, Giuliano's death, and the letter to Vettori makes it clear that Machiavelli was not composing a satire or an exposé of the evils of autocratic behavior; he was desperately seeking to return to Florence and to serve the Medici as a political adviser. On the Medici, see the family tree on p. 88. The form of the dedication reveals Machiavelli's devotion to antiquity; it is an imitation of the *Address to Nicocles* by the ancient Greek rhetorician Isocrates.

carefully, you will recognize in it my most earnest desire that you may achieve that summit of grandeur which Fortune and your other qualities presage for you. And if from that summit Your Magnificence will occasionally glance down at these humble places, you will recognize how unjustly I suffer from the great and continual malice of Fortune.

THE PRINCE

Chapter 1

Of the Many Different Kinds of States and the Different Ways to Acquire Them

All the states and governments that ever held or now hold sway over men were and are of two sorts: either republics or principalities. And principalities are also of two sorts: either hereditary, where the family of the rulers has been in control for a long time, or else they are new. And the new ones are either entirely new, as Milan was for Francesco Sforza,[1] or they are like new members grafted onto the hereditary state of the prince who has acquired them, as the kingdom of Naples was to the kingdom of Spain.[2] New acquisitions of this type are either accustomed to living under a prince, or used to being free, and they are acquired either with the force of other people's arms, or with one's own, either by Fortune or by prowess [*virtù*].

Chapter 2

On Hereditary Principalities

Setting aside any discussion of republics, about which I have spoken at length elsewhere,[1] I will concern myself only with principalities, and following the order set down above, I will describe how these states may be governed and preserved.

1. Francesco Sforza (1401–1466) was the second of the name. His father, originally named Giacomo or Muzio Attendolo, was a tough peasant who, when he became a professional soldier, took the name of Sforza, implying energy and ambition. His bastard son Francesco was also a professional soldier for many years, often on both sides of the same feud. When the ancient line of the Visconti expired in Milan in 1447, he first defended, then betrayed the republic that replaced it, and in 1450 had himself declared duke of Milan.
2. The Kingdom of Naples, including southern Italy and Sicily, had a tangled succession to which practically everybody in Europe had some sort of claim. After being partitioned between France and Spain by the Treaty of Granada in 1500, it was captured for Spain and King Ferdinand II of Aragon (1452–1516) by brute force of arms in 1503. This is the annexation to which Machiavelli alludes (see Chapter 3, p. 11, and Chapter 18, p. 57).

1. See the *Discourses*, Book 1.

Let me say, then, that hereditary states which have grown used to the family of their ruler are much less trouble to maintain than new ones are, for it is simply a matter of not upsetting ancient customs and of accommodating oneself to meet new circumstances. Hence, if such a prince is ordinarily industrious, he can always maintain his position, unless some unusual and excessive act of force deprives him of it. And even if he is deprived of it, any adversity experienced by the usurper will enable him to get it back.

We have an Italian example in the duke of Ferrara, who stood up against attacks from the Venetians in 1484, and those of Pope Julius in 1510, for no better reason than that his family had ruled that state for a long time.[2] Since a prince by birth has fewer reasons and less need to harm his subjects, it follows that they would love him all the more, and if he has no extravagant vices to make him hated, it is only natural that he should have the goodwill of his own people. And because of the antiquity and continuity of the government, people forget not only the reasons for innovations, but their very existence, because every new change provides a projecting stone[3] to serve as the base for another.

Chapter 3

On Mixed Principalities

But it is the new principality that causes all the problems. To begin with, if it is not entirely new but like a graft freshly joined to an established state, so that the two bodies together may be considered mixed, its problems initially spring from a natural difficulty, common to all new principalities, which is that all men are willing to change rulers in the hope of bettering themselves. In this belief, they take up arms against their ruler, but find themselves deceived when they discover through experience that things have gotten worse. And

2. Two dukes of Ferrara were involved in the two assaults. The first, Ercole d'Este (b. 1431; ruled 1471–1505), had to yield some of his territory to the Venetians in 1484 as a result of a dispute over a tax on salt. The second, Alfonso I d'Este (b. 1476; ruled 1505–34), refused to join the Venetians and the pope in what was called the Lega Santa, or Holy League, against the French and had to defend himself against both of them. He was attacked by Pope Julius II (b. 1443; pope 1503–13) and briefly driven out of his territories, but ultimately regained them. The house of Este had been established in Ferrara for four centuries, although Machiavelli's point would have been less clear-cut had he told us that Alfonso d'Este was a wily diplomat, a master strategist, a superb gunner, and one of the most skillful soldiers in Europe. His conflating of the gentle, culturally minded Ercole with the tough, resourceful Alfonso makes more impressive his point that a long-established regime is a stable one. Pope Julius II was known as the "warrior pope," and Machiavelli describes his impetuous character in Chapter 25 (see pp. 79–80).
3. Machiavelli uses the technical term *l'addentellato* to express the way in which one policy or institution of a long-enduring state can be deliberately designed to provide the basis for another one. His term, deriving from the Italian word for "tooth," refers to a stone jutting out from a wall on which another one could be securely placed.

the reason for this is another very natural and ordinary necessity, which is that a new prince must always harm those over whom he rules, both with his soldiers and with countless other injuries that are entailed in his takeover of that state. Thus you will have as enemies all those you harmed in occupying the principality, and you cannot maintain the friendship of those who helped to put you there, because you will not be able to satisfy them as they expected, nor can you make use of strong medicines against them, since you are under obligations to them. No matter how strong one's armies may be, one always needs the favor of the inhabitants to take over a country. It was for these reasons that Louis XII of France took Milan quickly and lost it just as quickly, and the first time Ludovico's own troops were sufficient to take it back from him, because the people who had opened the gates to him, finding themselves deceived in the opinion they had formed and about the rewards they had expected, could not bear the offenses of their new prince.[1]

It is true, of course, that once lands that have rebelled are conquered a second time, they are not so easily lost, because the ruler, using that rebellion as a pretext, will be less hesitant about securing his position by punishing offenders, exposing those he suspects, and strengthening himself in his weakest places. Thus, if all that was required for France to lose Milan the first time was for a Duke Ludovico to be making warlike noises on the borders, the second time it was necessary to have the whole world united against her in order to destroy her armies or chase them out of Italy, all of which was caused by what was said above.[2] And nevertheless, Milan was taken from her the second time as well as the first.

The general causes of the first loss have been discussed; what remains now is to describe the reasons for the second and to identify the remedies that were available to Louis, or those which someone else in his position might have had available to preserve more successfully what had been acquired than the French king did. Let me say, then, that those states which, once they have been acquired, are annexed to an old state of the conqueror's are either parts of the same province or share the same language, or they do not. If they do, it is perfectly easy to hold onto them, especially when they are not used to freedom. To keep a secure hold on them, it suffices to have extinguished the line of the prince who previously ruled them,

1. Louis XII, king of France (b. 1462; ruled 1498–1515), invaded Italy in 1499 and captured Milan on October 5. It was recaptured by Ludovico Sforza, Il Moro, duke of Milan (1452–1508; ruled 1494–99), on February 5, 1500; soon after that he was betrayed to the French by his own troops and spent the rest of his days in prison in France.
2. The French retook Milan a second time in April 1500 and held it for more than ten years until they were driven out of Italy by the Holy League of Julius II, which included the armies of Spain and Venice and, on paper at least, the Holy Roman Empire and England.

for in other matters, as long as they maintain their old way of life, and there is no change in customs, people will live quietly, as has been seen in the cases of Burgundy, Brittany, Gascony, and Normandy, which have been joined to France for such a long time,[3] and although there is some difference of language, their customs are nevertheless similar, and so they are able to get along easily with one another. Whoever acquires such states and wishes to hold onto them must keep two things in mind: the first is that the line of the previous prince should be extinguished, and the other is to avoid making any changes in either their laws or their taxes, so that, in the shortest possible time, they will form a single body together with the old principality.

But when states are acquired in a province that differs in language, laws, and customs, this is where the difficulties arise, and here one needs good luck as well as great industriousness to hold onto them. One of the best and most effective remedies would be for the new ruler who has acquired them to go and live there. This would make his possession of them more secure and longer-lasting, as it did for the Turk in Greece; even with all the other measures he took to hold onto that state, it would not have been possible to keep it, if he had not gone there to live. For by being on the spot, you can see troubles getting started and find remedies for them right away; when you do not live there, you hear about them only when they are huge, and there is no longer a cure for them. Besides this, the province will not be looted by your officials; your subjects will be satisfied because they have more direct access to their ruler; and if they want to be good, they will have more reason to love him, and if they do not, they will have more reason to fear him. Any foreigner who would want to attack that state will think twice about it, for the ruler who lives there can be deprived of it only with the greatest difficulty.

The other, even better remedy is to set up colonies in one or two places which will serve, so to speak, as the shackles of the state, for it is necessary either to do this or to keep a large force of cavalry and infantry there. Colonies do not cost much, and for little or no expense the prince can send them out and maintain them there. The only people hurt are those whose lands and houses he takes in order to give them to the new inhabitants, and they constitute a very small part of that state. Those whom he does injure, being poor and scattered, cannot possibly do him any harm, while all the others, who are unscathed, would remain peaceful for just that reason, on the one hand, and on the other, would be afraid of making a mistake,

3. Although Normandy was incorporated into France in 1204, the other three independent duchies were added only in the second half of the 15th century.

fearing that they would suffer the same fate as those who had been stripped of their possessions. I conclude that these colonies cost nothing, are more loyal, and do less damage, and those they do hurt cannot do any harm, since they are poor and scattered, as I said. And in this connection it should be noted that men should be either caressed or destroyed, since they will seek revenge for minor injuries, but will not be able to do so for more serious ones. Thus, any harm done to a man should be done in such a way that there is no need to fear his vengeance. If troops are kept there instead of colonies, the expense will be much greater, because you will be obliged to consume all the income you get from the state in order to guard it. In this way the acquisition turns into a loss, and much more harm is done, since the entire state is injured by the army's having to shift its quarters from place to place. All the people feel this inconvenience, and each one of them becomes an enemy, and these are enemies who can do harm, because, even though beaten, they remain in their own homes. On every count, then, this form of protection is as useless as that of colonies is useful.

In addition, the man who comes into an alien province, as I have said, ought to set himself up as the head and defender of his less powerful neighbors and try to weaken the strong ones, and he should make sure that no foreigner who is as powerful as he is somehow manages to get in. And it will always be the case that the foreigner will be invited in by those who are discontented either because of excessive ambition or out of fear, as was seen long ago when the Aetolians brought the Romans into Greece, and in every other province the Romans entered, they were always brought there by the local inhabitants.[4] The general rule is that as soon as a powerful foreigner enters a province, all of those in the area who are less powerful become his adherents, moved by their hatred for the man who held sway over them. Thus, with respect to the less powerful, the foreigner need not take pains to win them over, because they will, all together, quickly become part of the state he has acquired there. He only needs to take care that they do not acquire too much strength and authority. Then, with his own forces and the people's support, he can easily put down those who are powerful and become, in every way, the master of that province. And anyone who does not govern well in this way will quickly lose what he has acquired, and for as long as he manages to hold onto it, he will meet with countless difficulties and annoyances there.

4. In 211 BCE, the Aetolians, a relatively weak confederacy of cities and states in north and central Greece, called in the Romans to help them against Philip V of Macedonia (b. 238; ruled 221–179 BCE), who was an ally of the great Carthaginian general Hannibal Barca (247–183/181 BCE). Once established there, the Romans easily controlled the balance of power by the means indicated in the rest of this paragraph.

In the provinces they took over, the Romans followed these policies: they sent in colonies, kept the less powerful occupied without increasing their strength, put down the powerful, and did not allow powerful foreigners to acquire a reputation there. I will limit my examples just to the province of Greece, where the Romans temporized with the Achaeans and the Aetolians, humbled the kingdom of the Macedonians, and drove Antiochus out of the land.[5] They did not permit the merits of the Achaeans or the Aetolians to let them gain any additional territory and never allowed Philip to talk them into being friends until they had reduced his strength, nor could the power of Antiochus make them consent to let him maintain any sort of state in that province. For in these instances the Romans did what all wise princes ought to do: they have to keep an eye not only on present troubles but on future ones, and make every effort to oppose them. For if troubles are seen from afar, they can easily be remedied, but if you wait until they are on top of you, there is no time to use medicine, since the malady has become incurable. What doctors say about consumption applies here: in the early stages of the illness, it is difficult to diagnose and easy to cure, but as time progresses, if it was not diagnosed and treated at the start, it becomes easy to diagnose and difficult to cure. Thus it happens in affairs of state: if the evils that are developing are diagnosed from afar (something only a prudent man can do), they are quickly cured, but when they have not been diagnosed and have thus been allowed to grow to the point that everyone recognizes them, then a remedy is no longer possible.

Thus, the Romans, observing troubles from afar, always found remedies for them, never allowing them to develop in order to avoid going to war, because they knew that wars do not go away, but are merely postponed to the advantage of others. Therefore, they wanted to wage war with Philip and Antiochus in Greece so as not to have to deal with them in Italy, though at the time they could have avoided both wars, something they did not want to do. They never liked that saying which is constantly on the lips of the wise men of our day, "enjoy the benefit of time," but they trusted in their own prowess [*virtù*] and prudence, for time drives all things before it and can bring in the good as well as the bad and the bad as well as the good.

But let us return to France and see if she did any of the things just described, and I shall speak not of Charles, but of Louis since

5. The Achaeans were a federal league, similar to the Aetolians and opposed to them. Antiochus III the Great of Syria (b. c. 241; ruled 222–187 BCE), invited by the Aetolians and incited by Hannibal (who had taken refuge in the Middle East after his defeat in the Second Punic War), invaded Greece in 196 BCE; he provided a natural counterweight to Philip V of Macedonia. The decisive battle in which the Romans gained control of Greece by defeating Philip was that of Cynoscephalae (197 BCE); seven years later they destroyed the power of Antiochus at Magnesia in Asia Minor.

his mode of proceeding has been better observed, because he has controlled territory in Italy for a longer period of time.[6] You will see that he did the opposite of what should be done to hold onto an alien province.

King Louis was brought into Italy by the ambition of the Venetians, who wanted to gain control over half of Lombardy thanks to his invasion. I will not blame the king for his decision, because he wanted to gain an initial foothold in Italy, and not only did he not have friends in this province, but, once he was there, he found all the doors locked against him because of what King Charles had done.[7] Hence, he had to take what friendships he could, and if he had made no other mistakes in his maneuvering, he might have succeeded with his well-thought-out plan. Indeed, having taken Lombardy, the king quickly regained the reputation lost by Charles. Genoa capitulated, and the Florentines became his friends; the marquis of Mantua, the duke of Ferrara, the Bentivogli, the lady of Forlì, the lords of Faenza, Pesaro, Rimini, Camerino, Piombino, the Lucchesi, the Pisans, the Sienese—all approached him with professions of friendship.[8] And at this point the Venetians could see the folly of the decision they had made, since in order to gain a couple of towns in Lombardy,[9] they had made the king the master of a third of Italy.

Now consider with how little difficulty the king could have maintained his reputation in Italy if he had observed the rules laid down above and become the protector and defender of all those friends of his. They were numerous, they were weak, and they were afraid, some of them of the Church, others of the Venetians, so that they were always obliged to stick with him, and by their means he could have easily protected himself from the remaining great powers. But no sooner was he in Milan than he did the opposite, giving aid to

6. Charles VIII (b. 1470; ruled 1483–98) led the first French invasion of Italy in 1494 in order to claim the Kingdom of Naples, but his occupation was short lived, and he left the next year. His successor, Louis XII (b. 1462; ruled 1498–1515), invaded Italy again in 1499 and captured Milan, which remained as his foothold in the country. He partitioned Naples with Spain in 1500, but then fought with Spain over Naples from 1502 to 1505, joined with Julius II in a league against the Venetians in 1508, and was finally expelled from the peninsula in 1513.

7. Starting from his idea of claiming Naples, Charles dreamed of recapturing Constantinople from the Turks and then advancing through the East like another Alexander; no sooner had he actually appeared in Italy in 1494 than the Italians joined with Maximilian I, the Holy Roman Emperor (b. 1459; ruled 1493–1519), to drive him out the next year.

8. Machiavelli's list of Louis's friends deliberately includes rulers of both big and little states. They are, respectively: Francesco Gonzaga, marquis of Mantua; Ercole I d'Este, duke of Ferrara; Giovanni Bentivoglio, lord of Bologna; Caterina Riario Sforza, lady of Forlì; Astorre Manfredi, lord of Faenza; Giovanni Sforza, lord of Pesaro; Pandolfo Malatesta, lord of Rimini; Giulio Cesare da Varano, lord of Camerino; and Jacopo IV d'Appiano, lord of Piombino. All of these figures ruled cities and towns in northern Italy, and when he threw away their support, Louis weakened himself substantially.

9. Venice had been promised the towns of Brescia, Bergamo, Crema, and Cremona.

Pope Alexander so that he might occupy the Romagna.[1] Nor did he perceive that by this decision he was weakening himself, casting off his friends and those who had thrown themselves into his lap, while strengthening the Church by adding vast temporal power to the spiritual power which gives it so much authority. And having made this first error, he was forced to follow up on it, so that in order to put a stop to the ambition of Alexander and keep him from becoming the master of Tuscany, he was forced to come to Italy himself.[2] It was not enough for him to have made the Church powerful and to have deprived himself of his friends, but, desiring to have the Kingdom of Naples, he divided it with the king of Spain. And where before he alone was the arbiter of Italy, he brought in a partner to whom those in that province who were ambitious and dissatisfied with him might have recourse. And where he could have left in Naples a king who was his tributary, he expelled him only to bring in another one who was capable of driving out Louis himself.[3]

The desire to acquire things is perfectly natural and ordinary, and when men do it if they can, they will always be praised or not blamed, but when they cannot and try to get it anyhow, here they are in error and deserve to be blamed. If France, therefore, could have attacked Naples with her own forces, she should have done so; if she could not, she should not have divided it up. And if the division of Lombardy that she made with the Venetians deserved to be excused, since it gave her a foothold in Italy, this other division of Naples with Spain deserves to be blamed, since there was no such necessity to excuse it.

Thus Louis had made these five errors: he destroyed the lesser powers; he increased the power in Italy of one who was already powerful; he brought a very powerful foreigner into that country; he did not go and reside there; and he did not set up colonies. And still, had he lived, those mistakes would not have hurt him, if he

1. A region in north-central Italy bordering on the Adriatic Sea; included within it are the towns of Ravenna, Forlì, Arezzo, Pesaro, and Urbino. Pope Alexander was Alexander VI, born Rodrigo Borgia (1431–1503); he was pope from 1492 on and was the father of Cesare. He got the support of Charles by granting him a dispensation to divorce his wife.
2. The armies of Louis XII, led by the Italian condottiere Gian Giacomo Trivulzio (1440/1441–1518) during the first expeditions against Ludovico Sforza, required the presence of King Charles himself in August 1502, as a result of Cesare Borgia's preparations to attack Florence. However, Charles actually came to Italy to fight Spain for control of Naples. His claim to the throne there was based on dynastic arrangements involving its connection with the house of Anjou, but Naples, as the most remote of the Italian states, was obviously the hardest for a French army to annex or defend. Ferdinand II of Spain was the king with whom Louis arranged, by the Treaty of Granada (November 11, 1500), to share Naples: the French were to get Campania and the Abruzzi, while the Spanish got Puglia, Calabria, and Sicily.
3. He could have left Frederick I of Aragon (1431–1501), the original ruler, in Naples, taking away any real power from him but leaving him in nominal command of his kingdom. Instead, he installed Ferdinand, who promptly drove him out.

had not made the sixth one of taking the Venetians' state from them.[4] For if he had not strengthened the Church or brought Spain into Italy, putting down the Venetians would have been perfectly reasonable and necessary, but having made those initial moves, he should never have agreed to their ruin, because as long as the Venetians remained powerful, they would have always kept the others out of Lombardy, both because they would not have consented to it unless they could become the rulers there themselves, and partly because the others would not have wanted to take it from France in order to give it to the Venetians, and they would not have had the courage to attack the two of them together. And if someone should say that King Louis gave the Romagna to Alexander and the Kingdom of Naples to Spain in order to avoid a war, I would reply with the arguments given above: that one should never allow disorders to continue for the sake of avoiding a war, because war is not avoided, but merely deferred to your disadvantage. And if others should allege the oath that the king swore to the pope to undertake that enterprise for him, in exchange for the dissolution of the king's marriage and a cardinal's hat for Rouen, I would reply with what I will say later about the word of princes and how it should be kept.[5]

Thus King Louis lost Lombardy because he did not observe any of the rules followed by others who have taken countries and sought to hold onto them. Nor is this some sort of miracle, but perfectly ordinary and reasonable. And I talked over this subject at Nantes with Cardinal Rouen when Valentino (as people generally call Cesare Borgia,[6] the son of Pope Alexander) was occupying the Romagna. For when the cardinal of Rouen told me that the Italians knew nothing about war, I replied that the French knew nothing about statecraft, for if they did, they would never have allowed the Church to grow so great.[7] And experience has shown that the Church and Spain have become great in Italy because of France, and her ruin, because of them. From this may be drawn a general rule which

4. When he joined the League of Cambrai (1508) under the leadership of Julius II to take part in a war against the Venetians, Louis sealed his own doom. The victory at Vailà or Agnadello (May 14, 1509), which took from the Venetians the territory they held on the mainland (their "state"), led directly to the formation of the Lega Santa, or Holy League, which linked the pope, who had broken with the French in 1510, to Venice, whose armies were allowed to take on a subordinate role for the purpose of driving the French from Italy.

5. See Chapter 18 (pp. 54–57). Rouen was Georges d'Amboise (1460–1510), who was made the archbishop of Rouen in 1493. An adviser to Louis XII, he was made a cardinal when Louis became king in 1498. Rouen continued to serve him during the wars in Italy.

6. Cesare Borgia was called Valentino or Duke Valentino because when he resigned as a cardinal in 1498 to take command of the forces of his father, Pope Alexander VI, the French king Louis XII made him the duke of Valentinois.

7. Machiavelli was on a diplomatic mission to France in 1500, just when Cesare Borgia and his father were starting to gain control of the Romagna, and he must have talked with Georges d'Amboise, the cardinal of Rouen, at that time.

never, or rarely, fails to hold: that whoever is the cause of another's becoming powerful will ruin himself, because the source of that power is either his resourcefulness or his strength, and both of these qualities are suspect to the one who has been given that power.

Chapter 4

Why, after Alexander's Death, His Successors Did Not Lose the Kingdom He Had Acquired from Darius

Considering how difficult it is to hold onto a newly acquired state, someone might wonder why, after the death of Alexander, when he had become the master of Asia in just a few years and had scarcely occupied it, the whole land did not rebel, as would have seemed reasonable. Nevertheless, Alexander's successors maintained their hold on it and had no difficulties in keeping it other than those that arose among themselves because of their own ambitions.[1] I would reply that all principalities of which we have knowledge are governed in two different ways: either by a prince with everyone else as servants who, by his appointment and with his permission, assist him as his ministers in governing that realm; or by a prince and the barons, who hold that rank, not through the grace of their lord, but by having been born into an ancient family. Barons of this sort have states and subjects of their own, who recognize them as their lords and feel a natural affection for them. In states governed by a prince and his servants, the prince has more authority, because in his entire province there is nobody who recognizes anyone except him as their superior, and if they obey others, they obey them as his ministers and officials, and do not feel any particular love for them.

Examples of these two different sorts of governments in our own time are the Turk and the king of France. The whole monarchy of Turkey is governed by a single ruler; everyone else is his servant; and dividing his realm into districts, he sends different administrators to each one, and changes and moves them around as he thinks best.[2]

1. When Alexander died abruptly in 323 BCE, power was divided among his main lieutenants, Antipater, Antigonus, Ptolemy, and Perdiccas. As these men had already been granted wide governmental as well as military power (they were satraps of districts as well as generals of the army), they adapted easily to independent rule. The exception Machiavelli makes (in saying that the only difficulty they had came from their quarrels with one another) is accurate and not insignificant: those quarrels were continuous, immensely complex, and brutally destructive.
2. Two great sultans ruled Turkey in Machiavelli's time: Mehmed II, also known as Mehmed or Muhammad the Conqueror (b. 1432; ruled 1444–46, 1451–81), and his son Bayezid II (b. 1447; ruled 1481–1512). The first instituted and the second consolidated a highly efficient, centralized government, and to control enemies at home and abroad, both made use of the elite corps of janissaries, a standing army loyal to the sultan, which was created in the 14th century and was composed of well-disciplined Christian slaves. For the districts into which Turkey was divided, Machiavelli uses the word *sangiachi*, which is an Italianized form of the Turkish word *sanjaks*.

But the king of France is in the midst of a great many nobles of long standing, each recognized in that state by their subjects, and loved by them. They have their hereditary privileges, nor can the king take them away, except at his peril. Whoever considers these two states, then, will find that the acquisition of the Turk's state would be hard, but once it is conquered, it would be very easy to hold. And so, on the contrary, you will find that in some respects it would be easier to conquer the state of France, but very difficult to hold onto it.

The causes of the problems involved in gaining control of the kingdom of the Turk are that one cannot be invited in by the princes of that realm, or hope to facilitate his enterprise by means of a rebellion of those whom the ruler has around him. This happens for the reasons I have given above: because they are all slaves and obligated to their lord, it will be more difficult to corrupt them, and even if they were corrupted, one cannot hope they will be very useful, since they would not be able to bring the people along with them, for the reasons given. Therefore, whoever attacks the Turks should expect to find them united, and he should base his hopes more on his own strength than on the disorder of others. But once they are beaten and routed on the field of battle so that they can no longer regroup their armies, there is nothing else to worry about except the family of the prince, and once that is extinguished, there is no one left to fear, since the others have no credit with the people, and just as the conqueror, before his victory, could not hope for anything from them, so, after it, he has no nothing to fear from them.

The contrary occurs with realms governed like that of France, because you can easily get into them by winning over some of the barons in the kingdom, since there will always be malcontents and others who desire to make changes.[3] For the reasons I have already given, these people can open the way for you into that state and make your victory an easy one. But after that, if you wish to hold onto power, that will involve countless difficulties both with those who helped you and with those you have beaten. Nor is it sufficient for you to wipe out the family of the prince, because the nobles who remain will head up new rebellions, and since you can neither content them nor exterminate them completely, you will lose that state whenever that occasion presents itself.

Now, if you consider what kind of government Darius[4] had, you will find it similar to that of the Turk. And therefore Alexander first had to defeat him utterly and take the country from him. After that

3. Henry V of England had, for example, made expert use of the dukes of Burgundy to gain a foothold in France early in the 15th century; even as Machiavelli wrote, the duke of Savoy was intriguing with Austria for protection against annexation by France.

4. Machiavelli is referring to Darius III Codomannus, the last king of Persia, who was born c. 380 and ruled from 336 to 330 BCE.

victory, with Darius dead, the state remained secure in Alexander's possession for the reasons described above. And if his successors had been united, they could have enjoyed it at their leisure, because no other disturbances arose in the kingdom except those they themselves stirred up. But it is impossible to hold onto states like France's so peacefully. Hence, the frequent rebellions of Spain, France, and Greece against the Romans occurred because of the numerous principalities in those states.[5] As long as the memory of those things lasted, the Romans were always uncertain about their control, but they became the secure possessors of those states once those memories were extinguished because of the power and the long duration of the empire. And later, when the Romans were fighting among themselves, each one of them could attract followers from those provinces, depending on the authority he had acquired there, and since the families of their ancient rulers were extinct, they recognized no one except the Romans. All these things considered, then, no one should marvel at the ease with which Alexander maintained his control over all of Asia, and at the difficulties that others have had in preserving what they acquired, such as Pyrrhus[6] and many others. This was not the result of the greater or lesser ability [*virtù*] of the conqueror, but of the dissimilarities among those who were his subjects.

Chapter 5

How Cities or Principalities Are to Be Administered That Used to Live under Their Own Laws before Being Conquered

As I have said, when states are acquired that are used to living freely and under their own laws, there are three ways to hold onto them: the first is to destroy them;[1] the second, to go and live there in

5. Spain took a long time to become Romanized and resisted the process (especially among the mountain tribes) well into the empire. But Gaul, after its conquest by Caesar, was almost a model of docility—there were few, only short-lived revolts against Roman power. And Greece, apart from the incursion of 88–84 BCE by Mithridates VI of Pontus (b. 135; ruled 120–63 BCE), was almost as well behaved. Historical inaccuracy is unusual in Machiavelli, and his overstatements here suggest he may be concerned about making a categorical distinction between Asian dynasties (Darius, the sultans) and European governments (less centralized and more like a confederation of local powers).
6. Pyrrhus of Epirus (b. 319; ruled 306–302, 297–272 BCE) was a Greek king related to Alexander the Great. He was called into Italy in 281 by the city of Tarentum to help defend the Greek colonies along the southern coast of the peninsula, including Naples, and in much of the island of Sicily, against encroaching Roman power. He defeated the Romans in battle but failed to establish a permanent state in the peninsula.
1. What Machiavelli means by "destroy them" could be the physical demolition of the captured cities and the dispersal of their inhabitants. But nothing like that happened in Renaissance Italy, and Machiavelli is unlikely to have recommended this policy "seriously" because it is apparent that Florence itself is the city he is focused on.

person; the third, to let them live under their own laws, exacting tribute from them and creating a government there composed of a few people who will keep it friendly toward you, for such a government, being the prince's creation, knows that it cannot stand without his friendship and power, and that it has to do all it can to preserve his control there. And a city used to living in freedom can be held more easily by means of its citizens than in any other way—assuming you want to keep it.

As examples, there are the Spartans and the Romans. The Spartans held onto Athens and Thebes by creating within them governments consisting of a few people; nevertheless, they lost both of them.[2] In order to hold Capua, Carthage, and Numantia, the Romans destroyed them,[3] and so, they did not lose them. They wanted to hold Greece in almost the same way the Spartans did, by making it free and leaving it under its own laws, and when they did not succeed, they were forced to destroy many cities in that province in order to hold onto it. In truth, there is no sure way to hold onto such cities except by destroying them, and the man who becomes the master of a city accustomed to living in freedom and does not destroy it may expect to be destroyed by it, for during a rebellion the city always finds refuge in the name of liberty and its ancient ordinances, which are never forgotten despite the long passage of time or the benefits it has received. And no matter what measures are taken in the present or for the future, if the inhabitants are not separated or scattered, they will not forget that name and those ordinances, and at every opportunity, they will immediately have recourse to them, as Pisa did after one hundred years of being held in servitude by the Florentines.[4] But when cities or provinces are used to living under a prince and his family line is extinguished, since, on the one hand, they are used to obeying, and on the other, they no longer have their old prince, they cannot agree among themselves to choose a new one, nor do they know how to live as free men. As a result, they are slower to take up arms, and a prince can win them over with greater

2. After the fall of Athens to Sparta in 405 BCE, the city was ruled by an oligarchy controlled by the Spartans called the Thirty Tyrants until 403, when it was liberated by the Athenian Thrasybulus (c. 440–388 BCE). Although Thebes and Sparta had previously been allies, in 382 BCE Spartan forces occupied the citadel of Thebes until they were driven out of the city three years later.
3. After lengthy sieges, Capua in Italy, Carthage in Africa, and Numantia in Spain were captured in 211, 146, and 133 BCE, respectively. The buildings in the towns were completely destroyed, their populations scattered, and their laws and constitutions abrogated. All three were later reconstituted, but from scratch. Machiavelli may also be alluding to the capture of contemporary Capua on July 24, 1501, by a French army that was then fighting for control of Naples with the Spanish. The city was not destroyed, but there was terrible looting and a massacre of around seven thousand people.
4. Pisa, purchased by Florence in 1405 and subjugated in 1406, was very harshly treated throughout the 15th century. It liberated itself in 1494 when Charles VIII invaded Italy. After four bitter campaigns and sieges, Florence won it back again in June 1509.

ease and make himself secure among them. But in republics there is greater life, greater hatred, more desire for revenge; the memory of their ancient liberty does not, nor can it, allow them any rest, so that the safest course to take with them is either to exterminate them or to go and live there.

Chapter 6

On New Principalities That Have Been Acquired with One's Own Arms and Prowess[1]

No one should marvel if in speaking about principalities with a completely new prince and political arrangements, I will adduce the greatest examples. Since men almost always walk along the paths beaten by others and proceed to act by imitating them, and since they cannot always stay on others' paths or attain the level of skill [*virtù*] of those you imitate, a prudent man should always enter the paths beaten by great men and imitate those who were the very best, so that, if his own talent [*virtù*] does not measure up to theirs, at least it will give off something of its odor. And he will do what prudent archers do when the spot they want to hit seems too far away: knowing the strength [*virtù*] of their bow, they aim much higher than the target they have chosen, not because they expect their arrow to reach such a height, but to be able to hit their target by aiming above it.

Let me say, then, that a new prince in a completely new principality will encounter more or less difficulty in holding onto it depending on whether he, as its conqueror, is more or less capable [*virtuoso*]. And since this transition from private citizen to prince presupposes either skill [*virtù*] or Fortune, it seems that either one or the other of these two might partly mitigate many difficulties. Nevertheless, the one who has entrusted himself less to Fortune has had more success in maintaining his rule. It also makes things easier if the prince, who does not have any other states, is forced to go and live there in person. But to come to those who have become princes through their own ability [*virtù*] and not by means of Fortune, I say that the most outstanding are Moses, Cyrus, Romulus, Theseus, and the like. And although one should not discuss Moses, since he was merely carrying out the things he was ordered to do by God, nevertheless he should be admired, if only for the grace that made him worthy of talking with God. But let us consider Cyrus and the others who have acquired or founded states: you will find them all deserving of admiration, and if their particular actions and decrees are considered, they will not appear different from those of

1. Machiavelli uses the Latin word *virtus* here, the equivalent of the Italian *virtù*, and it has been translated similarly.

Moses, who had so great a teacher. And when examining their actions and their lives, it will be seen that they got nothing from Fortune but an opportunity, which gave them matter into which they could introduce whatever form they thought fit, and that without that opportunity the strength [*virtù*] of their spirit would have been extinguished, and that without that strength [*virtù*] the opportunity would have come in vain.[2]

It was thus necessary for Moses to find the people of Israel in Egypt, enslaved and oppressed by the Egyptians, so that they would be disposed to follow him in order to escape from servitude.[3] It was necessary that Romulus should not remain in Alba and should have been exposed at birth, so that he might become the king of Rome and the founder of that nation.[4] It was necessary that Cyrus should find the Persians discontented with the rule of the Medes, and the Medes soft and effeminate from long years of peace.[5] Theseus could not have displayed his ability [*virtù*] if he had not found the Athenians disunified.[6] These opportunities, therefore, allowed these men to prosper, and their own abilities [*virtù*] enabled them to spot their opportunities, so that they ennobled their countries and made them exceedingly prosperous.

Like these men, those who become princes through their prowess [*per vie virtuose*] have trouble acquiring their principality, but hold onto it with ease, and the difficulties they have in acquiring it arise in part from the new laws and measures that they are forced to introduce in order to found their state and make themselves secure. And it should be borne in mind that there is nothing more difficult to manage, or more uncertain of success, or more dangerous to handle than to take the lead in introducing a new order of things. For the innovator has enemies in all those who are doing well under the old order, and he has only lukewarm defenders in all those who would do well under the new one. This lukewarmness arises partly from fear of their adversaries who have the laws on their side,

2. The scholastic distinction between matter (*materia*) and form (*forma*) carried with it the notion that the former was feminine and the latter masculine. The male thus provided shape and a soul for what, without him, would have been a merely inchoate mass (*mola*). This sexual meaning is clearer in Machiavelli's Italian, for he speaks of "introducing" form "into" matter (*introdurvi dentro*), rather than, to use the more idiomatic English expression, "imposing" form "on" matter. Thus the prince's *virtù* is the male principle in the marriage between the ruler and his people.
3. For the story of Moses and the bondage of the Hebrews in Egypt, see the Bible, Exodus 2–6. It is noteworthy that Moses and the three other figures named here all founded long-lived states, but they could also be said to be mythical or are made to seem so in the stories told of them.
4. The story of Romulus's founding of Rome is recounted by Livy (*History of Rome,* 1.5–1.7); it was also in Plutarch's *Life of Romulus.*
5. Peace lasted from 600 to 560 BCE. The story of Cyrus and the Medes is told by Herodotus (*Histories,* 1.123–130).
6. The story of Theseus's unification of Athens is told by Plutarch in his *Life of Theseus;* Plutarch also compares Theseus with Romulus in his *Parallel Lives.*

and partly from the incredulity of men who do not truly believe in new things until they have had a solid experience of them. This is why, whenever those enemies have the occasion to attack, they do so with the zeal of partisans, while the others defend him tepidly, so that together with them, everything is put at risk.

Still, in order to treat this matter thoroughly, it is necessary to determine whether these innovators are able to stand on their own or are dependent on others; that is, whether, in order to conduct their affairs, they have to go begging or are able to resort to force. In the first case they always end up badly and do not accomplish anything, but when they depend on their own resources and can make use of force, then they are rarely at risk. This is the reason why all the armed prophets are victorious and the unarmed ones come to ruin. For, apart from what has already been said, people are by nature fickle, and it is easy to persuade them of something, but difficult to keep them persuaded about it. And therefore, it is necessary to arrange things so that when they are no longer believed, they can be compelled to believe by force.[7] Moses, Cyrus, Theseus, and Romulus could not have made people obey their laws for so long if they had been unarmed, which is what happened in our own times with Fra Girolamo Savonarola,[8] who, with his new laws, came to ruin as soon as the people began to lose their faith in him, and he had no way of keeping the believers in line or of turning disbelievers into believers. Therefore, such men as these encounter great difficulties in conducting their affairs, and all their dangers are met along the way and must be overcome by their talents [*virtù*]. But once they have overcome them, the people begin to hold them in veneration, and having destroyed those who envy their abilities, they remain powerful, secure, honored, and happy.[9]

To such exalted examples I want to add a lesser one, but one that certainly parallels the others in some measure, and I want it to suffice for all similar cases. This is the example of Hieron of Syracuse.[1]

7. Practically the first act of Moses when he descended from Sinai with the tablets was to get the sons of Levi to massacre the three thousand worshipers of the Golden Calf (Exodus 32.19–28). Romulus killed Remus and his associate Titus Tatius, acts that Plutarch describes and Machiavelli endorses in the *Discourses* (p. 119).
8. Girolamo Savonarola (1452–1498) was a religious reformer who denounced the worldliness of the Florentines and the corruption of the Church. When the Medici were exiled in 1494, he became the spiritual leader of the city, which he wanted to turn into a Christian republic. He was undone, less by the fickleness of his followers than by the hostility of Pope Alexander VI and the great houses of Florence, the Medici among them. Alexander excommunicated the Dominican friar in 1497, and at the order of papal representatives, he was arrested, tortured, convicted of heresy, hanged, and burned at the stake along with two of his followers on May 23, 1498.
9. My translation of Machiavelli's *felici*, which could also mean "prosperous."
1. Hieron (or Hiero) II of Syracuse ruled c. 271–216 BCE. Machiavelli could have learned about him from Livy, *History of Rome*, 21.49–51, and Polybius, *The Histories*, 1.7–9. He was an able general who made himself king of Syracuse. After initially siding with the Carthaginians, he became a dependable ally of the Romans during both of the wars they fought with Carthage.

From being a private citizen he rose to become the prince of Syracuse, nor did he owe anything to Fortune except the opportunity, for the Syracusans, being oppressed, elected him their captain, from which he earned the right to be made their prince. And he was a man of such ability [*virtù*], even as a private citizen, that someone who wrote about him said that "he lacked nothing to reign except a realm."[2] He abolished the old army and formed a new one, abandoned old alliances and acquired new ones, and when he had allies and soldiers of his own, he could build on such a foundation whatever edifice he wanted. Thus, for him it was really hard to acquire what he did, but it took little to maintain his hold on it.

Chapter 7

On New Principalities Acquired with the Arms of Others and by Means of Fortune

When private citizens are made into princes solely by means of Fortune and do so with little effort, it takes little effort to rise, but a great deal to hold onto their positions. And they have no difficulty along the way as they go flying onward, but all the difficulties arise when they have landed. These are the people who have gained control of a state either by means of money or because of a favor from someone who gives it to them, as happened to many men in Greece, in the cities of Ionia and the Hellespont, who were made princes by Darius in order to hold them for the sake of his own his security and glory; such were also those who from being private citizens became emperors[1] by bribing the soldiers. These men depend simply on the will and fortune of those who granted them their position, two things which are extremely volatile and unstable, and they do not know how, nor are they able, to hold onto that position. They do not know how because, unless they are men of great intelligence and ability [*virtù*], it is unreasonable to expect them to know how to command others after having spent all their lives as private citizens. Nor can they maintain their positions because they have no troops who are loyal and devoted to them. Besides, states that take root quickly, like everything else in nature that is born and grows rapidly, cannot develop their roots complete with all their branchings, so that they are

2. Machiavelli is citing (inaccurately) the Roman historian Marcus Junianus Justinus, *Epitome of the Philippic Histories of Pompeius Trogus,* 23.4.

1. Machiavelli means the Roman emperors who owed their thrones to the army or the Praetorian Guard; many of these emperors are discussed in Chapter 19 (see pp. 60–65), in which Machiavelli particularly emphasizes Septimius Severus as one who rose to power and maintained his rule by gratifying the army. Darius the Great, king of Persia from 522 to 485 BCE, created many local princedoms and satrapies, especially in the Greek city-states of Asia Minor and the Hellespont.

destroyed by the first storm that strikes—unless, as has been said, those who have become princes so quickly have such great ability [*virtù*] that they instantly know how to prepare themselves to preserve what Fortune has tossed into their laps and that afterward they are able to lay those foundations that others have done before becoming princes.

With regard to these two methods of becoming a prince—by ability [*virtù*] or by Fortune—I want to adduce two examples here of recent memory, and they are those of Francesco Sforza and Cesare Borgia. By using the appropriate means and with great cunning [*virtù*], Francesco[2] started out as a private citizen and became duke of Milan, and what he acquired with a thousand difficulties, he maintained with little effort. On the other hand, Cesare Borgia, called Duke Valentino[3] by the common people, acquired his state through his father's fortune and lost it in the same way, and that despite the fact that he used every means and did everything that a prudent and capable [*virtuoso*] man should do so as to put down his roots in those states which the arms and fortune of others had granted him. For, as noted above, he who does not lay his foundations in advance might be able, with great effort [*virtù*], to lay them later, although he would do so with inconvenience to the architect and danger to the building. If, then, one considers all the duke's proceedings, one will see that he had laid firm foundations for future power, which I do not judge it superfluous to describe, since I cannot imagine better precepts for a new prince than the example of his actions. And if he failed to profit from what he established, the fault was not his but resulted from the extraordinary and extreme malice of Fortune.

When Alexander VI set out to elevate his son, the duke, he faced many difficulties, both present and future. First, he saw no way of making him master of any state that had not belonged to the Church, and when he contemplated his taking over the possessions of the Church, he realized that the duke of Milan would not consent to it, nor would the Venetians because Faenza and Rimini were already under their protection. In addition, he saw that the armies of Italy, and especially the ones he might have been able to use, were in the hands of those who had reason to fear the pope's power, and therefore he could not trust them since they all belonged to the Orsini

2. On Francesco Sforza, see n. 1, p. 4.
3. See n. 6, p. 12. Cesare Borgia (c. 1476–1507) was the illegitimate son of Rodrigo Borgia, later Pope Alexander VI, and engineered the papal conquest of the Romagna between 1499 and 1502. When Alexander died in 1503, however, Cesare lost the state he had created, for he could not prevent the election of Giuliano della Rovere, an inveterate enemy of the Borgias, as Pope Julius II, and he suffered a series of misfortunes from then until his death in Spain in 1507. Machiavelli met him several times on various diplomatic missions and studied his behavior closely.

and Colonna families and their confederates.[4] It was therefore necessary to upset existing arrangements and create disorder in those states so as to gain secure control as the ruler of some of them. This was easy for him to do, because he found that the Venetians, moved by other considerations, had decided to allow the French to come back into Italy, something he not only did not oppose, but made easier by dissolving the first marriage of King Louis.[5] Thus, the king entered Italy with the aid of the Venetians and the consent of Alexander, and no sooner was he in Milan than the pope got troops from him for the campaign in the Romagna, which surrendered to him because of the king's reputation.[6]

When the duke had acquired the Romagna and beaten the Colonna, he wanted to keep that province and push on ahead, but two things held him back: the first, his troops, who did not seem loyal to him; the other, the will of France. That is, he feared that the troops of the Orsini he had been using would play him false and not only keep him from acquiring more territory, but take what he had already acquired away from him, and he also feared that the king would do the same thing. The Orsini confirmed this for him when, after the storming of Faenza, he assaulted Bologna and observed how coldly they acted in that assault; and as for the king, the duke perceived his intentions when, after he had taken the duchy of Urbino, he attacked Tuscany, and the king made him desist from that enterprise.[7] As a result, the duke decided he would no longer depend on the arms and fortune of others. And the first thing he did was to weaken the Orsini and Colonna factions in Rome by winning over all their followers who were noblemen: he made them *his* noblemen, giving them generous stipends and honoring them with military commands and offices, according to their station, so that in a few months their affection for their factions was extinguished in their hearts and was entirely

4. The Orsini and the Colonna were famous Roman families, who had been feuding with one another since time immemorial. On the pope's traditional difficulties in putting down one without exalting the other, see Chapter 11, pp. 37–38.

5. Cesare led a lavish expedition to France in 1498 and negotiated a treaty between his father and Louis XII that gave the latter a dispensation to set aside his first wife, Jeanne, in order to marry Charles VIII's widow, Anne of Brittany, thereby gaining Louis's support for the papacy's plan to conquer Naples. Cesare was also given the duchy of Valentinois in France and gained the king's support to extend the papal state in the Romagna.

6. Cesare made two formal campaigns in the Romagna. The first occurred in 1499–1500. Leading an army composed primarily of French, Gascon, and Swiss troops, he quickly subdued Imola (November 14, 1499) and Forlì (December 17, 1499). In the second campaign, leading a larger army that included many Italian mercenaries, he took Rimini, Pesaro, and Faenza between October 1500 and June 1501.

7. In 1502, Cesare conquered Camerino and Urbino for the pope and put pressure on Bologna, but never besieged it. In May 15 of that year, Florence hired the duke as its "protector," buying him off, proposing to give him a stipend of 36,000 ducats a year for three years. Thus the city maintained its independence, although it was also supposedly under the "protection" of France.

directed toward the duke. After this, having already dispersed those who belonged to the house of the Colonna, he waited for an opportunity to wipe out the Orsini, and when a good one turned up, he made even better use of it. For when the Orsini realized, too late, that the preeminence of the duke and the Church meant their ruin, they arranged a meeting at La Magione in the territory of Perugia.[8] This was the cause of the rebellion of Urbino and tumults in the Romagna and countless dangers for the duke.[9] He overcame all of them with the aid of the French, and once his reputation had been restored, he placed no trust in either France or any other forces from outside. In order to avoid putting himself at risk with them, he turned to deceit, and he knew how to dissemble his intentions so well that the Orsini were reconciled with him through the mediation of Signor Paolo.[1] Nor did the duke fail to reassure him by using every sort of courtesy, giving him money, clothing, and horses, so that the Orsini, in their simple-mindedness, went to Sinigaglia and put themselves in his hands.[2] Thus, having wiped out these leaders and turned their partisans into his friends, the duke had laid down really good foundations for his power, since he held the entire Romagna as well as the Duchy of Urbino, and most important, it seemed to him that he had acquired the Romagna as his friend, having won over all its people from the moment they began to taste the benefits of his rule.

And because this part is worthy of note and of being imitated by others, I do not want to leave it out. When the duke had taken the Romagna, he found it to have been ruled by impotent lords who would have sooner plundered their subjects than governed them, and who had given them cause for disunity rather than unity, so that the entire province was overwhelmed by robberies, quarrels, and abuses of every description. Consequently, he decided that, if he wanted to pacify the province and make it obedient to its sovereign once again, he had to provide them with good government. He therefore put Messer Remirro de Orco in charge, a cruel and decisive man, to whom he gave the fullest authority. In short order, this man restored peace and unity in the province, greatly enhancing his own reputation. After

8. Present at the gathering at La Magione, a castle near Perugia belonging to Giulio Orsini, on October 9, 1502, were not just the members of the Orsini family but also Pandolfo Petrucci of Siena, Ermete Bentivoglio, and some of the members of the Baglioni family of Perugia as well as several of Cesare's captains, including Vitellozzo Vitelli and Oliverotto da Fermo.
9. Cesare lost Urbino when the population revolted against his occupying forces and he decided to pull out of the city. His retreating troops were beaten at the village of Calmazzo on October 17, 1502, by a league formed by his ex-condottieri, led by Vitellozzo Vitelli.
1. Paolo Orsini was the head of the family, who swore allegiance to Cesare on October 25, 1502, at Imola.
2. Vitellozzo Vitelli and Oliverotto da Fermo were strangled at Sinigaglia on the last day of December 1502, as were Paolo Orsini and the count of Gravina-Orsini on January 18, 1503, at Castel della Pieve.

that, the duke decided that such excessive authority was unnecessary, because he feared it might become odious, and he set up a civil court in the middle of the province with a truly excellent judge presiding over it, in which each city had its own advocate. And because he knew that the rigorous measures of the past had generated a certain amount of hatred toward him, in order to purge it from the minds of the people and to win them over for himself completely, he determined to show that if any cruelty had occurred, it had not come from him, but was due to the harsh nature of his minister. And seizing the occasion to deal with the matter, one morning he had him put in the piazza at Cesena in two pieces, with a piece of wood and a bloody knife beside him. The ferocity of such a spectacle left those people feeling at one and the same time both stunned and satisfied.[3]

But to return to the place from which we departed, let me say that the duke now found himself quite powerful and partially secure from immediate dangers, since he had armed himself as he wished and had in good measure destroyed those forces which, were they nearby, might have harmed him. If he wanted to proceed with his conquests, he still had to deal with the king of France, because he knew that the king, who had belatedly become aware of his mistake, would not have supported them. And for this reason he began to seek out new alliances and to temporize with France while the French army was making its way toward the kingdom of Naples to confront the Spaniards, who were besieging Gaeta.[4] It was his intention to secure the support of the latter, which he would soon have succeeded in doing if Alexander had lived.[5]

These were his methods with regard to present matters. As for the future, the first thing he had to worry about was that a new successor in the Church would not be his supporter and might seek to take away what Alexander had given him. And he thought of four ways to deal with this situation: first, he would eliminate the families of those lords whom he had ruined so that the pope would not have an opportunity to make use of them; second, he would win over all the noblemen of Rome, as I have said, so that he could use them to keep the pope in check; third, to make the College of Cardinals as much

3. Remirro de Orco, or Ramiro de Lorqua, to call him by his Spanish name (1452–1502), was a condottiere whom Cesare appointed the lieutenant of the Romagna in March 1501. Brought before a civil tribunal presided over by Antonio del Monte that sat between October and November 1502 and imprisoned on December 22 of that year, de Orco was put to death the morning of December 26. Note that Machiavelli does not specify in this passage what the "two pieces" of Remirro's body were, or what the knife and the piece of wood symbolize.
4. A few miles north of Naples, Gaeta was the first center of fighting between the French and the Spanish after the breakdown of the Treaty of Granada of 1491.
5. Alexander VI died on August 18, 1503, of a sudden fever, with which Cesare was also afflicted. Francesco Todeschini Piccolomini (b. 1439) was elected pope as Pius III on September 22, but died on October 18, and was replaced by Giuliano della Rovere as Pope Julius II on November 1.

his own as he could; fourth, to acquire so much power before the pope died that he could, by himself, resist a first onslaught. Of these four things, he had achieved three by the time Alexander died; the fourth he had almost accomplished. For of the lords whom he had ruined, he killed as many as he could get hold of, and very few escaped; he had won over the Roman noblemen; and in the College he controlled the greatest number. As for new conquests, he had planned to become the lord of Tuscany and was already the master of Perugia and Piombino, and he had placed Pisa under his protection.[6] And since he no longer had to be concerned about France (for he did not have to do so any longer since the French had been stripped of the kingdom of Naples by the Spaniards so that both of them were obliged to buy his friendship), he assaulted Pisa. After this, partly to spite the Florentines and partly out of fear, Lucca and Siena would have yielded at once, for which the Florentines would have had no remedy. If he had succeeded (and he was doing so in the very year that Alexander died), he would have acquired for himself such strength and such prestige that he could have stood alone and would no longer have had to depend on other people's fortune and forces, but on his own power and ability [*virtù*]. But five years after the duke had first drawn his sword, Alexander died, leaving him with only the state of the Romagna consolidated, and all the others up in the air, between two very powerful enemy armies, and deathly ill. Yet, the duke possessed such great ferocity and so much energy [*virtù*], and so well did he understand that men were to be won over or destroyed,[7] and so sturdy were the foundations he had laid for himself in so short a period, that if he had not had those two armies on his back, or if he had been healthy, he would have surmounted every difficulty. And that his foundations were good was evident, since the Romagna waited more than a month for him; in Rome, even though half alive, he was still safe; and although the Baglioni, the Vitelli, and the Orsini came to Rome, they had no followers to oppose him; if he could not make the person he wanted pope, at least he could have prevented someone he did not want from being elected.[8] Still, had he been healthy when Alexander died,

6. Perugia was conquered on January 6, 1503, and Piombino on September 3, 1501. Pisa placed itself under his control in August 1503; it had relied on the French to maintain its independence from Florence, and when the Spanish dislodged the French from Naples and the Pisans could no longer depend on them for protection, they turned to Cesare instead.
7. Machiavelli's Italian here is *guadagnare o perdere*. This second verb can also be translated as "lost," which seems to complement "won over" better than "destroyed." However, in Machiavelli's thought, the true alternative to the prince's winning of people's allegiance is not a matter of his losing it—that is, leaving them indifferent—but of destroying them so that they are no longer a potential danger to him.
8. Cesare had many enemies, and when he was sick, they all tried to finish him off, but had little success in doing so. Pius III, who succeeded Alexander, supported him, but lasted only some ten days as pope.

everything would have been easy for him. And on the day that Julius II was elected, he told me himself that he had thought of what could happen at his father's death and had found a remedy for everything, except that he never thought that when his father was dying, he, too, would be close to death himself.[9]

Therefore, having reviewed all the duke's actions, I would not know how to reproach him. On the contrary, it seems to me right to propose him, as I have done, for imitation by all of those who by means of Fortune and the arms of others have risen to power. For having great courage and lofty goals, he could not have conducted himself otherwise, and his plans were frustrated only by the brevity of Alexander's life and his own illness. Anyone, therefore, who deems it necessary in his new principality to keep himself safe from his enemies, to win friends, to conquer either by force or by fraud, to make himself loved and feared by the people, followed and revered by his soldiers, to wipe out those who can or may do you harm, to renovate old institutions with new measures, to be both severe and kind, magnanimous and liberal, to eliminate an untrustworthy army and create a new one, to maintain alliances with kings and princes so that they must be either glad to help you or cautious about harming you—such a person cannot find recent examples that are better to imitate than the actions of this man. He can only be blamed for making Julius pope, where he made a bad choice, because, as I said, if he could not make a pope to his liking, he could have kept someone else from the office, and he should never have allowed any of those cardinals whom he had injured, or who, having become pope, might have had reason to fear him, to be elevated to the papacy.[1] For men injure others because of either fear or hatred. Those whom he had injured were, among others, San Pietro in Vincoli, Colonna, San Giorgio, Ascanio; all the others, if they had become pope, would have had reason to fear him except for Rouen[2] and the Spaniards, the latter because of family ties and obligations to him, the former

9. Machiavelli was sent by Florence to Rome for the papal conclave that lasted from October to December 1503. After Pius III died, it elected Julius II, who was Cesare's enemy.
1. In the elections of September 1503, which led to the brief papacy of Pius III, there were originally fifteen votes for Carvajal, a Spaniard; fourteen for della Rovere; and thirteen for Rouen. Pius was elected as a compromise candidate when all three of the leading candidates agreed to withdraw. In the October election, which made Julius II pope, there was no significant division since Rouen withdrew, and Julius was elected on the first ballot.
2. Cardinals may be known either by the Roman church to which they are assigned, or by their family names, or even by their first names. San Pietro in Vincoli was Giuliano della Rovere (1443–1513), who became Pope Julius II in 1503. Colonna was Giovanni Colonna (1456–1508), who was made a cardinal in 1480. San Giorgio was Raffaele Riario (1461–1521), a great-nephew of Francesco della Rovere, who had been Pope Sixtus IV (b. 1414; pope 1471–84). Ascanio was Ascanio Sforza (1455–1505), son of Francesco and brother of Ludovico il Moro. Captured by the French and taken to France in 1500, he was released thanks to the influence of Rouen (see n. 5, p. 12), who wanted his vote to be made pope.

because of his power, since he was closely tied to the king of France. Therefore, the duke, first and foremost, should have made a Spaniard pope, and if he could not, he should have agreed to its being Rouen and not San Pietro in Vincoli.[3] And anyone who believes that new benefits make great men forget old injuries is deluding himself. The duke thus made a mistake in this decision, and it was the cause of his final ruin.

Chapter 8

On Those Who Have Become Princes through Crimes

But because there are also two other ways of becoming a prince from being a private citizen, ways which cannot be attributed altogether either to Fortune or to ability [*virtù*], I do not believe I can omit them, even though one could be treated more fully in a discussion of republics.[1] These are: when one ascends to princely rule by some wicked and nefarious route; or when a private citizen becomes the prince of his country by the favor of his fellow-citizens. And in speaking of the first method, I will give two examples, one ancient, the other modern, without otherwise entering into the merits of this method, because I judge these examples will suffice for anyone to imitate who should find that necessary.

Agathocles the Sicilian became the king of Syracuse, not simply from being a private citizen, but from a base and abject position.[2] Born the son of a potter, he led a life of the utmost wickedness at every stage of his career, yet he coupled with his wickedness such vigor [*virtù*] of mind and body that, after joining the army, he rose through the ranks to become the military governor of Syracuse. Once established in that position, he decided to make himself prince and to seize by violence, without any obligation to others, that which had been granted to him by common consent. After coming to an understanding about his plan with Hamilcar the Carthaginian,[3] who with

3. Giuliano della Rovere had held a grudge against the Borgias during the ten years of bitter exile in France that they forced on him. His election after the death of Pius III was a foregone conclusion, but Machiavelli is of the opinion that Cesare might have done more for Rouen by manipulating the Spanish faction in the College of Cardinals. The French king Louis XII agreed, and when he heard of the election of Pius, he is said to have shouted, "That son of a whore [Cesare] has kept Rouen from the papacy!"
1. Machiavelli alludes here to his own *Discourses*.
2. Agathocles of Syracuse (361–289 BCE) came to power in 316, thanks to a military coup, and fought a series of wars against the Carthaginians for control of Sicily. Defeated by them, he consolidated his power base in Syracuse and turned his attention to southern Italy, which he sought to bring under his control, although his efforts were cut short when he was assassinated in 289. Machiavelli misrepresents Agathocles's humble origins: his father was the wealthy owner of a pottery factory.
3. Hamilcar was tried by the Carthaginians for having aided Agathocles and died during his trial in 313 BCE. He is not to be confused with Hamilcar Barca, who was also a Carthaginian general and the father of Hannibal.

his armies was waging war in Sicily, one morning he called together the people and the senate of Syracuse, as if he had things concerning the republic to deliberate about, and at a prearranged signal, he had his soldiers kill all the senators and the richest of the people. Once they were dead, he seized the city and ruled it as its prince without any civil dissension. And even though he was twice defeated by the Carthaginians and ultimately besieged, not only was he able to defend his city, but leaving part of his troops to defend it against the siege, he attacked Africa with the others, and in a short time he liberated Syracuse from the siege and placed Carthage in dire straits, so that they were obliged to come to terms with him and to be content with the possession of Africa while leaving Sicily to him.

Therefore, whoever examines the deeds and the ability [*virtù*] of this man will see nothing, or very little, that can be attributed to Fortune, in that, as I said above, he did not ascend to princely rule by means of anyone's help, but by rising up through the ranks of the army, each one of which he won by going through a thousand hardships and perils, and afterwards he maintained his position by a great many feats involving both courage and danger. Still, it cannot be called virtue [*virtù*] to murder one's fellow-citizens, to betray one's friends, to be without loyalty, without mercy, without religion; one may acquire power by means like these, but not glory. For if we consider the courage [*virtù*] Agathocles displayed when facing and escaping from dangers and the greatness of his spirit in sustaining and overcoming adversities, it is hard to see why he should be judged inferior to the greatest of captains. Nonetheless, his ferocious cruelty and inhumanity, along with his innumerable crimes, do not permit him to be celebrated as being among the truly excellent men. One cannot, therefore, attribute to Fortune or virtue [*virtù*] that which he achieved without one or the other.

In our own days, during the papacy of Alexander VI, Oliverotto da Fermo, who many years before had been left fatherless as a child, was raised by a maternal uncle named Giovanni Fogliani and was sent off in the early days of his youth to serve as a soldier under Paolo Vitelli,[4] so that once he had mastered that discipline, he might have been able to obtain an excellent position in the army. Then, after Paolo's death, he served under his brother Vitellozzo,[5] and in a very short time, being a clever person, possessing both a robust body and an equally robust mind, he became the leader of his army. But as it seemed to him servile to depend on others, he plotted to

4. Paolo Vitelli (b. 1461) was an Italian condottiere. He commanded the Florentine army attacking Pisa, but when he did not make sufficient progress in capturing the city, he was accused of treason and executed in 1499.

5. Paolo's brother Vitellozzo (b. c. 1458) was killed by Cesare Borgia at Sinigaglia on December 31, 1503.

capture the city of Fermo with the support of Vitellozzo and the help of some of its citizens, who preferred to see their native land enslaved rather than free. Consequently, he wrote to Giovanni Fogliani how, having been away from home for many years, he wanted to come to see him and his city, and to survey portions of his estate. And since he had not labored so hard in order to acquire anything other than honor, he would like his fellow citizens to see that he had not spent his time in vain, and so, he wanted to come with full honors, accompanied by one hundred of his friends and followers on horseback, and he begged his uncle to be so kind as to arrange an honorable reception for him by the people of Fermo, which would confer honor not only on him, but on his uncle as well, since Oliverotto had been his pupil. Accordingly, Giovanni did not fail in any courtesy due his nephew, and having had the people of Fermo receive him with honor, lodged him in his own house. After several days had passed, during which he made the secret plans necessary for his future wickedness, Oliverotto arranged for a most solemn banquet to which he invited Giovanni Fogliani and all the principal men of Fermo. And when the food had been consumed and all the other entertainments usual at such feasts were completed, Oliverotto artfully raised certain serious topics, speaking of Pope Alexander's greatness and that of Cesare, his son, and of their undertakings. As Giovanni and the others were responding to those comments, Oliverotto arose abruptly, saying that these were things to be discussed in a less public place, and withdrew into a room followed by Giovanni and all the other citizens. No sooner were they seated than out from their hiding places in the room came soldiers who killed Giovanni and all the rest.[6] After this slaughter, Oliverotto mounted his horse, rode through the city, and besieged the chief magistrate in his palace, forcing them out of fear to obey him and to form a government, of which he made himself the prince. And once everyone was dead whose discontent might have threatened him, he strengthened his position with new laws, civil and military, to such effect that within the space of the single year in which he ruled as their prince, not only was he secure in the city of Fermo, but he made himself the terror of all his neighbors. And his expulsion would have been as difficult as that of Agathocles, if he had not let himself be tricked by Cesare Borgia, when, as was said above, the latter captured the Orsini and the Vitelli at Sinigaglia. There Oliverotto, too, was captured one year after the parricide he had committed, and there, together

6. In this coup, Oliverotto Euffreducci da Fermo (1475–1502) killed not only his uncle but his uncle's son Gennaro, his son-in-law Raffaello della Rovere, and four others shortly after his arrival in the city on January 8, 1502. At the time of this story, both Oliverotto and Vitellozzo were in the service of Cesare Borgia.

with Vitellozzo, who had been his teacher in cunning [*virtù*] and wickedness, he was strangled.[7]

Someone might wonder how it happened that Agathocles and others of his ilk, after they had committed countless acts of treachery and cruelty, could live long, secure lives in their native cities, defend themselves from external enemies, and never be conspired against by their own citizens, whereas many others were unable, by means of cruelty, to maintain their states even in times of peace, not to speak of the uncertain times of war. I believe this depends on whether the cruelties are used well or badly. Those can be described as used well (if it is permissible to say "well" about something evil) when they are done all in one fell stroke, for reasons of self-preservation, and when such acts are not repeated after that, but are converted into the greatest benefits possible for one's subjects. Those are badly used which, although they are few at first, grow over time rather than being eliminated. The ones who observe the first method can find some remedy for their condition with God and men, as Agathocles did; it is impossible for those others to preserve themselves.

Thus, it is to be noted that in taking a state, its conqueror should calculate the sum of all those injuries he has to do, and do them all at once, so as not to have to do new ones every day. By not repeating them, he will reassure men and win them over by means of his benefits. Whoever acts otherwise, either because of timidity or bad advice, must always go around with a knife in his hand, nor can he ever make his subjects the foundation of his rule, because, with the fresh, recurring injuries they suffer, they are unable to feel secure with him. For injuries should be done all at one and the same time, because the less they are tasted, the less they will offend, whereas benefits should be distributed very gradually, so that they may be better savored. And above all, a prince should live with his subjects on such terms that no accident, whether bad or good, could make him change his conduct, for when necessities arise because of adverse conditions, you will not have time to resort to harsh measures, and the good things you do will not help you, because you are judged to have acted under pressure, and no one will thank you for that.

Chapter 9

On the Civil Principality

But coming to the other alternative, when a private citizen becomes prince of his native city, not through crimes or other intolerable acts of violence, but by the favor of his fellow citizens (this may be called

7. See n. 2, p. 23.

a civil principality, since achieving it does not necessarily depend either entirely on talent [*virtù*] or entirely on Fortune, but rather on a cleverness assisted by Fortune), I say that one ascends to that position either by the favor of the people or by that of the nobility. For in every city these two different humors[1] are found, and this arises from the fact that the people desire not to be commanded or oppressed by the nobility, while the nobility desires to command and oppress the people. And from these two different appetites one of three effects arises in cities: either princely rule, or liberty, or license.

Princely rule is created either by the people or by the nobility, depending on which of the two is presented with the opportunity. For when the nobility see that they cannot resist the people, they start to build up one of their own and make him prince, so that, under his shadow, they can unleash their appetites. In the same way, when the people see that they cannot resist the nobility, they start offering their support to one man and make him their prince in order to be defended by his authority. The man who achieves princely rule with the help of the great has more difficulty in maintaining his position than one who does so with the help of the people, because, as prince, he finds himself surrounded by many who think of themselves as his equals, and for this reason, he is unable to command and manage them as he would like. But the man who attains princely rule through the favor of the people finds that he is positioned there all alone and that there is no one, or very few, around him who are not ready to obey him. Besides this, there is no way to satisfy the nobility honorably and without injuring others, but one can certainly do so with the people, because the people's goal is more honorable than that of the nobility, since the latter desire to oppress others, while the former desire not to be oppressed.[2] Moreover, a prince can never make himself secure against a hostile people because there are too many of them; he can secure himself against the great, because there are so few of them. The worst that a prince can expect from a hostile people is to be abandoned by them, but from hostile noblemen he has to fear not just abandonment, but their active opposition as well, because, having more foresight and more cunning,

1. Machiavelli's identification of the people and the nobility as "humors" here suggests he sees the state as a "body politic," a notion that is also implied by his frequent references to princes seeking "remedies" for sick states. His use of the term *humors* derives from the fact that in Renaissance medicine the body was seen as being composed of four humors (blood, yellow bile or choler, white bile or phlegm, and black bile or melancholy). One enjoys good health when they are all in balance, but since they usually are not, people are open to diseases, including mental ones. For if the humors were seen as affecting the body, they were also seen as simultaneously affecting the mind, something apparent in the adjectives we still use for personality traits or temperaments: sanguine, choleric, phlegmatic, and melancholic.
2. Machiavelli's strong democratic and popular feelings here are echoed throughout the *Discourses* and especially when he argues that princes are more likely to be ungrateful than the people (see 1.29, p. 130).

they always have time to save themselves and to seek favors from those whom they expect to win. Furthermore, the prince must always live among those same common people, but he can do very well without that same set of noblemen, because he has the power to make and unmake them every day, and to take away and restore their reputations as he pleases.

And in order to clarify this point better, let me say that the nobility should be thought of principally in two different ways: either they conduct themselves as they proceed in such a way that they are entirely dependent on your fortunes, or they do not. Those who feel obligated to you and are not greedy must be honored and loved; those who feel no obligation have to be assessed in two ways. If they act that way out of pusillanimity and a natural lack of courage, then you should make use of them, especially those who are good counselors, since in prosperous times you will gain honor from them and in adverse ones you have no need to fear them. But when they deliberately and for reasons of ambition do not commit themselves to you, it is a sign that they are thinking more of themselves than of you, and the prince should be on guard against those men and fear them as if they were open enemies, because in adversity they will always contribute to his ruin.

Therefore, one who becomes a prince through the support of the people must keep them well disposed toward him, something which should be easy, since all they ask of him is not to be oppressed. But one who becomes a prince with the aid of the nobility and against the will of the people, should try before anything else to win over the latter, something which will be easy for him to do if he takes them under his protection. And because men, when they are treated well by those from whom they expected harm, feel more obligated to their benefactor, the people will quickly become better disposed toward him than if he had achieved princely rule with their support. And the prince can win them over for himself in many ways, but because these vary according to circumstances, no fixed rules can be given, and I will, therefore, leave them out. I will conclude that the only thing a prince needs is to have the friendship of the people; otherwise, he will have no remedy in times of adversity.

Nabis, prince of the Spartans, held out against a siege by the whole of Greece and by one of Rome's most victorious armies, defending his city and his own state against them, and when danger was near, he needed only to protect himself from a few of his subjects,[3] but if

3. Nabis was the tyrant of Sparta from 207 to 192 BCE. When Machiavelli speaks of the "few" who were hostile to Nabis, he probably has in mind the story that when Nabis was first besieged by the Roman general Flamininus in 195, he had eighty suspected citizens put to death (see Livy, *History of Rome*, 34.27).

the people had been hostile to him, this would not have been enough. And let no one contradict this opinion of mine with that trite proverb, that "he who builds on the people builds on mud," because that is true when a private citizen lays his foundation on them and lets himself think that the people would free him if he were oppressed by his enemies or by public officials. In this case he might often find himself deceived, as happened in Rome to the Gracchi and in Florence to Messer Giorgio Scali.[4] But when a prince who builds his foundations on them knows how to command and is a man of courage, someone who is not bewildered by adversities and does not fail to make other preparations, and who keeps up the spirits of the entire people by means of his courage and his orders, that man will never find himself deceived by them and will discover that the foundations he laid there were good.

These principalities are generally endangered when they are passing from a civil to an absolute government, because their princes either command in their own persons or by means of magistrates. In the latter case their position is weaker and more dangerous, because they depend entirely on the will of those citizens who are appointed as magistrates, and who can, especially in times of trouble, take their state from them with great ease, either by opposing them or by disobeying them. And in periods of danger, the prince has no time to seize absolute authority, because his citizens and subjects who are used to taking their orders from the magistrates are not about to obey his in such crises,[5] and in uncertain times he will always find a scarcity of men he can trust. This is why such a prince cannot lay his foundations on what he sees in quiet times, when the citizens have need of the state, because then everyone comes running, everyone makes promises, and each person is willing to die for him as long as death is far away. But in times of adversity, when the state has need of its citizens, then few of them are to be found. And this experience is all the more dangerous in that it is something one can only have a single time. And therefore, a wise prince must

4. In 1378, Giorgio Scali took part in the so-called revolt of the Ciompi (wool carders), one of the guilds that employed the lowest of the people. After briefly heading a democratic government, he and his fellow leaders were thrown out of power, and Scali was beheaded in 1382. The two Gracchi brothers, Tiberius Sempronius (162–133 BCE) and Gaius Sempronius (154–121 BCE), were popular reformers who sought to change the Roman constitution to increase the power of the people against that of the senate. Both met violent ends as a result of bitter aristocratic resistance: the first, elected tribune in 133, was slain in that year by a senatorial gang, while the second became tribune in 123 and had his slave kill him to avoid capture by his enemies two years later.

5. Here Machiavelli writes *frangenti*, which means "shoals or reefs"; he is possibly thinking of a metaphorical ship of state in danger of sinking. Machiavelli usually distinguishes between citizens, who have some participatory role to play in government, and subjects, who do not (often because they live outside the city proper). His reference to "citizens" here thus suggests that, as he imagines it, even in a princely state at least some people there have political rights and responsibilities.

think of a way by which his citizens will always and in all circumstances have need of his state and of him, and then they will always be loyal to him.

Chapter 10

How the Strength of All Principalities Should Be Measured

In examining the character of these civil principalities there is one other consideration to bear in mind, and that is whether a prince has such a power base that he can, in case of need, stand on his own, or whether he always needs to be defended by others. And to make the matter clearer, let me say that in my opinion, those princes are self-sufficient who have an abundance of men or of money, so that they can put together an adequate army and fight a battle in the field[1] against anyone who comes to attack them. And similarly, I judge those princes as always being in need of others who cannot take the field against their foes, but are obliged to seek refuge behind their walls and defend themselves there. The first case has already been discussed, and in the future we will say whatever is needed about it.[2] As for the second case, there is nothing I can say except to encourage such princes to fortify and provision their own towns and not to concern themselves with the surrounding countryside. And if someone has done a good job of fortifying his town and, with regard to the governing of his subjects, has dealt with them as I described above and will discuss below,[3] others will inevitably be hesitant to attack him, for men are always hostile to undertakings in which they see difficulties, nor can it ever seem easy to attack one whose town is strongly fortified and whose people do not hate him.

In Germany[4] the cities are completely free, have little surrounding countryside, and obey the emperor when they feel like it, nor do they fear him or any other neighboring power, because they are fortified in such a manner that everyone thinks that conquering them would be difficult and disagreeable. For they all have proper moats and walls, possess plenty of artillery, always keep enough food and drink and fuel for a year in public warehouses. Besides all this, in

1. Here Machiavelli writes *giornata,* an Italianized version of the French *journée,* which literally meant "day" but had acquired the specialized meaning of "battle in the field (during the course of the day)." In *Discourses* 2.17, Machiavelli explains that the normal Italian expression was *fatti d'arme* (feats of arms).
2. Machiavelli will return to the subject in Chapters 12 and 13, and has already mentioned it in Chapter 6 (see pp. 17–20).
3. See Chapters 9 and 19 (pp. 53 and 57–59).
4. In 1507, Machiavelli had been sent by Florence to negotiate with Maximilian I, the Holy Roman Emperor, and had traveled through Austria and the German-speaking areas of Switzerland. In 1508 (most likely), he wrote the short *Rapporto delle cose della Magna* (*Report on German Affairs*). Since Germany was not a nation in the Renaissance, what he means by that name is simply the German-speaking areas he had visited.

order to keep the lower classes fed without a loss to the public treasury, they always hold in reserve enough to give them work for a year in those trades that are the nerves and lifeblood of the city and of the industries by means of which the lower classes make their living.[5] In addition, they hold military exercises in high repute, and what is more, have many regulations for maintaining them.

Thus, a prince, who has a strong city and does not make himself hated, cannot be attacked, and if he were, the enemy would have to retreat with shame, for the affairs of this world are so variable that it is impossible for anyone to remain idle with his armies for a year while engaged in a siege. And should someone object that if the people have their possessions outside the city and see them burning, they will lose patience, and the long siege and their self-interest will make them forget the prince,[6] I would reply that a strong, courageous prince will always overcome all those difficulties, now by giving hope to his subjects that the evil will not last long, now by making them fear the enemy's cruelty, now by adroitly protecting himself against those subjects who seem too hot-headed. Moreover, it stands to reason that the enemy will burn and lay waste to the countryside upon their arrival, at a time when men's spirits are still ardent and they are determined to defend the city; and thus, the prince will have so much less to worry about, for after a few days, when their spirits have cooled down, the damage will have already been done, the evils suffered, and there is no longer any remedy for them. And then the people will rally around their prince all the more, for he appears to be obligated to them, since their houses have been burned and their possessions destroyed in his defense. And the nature of men is such that they feel obligated as much by the benefits they confer as by those they receive. Thus, all things considered, it should not be difficult for a prudent prince to keep the spirits of his citizens firm, both at first and later on during a siege, so long as he does not lack provisions or weapons for his defense.

Chapter 11

On Ecclesiastical Principalities

At present the only thing remaining for us to do is to speak of ecclesiastical principalities, concerning which all the difficulties occur before one takes possession of them, for they are acquired either

5. Here Machiavelli writes *de' quali la plebe pasca,* which means literally "on which the lower class feeds [itself]."
6. In his *History of the Peloponnesian War,* Thucydides describes the rage of the Athenians when they saw the lands outside the city's walls being ravaged. But Machiavelli most likely had in mind the recent example of the Pisans who saw their Florentine attackers attempting to divert the Arno from their city.

through ability [*virtù*] or through Fortune, and are maintained without one or the other. For they are sustained by the ancient institutions of religion, which are so powerful and of such a quality that they keep their princes in power whatever they do and however they live. These are the only princes who have states and do not defend them, subjects and do not govern them; and their states, though undefended, are not taken from them, and their subjects, though ungoverned, are not concerned about it, and neither do they think of severing their ties with them, nor are they capable of doing so. These, then, are the only principalities that are happy and secure. But since they are upheld by a higher cause, a cause the human mind cannot reach, I shall stop talking about them, for seeing as how they have been raised up and preserved by God, it would be the action of a presumptuous and foolhardy man to discuss them.[1]

Still, if someone asked me how it has happened that the Church has achieved such greatness in the temporal sphere, considering that prior to Alexander[2] the Italian powers—and not just those that were considered powers, but every baron or lord, however insignificant—used to have little esteem for it as a temporal authority, and yet now, a king of France trembles before it, and it has been able to throw him out of Italy and to ruin the Venetians[3]—still, although this is well known, it does not seem superfluous for me to rehearse it in some detail.

Before Charles, the king of France, came into Italy, this province was under the rule of the pope, the Venetians, the king of Naples, the duke of Milan, and the Florentines.[4] These powers necessarily had two principal concerns: one, that no foreigner should enter Italy by force of arms; the other, that none of those powers should occupy more territory.[5] Those they had to worry about the most were the pope and the Venetians. To hold back the Venetians, a union of all the rest was required, as was the case in the defense of Ferrara,[6] and to keep the pope down, they made use of the Roman barons, who, being divided into two factions, the Orsini and the Colonna, always had some reason for squabbling among themselves, and who stood with their arms in their hands right under the pope's eyes, keeping the

1. Machiavelli is being ironic here. His bitter view of the Church's role in Italian politics is most fully presented in the *Discourses* 1.11 (see pp. 124–25).
2. I.e., Pope Alexander VI.
3. Pope Julius II defeated the Venetians at Vailà (or Agnadello) on May 14, 1509, and he drove the French out of Italy in 1512 and died the next year just when he was about to have the French king condemned.
4. Guicciardini's *History of Italy* opens with a long and eloquent picture of the peace and prosperity of Italy at the time of the death of Lorenzo the Magnificent in 1492.
5. Machiavelli's word here is *stato*. That it cannot be translated as "state" testifies to the often slippery nature of Machiavelli's political vocabulary.
6. In 1484, Ferrara was defended from the Venetians by the combined forces of the pope, the king of Naples, the duke of Milan, and the Florentines in the so-called War of Ferrara.

papacy weak and unstable. And although occasionally a courageous pope, like Sixtus,[7] would appear, nevertheless, neither Fortune nor wisdom was ever able to liberate him from these inconveniences. The brevity of their lives was the reason for this, because in ten years, which on average is the life-span of a pope, he might with difficulty put down one of the factions; and if, for example, one pope had almost wiped out the Colonna, another one would emerge who was hostile to the Orsini, which would cause the resurgence of the Colonna, and yet he would not have time to eliminate the Orsini. Consequently, the temporal powers of the pope were little respected in Italy.

Then Alexander VI rose to power, who, of all the pontiffs who have ever existed, showed how much a pope with money and arms could accomplish, for with Duke Valentino as his instrument and the French invasion as his opportunity, he did all those things that I described earlier when speaking of the actions of the duke.[8] And although his intention was to make the duke great, not the Church, nevertheless, what he did redounded to the greatness of the Church, which, after he died and the duke was ruined, became the heir to his labors.

Then came Pope Julius, who found that the Church was already powerful, for it possessed all of the Romagna, had rendered the Roman barons utterly impotent, and had annihilated the factions that had been beaten down by Alexander. Moreover, he also found the way open for accumulating wealth by a method never used before the time of Alexander.[9] These practices Julius not only continued, but increased, and he planned to take Bologna, crush the Venetians, and drive the French out of Italy. And he succeeded in all these undertakings, and is worthy of all the more praise, since he did everything to increase the power of the Church and not that of any private individual. Moreover, he kept the Orsini and Colonna factions in the same conditions in which he found them, and although there were some leaders among them who wanted to make changes, nonetheless, there were two things that held them back: one was the greatness of the Church, which dismayed them, and the other, their not having cardinals of their own, who are the source of the conflicts between them. For these factions will never be at peace as long as they have cardinals, since they nourish factions inside and outside Rome, and those barons are forced to defend them. And so, from the ambition of

7. I.e., Sixtus IV (b. 1414, pope from 1471 to 1484), also referred to in the previous sentence. He was born Francesco della Rovere, a member of the same family as his nephew Julius II.
8. See Chapter 7 (pp. 21–27).
9. In a papal bull, Alexander pronounced 1500 a jubilee year and levied a tax on all of Christendom, ostensibly to support a crusade against the Turks. He also created cardinals in exchange for cash in order to support his son Cesare's campaigns in the Romagna, and he claimed the right to confiscate the wealth of those cardinals who died. Like Alexander, Julius sold Church offices and indulgences, perhaps less spectacularly, but on a wider scale.

prelates are born the discords and tumults among the barons. Thus, His Holiness, Pope Leo,[1] has found the papacy extremely powerful. One hopes that if those earlier popes made it great by force of arms, this pontiff, through his goodness and countless other virtues [*virtù*],[2] will make it very great and worthy of veneration.

Chapter 12

How Many Kinds of Troops There Are and on Mercenaries

Having described in detail all the characteristics of those principalities which I proposed to speak of at the beginning, and having considered to some extent the reasons for their successes and failures, and since I have also shown the methods by which many people have tried to acquire and preserve them, it remains for me now to discuss in general the kinds of offense and defense that can be used by each of the states I mentioned earlier. We said above how necessary it is for a prince to lay good foundations; otherwise, he is bound to come to ruin. The principal foundations of all states, whether new, old, or mixed, are good laws and good arms, and since there cannot be good laws where there are not good arms, and where there are good arms, there are bound to be good laws, I shall set aside the discussion of the laws and talk of arms.

Let me say, then, that the arms with which a prince defends his state are either his own, or they are mercenaries, or auxiliaries, or a mixture. Mercenaries and auxiliaries are useless and dangerous. If a man possesses a state founded on the arms of mercenaries, he will never be able to stand firm or feel secure, because they are disunited, ambitious, undisciplined, disloyal; bold among friends, among enemies cowardly; without fear of God, without loyalty to men; and ruin is deferred only so long as an attack is deferred; and in peace you are plundered by them, in war by the enemy. The reason for this is that they have no love or any other motive that keeps them in the field other than a meager salary, which is not enough to make them willing to die for you.[1] They are quite eager to be your soldiers as long as

1. Leo X (1475–1521), a member of the Medici family, was pope from 1513 on. Machiavelli's praise here is complicated because it seems sincere enough if one reads his treatise as a kind of "job application" dedicated to a member of the Medici family. That family, however, had undone the Florentine Republic, ruled the city for most of the rest of Machiavelli's life, and kept him in exile from 1512 until 1520.
2. Note that Machiavelli's use of *virtù* here is one of the relatively few instances in his work when the meaning of the term is close to what we would normally understand as moral virtue.

1. Machiavelli calls mercenaries here *soldati* (soldiers), using a word containing a double meaning that captures Machiavelli's criticism beautifully. A *soldato* was—and is—a soldier, but the word derives from the verb *soldare,* which means "to pay someone a salary," a *soldo.* That meaning was very much alive in Machiavelli's time and is more visible today in the Italian *soldato* than in the English soldier. This word sums up Machiavelli's criticism of mercenaries: they serve only for money, whereas a citizen army would fight for love of country.

you are not waging war, but when war comes, then it is: retreat or run away. I should not have to expend much effort to demonstrate this, because the present ruin of Italy is caused by nothing other than its having relied for many years on mercenary armies. These troops once did enable some men to get ahead, and they did appear courageous to one another, but when the foreigner arrived, they showed themselves for what they were. In consequence, Charles, king of France, was able to take Italy with a piece of chalk,[2] and the man who said that the cause of this was our sins spoke the truth, although they were not at all the sins he was thinking of, but the ones I have described, and because they were the sins of princes, they too have suffered the punishment for them.[3]

I want to demonstrate further the sorry nature of these troops. Mercenary captains are either excellent men or they are not: if they are, you cannot trust yourself to them, for they will always aspire to their own greatness, either by oppressing you, who are their master, or by oppressing others against your intentions; but if the captain is not skillful [*virtuoso*], he will usually ruin you. And if someone objects that whoever bears arms will do this, whether a mercenary or not, I would reply that armies must be commanded by either a prince or a republic: the prince must go in person and assume the office of captain; the republic has to send its citizens. And when it sends one of them who does not turn out to be capable, it must replace him, and if he is capable, it must restrain him by means of the laws from going beyond his proper authority. And one sees from experience that individual princes and armed republics make very great progress, and that mercenary armies do nothing but damage. Furthermore, it is harder to make a republic, armed with its own troops, submit to the rule of one of its own citizens than a republic armed with foreign soldiers.

For many centuries, Rome and Sparta stood armed and free. The Swiss are extremely well armed and enjoy the greatest freedom. As for mercenary armies in antiquity, there is the example of the Carthaginians: even though they had their own citizens as leaders, they were almost overcome by their mercenary soldiers after the end of the first war with the Romans.[4] After the death of Epaminondas,

2. I.e., when Charles VIII invaded Italy in 1494, he simply marked with chalk the doors of houses requisitioned for his troops. According to the *Mémoires* of the French historian Philippe de Commynes (1447–1511), it was Pope Alexander VI who made the remark in question.
3. In a sermon delivered on November 1, 1494, Fra Girolamo Savonarola claimed that the French invasion was God's punishment for the sins of the Italians, the Church, and the Florentines.
4. In the Mercenary War (241–237 BCE), which broke out directly after the end of the First Punic War (264–241 BCE), the Carthaginians' mercenary troops turned on their employers because the city was destitute after having lost the war with Rome and initially could not pay them. Machiavelli could have read about this war in the first book of Polybius's *Histories*.

Philip of Macedonia was made captain of their army by the Thebans, and after winning a victory, he took away their liberty from them.[5] After the death of Duke Filippo, the Milanese hired Francesco Sforza to fight the Venetians, and once he had overcome the enemy at Caravaggio, he allied himself with them to oppress the Milanese, his employers.[6] Sforza's father, being in the employ of Queen Giovanna of Naples, all of a sudden left her unarmed, so that she was compelled, in order to retain her kingdom, to throw herself into the lap of the king of Aragon.[7] And if the Venetians and the Florentines have in the past increased their dominions by means of these forces, and their captains have not made themselves the princes of those cities, but defended them, I reply that the Florentines in this case have been favored by luck, for of the capable [*virtuosi*] captains whom they could have feared, some did not win, some met with opposition, and others turned their ambition elsewhere. The one who did not win was Giovanni Acuto,[8] whose loyalty could not be known since he was not victorious, but everyone will confess that, if he had won, the Florentines would have been at his mercy. Sforza always had the Bracceschi as his rivals, and they kept an eye on one another. Francesco turned his ambition toward Lombardy, and Braccio turned his against the Church and the Kingdom of Naples.[9]

But let us come to what occurred a little while ago. The Florentines made Paolo Vitelli[1] their captain, a very prudent man who had risen from private life to achieve the greatest renown. If he had taken Pisa, no one would deny that the Florentines would have had to stick

5. The Thebans asked Philip II of Macedonia (382–336 BCE), Alexander's father, for help in fighting the Phocians, and less than a decade later, in 338 BCE, he turned on the Thebans and defeated them at the battle of Chaeronea.
6. Filippo Maria (b. 1392; ruled 1412–47) was the last of the Visconti line to rule Milan. When he died, the city became the Ambrosian Republic. It immediately engaged Francesco Sforza's services as a condottiere, and he led the city's troops to victory over the Venetians in the battle of Caravaggio on September 15, 1448. But Sforza defected to the Venetians the following October, and by March of 1450 he had made himself the master of the city. For more on Sforza, see n. 1, p. 4.
7. In her struggles with Pope Martin V, the childless Giovanna (or Joanna) II of Naples (b. 1373; ruled 1414–35) asked for aid at one point from Alfonso V of Aragon (b. 1396; ruled 1416–58), whom she named her heir. Alfonso came to Naples in 1421, but his relationship with Giovanna quickly soured, and she renounced him as her heir. Sforza led her troops against him, but then suddenly abandoned her, and although Alfonso soon returned to Spain, upon her death in 1435 he fought the French for control of Naples and finally established the Aragonese house there in 1442, becoming King Alfonso I. Machiavelli's brief account of what happened simplifies what was an extremely complicated historical situation.
8. I.e., Sir John Hawkwood (1320–1394), an English mercenary who served the Florentines from 1370 until his death. His band of mercenaries was known as the "White Company."
9. Braccio da Montone was born Andrea Fortebraccio (1368–1424). He and Francesco Sforza were contemporaries, fellow-students, and professional rivals among the condottieri fighting in the Romagna during the 15th century. In his *Florentine History* (5.2), Machiavelli sees the two as the leading mercenaries of the early 15th century; they stood for two opposed schools of military discipline. "Bracceschi": Braccio's followers.
1. See n. 4, p. 28.

with him, because, if he had been hired as a soldier by their enemies, they would have had no remedy for that, and if they had retained him, they would have been obliged to obey him.

As for the Venetians, if one considers the progress they made, we will see that they operated safely and gloriously as long as they made war with their own forces—that was before they directed their military operations to the mainland—and they fought most ably [*virtuosissimamente*] using their noblemen and their armed commoners, but when they began to fight on land, they left that skill [*virtù*] behind and followed the usual customs of Italy. At the beginning of their expansion onto the mainland, they did not have much to fear from their captains, because they did not have much territory there and they enjoyed great prestige, but as they expanded, which happened under Carmagnola, they got a taste of this error. For they saw that he was a most capable man [*virtuosissimo*] and that they had defeated the duke of Milan under his leadership, but, on the other hand, once they recognized how he had been cooling off when he was waging war, they judged that they could no longer win with him, because he did not want to do so, nor could they dismiss him for fear of losing again what they had acquired, and consequently, they were obliged, in order to be sure of him, to have him killed.[2] After that, they had as captains Bartolomeo da Bergamo, Roberto da San Severino, the count of Pitigliano, and the like, with whom they had to fear their losses, not their gains, as happened subsequently at Vailà, where in a single day they lost what in eight hundred years, with enormous effort, they had acquired.[3] From these armies come only slow, tardy, and weak conquests, but sudden and miraculous losses.

And since with these examples I have come to Italy, which has for many years been ruled by mercenary armies, I want to discuss them in greater depth, so that when we have seen their origins and developments, they can be more easily corrected. You must understand, then, that in recent times, when the empire was first being driven out of Italy and the pope began to win more prestige in temporal affairs,

2. Francesco Bussone, count of Carmagnola (c. 1380–1432), was not as victorious as Machiavelli describes him. He did win the battle of Maclodio (1427), which gave the Venetians Bergamo and Brescia, but in his later campaigns he was either inept or dilatory. The Venetians suspected him of treachery and had him executed in the spring of 1432.

3. Niccolò Orsini (1442–1510), the count of Pitigliano, was one of the leaders of the Venetian army in the battle of Vailà, also known as Agnadello, which was fought on May 14, 1509, against the forces of Julius II. In this engagement the Venetians lost their entire land empire in Italy—which was not everything they had gained in eight hundred years, but it came at the same time as losses at sea to the Turks and thus represented a staggering blow. Bartolomeo da Bergamo, better known as Bartolomeo Colleoni (1400–1475), was a relatively able commander and a disciple of Sforza, who is best known for the magnificent equestrian statue by Verrocchio that stands in front of the church of San Giovanni e Paolo in Venice and that was erected after his death in 1475. The other Venetian generals mentioned here were Colleoni's associates and subordinates. Roberto da San Severino d'Aragona (1418–1487) served Venice in the war against Ferrara (1482–84).

the result was that Italy was divided into multiple states, because many of the large cities took up arms against their noblemen who had been originally favored by the emperor and who held them in subjection. Now the Church began to favor ordinary citizens in order to increase its temporal power, and in many other cities citizens became princes.[4] Thus, since Italy was almost entirely in the hands of the Church and a few republics, and since the priests and the citizens were not accustomed to bearing arms, they began to hire foreigners as soldiers. The first to bring prestige to this kind of soldiering was Alberigo da Conio from the Romagna.[5] This man trained, among others, Braccio and Sforza, who were in their time the arbiters of Italy. After them came all the others who have commanded these armies down to our own times. And the result of their prowess [*virtù*] has been that Italy has been overrun by Charles, preyed on by Louis, raped by Ferdinand, and mocked by the Swiss.

The method they followed has been, first, to take away the prestige of the infantry in order to increase their own. They did this because they had no states themselves and lived by exercising their profession, and since they saw that a small number of foot soldiers would not have increased their prestige, and that they could not provide for a great many of them, they therefore limited themselves to cavalry, since with only a limited number of them they would be provided for[6] and honored. And things have now been reduced to such a state that in an army of twenty thousand soldiers, one cannot find two thousand infantry. Besides this, they have made every effort to spare themselves and their soldiers fear and hardship by not killing one another in skirmishes, but taking one another prisoner and never asking for ransom. They have not been in a rush to attack cities at night, nor would those in the cities have hastened out to attack the tents of their besiegers. Around their camps they made neither stockades nor ditches, and they did not campaign in winter. And all of these things were permitted by their rules of warfare and were contrived by them, as has been said, to avoid hardships and dangers, with the result that they have led Italy into a state of slavery and degradation.[7]

4. The historical developments to which Machiavelli refers started in the 13th century, especially in northern and central Italy. The empire in question is the Holy Roman Empire, under which many Italian noblemen, theoretically at least, held their lands as fiefs.
5. Alberigo da Barbiano, count of Conio (d. 1409), founded the first Italian mercenary army, the Company of St. George, and taught both Braccio Montone and the elder Sforza. He was responsible for making the mounted soldier the key fighting figure in the army.
6. The Italian verb here is *nutrire*, which means literally "to nourish."
7. This sentence contains a wonderful play on words that emphasizes Machiavelli's disdain for mercenaries. The word translated as "led" is *condotta* in Machiavelli's Italian, the past participle of *condurre*. However, the noun *la condotta* meant the "contract" signed by a mercenary to lead (*condurre*) troops into battle; indeed, his signing the *condotta* made him into a *condottiere* or a *condottiero*, the usual term for a mercenary leader. What Machiavelli is suggesting here, as he was with his use of the word *soldato* earlier, is that these *condottieri*, men who served only for the money promised by their contract (*la condotta*), have led (*condotta*) Italy into ruin.

Chapter 13

On Auxiliary, Mixed, and Citizen Soldiers

Armies made up of auxiliaries, who are equally useless, are those belonging to a power whom you have asked to come and help you by defending you with his troops, as Pope Julius did in recent times, because, having witnessed the sad showing of his mercenary forces in the Ferrara campaign, he turned to auxiliaries and arranged with Ferdinand, the king of Spain, to help him with men and arms.[1] These troops can be good and useful in their own right, but for the man who calls them in, they are almost always harmful, because if they lose, you are undone, and if they win, you wind up their prisoner. And although ancient history is full of such examples, nonetheless, I want to stay with this recent example of Pope Julius II, whose decision could not have been more ill-considered, for in his desire to take Ferrara, he put himself completely in the hands of a foreigner. But his good fortune produced a third development, with the result that he did not reap the effects of his bad decision. For after his auxiliaries had been beaten at Ravenna, the Swiss rose up and drove off the victors, much to his surprise and everyone else's, so that he was taken prisoner neither by the enemy, who had fled, nor by his auxiliaries, since he had won with arms other than theirs.[2] The Florentines, having no arms of their own, hired ten thousand Frenchmen to conquer Pisa, and because of this decision they exposed themselves to more danger than in any other period of their troubles.[3] The emperor of Constantinople, in order to put down his neighbors, brought an army of ten thousand Turks into Greece, who, when the war was over, refused to leave—and that began the servitude of Greece to the infidels.[4]

Anyone, therefore, who wants to make sure he cannot win, should avail himself of these forces, because they are much more

1. Julius II assaulted Ferrara and Bologna in 1510, using troops of different nationalities, including three hundred Spanish lancers supplied by Ferdinand I of Aragon. Initially victorious, he was driven out of Ferrara in the spring of 1511 and lost Bologna as well. He was defeated at Ferrara by its duke, Alfonso I, who was an extremely capable soldier (on Alfonso, see n. 2, p. 5).
2. At the battle of Ravenna, on April 11, 1512, the French defeated Julius and his auxiliaries, but the Spaniards inflicted crippling losses on the French, killing their leader, Gaston de Foix. Then, in May, twenty thousand Swiss came to the aid of the pope and defeated the French. The French were expelled from Italy the next year after the battle of Novara on June 6, 1513.
3. Florence got Gascon and Swiss troops from their ally, the king of France, for use against Pisa in the summer of 1500, but the troops mutinied for more pay, and so the entire enterprise collapsed. Machiavelli was one of the commissioners who had to explain the fiasco to Louis XII.
4. Here Machiavelli goes back a century and a half to 1353, when the Byzantine emperor John VI Cantacuzene (1292–1383; ruled 1347–54) made the fatal error of hiring Turkish troops to fight for him against the rightful heir to the Byzantine Empire, John V Palaeologus (1332–1391), thus giving the Turks their first foothold in Europe.

dangerous than mercenaries. With them, your ruin is ensured, since they are all united, all under the command of others, whereas with mercenaries, once they have won, they need more time and a better opportunity if they are to harm you, since they are not a unified body of men, but have been hired and paid by you, and with them, a third party whom you have made their leader cannot acquire sufficient authority quickly enough to hurt you. To sum up: with mercenaries, it is their reluctance to fight that is more dangerous; with auxiliaries, it is their ability [*virtù*] as warriors. Wise princes, therefore, have always avoided such soldiers and relied on their own troops, and have chosen sooner to lose with them than to win with those belonging to others, judging that it is not a true victory when it is gained by using the arms of outsiders.

I will never stop citing the example of Cesare Borgia and his actions. This duke entered the Romagna with auxiliary troops, leading an army composed entirely of Frenchmen, and with them he did take Imola and Forlì.[5] But as they did not seem reliable to him, he turned to mercenaries, considering them to be less of a danger, and hired the Orsini and the Vitelli. When he found, in using them, that they were undependable, disloyal, and dangerous, he got rid of them and turned to his own men. And it is easy to see the difference between these two sorts of armies if one considers the difference in the duke's reputation both when he had only the French and when he had the Orsini and Vitelli, as opposed to when all he had were his own soldiers and he depended only on himself: his reputation always increased, nor was he ever esteemed so highly as when everyone saw that he was the complete master of his army.

I did not wish to depart from recent Italian examples, but I cannot leave out Hieron of Syracuse, since he is one of those I have mentioned previously. This man, having been made, as I said, head of their armies by the Syracusans, recognized at once that mercenary armies were useless because they were composed of condottieri like our Italians'. And because he thought he could neither keep them on nor let them go, he had them all cut into pieces, and from then on he made war using his own troops, not those of others.[6]

I also want to call to mind an exemplary figure from the Old Testament who fits this argument. When David made the offer to Saul, saying he would go and fight Goliath, the Philistine challenger, Saul

5. Cesare led an army of French, Gascon, and Swiss troops into the Romagna in the late spring of 1499 and captured Imola on November 24 and Forlì on December 17. In a second campaign there from October 1500 to June 1501, he led a larger army that included mercenaries.

6. Machiavelli mentioned Hieron earlier (see n. 1, p. 19). The mercenaries with whom he struggled were known as Mamertines and had originally been hired by Agathocles. Hieron did not eliminate them because they were ineffective, but because they threatened his rule of Syracuse.

armed him with his own armor in order to give him courage. But when David had tried it on, he rejected it, saying that he could not demonstrate his true worth with it, and for that reason he wanted to meet the enemy with his own sling and his own knife.[7] In short, the arms of others will slip off your back, or weigh you down, or tie you up.

Charles VII, father of King Louis XI, having by means of his good Fortune and ability [*virtù*] liberated France from the English, recognized the necessity of arming himself with his own arms and established an ordinance in his kingdom for training cavalry and infantry. Afterward, King Louis, his son, abolished the law concerning the infantry and began to hire the Swiss, and this error, which was followed by others, is the cause of the dangers which that kingdom faces, as we now see in what has happened.[8] By giving such prestige to the Swiss, he discredited all his own troops, for he did away with his infantry and forced his cavalry to depend on the arms of others, and once accustomed to fighting with the aid of the Swiss, they began to feel that they could not win without them. As a result, the French are not strong enough to match the Swiss, and without the Swiss, they will not put themselves to the test against others. The armies of France have thus been mixed, partly mercenaries and partly her own citizens. Such armies, made up of forces combined together, are much better than those composed purely of auxiliaries or mercenaries, but much inferior to one's own troops. And the example already given should suffice, for the kingdom of France would be invincible if the ordinances of Charles had been developed or even just simply preserved. But because men are insufficiently prudent, they will start something, and because it then tastes good to them, the poison within it is not perceived, as I said above about consumptive fevers.[9]

Thus, anyone who does not recognize the ills in a principality the moment they arise is not truly wise—and this ability is given to few men. And, if one were to look for the first signs of the ruin of the Roman Empire, one will find it began with the hiring of the Goths as soldiers, because from that beginning the forces of the Roman Empire began to grow slack, and all that energy [*virtù*] which was taken from them was given to the Goths. I conclude, therefore, that unless it has its own armies, no principality is secure; on the contrary, it is completely dependent on Fortune, not having the valor [*virtù*] which puts up a reliable defense in the midst of adversity. And

7. For this story, see the Bible, 1 Samuel 17:38–40.
8. In the 1440s, Charles VII (b. 1403; ruled 1422–61), whom Joan of Arc had made the king of France, had to transform the French army that had been fighting the English during the Hundred Years' War. He formed a kind of civic militia and finally drove the English out of France in 1453. In 1474, his son, Louis XI (b. 1423; ruled 1461–83), repealed the ordinance and began replacing the citizen troops with Swiss and German mercenaries. The dangers facing the French in 1513 grew out of their losses at Ravenna (1512) and Novara (1513), which Machiavelli attributes to the poor quality of their infantry.
9. See Chapter 3 (p. 9).

wise men have always thought and said "that there is nothing so weak and unstable as a reputation for power not founded on one's own strength."[1] One's own troops are those that are composed of either subjects, or citizens, or your own dependents; all the others are either mercenaries or auxiliaries. And it will be easy to discover how to set up one's own army if one considers the methods of the four men I cited above,[2] and if one notes how Philip, the father of Alexander the Great, and how many republics and princes, have been armed and organized; to those methods I defer absolutely.

Chapter 14

What the Duties of the Prince Are with Regard to the Military

A prince, therefore, should have no other object, no other thought, nor should he adopt any other art as his profession, than war and its rules and discipline, for that is the only art[1] befitting one who commands. And it has such power [*virtù*] that it not only allows those who are born princes to keep their positions, but it often enables men of private station to ascend to that rank. On the other hand, it is evident that when princes have given more thought to the refinements of life than to arms, they have lost their states. And the chief cause of such a loss is to neglect this art, while the way to acquire a state is to be an expert in it.

From being a private citizen Francesco Sforza became the duke of Milan because he was armed; his sons, in order to avoid the hardships of war, from being dukes became private citizens.[2] For among the other bad effects being unarmed has on you is this: it makes you contemptible, which is a kind of infamy from which a prince must guard himself, as will be explained later.[3] For between an armed and an unarmed man there is no comparison whatsoever, and it is

1. *"Quod nihil sit tam infirmum aut instabile quam fama potentie non sua vi nixa,"* from Tacitus, *Annals,* 13.19; the quotation is slightly inaccurate.
2. The men in question are Cesare Borgia, Hieron of Syracuse, King David, and Charles VII of France. Machiavelli seems to be implying that the rule holds good no matter what the moral status of the ruler may be.

1. *Arte* in Italian; the word in Machiavelli's time meant something more like craft or profession or even guild, but since he is absolutely opposed to mercenary—that is, professional—armies "art" seems a better translation than "profession." Machiavelli would go on to write a treatise called *The Art of War* (*L'arte della guerra*), in which the term has a roughly similar meaning.
2. Machiavelli is thinking of two of Francesco Sforza's sons in particular, one of whom, Galeazzo Maria (1444–1476), ruled Milan for the last ten years of his life after his father's death. He was a patron of music, but was known for his cruelty and lechery and was finally assassinated by his enemies. Galeazzo's son Gian Galeazzo (1469–1494) inherited the duchy when he was seven, ruling it under the protectorship of his uncle Ludovico Maria, known as Ludovico il Moro (1452–1508), Francesco's other son, who finally became duke when his nephew died under mysterious circumstances. Ludovico il Moro was defeated twice by the French, the second time in 1499, when he was captured and sent to France, where he finally died in prison at Loches.
3. See Chapter 19 (pp. 57–58).

unreasonable to think that a man who is armed would willingly obey one who is unarmed, or that an unarmed one would be safe among armed servants. For since the former is disdainful and the latter suspicious, it is impossible for them to work well together. Thus, besides the other misfortunes that have already been mentioned, a prince who does not understand military matters cannot earn the esteem of his soldiers or place his trust in them.

The prince should, therefore, never stop thinking about this exercise of war, and in peacetime he must train himself for it more than when he is at war. He can do this in two ways: the first, through physical activities; the other, through study. As for his physical activities—aside from their keeping his soldiers well-disciplined and fit—he must always be out hunting, so that by doing so, he can accustom his body to hardships. At the same time, he must learn the nature of different terrains, getting to know how the mountains slope upward, how the valleys open out, and how the plains lie, while also coming to understand the nature of the rivers and the swamps—and on all this he should lavish the greatest care. Such knowledge is useful in two ways: first, he will get to know his country and understand better how to defend it; second, with his knowledge and experience of these different terrains, it will be easy for him to grasp the nature of any other site he may have to explore for the first time. For the hills, valleys, plains, rivers, and swamps that are in Tuscany, for instance, have a certain resemblance to those of other provinces, so that by knowing the terrain in one place, he will easily be able to understand it in others. And that prince who lacks this experience lacks the main thing a captain should have, because it teaches you how to find the enemy, select quarters, lead troops, organize them for battle, and besiege towns to your advantage.

Among the other things for which writers have praised Philopoemon, prince of the Achaeans, they say that in peacetime he thought of nothing except how to wage war, and when he was out in the country with his friends, he would often stop and reason with them: "If the enemy were up on that hill, and we found ourselves here with our army, which of us would have the advantage? How could we go after them without breaking formation? If we wanted to retreat, how would we do it? If they were to retreat, how would we pursue them?"[4] As they were going along, he would ask them to consider every situation that an army might confront; he would hear their opinions and tell them his own, supporting it with arguments, so that because of these continual discussions, no unexpected incident could arise when he was at the head of his army for which he did not have a remedy.

4. For these words from Philopoemon of Megalopolis (c. 253–182 BCE), who was a skilled general and strategist and the leader of the Achaean League, which conquered Sparta and most of the Peloponnese during his lifetime, Machiavelli has two sources: Plutarch, *Life of Philopoemon*, 4; and Livy, *History of Rome*, 35.28.

But as for exercising the mind, the prince must read histories and in them consider the actions of eminent men, see how they conducted themselves during their wars, and examine the causes of their victories and defeats in order to be able to avoid the latter and imitate the former. Above all, he must do what some outstanding men have done in the past: they chose to imitate someone before them who had been praised and glorified, always keeping his deeds and actions in their minds, as it is said Alexander the Great imitated Achilles; Caesar, Alexander; and Scipio, Cyrus.[5] Anyone who reads the life of Cyrus written by Xenophon will realize how much in Scipio's life his imitation of Cyrus contributed to his glory, and how closely he conformed, in chastity, affability, humanity, and liberality, to what Xenophon wrote about Cyrus.[6]

A wise prince must follow such methods as these and never remain idle in times of peace, but by being industrious he must make capital out of them in order to be able to profit from them in times of adversity, so that when Fortune changes, she will find him prepared to resist her.

Chapter 15

Of the Things for Which Men, and Especially Princes, Are Praised or Blamed

It remains now to be seen what the methods and procedures should be for a prince in dealing with his subjects and allies. And because I know that many have written about this, I fear that people will consider me presumptuous for doing so again, especially since, in discussing this subject, I will depart from the rules given by others. But since I intend to write something useful for anyone who understands it, it seemed to me more suitable to go after the effectual truth of the matter than what people have imagined about it.[1] And many have imagined republics and principalities for themselves that have never

5. These various stories of classical figures who imitated other classical figures are all taken from books. The story of Alexander's imitating Achilles comes from Plutarch, *Life of Alexander*, 8; of Caesar and Alexander, from Suetonius, *The Deified Julius*, 7; and of Scipio and Cyrus, from Cicero, *Letters to his Brother Quintus*, 1.8–23. Scipio was Publius Cornelius Scipio Africanus (236–183 BCE), a Roman general and statesman who beat the Carthaginians in Spain and then carried the war to Africa, where he decisively defeated Hannibal at the battle of Zama in 202 BCE.
6. Cyrus the Great (ruled 557–530 BCE) conquered a series of states to found the Persian Empire. Xenophon's "life" of Cyrus is really a didactic novel; its title, *Cyropaedia*, means *The Education of Cyrus*.
1. From antiquity to the Renaissance countless writers produced books of advice for princes, constituting a genre called the *Speculum principis* (The Mirror for Princes). In those works the prince was primarily taught that he must learn both religious and secular virtues and then practice them as a ruler. Machiavelli turns that advice on its head. Here he says he will write of the "effectual truth" (*verità effetuale*) because he is interested in a truth that has an *effect*—in other words, one that leads to action in the world—rather than turning the prince into a model of morality.

been seen or known to exist in the real world.[2] For there is such a distance between the way we really live and the way we ought to live that the man who abandons what is done for what ought to be done ensures his ruin rather than his preservation. For a man who wants to make a profession of goodness in everything is bound to come to ruin among so many who are not good. Hence, a prince who wants to preserve himself must learn how not to be good, and to use this knowledge and not use it as necessity requires.

Leaving aside, then, the imaginary things that have been said about the prince, and discussing those that are true, let me say that whenever men are spoken of, and especially princes, because they are positioned at a greater height, they will be judged for qualities that bring them either blame or praise. And this is why one man is considered generous, another miserly (I use a Tuscan term, because avaricious [*avaro*] in our language still means a man who wants to take possession of things by theft; we call a man miserly [*misero*] who is excessive in abstaining from the use of what is his own); one is considered a benefactor, another rapacious; one man cruel, another merciful; one treacherous, the other faithful; one effeminate and cowardly, the other fierce and courageous; one humane, the other proud; one lascivious, the other chaste; one straightforward, the other cunning; one tough, the other easygoing; one serious, the other frivolous; one religious, the other unbelieving; and so on. And I know everyone will admit that it would be a most praiseworthy thing for a prince to have all of the qualities mentioned above that are held to be good. But since it is impossible to have them and to practice them all perfectly, because the human condition does not permit it, a prince must be prudent enough to know how to avoid the infamy of those vices that would take his state away from him, and whenever possible, to be on guard even against those that might not lose it for him, but that, if he cannot resist them, he can indulge them with less concern. Furthermore, he should not worry about incurring the infamy of those vices without which it would be hard for him to save his state, for carefully taking everything into account, a man will discover that something resembling a virtue [*virtù*] would, if it were put into practice, result in his ruin, whereas something else, which seems a vice, would, if it were put into practice, result in his security and well-being.

2. Plato's *Republic* was certainly on Machiavelli's mind; More's *Utopia* was not yet published. But Machiavelli was doubtless thinking as well of the books of advice for princes discussed in the preceding note. For example, Egidio Colonna, or Giles of Rome (c. 1243–1316), archbishop of Bourges and Prior General of the Augustinian monastic order, insisted in his popular and often translated *De regimine principum* (*On the Governance of Princes*) of 1277–79 that princes had to have all the moral virtues, declaring that to lack just one of them was to lack them all.

Chapter 16

Of Liberality and Miserliness

Let me begin, therefore, with the first of the qualities mentioned above, by saying that it would be good to be considered generous; nevertheless, generosity used in such a way as to give you a reputation for being generous will harm you, because if it is put into practice virtuously [*virtuosamente*][1] and as it is supposed to be, it will not be recognized as such, and you will not avoid the infamy of its opposite. And therefore, if someone wants to maintain a reputation among men for generosity, he must not neglect any possible opportunity for sumptuous display. The result will be that a prince so disposed will inevitably use up all his wealth in such activities, and in the end, if he wants to maintain his reputation for liberality, he will be obliged to burden his people with exorbitant taxes, and to be strict and demanding about them, and to do everything possible in order to get money. This will begin to make him hateful to his subjects, and since he will now have become poor, he will lose everyone's respect. As a result, with this generosity of his he will have harmed many and benefited few, he will feel every little difficulty, and the first appearance of danger will put him at risk. When he recognizes this and seeks to change his ways, he will immediately incur the infamous charge of being a miser.

Therefore, since a prince cannot practice this virtue [*virtù*] of liberality in such a way as to acquire a reputation for it without harming himself, he must not mind, if he is prudent, to be considered a miser, because over time he will always come to be considered more generous when people see that because of his parsimony his income is sufficient, he can defend himself from anyone who makes war on him, and he can undertake enterprises without burdening his people. In short, he will be generous toward all those people from whom he takes nothing—and they are numberless—while being miserly to all those people to whom he gives nothing—and they are few. In our times, we have seen great things being accomplished only by those who have been considered miserly; the others have all been wiped out. Pope Julius II, although he had made use of his reputation for generosity in order to gain the papacy, decided not to preserve it afterwards, so that he would be able to wage war.[2] The present king of France has waged many wars without imposing an extra tax on

1. Machiavelli's "virtuously" here is another instance of his use of the idea of *virtù* in something like its modern sense—namely, doing a charitable thing without an ulterior motive.
2. Machiavelli's remarks about Julius II equate what would be called simony with generosity, but it is clear that he admired the pope's action (though with some reservations, as we discover in Chapter 25 [see pp. 79–80]).

his people, because his long-practiced parsimony took care of the additional expenses. If the present king of Spain had a reputation for generosity, he would not have undertaken and prevailed in so many campaigns.[3]

Therefore, in order not to have to rob his subjects, to be able to defend himself, to prevent his becoming poor and contemptible, and to avoid being forced to become rapacious, a prince should think it a matter of little moment to be called a miser, for this is one of those vices that will enable him to rule. And if someone should object that Caesar achieved imperial power through his generosity,[4] and that many others have reached the highest ranks because they were generous and were known to be so, I would reply: you are either a prince already, or you are on your way to becoming one. In the first case, such liberality is harmful; in the second, it is indeed necessary to be considered generous. And Caesar was one of those who wanted to achieve princely rule over Rome, but if, after having achieved it, he had survived and had not moderated those expenditures, he would have destroyed the power he had acquired.

And if someone might reply that there have been plenty of princes who have accomplished great things with their armies and have been reputed to be extremely generous, my answer to you is either that such a prince is spending his own wealth and that of his subjects, or he is spending the wealth of others. In the first case he must be frugal; in the second, he must not omit any aspect of liberality. And that prince who goes out with his armies and lives by looting, sacking, and extortion is making use of what belongs to others. For him such generosity is necessary; otherwise, his soldiers would not follow him. But with what does not belong to you or your subjects, it is possible to bestow gifts more generously, as did Cyrus, Caesar, and Alexander, for spending what belongs to others does not take away from your reputation, but actually enhances it. You only harm yourself by spending what is your own, and there is nothing that uses itself up so much as generosity: while you are practicing it, you lose the very means to practice it, and either you become poor and contemptible, or, in order to escape impoverishing yourself, you become rapacious and hated. And above all the things that a prince must guard against is being despised and hated, and liberality will lead you to become both. Therefore, it is wiser to be called a miser, which gives birth to an infamy free from hatred, than, because you want to be considered liberal, to be forced to acquire a reputation for rapacity, which gives birth to infamy as well as hatred.

3. Machiavelli's praise of Louis XII of France and Ferdinand II of Aragon seems justified: they were as fiscally prudent as they were committed to warfare.
4. On Julius Caesar's use of generosity to achieve power, see Cicero, *De officiis,* 1.14, and Suetonius, *Divus Iulius,* 11–12.

Chapter 17

On Cruelty and Mercy, and Whether It Is Better to Be Loved Than Feared, or the Contrary

Proceeding to the other qualities mentioned before, let me say that every prince should desire to be considered merciful and not cruel; nevertheless, he must take care not to use this mercy[1] badly. Cesare Borgia was considered cruel; still, that cruelty of his brought order to[2] the Romagna, united it, and restored it to peace and loyalty. If this is examined with care, it will be seen that he was much more merciful than the people of Florence, who, to avoid a reputation for cruelty, allowed Pistoia to be destroyed.[3] A prince, therefore, must not mind acquiring the infamy of being considered cruel in order to keep his subjects united and loyal, for by providing just a very few examples of cruelty, he will be more merciful than those who, because of their excessive compassion, allow disorders to continue, which lead to murders and looting, for these usually harm the whole community, while the executions ordered by the prince harm just single individuals. And the new prince, more than all the other types, cannot avoid a reputation for cruelty, because new states are full of dangers. And Vergil, speaking through Dido's mouth, says:

> Res dura, et regni novitas me talia cogunt
> Moliri, et late fines custode tueri.[4]

Nonetheless, the prince must be slow to believe things and to act on them, although he should not make himself fear his own thoughts, and he must proceed in a temperate manner, acting with prudence and humanity, so that too much confidence does not make him rash, and too much distrust does not render him insufferable.

From this there arises a question: whether it is better to be loved than feared, or the contrary. The answer is that one should like to be

1. Here Machiavelli writes *pietà,* which has no single English translation, for it means both "piety," in the sense of religious devotion, and "pity" or "mercy" or "compassion," in the sense of feeling sorrow for the suffering of others. The Latin *pietas* is at the root of the word and meant loyalty and devotion to family, friends, and the state as well as religious piety, and some of those ideas are attached to the Italian *pietà* as well. Finally, the term could also mean clemency in a political context. I have used "mercy" here and generally throughout the translation, except for "compassion" at one point, but all the other meanings are never to be excluded when the word appears.
2. Machiavelli's Italian verb here is *racconciare*, which literally means "to mend or sew up."
3. In 1501–02, Pistoia saw a small but desperate civil war break out between two factions, the Panciatichi and the Cancellieri, and although the nearby Florentines controlled the city and actually sent Machiavelli to investigate, they were afraid to intervene, allowing the two factions to tear the city apart.
4. *Aeneid*, 2.563–64: "Harsh necessity and the newness of my reign force me to take such measures and to watch over my borders with a widespread guard."

both the one and the other, but since it is difficult to mix them together, it is much safer to be feared than to be loved if you have to lack one of the two. For this can generally be said about men: that they are ungrateful, fickle, hypocrites and dissemblers, always dodging dangers, greedy for gain; and while you benefit them, they are all yours, offering you their blood, their belongings, their life, their children, as I said above, when the need for such things is far away, but when it actually comes closer, they turn aside. And the prince who has made their words his entire foundation, finding himself stripped naked of other preparations, will be ruined, for friendships that are acquired for a price and not by grandeur and nobility of spirit are purchased, but are not truly owned, and in critical moments, they cannot be spent. And men are less hesitant about injuring someone who makes himself loved than one who makes himself feared, for love is held together by a chain of obligation which, because men are a sad lot, is broken at every opportunity to serve their self-interest, but fear is maintained by a dread of punishment which never abandons you.

Nevertheless, a prince must make himself feared in such a way that he avoids hatred even if he does not obtain love, for to be feared and not to be hated can work very well together, and this will always be the case when he abstains from taking the property of his citizens and subjects, and their women, too. And if he is obliged to shed someone's blood, he should do so when there is proper justification and manifest cause, but above all, he must abstain from taking other people's property, for men sooner forget the death of their father than the loss of their patrimony.[5] Besides, reasons for taking property are never lacking, and he who begins to live by stealing always finds a reason for taking what belongs to others, whereas reasons for shedding blood are rarer and more quickly exhausted.

But when the prince is with his armies and has under his command a multitude of soldiers, then it is absolutely necessary not to care about being called cruel, for without that reputation, no one has ever kept an army united or ready for any sort of military action. Counted among the marvelous deeds of Hannibal[6] there is this one: that although he had an enormous army which was composed of men of countless races and nations, and which he led to fight in foreign lands, there never arose any dissension either among themselves or against their leader, whether his luck was bad or good. This could

5. There is no way to capture in English Machiavelli's comic, though cynical, wordplay in Italian on "father" and "patrimony" here. His clause says that men sooner forget the death of their "padre" than the loss of their "patrimonio": *padre* comes from the Latin *pater*, as does *patrimonio*, a linkage no educated Italian would miss.

6. Hannibal Barca (247–181 BCE), a Carthaginian general, repeatedly defeated the Romans during the Second Punic War (219–201), until he was beaten by Scipio in 202 and fled to Syria and then to Bithnia, where he poisoned himself lest he fall into the hands of his enemies.

not have arisen from anything other than that inhuman cruelty of his,[7] which, together with his numberless talents [*virtù*], always made him a figure of awe and terror in the sight of his soldiers, and without that, his other talents [*virtù*] would not have sufficed. And less thoughtful writers admire this accomplishment of his, on the one hand, and on the other, condemn the principal reason for it.

That it is true that his other abilities [*virtù*] would not have been sufficient can be seen in the case of Scipio, the rarest of men not only in his own times, but in all of recorded history, whose armies in Spain rebelled against him.[8] This arose from nothing other than his excessive compassion, which gave his soldiers more license than was consistent with military discipline. He was rebuked for this in the senate by Fabius Maximus,[9] who called him the corrupter of the Roman army. When Locri had been plundered by one of Scipio's legates, the Locrians were not avenged by Scipio, nor was the insolence of that legate corrected, all of which arose from his easygoing nature, so that someone in the senate who wanted to excuse him said that there were many men who knew better how not to err than how to correct errors in others.[1] In time such a disposition would have tarnished Scipio's fame and glory, had he persisted in it while commanding the armies, but since he lived under the control of the senate, this harmful quality of his was not only concealed, but brought him glory.

Therefore, returning to the question of being feared and loved, I conclude that since men love according to their own inclination and fear at the will of the prince, a wise prince must lay his foundation on what is his own and not on what belongs to others; he must only take pains to escape hatred, as I said.

Chapter 18

How Princes Must Keep Their Word

Everyone knows how laudable it is for a prince to keep his word and to live with integrity and not by means of cunning. Nevertheless, one sees from experience in our times that those princes who have accomplished great things have felt little concern about

7. Among the historians who applauded Hannibal's feats but deplored the "inhuman cruelty" that made them possible was Machiavelli's chief source, Livy, who uses that exact phrase himself; see his *History of Rome*, 21.4.
8. On Scipio, see n. 5, p. 48. On his troops' rebellion in Spain in 206 BCE, see Livy, *History of Rome*, 28.24.
9. Quintus Fabius Maximus Cunctator (d. 203 BCE) was the great opponent of Hannibal in the first, defensive phases of the Second Punic War. By refusing to fight when he knew he would lose, he was given the sobriquet of Cunctator, "the hesitator." He also opposed Scipio in the senate. For his accusation of Scipio as the "corrupter of the Roman army," see Livy, *History of Rome*, 29.19.
1. The southern Italian city of Locri was captured by Scipio in 205 BCE and placed under the control of his legate Quintus Pleminius, who outdid the Carthaginians in destructiveness without suffering even a minor rebuke from Scipio. He was eventually arrested and punished by the senate. See Livy, *History of Rome*, 29.21.

keeping their word[1] and have been able to confuse men's brains by cunning, and in the end, they have overcome those who made loyalty their foundation.

You must know, then, that there are two methods of fighting, one with laws, the other with force: the first one is proper to man, the second to beasts; but because the first one often does not suffice, one has to have recourse to the second. Thus, a prince must know how to make good use of the beast as well as the man. This procedure was taught to princes in symbolic form by the writers of antiquity, when they recounted how Achilles and many other ancient princes were sent to be reared by Chiron the centaur, who trained them in his discipline.[2] Having a teacher who was half-beast and half-man can only mean that a prince must know how to use both natures, and that the one without the other will not endure.

Since a prince must know how to make good use of the nature of the beast, he must choose the fox and the lion from among them, for the lion cannot defend himself from traps, and the fox cannot defend himself from wolves.[3] It is therefore necessary to be a fox to recognize traps and a lion to frighten off the wolves. Those who base their behavior simply on the lion do not understand all this. Therefore, a prudent ruler cannot and should not keep his word, when keeping it would work against him, and when the reasons which made him pledge it have disappeared. And if men were all good, this precept would not be good, but since they are a sad lot[4] and would not keep their word to you, then you, too, are under no obligation to keep it to them. Nor does a prince ever lack reasons to color over[5]

1. Machiavelli speaks here of keeping one's *fede*, or "faith," which I have translated as keeping one's "word" because "keeping one's faith" is unidiomatic. But I have also translated it as "loyalty" when that word seemed more appropriate. *Fede* could also mean "faith" or "belief" when used in a religious context, and since Machiavelli's treatment of religion in *The Prince* is generally ironic, readers may well be tempted to interpret the discussion of princes who keep—or do not keep—their *fede* ironically, too.
2. Centaurs were mythological beasts who had the upper portion of a man and the lower of a horse. Chiron is said to have taught not just Achilles, but Aesculapius and Jason. Although Chiron is mentioned in the *Iliad* and centaurs are discussed in Xenophon's *Cyropaedia*, which was clearly one of Machiavelli's favorite books, it is not clear which "ancient writers" he is referring to. (Centaurs also appear in Dante, but he is hardly an ancient writer.) Machiavelli's allegorization of Chiron seems to be highly original; it appears only in the work of the Renaissance mythographer Natale Conti (1520–1582), whose encyclopedic *Mythologiae* (*Mythologies*) was published in 1568 and whose interpretation of Chiron may well be indebted to Machiavelli's.
3. With these two allegorical beasts, as well as with the notion that the prince must know how to fight like a man, using the laws, and like a beast, using force and fraud, Machiavelli is referring to passages in Cicero's *De officiis* (1.11.34 and 1.13.41), but he is really doing more than that. He is deliberately setting himself up in opposition to Cicero—and the humanist tradition that followed him—since Cicero thoroughly condemned the use of force and fraud because it lowered men to the level of animals.
4. Machiavelli writes that men are *tristi*, the primary meaning of which is "sad," but the term had a moral dimension as well as a psychological one and implied that men are wicked. "Sad lot" captures some, but not all, of this subtlety.
5. *Colorire* in Machiavelli's Italian. *Color* (Lat.) was a key word in Renaissance rhetoric. It meant ornamentation—that is, figurative language, designed to make an utterance more striking. It could have a negative sense too and could mean covering up or hiding something from the listener or the reader.

his failure to keep it. Of this one could furnish innumerable modern examples, showing how many peace treaties, how many promises, have been made null and void by the faithlessness of princes, and how the man who enjoyed the greatest success was the one who knew best how to use the fox. But it is necessary to know how to do a good job of coloring over this character, and to be a great pretender and dissembler, and men are so simple-minded and so obedient to present necessities, that a deceitful man will always find someone who will let himself be deceived.

I do not wish to remain silent about one of these recent examples. Alexander VI never did anything, never thought of anything, other than deceiving men, and he always found a subject on whom he could practice. And never was there a man who was more effective in making assertions and affirming things with greater oaths, who observed them less. Nevertheless, his deceptions were always successful just as he wished, because he really knew this aspect of the world.

Therefore, it is not necessary for a prince to have all the qualities mentioned above, but it is absolutely necessary that he should seem to have them. Indeed, I will even be so bold as to say this: that having them and always observing them is harmful, but appearing to observe them is useful. In other words, it is good to appear merciful, faithful, humane, upright, and religious—and to be so—but to keep your mind so disposed that, when it is necessary not to be that way, you will be ready and able to change to the contrary.[6] And this has to be understood: a prince, and especially a new prince, cannot practice all those things for which men are considered good, because in order to preserve his state, he must often act against faithfulness, against charity, against humanity, against religion. And, therefore, he needs to have a mind disposed to shift about as the winds and variations of Fortune dictate, and as I said above, he should not depart from the good, if that is possible, but he should know how to enter into evil when necessity demands it.

Hence a prince should take great care never to let anything fall from his lips that is not imbued with the five qualities mentioned above, and to anyone seeing and hearing him, he should appear all mercy, all faithfulness, all integrity, all humanity, all religion. And nothing is more necessary than to seem to have than this last quality. And men in general judge more by their eyes than their hands, because everyone can see, but few can feel. Everyone sees what you appear to be, few feel what you are, and those few do not dare to take a stand against the opinion of the many, who have the majesty of the state to defend them. And in the actions of all men, and especially of

6. This recommendation to use hypocrisy has affected, negatively, the popular image of Machiavelli and his prince, but in the first book of his *Cyropaedia,* the young Cyrus was required to learn the same thing.

princes, where there is no court to which to appeal, one looks at the end.[7] Therefore, let a prince win victories and preserve his state: his means will always be considered honorable and praised by everyone, because ordinary people will always be taken in by appearances and by the outcome of an undertaking; and in the world there are only ordinary people, nor do the few have any place while the many have something they can lean on. A certain prince of our own times, whom it is just as well not to name, preaches nothing but peace and faithfulness, and to the one and the other he is extraordinarily hostile; and if, on many occasions, he had observed both of those things, he would have had either his reputation or his state taken from him.[8]

Chapter 19

On Avoiding Contempt and Hatred

But since I have talked about the most important of the qualities mentioned above, I should like to discuss the others briefly under this general rule: that the prince, as was noted above,[1] must concentrate on avoiding those things that would make him either hated or contemptible, and whenever he has avoided this, he will have carried out his duties and will not be put in danger because of his other infamous deeds. What makes him hated above all, as I said, is being predatory and usurping the property and women of his subjects.[2] He must refrain from such acts, and when men are not deprived of their property or their honor, in most cases they will live contentedly, and one will only have to contend with the ambition of a few, which can easily be restrained in a number of ways. What makes him contemptible is being considered changeable, frivolous, effeminate, cowardly, irresolute: a prince must guard himself against this as against a reef, and he must do his best so that in his actions people recognize his greatness, courage, dignity, and strength. Concerning the private affairs of his subjects, he should insist that his sentence be irrevocable, and he should maintain such a reputation that no one would think to deceive him or try to get around him.

7. Machiavelli's *si guarda al fine* (one looks at the end) has been used to support the notion that a prince's actions may appear to be evil, but can be justified by the good ends they produce. In other words, the end justifies the means. Machiavelli's statement, however, does no such thing. It is concerned with the way human psychology works: people's response to what is done is determined by how its end, its outcome, affects them. Machiavelli thus offers an ironic and satirical perspective on people who are, finally, less concerned about the morality of the prince's methods than about how his actions wind up either benefiting or harming them.
8. This not-very-covert allusion is to Ferdinand II of Aragon, also called Ferdinand the Catholic. Near the end of his life, he supposedly boasted that he had deceived Louis XII of France twelve times in a row. In general, Machiavelli does not like Ferdinand (see his treatment of Ferdinand in Chapter 19 [pp. 70–71]).

1. See p. 52.
2. See p. 53.

That prince who creates such an opinion about himself is highly esteemed, and it is difficult to conspire against and attack a man with such a reputation, provided that he is considered exceptional and is revered by his people. For a prince should have two fears: one internal, on account of his subjects; the other external, on account of foreign powers. From the latter he can defend himself with good arms and good friends, and if he has good arms, he will always have good friends. And internal affairs will always remain stable, when external ones are stable, unless they have already been disturbed by a conspiracy. But even though external conditions should change, if he has organized everything and lived as I have said, and does not lose control of himself, he will always be able to withstand every assault, just as I have said Nabis the Spartan did.[3]

But as for his subjects, when external conditions do not change, he has to fear that they may be hatching a secret conspiracy, from which the prince will be sufficiently secure if he avoids being hated or despised, and keeps the people satisfied with him, something that is necessary for him to do, as I explained above at length.[4] And one of the most potent remedies a prince has for conspiracies is to avoid being hated by the masses, for whoever conspires always believes that by killing the prince he will satisfy the people. But when he thinks he might offend them, he cannot summon up the courage to make such a move, because the difficulties on the part of the conspirators are infinite. Experience shows that there have been many conspiracies, but few have been successful. For anyone who conspires cannot do so alone, nor can he find accomplices except among those he judges to be discontented, and as soon as you have revealed your intention to a malcontent, you furnish him with the means to make himself content, since by revealing your plot he has everything to gain. Thus, seeing a certain gain on the one hand and one that is dubious and full of danger on the other, he must either be a rare kind of friend or an absolutely determined enemy of the prince if he is to remain loyal to you. To reduce the matter to a few words: let me say that on the part of the conspirator there is nothing but fear, jealousy, and the terrifying prospect of punishment, but on the part of the prince there are the majesty of the principality, the laws, and the protection of both his supporters and the state to defend him. And so, if the good will of the people is added to all these things, it is impossible that anyone would be so rash as to engage in a conspiracy, for whereas ordinarily a conspirator must live in fear before performing his evil deed, in this case,

3. On Nabis, see Chapter 9, pp. 32–33.
4. See Chapters 15–18.

since he has the people as his enemy, once he has committed his crime, he must live in fear then, too, nor can he hope to find any sort of refuge.[5]

One could give innumerable examples of this subject, but I will content myself with just one that took place within the memory of our fathers. Messer Annibale Bentivoglio, grandfather of the present Messer Annibale, was murdered when he was prince of Bologna by the Canneschi, who conspired against him, and he left behind no one but Messer Giovanni, who was in swaddling bands. Immediately after that murder, the people rose up and massacred all the Canneschi. This came about because of the good will the people felt toward the house of Bentivogli at that time, a good will so great that, when there was no one left in Bologna who could rule the state after Annibale's death, the Bolognesi found out that a member of the Bentivoglio family was in Florence who had up until then been considered the son of a blacksmith, and they came to seek him there and gave him control of their city, which he governed until Messer Giovanni came of age to rule.[6]

Thus I conclude that a prince should not be too concerned about conspiracies when the people are well disposed toward him, but when they are hostile and regard him with hatred, he should fear everything and everybody. And well-ordered states and wise princes have made every effort not to drive the aristocracy to desperation while satisfying the people and keeping them contented, for this is one of a prince's most important concerns.

Among the well-ordered and well-governed kingdoms of our time is that of France, in which one can find countless good institutions on which the liberty and security of the king depend, of which the chief is the parliament and its authority. For the founder of that realm, knowing the ambition of the nobility and their insolence, judged it necessary to put a bit in their mouths to keep them in check. On the other hand, he understood the hatred of the people for the nobility, a hatred based on fear, and desired to reassure them. Yet he did not want these things to be the particular concern of the king in order to spare him the dissatisfaction that he might stir up among the nobles for favoring the people and among the people for favoring the nobility. Consequently, he established a third judicial body that, without placing any burden on the king, might hold down the nobility and favor the lower

5. Machiavelli discusses conspiracies in a much more nuanced fashion in *Discourses* 3.6.
6. In 1445, Battista Canneschi murdered Annibale I Bentivoglio (b. 1415; ruled 1443–45); his son Giovanni II Bentivogli (1443–1508; ruled Bologna 1462–1506) did not come of age until seventeen years later, in 1462. Sante Bentivoglio (b. 1426; ruled 1445–62), the illegitimate son of Annibale's cousin Ercole, filled the gap. Giovanni was later succeeded by his son, the "present Annibale"—that is, Annibale II Bentivogli (1467–1540), who ruled for just two years, 1510–12.

classes.[7] There could not be a better or more prudent arrangement than this one, nor a greater source of security for the king and the kingdom. From this another noteworthy lesson can be drawn: that princes should have others carry out hateful tasks and reserve the pleasant ones for themselves. Again, I conclude that a prince should respect his nobles, but not make himself hated by the people.

Perhaps it might seem to many who have studied the lives and deaths of a number of Roman emperors that they provide examples contrary to this opinion of mine, since some of them always lived exemplary lives and showed great strength [*virtù*] of character, yet nevertheless lost the empire or were killed by their own people who conspired against them. Wishing therefore to respond to these objections, I will discuss the characteristics of some of these emperors and explain the reasons for their ruin, which do not differ from the ones I have presented, and in addition, I will point out those notable things that are worthy of being considered by anyone who reads the history of those times. Furthermore, it will be sufficient if I choose all those emperors who succeeded to the imperial throne from Marcus the philosopher to Maximinus: these were Marcus, his son Commodus, Pertinax, Julian, Severus, his son Antoninus Caracalla, Macrinus, Heliogabalus, Alexander, and Maximinus.[8]

Now the first thing to note is that whereas in other principalities one has to contend only with the ambition of the nobles and the insolence of the people, the Roman emperors had a third difficulty, that of having to cope with the cruelty and avarice of the soldiers. This difficulty was so great that it caused the downfall of many of them, for it was hard to satisfy the soldiers as well as the people, since the people loved peace and quiet, and consequently loved princes who restrained themselves, while the soldiers loved a prince with a

7. Machiavelli's ideas on the form and function of the French parliament are not quite accurate. The initial French parliament (or *parlement*) was that of Paris, and despite its name, it was a court of law, not a legislative body. It grew out of the king's court during the reign of Louis IX (b. 1214; ruled 1226–70), who often presided over it. Additional provincial parliaments developed in the 15th century. The idea of using the parliament as a means to achieve a balance among the ruler, the nobility, and the common people never really had the importance Machiavelli assigns it.

8. The period of Roman history Machiavelli covers here—namely 161–238 CE—is later than that covered by such great Roman historians as Suetonius and Tacitus. Machiavelli's likely source for all this information is the Greek historian Herodian, whose *Histories* had been translated into Latin by the Italian humanist Angelo Poliziano. The emperors discussed here, with the dates that they ruled, are Marcus Aurelius Antoninus (161–180); his son, Lucius Aelius Aurelius Commodus (180–193); Publius Helvius Pertinax (January to March, 193); Marcus Didius Julianus (March to June, 193); Septimius Severus (193–211); Marcus Aurelius Antoninus Caracalla (211–217); Marcus Opellius Macrinus (217–218); Heliogabalus—that is, Varius Avitus Bassianus (218–222); Marcus Aurelius Severus Alexander (222–235); and Gaius Julius Verus Maximinus (235–238). The reign of Marcus Aurelius has generally been seen as one of the high points of the Roman Empire. The emperors Machiavelli focuses on thus illustrate its steep decline.

martial spirit who was arrogant, cruel, and rapacious. They wanted him to behave that way toward the people in order to get double wages and to give vent to their avarice and cruelty. These were the reasons why those emperors who did not possess a great reputation, either given to them by nature or acquired through practice, so that by its means they could rein in both groups, invariably came to grief. And most of them, especially those who came to power as new princes, knowing the difficulties created by these two conflicting humors, devoted themselves to satisfying the soldiers, caring little if the people were harmed.[9] This was a choice they had to make, because princes, who cannot avoid being hated by somebody, must first seek to avoid being hated by everybody, and when they cannot achieve this, they should try as hard as possible to avoid the hatred of the most powerful group around. And therefore, those emperors, who were new princes and had need of extraordinary support, allied themselves with the soldiers rather than with the people. Nevertheless, whether this turned out to be useful to them or not depended on whether the prince knew how to maintain his reputation with the army.

For the reasons mentioned above, it turned out that Marcus, Pertinax, and Alexander, all of whom led lives of moderation and were lovers of justice, enemies of cruelty, humane, and benevolent, all, except for Marcus, came to a sad end. Marcus alone lived and died with the greatest honor, because he became the emperor by hereditary right and did not have to acknowledge that he owed it either to the army or to the people. Besides, being endowed with many virtues [*virtù*] that made people revere him, he kept both factions within bounds as long as he lived, and he was never hated or despised.[1] But Pertinax was made emperor against the will of the soldiers, who, being accustomed to a licentious life under Commodus, could not tolerate the honest life to which Pertinax wanted them to return, so that, having made himself hated—and since contempt was added to this hatred because he was old—he came to ruin at the very beginning of his reign.[2] And here it should be noted that hatred is acquired as much by good deeds as by sorry ones, and so, as I said above, a prince who wants to hold onto his state is often forced not to be good, for when that group whose support you think you need in order to rule, whether it be the people, the army, or the nobility, is corrupt, you must follow its humor and satisfy it, and in

9. Machiavelli's reference to "humors" here is based on the idea of the state as a body politic, and the citizens who inhabit it as the substances, the "humors," that make the body function; see also n. 1, p. 31.
1. Marcus Aurelius had been adopted as heir by the preceding emperor, Antoninus Pius.
2. Pertinax became emperor in his old age and against his will and lasted just three months in that position.

e, good deeds will be your enemies. But let us come to Alex-
ne was so good that among the other things for which he has
raised, there is this one: that in the fourteen years of his reign, he ne ver put anyone to death without a trial. Nevertheless, since he was considered effeminate and a man who allowed himself to be ruled by his mother, he came to be despised because of this, and the army conspired against him and murdered him.[3]

Considering now, by contrast, the qualities of Commodus, Severus, Antoninus Caracalla, and Maximinus, you will find that they were extremely cruel and rapacious, and so, to satisfy the army, they did not hesitate to inflict all sorts of injuries on the people, and every one of them, except for Severus, came to a sad end. For Severus had so much talent [*virtù*] that by keeping the soldiers his allies, even though the people were oppressed by him, he was always able to rule happily, for those abilities [*virtù*] of his made him so admirable in the eyes of the soldiers and the people that the latter remained, in a way, astonished and stupefied, and the former, respectful and satisfied.[4]

And because the actions of this man were very impressive in someone who was a new prince, I would like to show briefly what good use he made of the characters of the fox and the lion, whose natures, as I say above, a prince must imitate. Once he realized that the emperor Julian was indecisive, Severus persuaded his army, which he was leading in Slavonia,[5] that it was a good idea for them to go to Rome, in order to avenge the death of Pertinax, who had been killed by the Praetorian Guard, and under this pretext,[6] without revealing that he aspired to rule the empire, he moved his army against Rome and was in Italy before anyone knew of his departure. Upon his arrival in Rome, the senate, acting out of fear, elected him emperor, and he put Julian to death. After this beginning, Severus faced two remaining difficulties if he wanted to make himself master of the entire state: one in Asia, where Niger, head of the Asian armies, had had himself proclaimed emperor; and the other in the west, where Albinus[7] also aspired to imperial rule. And since he

3. Alexander Severus became emperor when he was just fourteen because of the murder of Heliogabalus. Neither fact about these emperors seems relevant to Machiavelli as he conducts his argument.

4. Machiavelli here equates the virtues (*virtù*) of Severus with those of Marcus Aurelius, thus identifying the prince's virtues (and vices) as those qualities that allow him to rule successfully (or to fail as a ruler).

5. I.e., the modern Slovenia. Julian was Marcus Didius Severus Julianus Augustus, who bought the Roman Empire at auction from the Praetorian Guard in March 193. He ruled it for only sixty-six days before Severus, who was commanding an army not far from modern Vienna, took it from him and had his head cut off.

6. Here, *colore*. On the ambiguous meaning of *color* in the rhetorical tradition, see n. 5, p. 55.

7. Decius Claudius Septimius Albinus, head of the legions in Gaul. He was beaten by Severus in 198 and taken to Rome, where he was executed. Niger was Gaius Pescennius Niger Augustus, who was proclaimed emperor by his legions in Antioch in 193. Beaten by Severus at Nicaea later that year, he was killed by his own soldiers.

judged it dangerous to reveal himself as the enemy of both, he decided to attack Niger and to deceive Albinus. To the latter he wrote that, having been elected emperor by the senate, he wanted to share that dignity with him, and he sent him the title of "Caesar" and, through a resolution of the senate, made him his co-equal. These things were accepted as true by Albinus. But when Severus had defeated and killed Niger, pacified things in the East, and returned to Rome, he complained in the senate that Albinus, hardly acknowledging the benefits received from him, had treacherously sought to murder him, and for this it was necessary for him to go and punish his ingratitude. He then went to find him in France, and he took away from him both his state and his life. Thus, whoever examines the actions of this man in detail will find that he was a most ferocious lion and a very clever fox, and will see that he was feared and respected by everyone, while not being hated by his armies. Nor will he be amazed that Severus, a new man, could have held onto so great an empire, for his enormous reputation always protected him from the hatred that the people might have conceived against him because of the looting he did.[8]

But Severus's son Antoninus was also a man of the most excellent qualities that made him admirable in the eyes of the people and popular with the soldiers, for he was a military man, who was quite capable of enduring any kind of hardship and despised all delicate foods and every sort of easy living, which made him loved by all the armies. Nevertheless, his ferocity and cruelty were so great and so unheard of that—because, after countless individual murders, he put to death a large part of the populace of Rome and the entire populace of Alexandria[9]—he came to be thoroughly hated by absolutely everyone and began to be feared even by those whom he had about him, with the result that he was murdered by a centurion even though he was surrounded by his army. From this it is to be noted that assassinations such as these, which result from the deliberation of a man of obstinate spirit, are impossible for princes to avoid, since anyone who does not fear to die himself can do him harm. The prince need not fear such attacks very much, however, since they are extremely rare. He must only guard against inflicting serious injury on those who serve him and those whom he keeps near him

8. Machiavelli omits the fact that Severus terrorized the senate. Having created a law punishing anyone who murdered a senator, he first had his enemies removed from the senate and then had them killed. This might have enhanced his reputation, but not in a positive way. His son Caracalla was apparently half insane. He murdered his brother Geta in their mother's arms, turned over the government to her, and wandered from one remote military outpost to another, seeking the death with which his own soldiers finally obliged him. His murderer, Macrinus, thereby became emperor, but held the position for less than a year.
9. Machiavelli exaggerates here, but Herodian does speak of numerous murders in both cities.

in the service of the state, as Antoninus had done, for he had shamefully put to death a brother of that centurion, and threatened the man himself every day, though he still kept him in his bodyguard. This was a rash thing to do, and as it happened, one that led to his ruin.

But let us come to Commodus, for whom it was very easy to hold onto the empire, since it came to him by hereditary right, as the son of Marcus [Aurelius], and it would have been enough for him to have simply followed in his father's footsteps and to have satisfied the army and the people. But being of a cruel and bestial disposition, in order to be able to exercise his rapacity on the people, he turned to indulging the soldiers and encouraging their licentiousness. On the other hand, he did not maintain his own dignity, often descending into the theater to fight with the gladiators and doing other truly degrading things unworthy of his imperial majesty, until he became contemptible in the sight of the soldiers. And since he was hated on the one hand and despised on the other, a conspiracy was formed against him, and he was murdered.

The qualities of Maximinus remain to be described. He was an extremely warlike man, and since the armies were disgusted with the softness of Alexander, which I discussed above, they elected him emperor after Alexander's death. He did not possess that position for very long, because two things made him hated and despised: the one was his very base birth, for he had once herded sheep in Thrace (something that was well known everywhere and made him lose considerable dignity in everyone's eyes); the other was that at the beginning of his reign he had put off going to Rome to take possession of the imperial throne, and he had acquired a reputation for great cruelty since he had, acting through his prefects, committed many cruel deeds in Rome and in other parts of the empire. Consequently, the whole world was moved by scorn for his base blood and by a hatred caused by fear of his ferocity, so that Africa was the first to rebel, followed by the senate together with all the people of Rome, until finally, all of Italy conspired against him. To this was added his very own army: besieging Aquileia and finding it difficult to capture, disgusted by his cruelty, and fearing him less because they saw he had so many enemies, they murdered him.

I do not want to speak of Heliogabalus, Macrinus, or Julian, who were quickly eliminated since everyone despised them. But let me come to the conclusion of this discourse and say that the princes of our times have to deal less with the difficulty of having to resort to extraordinary means to satisfy the soldiers under their command: although some consideration has to be given to them, nevertheless problems are quickly solved, because none of these princes have standing armies entrenched in the government and administration of provinces, as were the armies of the Roman empire. And therefore, if it was necessary at that time to satisfy the soldiers more than the people, that was because the soldiers had more power than the people; now, it is necessary for all princes, except the Turk and the Sultan,[1] to satisfy the people more than the soldiers, for the people have more power than the soldiers do. I except the Turk here, because he always keeps about him twelve thousand infantry and fifteen thousand cavalry, on whom the strength and security of his rule depend, and it is necessary for that lord to set aside every other consideration so as to keep them his friends. Similarly, since the realm of the Sultan is entirely in the hands of the soldiers, he, too, must keep them his friends, without any regard for the people. And it should be noted that this state of the Sultan is unlike all the other principalities, for it is similar to the Christian pontificate, which cannot be labeled either a hereditary principality or a new principality, because it is not the sons of the old prince who are his heirs and succeed him as rulers, but rather the man who is elected to that position by those who have the authority to do so. And since this system is an ancient one, it cannot be called a new principality, because in it there are none of those difficulties inherent in new ones, for although the prince really is new, the institutions of that state are old and are set up to receive him as if he were their hereditary lord.

But let us return to our topic. I say that whoever studies the preceding discourse will see that either hatred or contempt was the reason for the ruin of those emperors who were mentioned above, and he will also understand how it comes about that, while some of them proceeded in one way and some in a contrary manner, in each group one man had a happy ending and the others an unhappy one. Because for Pertinax and Alexander, being new princes, it was useless and harmful for them to try to imitate Marcus [Aurelius], who ruled the state by hereditary right; and similarly, for Caracalla, Commodus, and Maximinus, it was disastrous for them to imitate Severus, since they did not have sufficient ability [*virtù*] to follow in his footsteps. Thus, a new prince in a new principality cannot imitate the actions of Marcus, nor is it necessary for him to follow those of Severus either, but he should take from Severus those qualities that are necessary to found his state, and from Marcus those that are proper and glorious in order to preserve a state that is already established and secure.[2]

1. I.e., the ruler of the caliphate that was established by Muhammad as an elective monarchy. In its later Egyptian manifestations, there were frequent power struggles, and efforts were made by various caliphs to have their sons succeed them. "The Turk": the hereditary ruler of the Ottoman Empire. Machiavelli is possibly thinking of such figures as Bayezid II (b. 1447; ruled 1481–1512) and his son Selim I (b. 1465; ruled 1512–20).
2. It could be argued that Machiavelli has been playing fast and loose with history to some extent, making the accounts of the different emperors' lives fit the different ends they came to. Alexander Severus, for example, was not a new prince, and the virtues that were fatal to him brought about the success of Marcus Aurelius.

Chapter 20

Whether Fortresses and Many Other Things Utilized Every Day by Princes Are Useful, or Not

In order to maintain a secure hold on their states, some princes have disarmed their subjects; some others have kept their subject lands divided; some have nourished hostilities against themselves; others have devoted themselves to winning over those who were suspect at the beginning of their reign; some have built fortresses; some have reduced them to ruins and destroyed them. And although one cannot provide a definitive judgment about all these things without going into the particular circumstances of those states in which some similar deliberation had to be made, nevertheless I will speak in as general a way as the subject matter itself will allow.

There has never been a case, then, when a new prince has disarmed his subjects; on the contrary, when he found them disarmed, he has always armed them, for when they are armed, those arms become yours, those whom you suspect become loyal, and those who were loyal maintain their allegiance and from being subjects make themselves into your partisans. And since all subjects cannot be armed, when the ones you do arm receive benefits, you can deal more securely with the others. And this difference in treatment toward themselves that the armed ones recognize makes them feel more obligated to you; those others excuse you, judging it necessary that those who face more danger and have more responsibilities should get greater rewards. But when you disarm them, you begin to offend them, and you show that you distrust them either because of their cowardice or lack of loyalty, and both of these opinions generate hatred against you. And since you cannot remain unarmed, you are obliged to turn to a mercenary army, whose character was discussed above;[1] and even if they were good, they could not be strong enough to defend you from powerful enemies and distrustful subjects. Therefore, as I have said, a new prince in a new principality has always created an army there. History books are full of such examples. But when a prince acquires a new state, which is attached to his old one like an appendage, then it is necessary to disarm that state, except for those who were your partisans when you were acquiring it, and when time and opportunity serve, even they must be rendered soft and effeminate, and things must be arranged in such a way that all the arms of your state are in the hands of your own soldiers who live near you in your old state.

1. See Chapter 12, pp. 38–42.

Our ancestors and those who were considered wise used to say that Pistoia was to be held by means of factions and Pisa by means of fortresses, and consequently they nurtured factional strife in some of their subject towns in order to hold onto them more easily.[2] In those times when Italy had, to some extent, a balance of power, this wisdom may have served well, but I doubt it can be given as a rule today, for I do not believe that factions ever did any good.[3] On the contrary, it is inevitable that when the enemy approaches, divided cities are lost immediately, for the weaker party will always attach itself to the forces outside, and the stronger one will not be able to hold out against them.

I believe that the Venetians were moved by the reasons stated above to nourish the Guelf and Ghibelline factions in their subject cities,[4] and although they never allowed things to reach the point of bloodshed, they still nourished these quarrels among them, so that the citizens would not unite against them, being occupied with those disagreements of theirs. As has been seen, this did not then turn out to their advantage, because, after the defeat at Vailà, one of those factions was immediately emboldened and took their entire state from them.[5] Such methods, therefore, argue weakness in a prince, for in a strong principality divisions of this sort will never be permitted, because they are profitable only in peacetime, enabling subjects to be managed more easily by such means, but when war comes, an arrangement like that reveals its defectiveness.

Without a doubt, princes become great by overcoming the difficulties and obstacles placed in their way, and therefore, especially when Fortune wants to enhance the reputation of a new prince, who has more need of acquiring prestige than does a hereditary prince, she creates enemies for him and has them undertake campaigns

2. Machiavelli is usually impatient with proverbial sayings and customary beliefs. In the case of Pistoia he had seen the consequences of factional rioting there; see n. 3, p. 52.
3. The period in which Italy enjoyed something like a balance of power stretched from the signing of the Treaty of Lodi (also called the Peace of Lodi) in 1454 by Florence, Milan, and Naples to the death of Lorenzo the Magnificent in 1492 and the invasion of Italy by Charles VIII of France in 1494. The concept of balance of power is usually credited to Francesco Guicciardini's *History of Italy* (1561–64), although it was implicit in the foreign policies of the various states in the peninsula well before then, as they continually formed and re-formed alliances when any one state seemed to become more powerful than the others. Machiavelli's statement here suggests that he formulated a version of the concept before Guicciardini did.
4. In the Middle Ages, Italian city-states tended to be divided between the Guelfs, a faction (here referred to as a *setta,* or sect, by Machiavelli) that favored the papacy, and the Ghibellines, a faction that favored the Holy Roman Empire. By Machiavelli's time, the terms had lost their specific meanings and were simply another way of saying "faction."
5. After they lost the battle of Vailà, also known as Agnadello, which was fought against the forces of the League of Cambrai, led by Pope Julius II, on May 14, 1509, the Venetians had to face rebellions in many of the principal cities they held, including Brescia, Verona, Vicenza, and Padua, but they essentially decided to let their possessions on the mainland go rather than fight to retain them. The city lost none of its overseas possessions, which were the real source of its wealth and power.

against him, so that he may have reason to overcome them and to climb up higher on the ladder which his enemies have brought him. For this reason, many hold that a wise prince, when he has the opportunity, should cunningly nourish such hostility, so that by suppressing it he can augment his greatness.

Princes, and especially those who are new, have found more loyalty and more usefulness in those men who were considered suspect at the beginning of their reign than in those whom they trusted at the start. Pandolfo Petrucci,[6] prince of Siena, ruled his state more with men he did not trust than with the others. But on this matter one cannot speak in generalities, because it varies according to the case involved. I will only say this: that the prince will always have no trouble at all in winning over those men who had been his enemies at the founding of the principality, the kind of men who need support in order to maintain themselves, and they will be even more obliged to serve him loyally in that they recognize the need to cancel the bad opinion he had of them because of what they did. And thus the prince always gets greater use out of them than out of those who, serving him from positions of too much security, neglect his affairs.

And since the subject requires it, I do not wish to fail to remind princes who have recently acquired a new state by means of assistance from its inhabitants that they should consider carefully what reason may have moved those who supported them to have done so; and if it is not natural affection for him, but only because they were unhappy with the preceding state, he will be able to keep them his friends only by means of hard work and with great difficulty, because it will be impossible for him to satisfy them. And by carefully considering the reason for this, using examples drawn from antiquity and modern times, he will see that it is much easier to win the friendship of those who were content with the state before and were therefore his enemies, than those who became his friends and helped him to occupy it because they were dissatisfied with it.

In order to hold their states more securely, it has been customary for princes to build fortresses that may serve as the bridle and bit for those who might plan to act against them, and in order to have a secure refuge against an unexpected attack. I praise this policy because it has been used since antiquity. Nevertheless, in our own times Messer Niccolò Vitelli was seen to demolish two fortresses in Città di Castello as a means of holding onto that state. Guido Ubaldo, duke of Urbino, upon returning to his dominion from which Cesare

6. Pandolfo Petrucci (1452–1512), the ruler of Siena from 1500 until his death, was the leader of the aristocratic faction in the city. He may have ruled with the aid of men he did not trust, but no historian shares this opinion. Machiavelli knew that he was himself in the position of those men who could not be trusted by the Medici after they had retaken Florence in 1512. Machiavelli is implying that since Petrucci was highly respected, successful, and had just died, he provides a good precedent for the Medici to follow.

Borgia had driven him, razed all the fortresses in that country down to their foundations and concluded that without them it would be more difficult for him to lose that state a second time. The Bentivogli took similar measures after returning to Bologna.[7] Thus, fortresses are useful, or not, depending upon the times, and if they help you in one way, they harm you in another. The question can be dealt with this way: the prince who fears his own people more than foreigners ought to build fortresses, but the one who fears foreigners more than his people ought to do without them. The castle that Francesco Sforza built in Milan has brought and will bring more wars upon the house of Sforza than any other disorder in that state.[8] Therefore, the best fortress that exists is not to be hated by the people, for although you may have fortresses, they will not save you if the people hate you, because once the people have taken up arms, they will never lack foreigners to come to their assistance. In our times no one has seen a fortress to benefit any prince except the countess of Forlì after her consort, Count Girolamo, was murdered, for thanks to her castle she was able to escape a popular uprising, wait for help from Milan, and retake her state.[9] The times were such that at that moment no outsider could come to the assistance of the people, but later on, fortresses were of little value to her when Cesare Borgia attacked her, and the people, because of their hostility to her, joined with the outsiders. Therefore, at that time, as well as earlier, it would have been safer for her if, instead of having fortresses, she had managed to avoid being hated by the people.

Everything considered, then, I will praise those who build fortresses and those who do not, and I shall blame anyone who, trusting in fortresses, thinks it of little moment to be hated by the people.

7. These various instances of fortress razing involve somewhat different motives. Niccolò Vitelli, the father of Vitellozzo and Paolo, was chased from his city by Pope Sixtus IV in 1474, but when he returned from exile with the help of Florence in 1482, he destroyed the castles built there by the pope as a gesture of confidence in his people. Guido Ubaldo, or Guidobaldo, da Montefeltro (1472–1508), was the duke of Urbino from 1482 on. He was driven out of his state by Cesare Borgia in 1502, but regained it the next year; his court is celebrated in Baldesare Castiglione's classic *Book of the Courtier.* He destroyed his castles because he found they were more useful to the enemy than to him. When the Bentivoglio family of Bologna, who were driven out of their city by Julius II in 1506, regained it in 1511, they destroyed the castle of Porta Galliera that the pope had erected to command the city and that served as an emblem of his power.
8. Shortly after he became the duke of Milan, Francesco Sforza built the castle, now known as the Castello Sforzesco, which still stands in the heart of the city. The Sforza rulers of Milan had relied on the protection of their castle when oppressing the people in the city, but twice within recent memory during Machiavelli's lifetime Ludovico lost his state to the French without a shot being fired.
9. The countess of Forlì was Caterina Sforza, the niece of Ludovico il Moro. After her husband, Girolamo Riario, was murdered by plotters in 1488, she took refuge in her castle and held out until her uncle came to her rescue from Milan. But Cesare Borgia attacked and defeated her in 1500. Machiavelli may have admired her for her courage, but he still felt that her reliance on her castle rather than the people was a mistake.

Chapter 21

How a Prince Should Act to Gain Renown

Nothing makes a prince esteemed so much as undertaking great enterprises and setting extraordinary examples for others. In our times we have Ferdinand of Aragon, the present king of Spain.[1] He may almost be called a new prince, because from being a weak king he has become, through his fame and glory, the leading king of Christendom, and if you consider his deeds, you will find them all very grand and some even extraordinary. At the beginning of his reign he attacked Granada, and that undertaking was the foundation of his state. First, he did it when his country was at peace and without a hint of opposition: he kept the minds of the barons of Castile occupied with this undertaking, and as long as they were thinking of that war, they did not consider making any political changes, and thus he acquired prestige and power over them without their becoming aware of it. He was able to nourish his armies with money from the Church and the people, and through that long war he was able to lay the foundation for his own army, which has since brought him honor. Besides this, in order to be able to undertake greater enterprises, he always used religion for his own purposes and had recourse to a pious cruelty in driving the Marranos out of his kingdom and seizing their property—no example of his actions could be more pitiful or more extraordinary.[2] Under this same cloak of religion, he attacked Africa, carried out his Italian campaign, and has finally attacked France.[3] Thus he has always accomplished great feats which he contrived for himself and which have always kept his subjects' minds in

1. Machiavelli both admires and disapproves of Ferdinand the Catholic. He was a "new prince" in the sense that he acquired the Kingdom of Castile through marriage and ruled it, as well as Aragon, from 1474 to 1504. Because Castile actually belonged to his wife, Isabella, it is not surprising that he chose to distract the nobility of that kingdom with a series of foreign wars. It was Ferdinand's armies that finally drove the Moors from Spain in 1492 with the capture of their last stronghold in Granada.
2. The Marranos were Jews or Moors who had converted to Christianity but were distrusted by the Spaniards; using religion as a pretext, Ferdinand drove them out of Spain in 1502. Machiavelli's comment on this event as something "pitiful" and "extraordinary" (*miserabile* and *raro* in Italian) suggests his mixed feelings about it, despite his recognition that such things contributed to Ferdinand's reputation. Ironically, the expulsions of the Marranos deprived Spain of many members of its middle class, who might have been able to do something to avert the economic and political decline the country experienced in the course of the 17th century.
3. Machiavelli's sentence hurries through a number of wars undertaken by Ferdinand, thus suggesting the incredible energy animating his exploits. The examples do not come in chronological order. Ferdinand pursued his war against the Moors in 1509 by invading Africa. His Italian campaign began with his capture of Sicily from the French in 1496 and the entire Kingdom of Naples from them in 1504. His expulsion of the French from Italy occurred between 1511 and 1513. Finally, Ferdinand attacked France in 1512, taking the southwestern Kingdom of Navarre from it by 1515.

suspense and amazement, and occupied with their outcome. And these actions of his have sprung one out of the other in such a way that in between them he never gave men the space to be able to work at leisure against him.

It also helps a prince a great deal to give extraordinary examples of how he handles internal affairs, like those reported of Messer Bernabò of Milan.[4] Whenever it happens that someone does something extraordinary, whether for good or for ill, in civic life, the prince should choose a method of rewarding or punishing him that will be much talked of. And above all, a prince should strive in his every action to create the impression that he is a great man of exceptional intelligence.

A prince is also esteemed when he is a true friend and a true enemy, that is, when he declares himself without reservation in favor of one person and against another. This policy will always be more useful than staying neutral, because if two powerful neighbors of yours come to blows, either they are such people that if one of them wins, you will have to fear the victor, or they are not. In either of these two cases, it will be more useful for you to declare yourself and wage open war, because in the first case, if you do not declare yourself, you will always be the prey of the winner, to the delight and satisfaction of the one who has been defeated, and you will have no reason or anything else to defend you, nor will anyone offer you refuge. For whoever wins does not want suspect friends who would not help him in adversity; whoever loses will not take you in, because you were not willing, sword in hand, to take your chances with him.

Antiochus[5] came into Greece, sent there by the Aetolians to drive out the Romans. He dispatched ambassadors to the Achaeans,[6] who were allies of the Romans, to encourage them to remain neutral, while on the other side, the Romans were urging them to take up arms on their behalf. The matter came up for debate in the Achaeans' council, where Antiochus's legate urged them to remain neutral, to which the Roman legate replied: "As to what these men are saying about how you should not get involved in the war, nothing is

4. Bernabò, or Barnabò, Visconti (1323–1385) was duke of Milan from 1354 on, but divided the rule of the city with his nephew Giovanni (Gian) Galeazzo Visconti (1351–1402), who eventually killed his uncle and became the sole ruler. All the Visconti were infamous for the hideous ingenuity and cruelty of their punishments, but Messer Bernabò was the worst. In addition, he sired over thirty children, legitimate and illegitimate, whom he married off for their advantage and his own. Machiavelli is probably serious about the need for the prince to distinguish himself in handling internal affairs, but he may be using this example ironically.
5. Antiochus III, also known as "the Great" (b. c. 241; ruled 223–187 BCE), was the king of Syria and allied to the city-states of northern and central Greece that made up the Aetolian League.
6. A confederacy of Greek city-states. The Romans defeated the Achaeans in 197 and the Aetolians, along with Antiochus, in 190.

farther from your interests; without thanks, without dignity, you will be the prize of the victor."[7]

And it will always be the case that the one who is not your friend will seek your neutrality, while the one who is your friend will ask you to declare yourself by taking up arms. And most of the time, irresolute princes, in order to avoid present dangers, follow that path of neutrality and come to ruin. But when the prince declares himself vigorously in favor of one party, even if the one to whom you have allied yourself wins, and he is powerful and you remain at his discretion, he does feel obligated to you and there does exist a bond of friendship contracted between you, and men are never so dishonorable that they will make themselves into so great an example of ingratitude by oppressing you. Moreover, victories are never so decisive that the victor can avoid having some concerns, especially with regard to justice. But if the one to whom you are allied loses, you will be given refuge by him, and while he can, he will aid you, and you will become the comrade of one whose fortune may rise again.

In the second case, when those who fight one another are such that you do not have to fear the one who wins, taking sides is still so much more prudent. For you proceed to bring about the ruin of one with the help of another who ought to have saved him if he had been wise, for when he wins, he remains at your discretion, and with your help, it is impossible that he should fail to win. And here it is to be noted that a prince should never ally himself with someone more powerful than himself in order to attack others, unless necessity compels it, as was mentioned above, for if he wins, you remain his prisoner, and princes should avoid as much as possible being left at the discretion of others. The Venetians allied themselves with France against the duke of Milan, and they could have avoided making that alliance, which resulted in their ruin.[8] But when such an alliance cannot be avoided, as was the case with the Florentines when the pope and Spain went with their armies to attack Lombardy, then the prince should take sides, for the reasons stated above.[9] Nor

7. The episode Machiavelli describes comes from Livy, *History of Rome,* 35.48–49, and he cites, slightly inaccurately, the Roman legate's words in Latin: *"Quod autem isti dicunt non interponendi vos bello, nihil magis alienum rebus vestris est; sine gratia, sine dignitate, praemium victoris eris"* (35.49).
8. They did this in 1499 when Louis XII drove Ludovico Sforza from Milan.
9. Florence maintained its alliance with France in 1512, when Julius II and Ferdinand of Aragon formed the Holy League to drive the French out of Italy. Machiavelli's fairly vague references here may be a strategic move so that he does not have to say what really happened. The leader of Florence, Piero di Tommaso Soderini (1450–1522), usually referred to as Pier Soderini, whose temporizing policies Machiavelli disliked, failed to support the French, but did not really support the pope and the Spanish either. The result was the sack of Prato in 1512 in which a Spanish army routed the Florentine militia that Machiavelli had trained, the downfall of Soderini's republican government and the restoration of the Medici to power, Machiavelli's own dismissal from political office as the head of the Second Chancery (and as Soderini's close confidant), and the beginning of Machiavelli's own eight-year exile from the city.

should any state ever believe that it can invariably choose safe courses of action; rather, it should recognize that its only choices are doubtful ones. For it is in the nature of things that whenever we strive to avoid one difficulty, we run into another one, but prudence consists in knowing how to recognize the nature of the difficulties and in choosing the least sorry one as the better.

A prince must also show himself a lover of virtue [*virtù*], give recognition to virtuous men [*uomini virtuosi*], and honor those who excel in any particular art. Moreover, he should encourage his citizens to practice their trades in peace, whether in commerce, or agriculture, or any other human activity. This man should not be afraid to improve his holdings for fear that they will be taken from him, or that man to start a commercial enterprise for fear of taxes. Instead, the prince must prepare prizes for whoever wants to do these things and for anyone who thinks in whatever way to enrich his city or his state. Besides this, he must, at appropriate times during the year, keep the people occupied with festivals and spectacles. And as every city is divided into guilds or neighborhoods,[1] he should take account of those groups, join their gatherings from time to time, and give them examples of his humanity and magnificence, while always firmly maintaining the majesty of his position, for this should never be deficient in any way whatsoever.

Chapter 22

On the Secretaries of Princes

The choosing of ministers[1] is a matter of no small importance to a prince: whether they are good, or not, depends on his prudence. The first conjecture that one makes of a ruler's intelligence comes from seeing the men he has around him, and when they are capable and loyal, he may be considered wise because he knew how to recognize their ability and command their loyalty. But when they are otherwise, one can always arrive at a negative judgment of him because the first mistake he makes is made in this choice.

1. Machiavelli's word, *tribú*, literally means "tribes" and could be rendered as such or as "clans." But Machiavelli is really thinking of the neighborhoods, or *quartieri*, in Florence that were usually centered on their local churches.

1. Machiavelli uses the word *minister* (*ministro*) in this chapter, rather than *secretary*, although the Latin title of the chapter points to the latter. There Machiavelli's word for "secretaries" is the late Latin phrase *a secretis* (literally, "from or by the secrets"), a shorthand expression for someone who was the keeper of his employer's secrets. From the title of the chapter and from what Machiavelli says in it about the activities of the "minister," it should be clear that by this word he means someone who did not do what we would call secretarial work, such as composing letters, but who was more like what we would call a "confidential adviser." In various writings, Machiavelli identified himself as a "secretary" (*secretarius* in Latin).

There was no one who knew Messer Antonio da Venafro,[2] the minister of Pandolfo Petrucci, prince of Siena, who did not judge Pandolfo to be a thoroughly worthy man since he had that man as his minister. And there are three kinds of brains: the one understands things on its own; the other discerns that which others understand; the third understands neither by itself nor through others.[3] That first kind is most excellent, the second excellent, the third useless. Therefore, it necessarily must have been the case that, if Pandolfo was not in the first group, he was in the second. For whenever a man has enough intelligence to recognize the good or evil that another man does or says, even if he lacks that imaginative power himself, he can still recognize the good deeds as well as the sorry ones of his minister, and he will extol the former and correct the others; nor can the minister hope to deceive him, and he will therefore continue to be good.

But as to how a prince may recognize a minister, there is this method that never fails. When you notice that your minister is thinking more of himself than of you, and that in all his actions he pursues his own self-interest, a man like that will never be a good minister, nor will you ever be able to entrust yourself to him. For the man who holds another's state in his hands should never think of himself but always of his prince and must never call to mind anything except that which concerns the prince. And on the other side, the prince who wants to keep his minister loyal must think about him, bestowing honors on him, enriching him, making him feel a sense of obligation, sharing honors and responsibilities with him, so that the minister will see that he cannot exist without the prince, and so that his many honors will prevent him from desiring yet more honors, his great riches will stop him from desiring yet more riches, and his many offices will make him fear changes. Therefore, when ministers as well as princes stand on these terms with regard to their ministers, they can have confidence in one another, and when it is otherwise, the outcome will always be harmful, either for one or for the other.

Chapter 23

How Flatterers Are to Be Avoided

I do not want to omit an important subject and an error from which princes find it hard to defend themselves if they are not extremely

2. Antonio Giordani da Venafro (1459–1530), a lawyer and a professor in the *Studio* (University) of Siena, served as Pandolfo Petrucci's counselor for a long time and was widely recognized for his knowledge of the law and his eloquence. On Petrucci, see n. 6, p. 68.
3. See Livy, *History of Rome,* 22.29. However, the distinction was something of a commonplace, and Machiavelli could have found it elsewhere, such as in Hesiod's *Works and Days,* 293–97, or Cicero's speech *Pro Cluentio,* 31.

prudent or they do not make good choices. And these are the flatterers, of which the courts are full.[1] Because men take such pleasure in their own concerns, they deceive themselves in such a way that they can defend themselves only with difficulty from this plague. Besides, in wishing to defend themselves against it, one runs the risk of incurring contempt. For there is no way to guard oneself against flattery except by letting men understand that they will not offend you by telling you the truth, but when anyone can tell you the truth, you lose respect. Hence, a prudent prince should hold to a third course by choosing wise men for his government and giving them and them alone complete freedom to speak the truth to him—and only on those things which he asks them about and not on others. But he should ask them about everything and listen to their opinions; afterwards, he should deliberate by himself, according to his own style. With these counsels and with each of his ministers he should conduct himself in such a way that everyone recognizes that the more freely they speak, the more they will please him. Apart from these men, he should refuse to listen to anyone, and he should pursue what he has deliberated on and stand firmly by his decisions. Whoever does something else either fails because of the flatterers, or frequently changes his mind in the face of all the varied opinions, as a result of which he will get little respect.

In this connection I want to offer a modern example. Father Luca, a servant of Maximilian, the present emperor, speaking of his majesty, said that he never took counsel with anyone, and never did anything the way he wanted.[2] The reason for this was that he did things in a way exactly contrary to that described above. For the emperor is a secretive man, he communicates his plans to no one, he takes no advice about them; but when people start noticing and understand what his plans are as they are being put into effect, then those he has about him begin to criticize them, and he, being easily swayed, is diverted from them. As a result, what he does one day, he undoes the next, and no one ever understands what he wants or plans to do, and no one can rely on his decisions.

A prince should always take counsel, therefore, but when he wants to, not when others do; on the contrary, he must discourage anyone from giving him advice on any matter unless he asks the man about it. But he must certainly be a liberal questioner, and afterwards, patiently listen to the truth concerning the things he asked about.

1. Many works in the tradition of the Mirror for Princes actually devote substantial space to this topic, as does Castiglione in his slightly later *Book of the Courtier* (1528).
2. Father (Pre' or Prete) Luca Rainaldi was a bishop as well as being a counselor and ambassador who served the Holy Roman Emperor Maximilian I of Austria. Machiavelli got to know Rainaldi during a diplomatic mission to Maximilian in 1507–08. He wrote several reports about it, emphasizing how Maximilian's erratic and wavering conduct canceled out his good qualities as a soldier and statesman.

Indeed, if he learns that anyone, for whatever reason, is not telling him the truth, he ought to become angry. And since many people think that any prince who is considered prudent gets that reputation, not because of his own nature, but because of the good counselors he has around him, without a doubt they deceive themselves. For this is a general rule that never fails: a prince who is not wise in his own right cannot be well advised, unless by chance he has put himself entirely in the hands of one single person who is an extraordinarily prudent man and governs him in everything. In this case he might be all right, but it would not last long, because in short order such a governor would take his state away from him. If he consults with several different advisers, however, a prince who lacks wisdom will never get a unified set of opinions, nor will he be able to put them all together by himself. Each of his counselors will think of his own interests, nor will the prince see them for what they are or know how to correct them. And one cannot find counselors who are any different, because men will always turn out badly for you unless by some necessity they are forced to be good. Therefore, to conclude: good counsel, from whomever it may come, must necessarily derive from the prudence of the prince, and not the prince's prudence from good counsel.

Chapter 24

Why the Princes of Italy Have Lost Their States

The things written above, if prudently observed, will make a new prince seem like an old one and quickly make him more secure and more firmly established in his state than if he had been there a long time. For the actions of a new prince are watched much more closely than those of a hereditary one, and when those actions are recognized as being shrewd [*virtuose*], men are much more taken by them and are made to feel much more obligated to him than they would to ancient blood. For men are much more taken by present matters than by those of the past, and when they find things good in the present, they enjoy them and seek nothing more. On the contrary, they will seize every means to defend their prince as long as he himself does not fail otherwise. And so he will have the double glory of having established a new principality and adorned it and strengthened it with good laws, good arms, good friends, and good examples, just as that man who was born a prince will be doubly shamed if he loses his state because of his lack of prudence.

And if one considers those rulers in Italy who have lost their states in our times, such as the king of Naples, the duke of Milan, and others, one will discover in them, first, a common defect insofar as armies are concerned, for the reasons that were discussed at length above.[1] Then one sees that some of them either had the people as their enemy, or if they had the people as their friends, they did not know how to protect themselves against the nobility. For without these defects, states are not lost that have enough strength[2] to keep an army in the field. Philip of Macedonia, not the father of Alexander the Great, but the one who was defeated by Titus Quintius,[3] did not have much of a state compared to the grandeur of the Greeks and Romans who attacked him, but because he was a military man who knew how to maintain his hold on the people and to secure himself against the nobility, he succeeded in waging war against the Romans for many years; and if at the end he lost control of several cities, he still kept his kingdom.

Therefore, these princes of ours, who had been in their principalities for many years and then lost them, should not blame Fortune, but rather their own indolence, for they never thought, during quiet times, that things might change (which is a common defect in men, not to reckon on storms in a calm), and then, when adverse times arrived, they thought of fleeing and not of defending themselves, and they hoped that the people, angered by the insolence of the conquerors, would recall them.[4] When there are no other plans, this one is good, but it is truly bad to have abandoned other remedies for this one, for you should never wish to fall down in the belief that you will find somebody to pick you up. This either does not happen, or if it does, it does not make for your security, since that is a cowardly kind of defense and does not depend on your own efforts. And only those defenses that depend on you yourself and on your ability [*virtù*] are good, certain, and lasting.

1. The king of Naples is Federico of Aragon. The duke of Milan is Ludovico Sforza, also known as Ludovico il Moro. Machiavelli discusses the issue of what sort of armies to use in Chapters 12 and 13. His real focus in this chapter is on Ludovico Sforza, who was lazy, dissolute, and deceitful—no warrior and no leader. If he had been half the man his father was, the French would never have taken Milan so easily or held it for so long. Because Federico of Aragon was dispossessed of the Kingdom of Naples by the combined powers of France and Spain, he hardly seems as "guilty" of failure as Sforza does.
2. Machiavelli's word here is *nervo,* which might seem cognate with the English "nerve," as in "he had the nerve to . . ." But the word looks back to the Latin *nervus,* which meant "sinew or muscle," and by extension "force, power, sexual virility" and was even slang for "penis."
3. Philip V of Macedonia (b. 238; ruled 221–179 BCE) fought two wars against the Romans. In the second one the Romans were led by Titus Quinctius Flamininus (229–174 BCE), who finally defeated Philip at the battle of Cynoscephalae in 197 BCE. Philip was forced to give up all the territory he had taken in Greece, but the Romans allowed him to keep his kingdom and his army.
4. Once again Machiavelli may well be thinking of Ludovico Sforza of Milan: after the first invasion by the French, he ran away, but was recalled when the populace rose against their conquerors. After he was defeated a second time, the French took him back to France, where he died in prison. See also n. 1, p. 6.

Chapter 25

How Much Fortune Can Do in Human Affairs, and How She Is to Be Resisted

It is not unknown to me that many people have been—and still are—of the opinion that the affairs of this world are governed by Fortune and by God in such a way that men with their prudence cannot control them, indeed, that there is no remedy for them whatsoever, and for this reason, they would conclude that it is pointless to sweat much over anything, and that we should rather let ourselves be ruled by chance.[1] This opinion has had more credibility in our times because of the great changes that have been seen, and continue to be seen, every day, changes that go beyond what anyone could have imagined. Sometimes when I think about it, I am inclined toward this opinion of theirs to a certain extent. Nevertheless, in order not to extinguish our free will, I think it may be true that Fortune is the arbiter of half of our actions, but she still leaves the other half of them, more or less, to be governed by us.[2] And I compare her to one of these destructive rivers that, when they are raging, flood the plains, demolish trees and buildings, taking up earth from this side and putting it down on the other; everyone flees before them, everyone yields to their onslaught without being able to oppose them in any way. And although this is how they are, it does not follow that when the weather is calm, men cannot make provision against them with dikes and embankments, so that when they rise again, either they would be channeled off, or their impetus would not be so disorderly or so destructive. It happens similarly with Fortune: she shows her power where there is no organized force [*virtù*] to resist her and directs her onslaught there, where she knows that no embankments and dikes have been made to hold her. And if you consider Italy, which is the locus of these changes, and the one who has set them in motion, you will see a countryside without embankments and without any dikes at all; for if it had been protected by proper valor [*virtù*], as Germany, Spain, and France are, either this flood would not have caused the great changes that it has, or it would not have come upon us at all. And let this be enough to have said in general about opposing Fortune.

1. Fortune (*Fortuna* in Latin) was imagined from late antiquity through the Renaissance as being synonymous with the contingency and disorderliness of events, both natural and historical, in this world. On this key term in Machiavelli's lexicon, see the Introduction (p. ix).
2. There is no theological or philosophical system that argues for a fifty-fifty split between Fortune and free will. Rather, Machiavelli's "saving" of free will may be shaped by his tendency to analyze human experience in terms of dichotomies.

But restricting myself more to particulars, let me say that one sees this prince happy[3] today and ruined tomorrow without having seen him change his nature or any one of his traits. I think this happens, first of all, as a result of the causes that have already been discussed at length: namely, that a prince who relies entirely on Fortune comes to ruin as she changes. I also believe that the man who adapts his mode of proceeding to the nature of the times will be happy, and similarly, that the man whose mode of proceeding is not in accord with the times will be unhappy.[4] For one can see that in those affairs that lead men to the end each one has in view, namely, to glory and riches, they proceed in different ways: one with caution, the other with impetuosity; one by means of violence, the other with stealth; one through patience, the other with its contrary; and each can reach his goal using these different means. One also sees that of two cautious men, one will succeed with his designs, while the other will not, and in the same way, two will be equally happy by following two different procedures, one by being cautious and the other impetuous. And this arises from nothing other than the nature of the times, which are, or are not, in conformity with the way they proceed. This follows from what I said: that two men, operating differently, will achieve the same outcome; and of two men, operating in the same way, one will arrive at his goal, and the other will not. On this also depends the variation in what is good, for if one governs oneself with caution and patience, and if the times and circumstances turn in such a way that his behavior is good, he is going to be happy, but if the times and circumstances change, he will come to ruin, because he does not change his mode of proceeding. Nor can any man be found who is so prudent that he knows how to adapt himself to this, both because he cannot deviate from that to which he is inclined by nature, and also because, when he has always prospered by walking down one path, he cannot be persuaded to depart from it. And thus, the cautious man, when it is time to act impetuously, does not know how to do so and is ruined as a result, for if he could only change his nature with the times and circumstances, Fortune would not have changed.

In everything he undertook, Pope Julius II acted impetuously, and he found the times and circumstances so in conformity with that mode of proceeding of his, that he always achieved felicitous results. Consider the first campaign he made against Bologna while Messer

3. Machiavelli writes *felicitare,* which means "to rejoice" and thus to be happy. His verb derives from the adjective *felice,* which retains something of the meaning of its Latin root *felix*—namely, happy in the sense of being fortunate or lucky, and by extension, prosperous and fruitful. To say "happy" is thus to imply "prosperous."

4. See *Discourses* 3.8, pp. 157–60, for another statement of Machiavelli's view that success in ruling depends on one's ability to adapt to circumstances.

Giovanni Bentivoglio was still alive.[5] The Venetians were unhappy with it, and so was the king of Spain; Julius was in the midst of negotiations with France about the campaign; and nevertheless, with his usual ferocity and impetuosity, he set out on this expedition in person. This move made both Spain and the Venetians stop and hesitate, the latter out of fear and the other out of a desire to recover the entire Kingdom of Naples.[6] On the other hand, Julius dragged the king of France along behind him, because, when the king saw the pope make this move, and desiring to turn him into his ally in order to put down the Venetians, he judged that he could not deny the support of his troops without openly offending him. Thus, with his impetuous move Julius achieved that which no other pontiff, even with the utmost human prudence, would have accomplished, because, if he had waited until the negotiations were concluded and everything was settled in order to depart from Rome, as any other pontiff would have done, he would never have succeeded, for the king of France would have found a thousand excuses, and the other powers would have stirred up a thousand fears. I wish to omit the other deeds of his, which were all similar and which all turned out well for him. And the shortness of his life prevented him from having the opposite experience, for if times had come in which it was necessary to proceed with caution, he would have been ruined, for he never would have deviated from these methods to which his nature inclined him.

I conclude, then, that since Fortune changes and men remain set in their ways, they will be happy as long as the two are in accord with one another, but unhappy when the two are not. I certainly believe this: that it is better to be impetuous than cautious, because Fortune is a woman, and it is necessary, if you wish to keep her down, to beat her and knock her about. And one sees that she lets herself be conquered by men of this stripe more than by those who proceed coldly. And therefore, like a woman, she is always a friend of the young, because they are less cautious, fiercer, and command her with more audacity.

5. At that time (1506), Machiavelli was in the field with the pope and his army, and in his *Legazione seconda alla corte di Roma* (*Second Legation* [i.e., *Diplomatic Mission*] *to the Court of Rome*), he wrote about Julius's rashness, including his gambling on French support. Giovanni Bentivoglio (1438–1508) ruled Bologna from 1462 until Julius drove him out in 1506; he died two years later in exile.

6. Julius II took to the field against the Baglioni of Perugia and the Bentivogli of Bologna on August 26, 1506. He took Perugia on September 13, and Bologna on November 11. Ferdinand II of Aragon wanted to recuperate the Kingdom of Naples because he had ceded several ports in Puglia to the Venetians in 1494; he finally regained them in 1508.

Chapter 26

An Exhortation to Seize Italy and Liberate Her from the Barbarians

Having considered, therefore, all the things discussed above, and asking myself whether at present the times are ripe to honor a new prince in Italy, and if there were material here which might give a prudent and capable [*virtuoso*] man an opportunity to introduce a form into her that would confer honor on himself and benefit all her people, it seems to me that so many things are coming together in favor of a new prince that I do not know what time was ever more suitable for him. And if, as I have said, it was necessary, in order to see the ability [*virtù*] of Moses, that the people of Israel should be slaves in Egypt, and to recognize Cyrus's greatness of spirit, it was necessary for the Persians to be oppressed by the Medes, and for the excellence of Theseus, that the Athenians should be scattered, so, at present, in order to recognize the capabilities [*virtù*] of an Italian spirit, it was necessary that Italy should be reduced to her present condition, and that she should be more enslaved than the Hebrews, more servile than the Persians, and more widely dispersed than the Athenians, without a head, without order, beaten, despoiled, torn apart, overrun, and having endured every sort of ruin.[1]

And though, before now, some gleams of light may have shown themselves in a certain man,[2] leading people to the conclusion that God had ordained him for the redemption of Italy, yet afterwards we saw how, at the height of his career, he was cast down by Fortune. Thus Italy, left almost lifeless, waits for a man who is the one to heal her wounds and put an end to the plundering of Lombardy, to the taxes imposed on the Kingdom [of Naples] and on Tuscany, and to cure her of those wounds which have been festering for so long.[3] Behold how she prays to God to send someone to redeem her from these barbarous cruelties and insults. Behold, as well, how ready and willing she is to follow any banner, if only there were someone who would lift it up. At present, there is no one in sight from whom she has more to hope than from your illustrious house, for, with its fortune and its virtue [*virtù*], favored by God and by the

1. See Chapter 6, pp. 17–19, for Machiavelli's discussion of Moses, Cyrus, and Theseus.
2. I.e., Cesare Borgia, whose bad luck is detailed in Chapter 7, pp. 21–27.
3. From the French invasion of 1494 on, Lombardy was often the scene of battles fought in Italy among the French, the Spanish, the Holy Roman Empire, and the various city-states. In particular, the French plundered Tortona in 1499 and Brescia in 1512. "Taxes": large sums paid by cities to prevent the mercenary armies that had besieged them successfully from sacking and pillaging them as well.

Church, of which it is now the head, your house could make itself the leader in this work of redemption.[4]

This will not be very difficult if you keep before your eyes the actions and lives of those who were described above. And although those men were rare and marvelous, they were nevertheless men, and each of them had less of an opportunity than you have at present, for their missions were not more just than this one is, nor any easier, nor was God more a friend to them than to you. For your cause is truly just: "that war is justified when it is necessary, and those arms are pious when there is no hope except in arms."[5] Here people are ready and willing, and where there is great enthusiasm, there can be no great difficulty, provided that your house imitates the methods of those whom I have proposed for you to aim at. Besides this, extraordinary, unprecedented things have been seen to have been performed here by God: the sea has been divided; a cloud has shown you the road; the rock has poured forth water; here it has rained manna; everything has come together for your greatness.[6] The rest you must do yourself. God does not want to do everything lest He deprive us of our free will and a portion of the glory that belongs to us.

And it is no wonder that none of the Italians mentioned before was able to do what we might hope your illustrious house will achieve, and that, in so many upheavals in Italy and so many military campaigns, it always seems as if her military skill [*virtù*] is extinct. This has happened because her ancient military methods were no good, and there has been no one who has been able to find new ones. And nothing confers so much honor on a man newly risen to power as do the new laws and the new institutions he has introduced. When these things have good foundations and possess greatness, they will make him revered and admired, and in Italy there is no lack of matter into which all sorts of forms can be introduced.[7] There is great strength [*virtù*] in her members, were it not for the lack of it in her heads.[8] Observe how, in duels and in combats involving just a few men, Italians reveal their superiority in strength, in dexterity, in

4. The cardinal Giovanni de' Medici was made Pope Leo X in 1513.
5. Machiavelli is quoting the speech of the Roman leader Gaius Pontius to the Samnites as given in Livy, *History of Rome,* 9.1: "*iustum enim est bellum quibus necessarium, et pia arma ubi nulla nisi in armis spes est.*"
6. All of these "extraordinary things" are the well-known Mosaic miracles God performed for the Hebrews when they were in the wilderness; see, respectively, Exodus 14.21, 13.21–22, 17.5–6, and 16.13–15. It is not clear what parallel contemporary events Machiavelli was thinking of here; he may be speaking ironically.
7. Machiavelli once again uses the Scholastic distinction between matter and form; see n. 2, p. 18.
8. Machiavelli's metaphors here imply the notion that the state is like the human body, with the people being its members and the heads its leaders.

ingenuity.[9] But when it comes to armies, they are no match for others. And all of this derives from the weakness of their heads, for those who have the know-how are not obeyed. Of all of those who think they know best, up to now, there has been no one who has been able to raise himself up through his valor [*virtù*] and good fortune so that the others would yield to him. This is the reason why in so much time, in so many wars waged during the last twenty years, whenever there has been an army composed entirely of Italians, it has always made a poor showing. Bearing witness to this, first there is Taro, then Alessandria, Capua, Genoa, Vailà, Bologna, Mestre.[1]

If, then, your illustrious house is to follow those excellent men who redeemed their native lands, it is necessary before anything else, to provide yourself with your own army, which is the true foundation of every undertaking, for you cannot have more loyal, or truer, or better soldiers. And although each one of them may be good individually, united together they will become even better when they see themselves commanded by their own prince who will honor and provide for them. It is necessary, therefore, to prepare oneself with such arms as these so that you will be able, using Italian valor [*virtù*], to defend yourself from foreigners. And although the Swiss and Spanish infantry are considered terrifying, nonetheless they both have defects, so that a third kind of force would not only be able to confront them, but feel confident of overcoming them. For the Spaniards cannot stand up against cavalry, and the Swiss will have to fear the infantry they encounter in combat who are as resolute as they are. For we have seen—and experience will show—that the Spaniards cannot withstand the French cavalry, and that the Spanish

9. While Machiavelli's claim about Italians' superiority in dueling may seem a pure fabrication designed here to advance his argument, his remark about their superiority in "combats involving just a few men" (*congressi di pochi*) may be related to a celebrated chivalric combat that took place on February 13, 1503, in which thirteen Italian champions decisively defeated thirteen French champions. The Spanish and French armies had been fighting in the Kingdom of Naples, and a French knight had made a disparaging comment about Italian valor, apparently responding to the performance of a contingent of Italian mercenaries fighting for the Spanish. Because the Spanish army was encamped in Barletta, a city in the province of Puglia, which is in the southeastern part (the "heel") of Italy, the challenge and the subsequent combat became known as *La disfida di Barletta* (The Challenge of Barletta).

1. Machiavelli's sad list of Italian defeats is arranged in strict chronological order and covers the period from the first invasion of the peninsula by Charles VIII in 1494 up to 1513, when Machiavelli was beginning to write *The Prince*. He starts with the battle of Fornovo on the Taro River on July 6, 1495, when the army of Francesco Gonzaga met that of Charles VIII in retreat; although the former won the field, Charles really won in that he was able to continue to withdraw. Alessandria was conquered by the French in 1499, Capua in 1501, and Genoa in 1507. At the battle of Vailà, or Agnadello, on May 14, 1509, the Venetians were beaten by the French in league with the papacy and lost all their holdings on the mainland as a result. Bologna was abandoned to the French by the Holy League in 1511. Mestre was burned just before the battle of Vicenza (usually referred to as the battle of La Motta) on October 7, 1513, in which the forces of Spain and the Holy Roman Empire decisively beat the Venetian army.

infantry can defeat the Swiss. And although we have not had a complete experience of the latter, still, we have had a taste of it in the battle of Ravenna, when the Spanish infantry confronted battalions of Germans, who make use of the same battle formation as the Swiss.[2] There, the Spanish used their physical agility and, with the help of their spiked bucklers, got in between and under the Germans' pikes where they were safe to attack them without the Germans having any remedy for it; and if it had not been for the cavalry that charged them, the Spaniards would have devoured them. Therefore, when the defects of both of these kinds of infantry are recognized, a new kind can be organized that will stand up to cavalry and will have no fear of foot soldiers; this will be accomplished by creating a new army and a change in battle formations. And these are among the things which, when newly introduced, create a reputation for a new prince and confer greatness on him.

This opportunity must not, therefore, be allowed to pass by, so that Italy may behold her redeemer after so long a time. Nor can I express with what love he would be received in all those provinces which have suffered because of these foreign inundations, with what thirst for vengeance, with what steadfast loyalty, with what devotion, with what tears. What doors would be closed against him? What people would refuse him obedience? What envy would oppose him? What Italian would refuse him homage? This barbarian domination stinks in everyone's nostrils.[3] May your illustrious house therefore take up this task with that courage and that hope with which just enterprises are begun, so that under your banner this country may be ennobled, and under your auspices the words of Petrarch may prove true:

> Virtù contro a furore
> prenderà l'arme; e fia el combatter corto:
> ché l'antico valore
> nelli italici cor non è ancor morto.[4]

2. The battle of Ravenna on April 11, 1512, between the Spanish and the French was one of the most desperately fought of the Italian Wars; on it, see n. 2, p. 43. Machiavelli ignores the decisive role played by artillery in the battle—possibly because he prefers to think in binary oppositions, in this case those between the Swiss and the Spanish and between foot soldiers and cavalry.
3. Machiavelli echoes the war cry of Julius II: "*Fuori i barbari!*" (Out with the barbarians!), but this was not the sentiment of a nationalist, although many 19th-century Italians saw him as such. In opposition to the Spanish, the French, and the Germans, Machiavelli might dub himself an Italian, but at heart he was a Florentine.
4. This excerpt comes from Petrarch's canzone "*Italia mia*" (*Canzoniere,* 128.93–96): "Virtue [*virtù*] against furor / will take up arms; and the combat will be short, / for ancient valor / in Italian hearts is not yet dead." The canzone is directed against "*la tedesca rabbia*" (German rage).

BACKGROUNDS

North-Central Italy in Machiavelli's Time

Medici Family Tree: A Rough Diagram

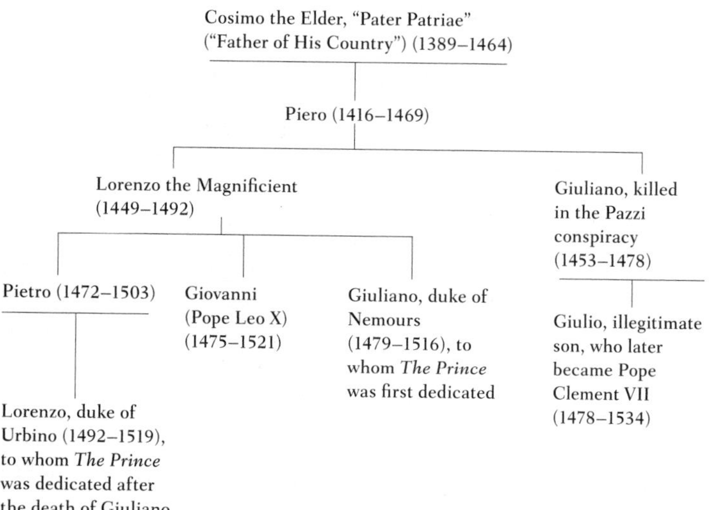

Popes during Machiavelli's Lifetime

Note: For more information on Machiavelli's relationships to the popes below, see Niccolò Machiavelli: A Chronology of His Life and Times (pp. 329–35).

1471–84: Sixtus IV (Francesco della Rovere). Intent on expanding the temporal power of the Church, Sixtus fought wars with Florence and Venice, among others, increased Church taxes and the selling of indulgences, and built the Sistine Chapel (later to be decorated by Michelangelo).

1484–92: Innocent VIII (Giovanni Battista Cibo). An enemy of King Ferdinand I of Naples, he invited King Charles VIII of France to invade Italy and defend his claim to the Kingdom of Naples. Charles did so in 1494, thus beginning the Italian Wars, which eventually led to the domination of Italy by Spain and the Holy Roman Empire.

1492–1503: Alexander VI (Rodrigo Borgia, or Borja**).** He increased the money-gathering powers of the Church to finance campaigns to expand the Church's temporal powers in Italy. He had four illegitimate children, including Lucrezia and Cesare. The latter was his father's political instrument and had almost consolidated the Church's holdings in central Italy, in the region known as the Romagna (part of the so-called Papal States) when Alexander died. Sick himself at the time, Cesare managed to get a neutral figure, Pius III, elected pope, but Pius died shortly after his election and was succeeded by Julius II, an inveterate enemy of the Borgias. Both Alexander and Cesare are central figures in *The Prince.*

1503: Pius III (Francesco Todeschini Piccolomini). A compromise candidate between the Borgia and della Rovere factions in the College of Cardinals, he was elected pope on September 22, ordained on September 30, crowned on October 8, and died because of an ulcer on his leg brought about by gout on October 18.

1503–13: Julius II (Giuliano della Rovere, nephew of Sixtus IV**).** Known as the "warrior pope," Julius led his own armies into battle, seeking to consolidate papal power in the peninsula. He allied himself with Spain and the Holy Roman Empire against France, which eventually led, after his death, to the expulsion of France from Italy and the subjection of all the states in the peninsula, except Venice, either directly or indirectly to Spain and the Empire.

1513–21: Leo X (Giovanni de' Medici). The second son of Lorenzo de' Medici, "the Magnificent," he patronized artists such as Michelangelo and Raphael and financed the rebuilding of St. Peter's Basilica with the sale of indulgences. Those indulgences influenced the German theologian Martin Luther to attack the Church with his Ninety-Five Theses in Wittenberg on October 31, 1517, and led to the Protestant Reformation.

1522–23: Adrian VI (Adriaan Floriszoon Boeyens). The only Dutchman ever to be pope, Adrian was elected as a compromise candidate between the Spanish and Italian factions in the College of Cardinals. Contrary to his wishes, he failed to reform the Church, could not check the expansion of the Ottoman Empire, and was unable to put an end to the Protestant Reformation. He was elected on January 9, 1522, crowned on August 31, and died on September 14, 1523.

1523–34: Clement VII (Giulio de' Medici, cousin of Leo X). Known for his political ability, Clement wavered between France and Spain in their struggle to dominate the Italian peninsula. He was pope during the infamous Sack of Rome that began on May 6, 1527, and was imprisoned in the Castel Sant'Angelo for six months, escaped, and then returned to the devastated city. He installed Alessandro de' Medici, the illegitimate son of Lorenzo II de' Medici (or possibly of Clement himself) and a black maid in the Medici household, as the ruler of Florence in 1530. Clement was responsible for allowing Machiavelli to return to Florence in 1520, made him the official historiographer of the city, and had him write his *Istorie fiorentine* (*The History of Florence*), which he presented to the pope in May 1526.

Machiavelli the Working Diplomat

Starting in 1498, Machiavelli was the secretary both of the Second Chancery, which was mostly concerned with military and diplomatic matters, and of The Ten, a committee of ten men who were appointed in times of crisis, mostly to handle military matters. "The Ten" is short for *I dieci di libertà e pace,* which means something like "The Council of Ten Men Responsible for Liberty and Peace." A version of this committee had been in existence since the late fourteenth century, although before 1498 it was called *I dieci di balia,* which could be rendered as "The Council of Ten Men Responsible for the Welfare of the State" (*balia* means "wet-nurse" and thus indicated that the committee had a nursing or nurturing function vis-à-vis the state). Before 1498, The Ten was created only occasionally, sometimes just to deal with domestic affairs, but from 1498 to 1512, the committee was made permanent since the Florentine Republic—like Italy—was going through something like a permanent crisis (see the Introduction on this subject). As secretary to The Ten, Machiavelli had a fairly important position, because his charge included writing letters to various Florentine officials outside the city, reforming the military, and undertaking diplomatic missions both inside and outside of Italy. Technically, he went on those missions as a *mandatario* (an envoy), not an *oratore* (an ambassador), and although that meant he could not participate in diplomatic ceremonies or sign treaties, he did draft agreements with other states, deliver important messages, gather information, and negotiate with various rulers on Florence's behalf. Between 1498 and 1512, Machiavelli went on more than twenty-five diplomatic missions to nearby places, such as Pisa and Siena, to other Italian city-states such as Mantua and Rome, and to foreign states such as France and the Holy Roman Empire. Such work was difficult and demanding both because of the often delicate negotiations Machiavelli had to conduct and because travel itself was difficult, especially in winter when snowy mountain passes had to be crossed. The first of Machiavelli's reports to The Ten included here is from *The Legation to Cesare Borgia* and discusses one of those difficulties: the issue of having to obtain fresh horses and having to leave baggage behind in order to travel quickly. These extracts provide a glimpse of Machiavelli as a hardworking envoy. They also reveal his admiration—or better, his fascination—with Cesare Borgia, who plays such an important role in *The Prince.* Some of Cesare's most cunning and ruthless actions as prince Machiavelli saw firsthand and recorded in these dispatches.

NICCOLÒ MACHIAVELLI

From The Legation to Cesare Borgia†

1. The Commission

Commission given to Niccolò Machiavelli, formulated by our esteemed masters on the fifth of October, 1502.

We send you with these credentials to meet with His Excellency the Duke Valentino at Imola, and to go there on horseback as quickly as you can.[1] In your first conference with him you will explain that, in the last few days, since his return to the Romagna, we have learned of the estrangement and departure of the Orsini from His Excellency and their gathering together to meet with their adherents at La Magione in the territory of Perugia.[2] We have also heard the rumor that the duke of Urbino and Signor Bartolommeo d'Alviano will be there to negotiate with them and deliberate about a plot against His Excellency, a plot which we also consider to be directed against the Most Christian King.[3] We, too, have been cunningly invited to send our representative in order to reach an agreement with them, but we continue to hold to our old view and desire to remain good friends with Our Master and His Excellency, and we have firmly resolved not to separate ourselves from them or abandon our devotion to the king of France, on whose friendship and protection this city relies.[4] And when it is a question of the king's interests and those of His Excellency's friends and dependents, we cannot do otherwise than to make known everything that

† From *Legazione al duca Valentino,* in *Le Legazioni e commissarie,* edited by Luigi Passerini and Gaetano Milanesi, vol. 2: 64–72, 249–51, 253–54, 258–61 (Firenze: Tipografia Cenniniani, 1875). Translated and annotated by the editor of this Norton Critical Edition.

1. Duke Valentino is another name for Cesare Borgia (on this title, see *The Prince* n. 6, p. 12). Imola is in the Romagna on the other side of the Appenines from Florence. Although the distance between the two cities is only about fifty miles, it normally took a day of hard riding to get there because of the mountains.
2. The assembly at La Magione, in a castle belonging to Cardinal Giambattista Orsini (b. c. 1450; cardinal 1493–1503), convened on October 9, but was much talked about in advance. It included members of the Orsini family as well as local rulers from the Romagna.
3. The duke of Urbino was Guidobaldo da Montefeltro (b. 1472; ruled 1482–1502, 1503–08), who was forced to flee his duchy by Cesare earlier in 1502, but returned to it in 1503 after the death of Alexander VI. Signor Bartolommeo (or Bartolomeo) d'Alviano (1455–1515) was a condottiere who fought for the Orsini from 1496 to 1503. The plot was directed against Cesare as well as his two chief supporters: his father, Pope Alexander VI, referred to as "Our Master" in the next sentence, and Louis XII of France, the "Most Christian King."
4. The words *amici* and *amicizia,* which are used here, have been translated as "friends," and "friendship," but they really refer to what we would now call "allies," and I have sometimes translated them accordingly. Readers should be aware that those terms define a political and diplomatic more than a personal relationship.

is going on and that we hear about, and to perform all the duties of good friends. And it is for this reason that we have sent you post-haste to His Excellency, since it seemed to us that the importance of the business requires it. You should tell him again that, in the midst of these movements of our neighbors, we intend to maintain the greatest respect for his interests and to preserve the same esteem for him that we have always had. For we consider all the friends of France to be our friends, and where it is a question of their interests, it is also a question of ours. And this, it seems to us, ought to be enough for your first audience, in which you will make it as clear as possible to His Excellency that we place great confidence and hope in him. And you may enlarge upon this theme as much as you think the occasion warrants, amplifying your remarks with all the details that the subject permits, and which do not need to be discussed here, as you are fully informed about the matter. Nor do we want you to talk of anything outside of it, or deal with it in any other way, and should His Excellency try to get you to go beyond this, we want you to hold back and tell us about it and then to wait for our reply. And after your initial discussion, either in this first audience or a later one, will you thank His Excellency most cordially for the benefit he has conferred on our merchants, which we consider a benefit conferred on us and on our Republic, by ordering the restoration of that cloth which has been held for several months at Urbino, and about which we have just had news today from those merchants that it has been handed over according to their instructions. Do all this in a friendly manner, and show that this, too, is part of your commission. And after that, when you think the occasion right, you will request of His Excellency, in our name, security and safe conduct through his states and territories for the goods of our merchants coming from and going to the East. This is a matter of considerable importance, something which you could call the very stomach of our city, and which you must pay particular attention to and use your best efforts to achieve the outcome we desire.

2. *Machiavelli to The Ten*

Magnificent and Distinguished Lords, my most exceptional masters. Finding myself ill-provided with horses at my departure, and believing my commission required haste, I took a post-horse at Scarperia and arrived here, without any loss of time, at about six o'clock.[5] And because I had left my own horses and servants behind, I presented

5. Instead of riding his own horse all the way, Machiavelli rented a succession of horses at places where couriers carrying the mail would normally stop and get fresh horses in order to make their deliveries as quickly as possible. Scarperia is a village about fifteen miles north-northeast of Florence on the road to Imola.

myself immediately, in my traveling clothes, to His Excellency, who greeted me warmly, and having given him my credentials, I explained to him the reason for my coming, starting off by thanking him for the restitution of our merchants' cloth. Then I turned to the defection of the Orsini and to the meeting they were having with their adherents and how they had cunningly invited Your Lordships to join them. Next, I reminded him of the views you hold regarding your friendship with the king of France and your devotion to the Church, amplifying with all the eloquence at my command what compels you to preserve your friendship with the king and the Church, and to avoid complicity with their adversaries. Furthermore, I assured him that in all circumstances, Your Lordships would have every concern for his particular interests, a concern consistent with the friendship you have with the king of France and the devotion you have always felt for his regime, since you consider all the friends of France to be your greatest friends and allies.

His Excellency made no reply on the subject of the restitution of the cloth, but turning to the other matters, he thanked Your Lordships for this kind and welcome expression of affection. Then he said that he had always desired a friendly alliance with Your Lordships, and if he had never obtained it, it was due to the malice of others more than to any fault of his own, adding that he wanted to explain to me in particular what he had never told anyone else with respect to his coming to Florence with his army.[6] Then he said that after the capture of Faenza and his attempt to take Bologna, the Orsini and Vitelli were on his back, trying to persuade him to return to Rome by way of Florence, and when he said no, because the pope, in a brief, had given him different instructions, Vitellozzo had thrown himself down at his feet in tears, begging him to go that way and promising that they would do no harm either to the city or the surrounding countryside. Although he did not want to consent to this, they kept at him with similar prayers to such an extent that he yielded and agreed to go that way, but with the proviso that the countryside should not be harmed and there would be no talk of the Medici. But since he was now going to Florence, he thought he would profit from the occasion by making an alliance with Your Lordships, and this is proved by the fact that in all the negotiations he said little or nothing about the Medici, as the commissioners

6. In May 1501, Cesare Borgia took his army into Florentine territory. One of his chief captains, Vitellozzo Vitelli, encouraged this move, since the Florentines had executed his brother Paolo, also a mercenary soldier, in 1499 for treason because he had withdrawn the Florentine army when it was attacking Pisa, thus disobeying the orders he had been given. Cesare entered into negotiations with the Florentines in the town of Campi, some six miles from the city, and because they were always afraid that someone would attempt to bring back the Medici, who had been driven from power in 1494, they signed a treaty with Cesare on May 15. He was made the "protector" of the city, receiving a *condotta* (contract) that put him in charge of three hundred lances and gave him an annual salary of 36,000 ducats.

who dealt with him know very well, and that he never allowed Piero[7] to come to his camp. While they were at Campi, he says the Orsini and Vitelli often asked for his permission to make a show of force before the gates of Florence or Pistoia, to demonstrate that those were feasible enterprises. But he never gave his consent; on the contrary, he made them understand by a thousand protestations that he would fight against them. Once the treaty had been concluded, it seemed to the Orsini and the Vitelli that he had gotten what he wanted, whereas they had not, and that their coming there had been to his profit and their loss, and so they set about to break the treaty by dishonest means and did all they could to make trouble for Your Lordships and upset the accord you had with him. And he could not properly set things right, partly because he could not be everywhere at once, and partly because Your Lordships had not come through with the advance which had been agreed on and which once seemed about to be paid.[8] Things stayed that way up to the end of June, when the rebellion of Arezzo occurred,[9] which, he said, he had never had any knowledge of beforehand, as he had already told the bishop of Volterra—but he certainly welcomed it, for he believed it offered him a chance to gain recognition from you. Yet even then, nothing was done, either because of bad luck on both sides, or because your city was not then in a position to deliberate and reach a decision about an arrangement that would have been mutually beneficial, something which he said had not bothered him very much. Yet, still being disposed to perform some beneficial service on your behalf, and knowing the wishes of the king, he wrote and sent men directly to Vitellozzo, telling him to withdraw from Arezzo. And not content with this, he went off with his troops toward Città di Castello and could have taken Vitelli's state from him, because the chief men of the city came to offer their support to him. This, he says, was the initial cause of Vitellozzo's anger and discontent. As for the Orsini, he said he did not know the source of their anger at the French court, which they left without leave of His Holiness.[1] But

7. Piero de' Medici (1472–1503) ruled Florence from the death of his father, Lorenzo the Magnificent, in 1492 until 1494, when he was forced to surrender the city to the French and fled from it along with the rest of his family. They went to Venice; and in 1503, fighting in the Battle of Garigliano on the losing side, Piero was drowned in the river for which the battle was named while attempting to flee. Not surprisingly, he became known as Piero the Unfortunate (Piero lo Sfortunato) or Piero the Fatuous (Piero il Fatuo).
8. On May 17, 1501, just two days after Cesare had signed a treaty with the Florentines, he sent for the first quarterly installment of the 36,000 ducats he was to have as an annual salary. The Florentines refused to pay it.
9. Incited by Cesare's lieutenant Vitellozzo Vitelli, Arezzo as well as several other subject cities rebelled against Florentine rule in June 1502, but the French governor of Milan quickly sent troops into Tuscany, forced Vitelli to withdraw, and restored Arezzo to Florence.
1. This passage in Machiavelli's report is somewhat unclear. In the summer of 1502, Louis XII went to Italy and moved from place to place with his court. Cardinal Giulio Orsini went to meet with him in Asti, seeking to incite the king to join his party and oppose Cesare and the pope. The cardinal's trip to Asti is most likely what Machiavelli is referring to with the phrase "without leave of His Holiness," in that he did not have the pope's permission to meet with the king and clearly left, also without the pope's permission, dissatisfied.

Cesare did see that the French king had given him better treatment than he gave Cardinal Orsini and that the king had bestowed great honors on him; and then there were rumors that he was going to take away their territory—so, acting on that, they withdrew and now found themselves at this meeting of bankrupts.[2] And although he had received various messages from Signor Giulio Orsini, protesting that he was not going to oppose him, etc., and it would be unreasonable for them to declare themselves openly against him because they had taken his money, still, when they did declare themselves, he would look on them as greater fools than he already thought they were, for not having known how to choose the right time to attack him.[3] For the king of France was in Italy, and His Holiness the pope was still alive, and those two things lit such a fire under him that putting it out would require a different water than theirs. Nor did he worry about their shaking up Urbino, because he had not forgotten the way to get it back if he should lose it.[4]

And then he suggested that now was the time, if Your Lordships wanted to be his friends, to bind yourselves to him because he could now enter into an alliance with you without regard for the Orsini, something he had never been able to do in the past. But if Your Lordships delayed, and he was reconciled in the meantime with the Orsini, who are still pursuing him, then the same old problems would come back; and as the Orsini could scarcely be satisfied with any deal unless it involved the restoration of the Medici, then Your Lordships would once again face the same difficulties and suspicions as before. Thus, he thinks Your Lordships should, in any case, declare yourselves immediately to be his friends or theirs, because if you put it off, the two parties could reach an agreement at your expense, and one of the parties could emerge victorious, and in the hour of victory, they would either be hostile, or feel themselves under no obligation to Your Lordships.[5] And he thinks that when you come to make your decision, which you will necessarily have to do, he does

2. This part of the passage is especially ambiguous: it may be Cesare or the Orsini who had seen the different treatments he and the cardinal received from the French, but either way, it would seem that Cesare actually did know why the Orsini were dissatisfied. It is also unclear just who was going to deprive whom of his territory: it could be Cesare depriving the Orsini of theirs, or the Orsini depriving the French king of his possessions in Italy. Note that Cesare had met with the king years before, in 1498, when he was sent as papal legate to the French court, bearing the order that annulled Louis's marriage with Jeanne of France and thus enabling him to marry Anne of Brittany, a much more useful match. The "meeting of bankrupts" was the one that took place at La Magione; on it see n. 2, p. 92. Machiavelli discusses these events in Chapter 7 of *The Prince* (see pp. 23–24).
3. Cesare had made it his business to seem conciliatory and even generous toward the Orsini and the Vitelli, only to lure them into a trap at Sinigaglia. On this subject, see the fourth and fifth reports in the *Legation* (pp. 100–03).
4. Only two days before, on October 5, Urbino had revolted against Cesare as part of a general uprising against him in the Romagna, which was coming to a head with the meeting at La Magione.
5. Machiavelli develops this idea in Chapter 21 of *The Prince* (see pp. 71–73).

not see how Your Lordships can take a different course from that on which His Majesty the King and His Holiness, Our Lord the Pope, have agreed. He added that it would please him a great deal, if Vitellozzo or anyone else should make a move against one or another of his states, you would have whatever forces you possess martial themselves in the vicinity of Borgo or near his borders in order to enhance the reputation of his enterprise.[6]

I listened attentively as His Excellency went over the things mentioned above. I have written down what he said in great detail, giving you not just the general import of what he said, but using the very same words, so that Your Lordships will be able to form a better judgment of it all. I will not write down for you what I said in response, for it is not necessary to do so: I did my best not to go beyond my commission. With regard to the part about your troops, I made no answer at all, but only said that I would write to Your Lordships and transmit his exact thoughts from which you would derive a most singular pleasure. And although His Excellency, as you see, appeared to have a great desire for you to promptly conclude a treaty with him, still, despite my pressing him closely to get some particular details out of him, he always talked in generalities, nor could I get anything from him other than what I have written.

Having heard on my arrival that there had been some disturbances in the state of Urbino, when His Excellency said during our discussion that he did not care about the troubles in that duchy, it occurred to me, in responding, to ask him what had happened. His Excellency replied to this: "My clemency and my having paid too little attention to what was going on are what harmed me. I took that duchy, as you know, in three days and did not touch a hair on anyone's head, except for Messer Dolce and two others who had acted against His Holiness the Pope. On the contrary, I went even further and appointed many of the principal citizens to offices in the state, putting one of them in charge of certain walls I was having built in the castle of San Leo.[7] And two days ago he put the final touches on a plot with certain peasants from the countryside, who pretended they were hauling up a beam, with the result that he forced open the gate and the castle was lost. Some say that the cry that went up was 'Marco,' others 'Vitelli,' and others 'Orsini,' but up to now no one has revealed himself.[8] Although I consider that duchy was lost

6. Borgo is Borgo San (or: Santo) Sepolcro and is located quite close to the border between Florentine territory and the Papal States Cesare had recently been enlarging for his father. The suggestion here is that the Florentines should make an aggressive move so that Cesare could order Vitellozzo, still under his command, into a disadvantageous position.
7. The castle or fortress of San Leo belonged to the duchy of Urbino and was located on the border of The Marches (*Le Marche*) and the Romagna.
8. These cries are the cheers of the men occupying the castle that identified them with one party or another. The cry "Marco" means Venice, since its patron is San Marco, or Saint Mark. But so far, Cesare says, no party has revealed itself as the conqueror.

because it is a weak, tired state and those men are discontented because I burdened them too heavily with my troops,[9] I still hope to take care of everything. And you will write to your Masters that they should consider their affairs carefully and let us hear from them promptly, because if the duke of Urbino returns and he comes from Venice, it will not be to their advantage and still less to ours—all of which means that we have even more reason to trust one another."[1]

This is, in effect, all I can write to Your Lordships at present, and although my duty would require that I write to you about how many troops this lord has, where his lodgings are, and many other particular details about the state of things here, still, since I only arrived today, I cannot know for sure what is true, and therefore I will reserve all that for another time, and commend myself to Your Lordships.

Your servant, Nicolaus Machiavellus. At Imola.

October 7, 1502
E. V. D.[2]

I have kept this letter until four p.m. today, because the courier had no horse and I had not found a mount until now. And what is left for me to write to you is that yesterday, while His Excellency was talking with me, he told me that the day before, Pandolfo Petrucci had sent him a messenger in disguise to swear to him that he was not about to favor anyone who was opposed to His Excellency and that the man went on to speak at length to that effect.[3]

On my way here yesterday I met Messer Agapito, with seven or eight horsemen, some two miles outside of town, and when he recognized me, I told him where I was going and who it was that sent me. He gave me a hearty welcome and continued on ahead for only a short distance before turning back. This morning I realized that the said Messer Agapito was going to your Lordships: he had been sent there by this duke and that he turned back because of my coming here.[4]

Farewell again.

9. Burdening the people of Urbino with soldiers means that too many of the latter were billeted with the local population, who had to feed and house them.

1. Florence had already fought against soldiers supplied by Venice in its wars with Pisa during the last decade of the 15th century, and the city thus had reason to fear that the duke might return with a Venetian army.

2. *Excellentissimae Vestrae Dominationis (Servitor)*: The Servant of Your Most Excellent Lordship.

3. Pandolfo Petrucci (1452–1512) ruled the Republic of Siena, which was a longtime opponent and rival of Florence, from around 1497 until his death.

4. Messer Agapito Geraldini (1450–1515) was made the secretary of Cardinal Giovanni Borgia in 1497 and became Cesare's secretary the following year. Machiavelli is saying that he was being sent to Florence by Cesare, who clearly needed the Florentines as much as they needed him.

October 8, 1502

I have given the present horseman two ducats on the understanding that he should be there tomorrow morning before daybreak which will be the ninth. Would you please reimburse Ser Agostino Vespucci for this.[5]

3. *Machiavelli to The Ten*

Magnificent Lords, etc. I wrote my last letter to Your Lordships on the way to Bagno, and having written at length in it about the departure of the French, and having discussed the matter at length, it consequently does not seem necessary for me to say anything else about it.

The day before yesterday Ardingo's boy, the courier, arrived with two of Your Lordships' letters of the twentieth and the twenty-second, and although I have made every effort after receiving them to talk to the duke, I was unsuccessful, because the only time I had to do so was yesterday, and His Excellency was busy then reviewing his infantry as well as with his other holiday pleasures, so that I could not get to see him. And this morning he rose early and went off to Santo Arcangelo with his entire army, fifteen miles from here and five miles from Rimini. Tomorrow morning I will get up and go to Rimini, since I cannot stay any closer because of the limited lodging available, although people say he does not intend to stay here for long, but to move on by long marches in the direction of Pesaro. No one knows what he intends to do then: some think he wants to attack Sinigaglia, and some, Ancona.[6] And as far as his forces are concerned, he has those men in the list I sent you recently as well as about thirty newly recruited Albanian auxiliaries.[7] Plus, there are 2,500 infantry from beyond the mountains and about the same number of Italians, some of whom passed in review yesterday and the day before. And you can figure that for every thousand infantry there are fifty horsemen capable of serving as cavalry. The artillery have taken the same route as he did, with all the necessary powder and shot. No one knows how many troops the Orsini and Vitelli can count on; we will know better on the day when the two forces are closer to one another.

As I have written to Your Lordships many times, this duke is very secretive, and I do not believe that anyone other than he knows what

5. Agostino Vespucci, cousin of the famous Amerigo Vespucci, was a Florentine chancellery clerk who was an assistant to Machiavelli and would have held the money for him.
6. Pesaro, Sinigaglia (the modern Senigallia), and Ancona are cities twenty to twenty-five miles apart on the Adriatic coast. Cesare's real aim was to capture the conspirators of La Magione, wherever they might be. They had, in fact, taken Sinigaglia and wanted to present it to Cesare as a peace offering. He took it—and them.
7. These were both foot soldiers and cavalry who were recruited in Albania by the Venetians. Dressed in the Turkish fashion, except for the turbans, they were known for their bravery.

he is about to do. His chief secretaries have often assured me that he never reveals anything until he is carrying it out, and he carries it out when forced to by necessity and when the time is ripe, not otherwise. Therefore, I beg Your Lordships to excuse me and not to impute it to negligence on my part if my information does not satisfy Your Lordships, for most of the time I do not even satisfy myself.

Concerning San Leo and his negotiations with duke Guido there is no further news. As for Camerino, I wrote at another time what the duke had told me, who was there on official duties, and after that I wrote as much as I had extracted from that secretary of Cardinal Farnese's, who told me he had little hope, especially because of the departure of the French. Yesterday the bishop of Euna told me that the affair was practically arranged: I will wait for the final outcome in order to avoid making an error again.

This morning Messer Rimirro was found in two pieces in the piazza, where he still remains, and all the people here could see him. No one knows for sure the reason for his death, other than that it pleased the prince, who shows that he knows how to make and unmake men at his will, according to their merits.[8]

The courier named above brought me twenty-five gold ducats and sixteen yards of black damask. I thank Your Lordships heartily for both things.

Because the court is about to move on, no man has been assigned to me to collect the three mares that Your Lordships say are at Poppi. The only thing I have been told is to ask Your Lordships to have them well cared for until orders have been given to bring them here.

Messer Bartolommeo Marcelli dal Borgo, on whose behalf the baron of Bierra recently wrote to our exalted masters, asks nothing but that a little time be granted to him before his appearance so that he can travel there. He is writing about it to Piero di Braccio Martelli who is managing his case, and I recommend him to Your Lordships once again. May all your affairs go well.

From Cesena, December 26, 1502, at ten p.m.
E. V. D.

Your servant, Nicholaus Machiavellus, Secretary

4. Machiavelli to The Ten

Magnificent Lords, etc. The day before yesterday I wrote to Your Lordships from Pesaro what I understood about Sinigaglia. Yesterday I went to Fano, and early this morning His Excellency the duke left

8. Compare Machiavelli's description of Cesare's treatment of Messer Remirro de Orco in *The Prince*, Chapter 7, pp. 23–24.

with his entire army and came here to Sinigaglia where all the Orsini and Vitelli were gathered, who, as I wrote before, had taken this city for him. They went out to meet him, and once he had entered the city with them at his side, he turned to his guard and had them all taken prisoner. And in this way he has captured all of them, and the city is being sacked. It is now eleven p.m., and I am overwhelmed with work. I do not know if I will be able to send this letter, having no one whom I can send with it. I will write more fully in another one. In my opinion, they will not be alive tomorrow morning.

In Sinigaglia, the last day of December, 1502.

All of their troops have also been taken, and the documents being drawn up about them say that the traitors have been captured, etc.

I have paid the present bearer three ducats, and You Lordships will give him another three, and on my account reimburse Biagio.[9]

5. *Machiavelli to The Ten*

Magnificent Lords, etc. Yesterday I wrote two letters to Your Lordships about what happened after the arrival of His Excellency the Duke in Sinigaglia, how he captured Paolo and the duke of Gravina Orsini, and Vitellozzo, and Oliverotto. In the first I simply gave you notice of the event, and in the second I narrated everything in detail, adding what His Excellency had said to me and an account of public opinion here concerning this lord's actions.[1] I would repeat those letters in detail if I thought they had not reached you safely. But having sent the first with the advantage of six ducats and the second with the advantage of three, using carefully selected men, one a Florentine, the other from Urbino, I am quite hopeful about their delivery. Still, out of an abundance of caution, I will repeat everything in summary fashion to Your Lordships in case those letters have not made an appearance.

This Lord left Fano yesterday morning, and with his entire army he went up to Sinigaglia, which had been occupied, except for the fortress, by the Orsini and by Messer Oliverotto da Fermo. The day before, Vitellozzo had come to the area from Castello. One after the other they went to meet the duke, then accompanied him into the town and into a house, and when they had gone into a single room with him, His Lordship had them all taken prisoner. Then he had their soldiers disarmed, who were in the suburbs outside the city, and he sent half of his forces to disarm their men-at-arms in certain castles about six or seven miles from Sinigaglia. Afterwards he summoned me at around two o'clock in the night, and with the most cheerful expression in the world, he rejoiced with me over his success,

9. Biagio Buonaccorsi (1472–1521/1522) worked in the Florentine chancery and was one of Machiavelli's closest friends.
1. The second letter has been lost.

saying that he had spoken with me about the matter the day before, but had not revealed everything, which was true. Then he added some wise and extraordinarily affectionate words about our city, presenting all the reasons that made him desire your friendship, provided that it was not unreciprocated by you, so that he left me in a state of astonishment. But I will not repeat anything else since I described it all at length in yesterday's letter.

Finally, he concluded that I should write three things to Your Lordships on his behalf. First, that I should rejoice with you over his success in having exterminated the principal enemies of the king, of himself, and of you, and having removed all the seeds of trouble and dissension which were set to ruin Italy, for which Your Lordships ought to feel much obliged to him. Next, that I should request, indeed beg, on his behalf that, in this matter, Your Lordships should be so kind as to show the entire world that you are his friends by sending your cavalry to Borgo, and having the infantry join them there, so that, together with him, you can strike at Castello or Perugia, should it be necessary. He said he wanted to turn in that direction right away and that he would have left the evening before if he had not been afraid that Sinigaglia would be sacked because of his departure. And he requested yet again that I should write and ask you to make every possible demonstration of your friendship for him, saying that at present you had neither fears nor suspicions to hold you back, since he was well armed and all of your enemies had been captured. *Finally,* he asked me to write to Your Lordships that if Duke Guido [da Montefeltro], who is at Castello, should take refuge in your territory after the capture of Vitellozzo, it was his particular desire that you should detain him. And when I said that it would not be in keeping with the dignity of the city for you to hand the duke over to him, and that you would never do it, he replied that what I told him was well said, but that it was sufficient for Your Lordships to hold him and not let him go without getting His Excellency's consent. I promised to write down everything, and he awaits your reply.

In my letter from yesterday I also wrote that I had been reminded by many well-informed men who are friends of our city that Your Lordships have a great opportunity to do something good to adjust your city's strategic position. Everyone thinks that as far as the French are concerned, Your Lordships can safely trust them, and that, in their judgment, considering the recent turn of events, this is an opportune moment for you to send one of your leading citizens here as ambassador. Furthermore, they think you should not delay in doing so, for if a man of some importance comes here with proposals to establish relations, they believe he will get a favorable hearing. I have been reminded of this matter time and time again by those who wish our city well, and I am communicating it to Your Lordships out of the same feeling of loyalty with which I have always served you. And this is, in brief, what I wrote to you in my second letter yesterday, albeit in much greater detail.

Since then, at ten o'clock at night, this lord had Vitellozzo and Messer Oliverotto da Fermo put to death. The other two are still alive, and people believe that the duke is waiting to see if the pope will have gotten his hands on the cardinal and the others in Rome, and that once he thinks the pope has done so, then they will deal with the whole gang of them at the same time.

The fortress of Sinigaglia surrendered to the duke this morning at an early hour, and it is now in his possession. His Lordship left there this same morning and has come here with his army, and they will be heading to either Perugia or Castello for sure, and possibly to Siena. Then he will go down in the direction of Rome, taking care of all those castles that belong to the Orsini, and his plan is to take Bracciano by storm, and the others will be as easy as setting straw ablaze in a fire. All this, however, is just a matter of people's opinions. We will be here the entire day tomorrow, and then the next day we will go to stay in Sassoferrato. The weather is as bad as it can be for waging war, and you would not believe it if I wrote to you and described the hardships these troops are experiencing, such that things can be said to be going well for any guy who is lucky enough to have a roof over his head.

Messer Goro da Pistoia, an enemy of our city and a rebel against it, was with Vitellozzo and is now here, a prisoner in the hands of certain Spaniards.[2] I believe that for a couple hundred ducats, if Your Lordships wanted to spend them, it could be arranged for whoever is holding him to turn him over to one of your officials. May it please Your Lordships to consider this matter and to advise me as to what you think about it. I commend myself to Your Lordships and hope that all is well with you.

From Corinaldo, the first day of January, 1503
E. V. D.

Your servant, Nicolaus Machiavellus, Secretary

2. Goro da Pistoia was an agent working for the Medici as they sought to overthrow the Republic and thus an enemy of Machiavelli and The Ten.

Machiavelli the Republican

Machiavelli was writing the *Discourses* when he interrupted that project to compose *The Prince* in 1513, but how much of the *Discourses* he had done when he started *The Prince* is unknown. The difference between the two can be explained in part by their audiences: *The Prince* was addressed to the Medici, the rulers of Florence, from whom Machiavelli was seeking employment and a chance to return to Florence; the *Discourses* was dedicated to two like-minded republicans who shared in the political discussions that Machiavelli was having with friends in the Orti Oricellari, the gardens of the Rucellai family. Thus there is no mention of tyranny in *The Prince,* whereas in the *Discourses,* Machiavelli feels freer to state his own, decidedly republican preferences and to argue for the superiority of republics to principalities without any hedging whatsoever. The *Discourses* is written as a commentary on Livy's *History of Rome,* whose Latin title is *Ab urbe condita* (*From the Founding of the City*); of the 142 books that originally made up Livy's work, only some 35 remain, and the first lacuna occurs after Book 10. Machiavelli's full title of his own work indicates that he will focus on the first "decade"—that is, the first ten books—of that history. Those books cover Roman history from the founding of the state in 509 BCE to the end of Rome's third war of expansion against the Samnites in 293 BCE; in other words, Machiavelli is focusing on the development and expansion of *republican* Rome. He does, however, mention events from later Roman history, especially because he sees the Roman Republic as the ideal state and a model for future republics and because he wants to make sure his readers understand that Rome's real decline began when Julius Caesar took the quasi-regal power accorded a Roman dictator on a temporary basis and made it permanent. Caesar's attempt to make himself emperor was cut short by his assassination, but it was imitated more successfully by Augustus, whose ascent to power marked the end of Roman greatness in Machiavelli's view. The *Discourses* is divided into three books. Book 1 is concerned with the development of Rome's republican institutions; Book 2 treats the expansion of the Roman state through the conquest of its neighbors; and Book 3 covers a variety of topics, but emphasizes Rome's good fortune in having many great men who saved the republic, often by taking the state, which was becoming corrupt, and leading it back to its republican roots.

NICCOLÒ MACHIAVELLI

From Discourses on the First Ten Books of Titus Livy†

BOOK I

Preface

Although the envious nature of men, readier to blame than to praise the actions of others, makes the discovery and introduction of any new principles and institutions as dangerous as the exploration of unknown seas and lands, yet, animated by that natural desire I have always had to do, without hesitation, what may be for the common good, I have resolved to open a new route, which as yet has not been trodden by anyone, and which may prove difficult and troublesome, but may also bring me some reward in the approbation of those who will consider kindly what I aim at in these efforts of mine. And if my poor talents, my scant experience of present events, and my limited knowledge of antiquity should make the result of my labors defective and of little utility, they will at least have shown the way to someone who will carry out my intentions with greater ability [*virtù*], analytical skill, and judgment, so that if I do not merit praise, I should at least not incur censure.

When I consider how much honor is accorded antiquity, and how often—to say nothing of countless other examples—a great price is paid for some fragments of an ancient statue, which we are eager to own in order to adorn our houses, or want to have imitated by those who take pleasure in that art and will, with great industriousness, make every effort to replicate it in their own works, and when I see, on the other hand, that the most virtuous [*virtuosissime*] actions which history shows us have been performed in ancient kingdoms and republics by kings, captains, citizens, lawgivers, and others, all of whom have labored for their countries—when I see these things and these actions, I say, being more often admired than imitated, or, on the contrary, so much neglected, down to the smallest detail, so that not the least trace of the virtue [*virtù*] of the ancients remains, I cannot help but be at the same time as much surprised as affected.

† From *The Historical, Political, and Diplomatic Writings of Niccolò Machiavelli*, trans. Christian E. Detmold (Boston: Houghton Mifflin, 1882); revised translation and annotations by the editor of this Norton Critical Edition. Italian text from Niccolò Machiavelli, *Discorsi sopra la prima deca di Tito Livio*, in *Opere*, edited by Niccolò Conti, vol. 3: 227–29, 234–40, 248–53, 261–64, 269–76, 279–81, 308–14, 324–27, 330–34, 381–89; vol. 4: 5–8, 50–52, 112–15, 135–36, 167–73, 200–01, 267–69 (Firenze: N. Conti, 1820).

And all the more so when I see that in the legal disputes that arise among citizens, or in the maladies to which they are subjected, they always have recourse to the judgments made and the remedies prescribed by the ancients. For the civil laws are in fact nothing but decisions made by ancient jurists, which, reduced to a system, teach our present jurists how to judge things. And medicine is nothing other than the experiments made by ancient physicians, on which contemporary physicians have based their own diagnoses. And yet, to found a republic, maintain states, rule kingdoms, organize an army, conduct a war, dispense justice to subjects, and extend empires, one cannot find a prince or a republic that has recourse to the examples of antiquity.

This neglect, I believe, arises not so much from the weakness into which our religion has brought the world, or from the harm that a certain ambitious indolence has done to many Christian states and cities, as from not having a true understanding of histories, because in reading them, we do not extract the sense or taste the flavor that is in them. Thus, the countless individuals who happen to read them take pleasure from hearing about the variety of events they contain, without otherwise thinking to imitate them, deeming that such imitation is not just difficult, but impossible—as if heavens, the sun, the elements, and men had changed their motions, order, and powers from what they were in antiquity.

Wishing, therefore, to draw men away from this error, I have thought it necessary to write about all those books of Titus Livy which, in spite of the malice of time, have not been taken away from us, and to say what I, thanks to my knowledge of ancient and modern affairs, feel is necessary for a greater understanding of them. Thus, those who read these remarks of mine might more easily extract from them that profit which is the reason why one should study history. And although this undertaking is difficult, nevertheless, aided by those who have encouraged me to take up this burden, I believe I can carry it so far that only a little way will be left for some other person to bring it to its destined end.

* * *

Chapter 2

On How Many Kinds of Republics There Are, and of What Kind the Roman Republic Was

I will leave aside what might be said of those cities that from their birth have been subject to some other power, and will speak only of those that were originally far removed from any kind of external servitude, and from the start have been governed by their own wishes, either as republics or principalities, and have had diverse laws and institutions just as they had diverse beginnings. For either at the start or shortly afterwards, some were given their laws at one stroke by some individual, like those that were given by Lycurgus to the Spartans;[1] others have acquired them by chance and at different times as occasions arose, which was the case with Rome.

Happy indeed may one call that republic which produces a man so prudent that he can give it well-organized laws under which it can live in security without ever having to correct them. Sparta, we know, observed its laws for more than eight hundred years without corrupting them and without any dangerous disturbances. Unhappy to some degree, on the other hand, is that city that did not chance to meet with a prudent legislator and had to effect reforms all on its own. And of those states, more unhappy still is the one that is farther away from having a well-ordered constitution, and that state is the farthest away from being well ordered that with its legal system strays away from the right road which could lead it to its true and perfect goal. For it is almost impossible that states in this condition could, by any chance, put themselves in order, whereas those which do not have a perfect system of laws, but have made a good beginning and are capable of improvement, can become perfect if events present them with the opportunity to do so. It is very true, however, that those states will never put themselves in order without danger, because the majority of men will never agree with one another about a new law aiming to establish a new constitution for their city unless necessity makes it clear that it is imperative for them to do so, and since this necessity cannot arise without danger, the state may actually come to ruin before it has perfected its constitution. The Republic of Florence offers complete proof of this, for it was reorganized after what happened in Arezzo in 1502 and it was disorganized after what happened in Prato in 1512.[2]

Since I want to discuss the kind of constitutional system established in the city of Rome and the events that led to its perfection, let me say that some people who have written about states declare that there are three kinds of governments in them, governments they call princely, aristocratic, and democratic, and that those who set up a government in a city must turn to one of these, depending on what seems most suitable to them. Others, who are wiser in many

1. Plutarch claims in his *Life of Lycurgus*, a partly legendary lawgiver who lived in the 9th century BCE, that, after traveling around Greece, Lycurgus settled in Sparta, undertook the reformation of its laws, and finally gave its inhabitants a complete constitution. Machiavelli's source here is Polybius, *The Histories*, 6.10.
2. When Arezzo rose up against Florentine rule in 1502, the rebellion was put down with the aid of French troops. Prato was sacked by Spanish troops in 1512, which led to the fall of Soderini's republican government, the restoration of the Medici as the rulers of the city, and Machiavelli's exile to his farm in Sant'Andrea in Percussina.

people's opinion, think that there are six types of government, three of which are very bad, and the other three good in themselves, but so easily corrupted that they, too, will become pernicious. The three good ones are the three mentioned above; those that are bad are the three others that derive from the first ones, each one being similar to the one closest to it, so that the transition from one form to the other is quite easy. Thus, princely rule effortlessly becomes tyrannical; the transition from aristocracy to oligarchy is an easy one; and democracy, without difficulty, turns into anarchy. Thus, if the founder of a state establishes one of these three types of government in a city, he will be establishing it there for only a short time, because there is no remedy capable of preventing it from slipping into its contrary because of the similarity that exists, in this case, between virtue and vice.[3]

These varied kinds of government arose among men by chance, for at the beginning of the world, the inhabitants were few in number, and they lived for a time scattered in the manner of the beasts. Then, as their offspring increased, they came together, and in order to be able to defend themselves better, they looked among themselves for one who was stronger and more courageous, and made him their head and obeyed him. From this they acquired an understanding of things that are honest and good, as distinct from those that are pernicious and evil, for seeing someone harm his benefactor aroused in them feelings of hatred and compassion, as they blamed the ingrate and honored those who conferred benefits on them. Moreover, thinking that the same injuries could be done to them, they decided that, in order to prevent similar evils, they set to work making laws and instituting punishments for those who contravened them. Thus, the notion of justice came into being.

The result of this was that afterwards, when they had to choose a prince, they did not go after the strongest person, but the one who was the most prudent and the most just. But later, when they began to make the prince a hereditary ruler instead of electing him, the heirs quickly degenerated from the level of their ancestors, and forsaking virtuous [*virtuose*] deeds, they thought that princes had nothing else to do other than to outdo all the rest in luxury, lasciviousness, and every other kind of licentious behavior. Thus, the prince began to be hated, and since he was hated, to feel fear, fear quickly led to the inflicting of injuries, and soon afterwards, tyranny was born. This quickly led to the beginnings of their ruin and to conspiracies and plots against their princes, not planned by those who were timid or weak, but by those who, surpassing others in liberality,

3. Machiavelli's source for this political model of *anacyclosis,* or the cyclical movement from one form of government to another, is Polybius, *The Histories,* 6. Polybius's classification is, in turn, derived from Book 3 of Aristotle's *Politics.*

magnanimity, wealth, and nobility, could not stand the dishonorable life of their ruler.

Following the lead of those powerful men, the masses[4] then took up arms against the prince, and when he was eliminated, they made themselves the subjects of those men whom they regarded as their liberators. The latter, to whom the very term "sole leader" had become odious, formed a government made up of themselves, and at first, still mindful of the tyranny left behind them, they conducted themselves according to the laws that they themselves had established, subordinating what was beneficial for themselves to the common good, and using the greatest care, they governed and preserved order in both private and public matters. Then, when the administration passed to their children, who had no knowledge of Fortune's changeability, had never experienced bad times, and were ill-disposed to remain content with this political equality, they gave themselves up to avarice, ambition, and the taking of other men's wives, turning an aristocratic government into an oligarchy with no respect for the norms of civic life. Thus, in a short time, the same thing that happened to the tyrant happened to them, for the masses, sick of their conduct, made themselves the instruments of anyone who aimed to harm their rulers in any way, so that one man soon arose who, with the aid of the masses, destroyed the oligarchy. And since the memory of the prince and of the injuries received from him was still fresh, and since they had destroyed the government of the few and were unwilling to restore that of the prince, they turned to government by the people and organized it in such a way that neither a few powerful men nor a prince would have any authority in it. And because all governments are looked up to with a certain reverence at the beginning, this government of the people did maintain itself for a while, but not for long, especially when the generation that had set it up had passed away, for it quickly turned into anarchy in which there was no fear of either private men or public officials. The result was that, with each person living as he pleased, a thousand injuries were committed every day, so that, constrained by necessity, or at the suggestion of some good man, or for the purpose of escaping such licentiousness, they returned once again to princely rule; and from this they then went back, step by step, toward anarchy, in the manner and for the reasons we have just given.

This, then, is the cycle through which all states pass, whether they are being governed or govern themselves. Rarely, however, do they return to their original forms of government, because practically no

4. Machiavelli's word here is *la moltitudine*. He uses it as a rough equivalent to *plebs* (plebeians) and *il populo* (the people) when he speaks in the *Discourses* of the lower classes of Rome, as opposed to the patricians or members of the senatorial class.

state has such vitality that it can pass through these changes many times and still remain standing. Rather, it may well happen that while it is struggling, such a state, which always lacks counsel and strength, will become subject to a neighboring state that is better organized than it is. Should this not be the case, however, then a state might be prone to go on cycling endlessly through all these forms of government.

I say, then, that all the forms of government mentioned above are disastrous because of the short-lived nature of their three good forms and the malignant character of the three bad ones. Thus, since those who have been prudent in establishing laws have recognized these defects, they have avoided each of these forms in itself and have chosen a government that partakes of them all, judging it to be steadier and more stable, for when one and the same city-state is a principality, an aristocracy, and a democracy, then each one of these keeps watch over the other.

Among those who have merited real acclaim for creating constitutions of this sort is Lycurgus, who established his laws in Sparta, and to his great credit, by assigning the kings, the nobles, and the people their respective powers, he created a state that enjoyed peace and quiet and that lasted more than eight hundred years.

Quite the contrary thing happened to Solon, who established the laws of Athens, for by setting up a purely popular form of government, he made it so short-lived that before his death, he saw the birth of the tyranny of Peisistratos.[5] And although forty years later the latter's heirs were driven out and Athens recovered its liberty, that did not last more than a hundred years, because they re-established their democracy according to Solon's laws. Although they did make many constitutional changes in order to repress the insolence of the nobility and the licentiousness of the masses, things which Solon had not considered, nevertheless, Athens lived a very short time in comparison with Sparta, because it did not combine popular government with princely rule and the rule of the nobility.

But let us come to Rome. Although it had no Lycurgus to give it a constitution at the beginning to secure its liberty for a lengthy period of time, nevertheless, because of the discord that existed between the plebeians and the senate, so many unexpected things happened in it that chance did for it what a founder had not done. Thus, if Rome did not get the first gift from Fortune, it got the second, for its first institutions, though defective, did not depart from

5. Peisistratos (d. 527 BCE) was a successful general and the head of a political faction in Athens. He defeated all rival factions around the year 546 and established a tyranny in the city that lasted thirty-six years. Solon (640–558 BCE) was an Athenian lawgiver who gave the city its most democratic constitution. Machiavelli's source for information about Solon and Peisistratos is Plutarch's *Life of Solon,* 18.

the right path that might lead it to perfection, in that Romulus and all the other kings made many good laws quite compatible with freedom. Because their goal was to found a kingdom and not a republic, however, when that city became free, it lacked many things necessary for the establishment of liberty that had not been instituted by those kings. So, when those kings lost their power for the reasons and in the ways described earlier, yet the people who expelled them immediately appointed two consuls in place of the king, so that what they got rid of in Rome was the title of king, not his royal power. Thus, since that republic had consuls and a senate, the result was a mixture of just two of the three elements mentioned above, that is, princely and aristocratic rule.

The one thing remaining to be done was to find a place in the state for democracy. In the course of time, when the Roman nobility became arrogant for the reasons that will be discussed below, the people rose up against it, with the result that, in order not to lose everything, the nobility was forced to grant the people a role in the government, while, on the other hand, the senate and the consuls still retained sufficient authority to preserve their position in the republic. And thus came about the creation of the tribunes of the people, after which the government of that republic became more stable, for all three kinds of rule had their place in it. And Fortune was so favorable to Rome that although it passed from government by kings and aristocrats to that of the people, going through the same stages for the same reasons discussed above, nevertheless, they never took away all the authority possessed by the kings in order to bestow it on the nobility, nor did they completely eliminate the authority of the nobility to give it to the people. But since authority was mixed, it produced a perfect republic.

* * *

Chapter 6

Whether in Rome It Was Possible to Establish a Government That Would Have Put to an End to the Enmity between the People and the Nobility

We have discussed above the effects of the controversies between the people and the senate. Since these same controversies continued into the time of the Gracchi,[6] when they caused the ruin of liberty, one might wish that Rome would have done the great things it

6. Two brothers, Tiberius Gracchus (c. 169–c. 133 BCE) and Gaius Gracchus (154–121 BCE), were tribunes and popular reformers who fought for the redistribution of agricultural land to the plebeians. Both came to violent ends because of the resistance of the aristocratic (i.e., senatorial) party.

did without the existence of such internal hostilities. It therefore seems to me worthwhile to examine whether Rome could have established a government that would have prevented such controversies. And in order to investigate this subject, it is necessary to consider those republics that have remained free for a long time but without such enmities and tumults, and to see what sort of government they had and whether it could have been introduced into Rome.

Among the ancients there is the example of Sparta, and among the moderns, Venice, as I noted before.[7] Sparta set up a king and a small senate to govern it; Venice did not make distinctions by means of titles among the members of the government, but all of those who were eligible to serve in the administration were grouped together under a single appellation and were called gentlemen.[8] This latter arrangement was due to chance more than to the prudence of its law-givers, for having taken refuge on those rocks where the city is located nowadays, * * * once its inhabitants had grown so numerous that it was necessary for them to establish laws if they wanted to live together, many of them devised a system of government and would frequently assemble in councils to deliberate about the city's affairs. When it seemed to them that they were sufficiently numerous to form a body politic, they barred the way for all of those others who had recently come there to live to be able to share in the government.[9] And when, over time, they found that there were enough inhabitants who remained outside the government, in order to give prestige to those who were inside, they called them gentlemen, and the others, commoners.[1]

It was possible for this form of government to arise and maintain itself without disturbances, because when it came into being, whoever was then dwelling in Venice became part of the governing class so that no one had any reason to complain. Those who came to live there afterwards, finding the government firmly established, had neither motive nor means to create disturbances. They had no motive because they had not been deprived of anything; they had no means because those who ruled kept them in check and did not employ them in matters that might offer them the possibility of acquiring

7. Machiavelli discusses the two states in the first and second chapters of this book of the *Discourses*. His source for information about Sparta is Polybius, *The Histories*, 6.48–52.
8. Sparta had what it called the *gerusía*, a college composed of twenty-eight men, presided over by two kings. The members of the college were elected for life and were chosen from among those who had passed the age of military service, to wit, seventy years. The "gentlemen" in Venice were members of the patrician class and constituted an oligarchy of sorts.
9. This permanent separation between citizens who had political power and those who did not occurred on February 28, 1297, at the meeting of the *Maggior Consiglio* (the Great Council), which replaced all former councils and became the dominant governing body in Venice. The meeting in 1297 was known as the *Serrata* (the Lockout).
1. Machiavelli's word here is *Popolani*, meaning "members of the popular, or ordinary people's, class." "Commoners" is more idiomatic English.

authority. Besides, there were not many people who came later to live in Venice, and they were not sufficiently numerous to create an imbalance between those who ruled and those who were ruled. For the number of gentlemen was either equal to, or greater than, that of the others. And so, these were the reasons that Venice could set up this form of government and maintain its unity.

Sparta, as I have said, was governed by a king and a limited senate. It was able to maintain itself in this way for a long time because it had only a few inhabitants and they had eliminated any way for others to come there to live. Moreover, they had embraced the laws of Lycurgus, and since those laws were observed, they removed every opportunity to cause disorder, so that the Spartans were able to live united for a long time. For by means of his laws, Lycurgus created in Sparta more equality with regard to material possessions and less with regard to rank, because everyone had an equal share of poverty, and the plebs were less ambitious since the offices in the city were open to only a few citizens and the plebs were excluded from them, nor did they ever feel any desire for them because they were ill-treated by the nobility. This was due to the position of the kings of Sparta in the state, for they were placed in the midst of the nobles and had no better remedy to prevent the loss of their authority than to protect the plebs from every injustice. As a result, the latter neither feared that authority nor desired to have authority themselves, and since they neither feared nor desired it, any potential rivalry with the nobility was eliminated, as was any ground for disturbances, and they were able to live together in unity for a long time. This unity, however, had two principal causes: first, the inhabitants of Sparta were few in number and could thus be governed by just a few; and the other was that, by not accepting foreigners into their state, they had no opportunity to become corrupt or to grow so numerous that they would be an unmanageable burden for the few men who ruled over them.

If one considers all these things, then, it is clear that the legislators of Rome had to do one of two things if they wanted their city to enjoy the same tranquility as the republics discussed above: either they should not employ the plebs in war, like the Venetians, or they should not open their gates to foreigners, like the Spartans. And yet, Rome did both of those things, which strengthened the plebs, increased its numbers, and provided countless opportunities for disturbances. But if the Roman republic had turned out to be more tranquil, this inconvenience would have ensued, namely that it would have been weaker because it would have cut off the route by which it was able to reach the greatness that it achieved, so that in seeking to remove the causes of its tumults, Rome would have also removed the causes of its expansion.

And thus, in all human affairs, one notices, if one examines them with care, that it is impossible to eliminate one inconvenience without having another one crop up. Therefore, if you want your people to be numerous and to arm them so that you can create a great empire, you will be fashioning them in such a way that, afterwards, you will not be able to manage them as you please. If you keep their numbers small or refrain from arming them so that you can control them, then, should you acquire other dominions, you will not be able to hold onto them, or they will become so debased that you will become the prey of whoever assaults you. Hence, in all of our deliberations, we have to consider which alternative involves fewer inconveniences and take that as our best choice, because one never finds anything that is clear cut and beyond dispute. Just like Sparta, then, Rome could have created a prince for life and established a small senate, but it could not, like Sparta, prevent its population from increasing, since it wanted to become a great empire, which meant that creating a king for life and a small senate would not have been of much use insofar as maintaining the unity of the state was concerned.

If anyone, therefore, wants to establish an entirely new republic, he would have to think about whether he wants it, like Rome, to expand its power and territory, or to remain confined within narrow limits. In the first case, it is necessary to organize it like Rome and, managing things the best he can, to leave room for tumults and disputes of all sorts, because without a large number of men, and these well-armed, a republic will never be able to grow or to hold onto what it has if it does grow. In the second case, you can organize it like Sparta and Venice, but because expansion is poison to such republics, whoever organizes them should, in every way possible, prevent them from acquiring territory, because such acquisitions, which have a weak republic as their foundation, will absolutely lead to its ruin. This is what happened to Sparta and Venice. The first of them, after having subjugated almost all of Greece, revealed the weakness of its foundation on the occasion of an insignificant incident, for when the rebellion of Thebes occurred, led by Pelopidas, the other cities [of Greece] rebelled, and Sparta was completely ruined.[2] In like manner, Venice, having occupied a great part of Italy, and most of it not by war, but by means of money and clever dealings, lost everything in a single battle when it had to put its forces to the test.[3] I am firmly convinced that in order to found a republic which would last a long time, the way to do it would be to

2. In 379 BCE, Pelopidas of Thebes (c. 410–364 BCE) led a successful revolt against the Spartans, who had conquered the city in 383 or 382. After beating Sparta in several more battles, Thebes displaced it as the main military power in Greece.
3. On the battle of Vailà or Agnadello, see *The Prince*, n. 4, p. 12.

organize it internally like Sparta or to locate it, like Venice, in some strong place and to make it so powerful that no one would believe it could be overcome swiftly, and on the other hand, not to make it so great that it would be frightening to its neighbors. In this way it should be able to enjoy its form of government for a long time. For there are two reasons for waging war against a republic: one is to become its ruler; the other is the fear that it will subjugate you. Both of these reasons will be almost entirely removed by the mode of governing described above. For if it is difficult to take a republic by an assault since its defenses are well organized, as I am presupposing, then it will never, or very rarely, happen that someone would make plans to subjugate it. If it stays within its boundaries, and if experience shows that it has no ambitions, the fear of its power will never make anyone wage war against it, and this would even more certainly be the case if its expansion were prohibited by its constitution or one of its laws. And I have no doubt that if this balance could be maintained, this would be the true form for political life and the source of real tranquility in a city.

But since all human affairs are constantly in flux and can never stand still, they must either ascend or descend, and necessity will induce you to do many things which reason cannot bring you to do, so that, having set up a republic disposed to maintain itself without expanding, if necessity should then compel it to expand, you will see its foundations give way and watch it soon turn into a ruin. And thus, on the other hand, should Heaven be so benevolent that it does not have to wage war, the result would be that its idleness will either make it effeminate or give rise to internal divisions, and those two things, taken together or separately, would cause its ruin.

Consequently, in my opinion, since there is no way to balance these things and maintain a precise middle course, one ought to think, when organizing a republic, about its more honorable aspects, and to set it up in such a way that if necessity should force it to expand, it would be able to preserve what it has acquired. And to return to our first argument, I think it is essential to imitate the Roman constitution, not those of the other republics, because I do not believe a middle way between the two of them can be found, and to tolerate those antagonisms that arise between the people and the senate as a necessary inconvenience in order to achieve Roman greatness.

* * *

Chapter 9

How It Is Necessary to Act Alone If One Wants to Set Up a Brand New Republic or to Reform It Thoroughly Regardless of Its Ancient Institutions

It may perhaps appear to some that I have gone too far along in Roman history without having yet made any mention of the founders of that republic or of its laws concerning religion and the military. And therefore, not wishing to keep the minds of those who want to know something about this subject any longer in suspense, let me say that many will perhaps judge it to be a bad example that the founder of a civil society, such as Romulus, should first have killed his brother and then acquiesced in the death of Titus Tatius, the Sabine, whom he had selected as his coruler in the kingdom.[4] From this, they might conclude that a prince's subjects, using him as their model, might, because of their ambition and desire to rule, do harm to those who opposed their authority. This opinion would be correct, but only if the end for which Romulus committed such a murder were not taken into consideration.

One should take it as a general rule that rarely, if ever, does it happen that a republic or a kingdom is well ordered at the start, or totally reformed with complete disregard for its old institutions, unless this is done by one individual; in fact, it must be one man alone who determines the method and on whose mind any organization of this sort depends. Thus, the prudent founder of a state, who intends to serve not himself, but the public good, and not his own heirs, but his fatherland[5] which all share in common, must do his utmost to concentrate all authority in himself. Nor will a wise man ever blame anyone for any deed, however extraordinary, if he is acting in order to organize a kingdom or establish a republic. It is certainly appropriate to say that although the deed accuses him, its outcome excuses him, and when what is done is good, as was the case with Romulus, it will always excuse him, for the man ought to be reprehended who uses violence for the purpose of destroying things, rather than for the sake of mending them.[6]

4. Romulus was the legendary founder of Rome, who supposedly ruled between 753 and 715 BCE. He and his twin brother, Remus, were foundlings, initially nurtured by a she-wolf. The two of them founded Rome, but in a dispute over which of seven hills was to be the location of the city, Remus was slain by Romulus, after whom the city is named. Titus Tatius was the king of the Sabines, a neighboring people, and was made coruler of Rome along with Romulus in order to unite the two peoples. Titus was killed by a mob in mysterious circumstances while officiating at a religious ceremony.
5. Here Machiavelli uses the Italian *patria*. For him, this word would have recalled the Roman ideal of the state, and so, I have chosen it here and elsewhere despite its inevitable association with Hitler's Third Reich in modern times.
6. Whereas in *The Prince*, the end—the prince's acquisition and preservation of his state—can never justify the perpetrating of evil, in the *Discourses*, since the end is the "public good," evil means may be excused.

Such a man must certainly be sufficiently prudent and virtuous [*virtuoso*] not to bequeath the authority he has assumed to another, for, men being more prone to evil than to good, his successor might employ for the sake of ambition what he had used virtuously [*virtuosamente*]. Besides, although one man is all it takes to organize a government, that which he has organized will not last long if it rests on the shoulders of a single individual. However, it will endure if it is left in the care of many, provided that preserving it is something dear to their hearts. For just as the many are not competent to organize a government, since the diversity of the opinions they hold prevents them from understanding what is best, so, once they have understood that they have such a good government, they will never agree to abandon it. And that Romulus was among those who might deserve to be excused for the deaths of his brother and his co-ruler, and that he did what he did for the common good and not for the gratification of his personal ambition—this is proved by the fact that he immediately established a senate with which to consult and on whose opinions he based his deliberations. Moreover, anyone who considers carefully the authority which Romulus reserved for himself will see that he only kept the authority to command the army when war had been decided as well as that of convoking the senate. This was seen later on, for when Rome became free after the expulsion of the Tarquins, none of its ancient institutions were changed, except that instead of a permanent king, they had two consuls chosen annually.[7] This bears witness to the fact all the original institutions of that city were more consistent with a free and civil society than with an absolute and tyrannical government.

The things stated above could be corroborated by any number of examples, such as those of Moses, Lycurgus, Solon, and other founders of kingdoms and republics, men who were able to fashion laws concerned with the common good because they had seized the authority to do so. However, I wish to omit this since it is well known. I will adduce only one example, not so celebrated, but worth considering by those who might desire to be the framers of new laws, and here it is. Agis, the king of Sparta,[8] wanted to bring the Spartans back to the limits within which the laws of Lycurgus had confined them, for it seemed to him that, having deviated from them to some

7. The Tarquins were a Roman family of Greco-Etruscan origins, two of whom were among the semilegendary early kings of Rome. The last one, who was also the last king of Rome, was Lucius Tarquinius Superbus ("the Proud"), who ruled from 534 to 510 BCE. After his son, Sextus Tarquinius, raped the Roman matron Lucretia, who committed suicide as a result, the people—led by her father; her husband, Lucius Tarquinius Collatinus; Publius Valerius Publicola; and Lucius Junius Brutus—rose against him, drove him out of the city, and established the Roman republic, of which they were appointed the first consuls.

8. Agis (c. 262–241 BCE) ruled Sparta for only three or four years before he was killed.

extent, his city had lost a great deal of its ancient vitality [*virtù*], and consequently, of its power and its empire. However, he was killed at the very start of his project by the Spartan ephors[9] who saw him as someone who wanted to become a tyrant. Cleomenes succeeded him as king,[1] and having found some of Agis's records and writings, and having learned what Agis's ideas and intentions were, he felt the same desire arise in him. He realized, however, that he could not bestow this benefit on his fatherland unless he became the sole authority there, for he felt that, because of the ambitious nature of men, he could not do something beneficial for the many against the will of the few. And so, availing himself of a suitable opportunity, he had all the ephors slain as well as anyone else who might oppose him, after which he restored the laws of Lycurgus in their entirety. This decision was on track to resuscitate Sparta and to earn a reputation for Cleomenes equal to that of Lycurgus—had it not been for the power of the Macedonians and the weakness of the other Greek republics. For just after that reorganization, he was attacked by the Macedonians, and since his forces were inferior and he could not get help from outside, he was defeated, and thus his project, however just and laudable, was never brought to completion.

Considering, then, all these things, I conclude that to found a republic, one must act alone, and that Romulus deserves to be excused, not condemned, for the deaths of Remus and Titus Tatius.

* * *

Chapter 11

On the Religion of the Romans

Although Rome had Romulus as its first lawgiver, and like a daughter, she owed her birth and her education to him, nevertheless, the heavens decided that Romulus's laws would not suffice for so great an empire, and they inspired the Roman senate to elect Numa Pompilius[2] as his successor, so that he might include those things omitted by Romulus. Finding a very savage people and wishing to lead

9. Five magistrates, elected annually, who were intended to constitute a counterweight to the power of the Spartan kings. Machiavelli's source here is probably Plutarch's *Lives of Agis and Cleomenes*.
1. Cleomenes III was one of the two kings of Sparta from about 235 to 222 BCE. He did indeed attempt to restore Lycurgus's laws, but his efforts at reform were cut short when his army was beaten by the Macedonians and the Achaean League at the battle of Sellasia in 222. Having fled to Egypt, Cleomenes attempted to stir up a revolt, but when it failed, he committed suicide in the winter of 220/219. Machiavelli's sources here are Polybius, *The Histories,* 2.45–70, and Plutarch's *Lives of Agis and Cleomenes.*
2. Numa Pompilius (b. 753; ruled 715–673 BCE) was the legendary second king of Rome. A Sabine, he established most of the basic rites and practices of Roman religion. On Numa, see Livy, *History of Rome,* 22.53.

them to civil obedience by means of the arts of peace, Numa turned to religion as an institution, necessary beyond all others, for the maintenance of a civil society, and he established it in such a way that for many centuries nowhere was there such fear of God as in that republic, which facilitated whatever enterprise the senate or the great men of Rome decided to undertake.

Whoever examines the numberless exploits of the Roman people as a whole, or of many individual Romans, will see that those citizens were much more afraid of breaking an oath than of breaking the laws, since they respected the power of God more than that of men. This is clearly manifested in the examples of Scipio and Manlius Torquatus.[3] For after Hannibal had routed the Romans at Cannae, many citizens had assembled together and, despairing of their fatherland, agreed to abandon Italy and go away to Sicily. When Scipio heard of this, he sought them out and with his unsheathed sword in his hand, he forced them to swear not to abandon their country. Lucius Manlius, the father of Titus Manlius, later called Torquatus, had been indicted by Marcus Pomponius, Tribune of the People, and before the day of the trial arrived, Titus went to find Marcus, and threatening to kill him if he did not withdraw the accusation against his father, forced him to swear it, and Marcus, having sworn out of fear, withdrew his accusation. And thus those citizens, who could not be kept in Italy by the love of their fatherland and its laws, were kept there by an oath they were forced to take, and that tribune set aside the anger he had at Titus's father, the injury the son had done him, and his own honor, in order to obey the oath he had taken—which came from nothing other than the religion which Numa had introduced into that city.

And those who read Roman history attentively will see clearly how much religion helped in commanding armies, in encouraging the plebeians, in producing good men, and in making the wicked feel shame.[4] Thus, if it were a question about the prince to whom Rome owed the most, whether Romulus or Numa, I think that Numa should easily obtain the first prize, for where there is religion, one

3. Titus Manlius Imperiosus Torquatus came from a very prominent patrician family and was elected consul in 235 and 224, and censor in 231 BCE. In 215 BCE, he defeated the Carthaginians when they were attempting to reclaim the island of Sardinia, which they had previously lost to the Romans. Renowned for his sense of filial duty and his severity, he was called "Torquatus" because of the golden torque, the metal collar or neck chain, he took from the body of a Gaul he defeated in a duel. One story has him executing his own son for having fought a duel against orders. For the incident Machiavelli is going to describe about him, see Livy, *History of Rome,* 7.4–5. Publius Cornelius Scipio Africanus, the Elder (236–183 BCE) was a Roman general and consul who is considered one of the city's greatest strategists. He defeated Hannibal and the Carthaginians in the Second Punic War at the battle of Zama in 202, for which he was given the nickname "Africanus" (the African). For the incident concerning him that Machiavelli is about to describe, see Livy, *History of Rome,* 22.53.

4. On the Romans' use of religion, see Polybius, *The Histories,* 6.56.

can easily introduce men to the use of arms, but where there are arms, but no religion, it is difficult to introduce the latter. And it is clear that Romulus did not need to invoke the authority of God in order to set up the senate and establish other civil and military institutions, but that divine authority was certainly necessary for Numa, who pretended to be on familiar terms with a nymph who advised him about the advice he had to give to the people, and the reason for all of this was that he wanted to introduce new and unfamiliar institutions into that city and doubted whether his own authority would suffice.[5]

And in truth, there was never a legislator who, in introducing extraordinary laws to a people, did not have recourse to God, because otherwise they would not have been accepted, for they offer many benefits of which a prudent man is aware, but which are not so clear to reason that he can convince others of them. Therefore, wise men who want to obviate this difficulty have recourse to God. This is what Lycurgus did, as did Solon, and many others who had the same end in view. Thus, marveling at Numa's goodness and prudence, the Roman people accepted every decision he made. It is true, to be sure, that those were very religious times and the men with whom he had to work were so simple that they made it very easy for him to implement his plans, since he could impress on them any new form he wanted. And doubtless, if anyone wanted to create a republic at the present time, he would find it much easier to do so among the uncivilized men living in the mountains than among those who are accustomed to living in cities, where civilization is corrupt—just as it will be easier for a sculptor to make a beautiful statue out of a rough piece of marble than out of one that has been badly carved by someone else.

Considering everything, then, I conclude that the religion introduced by Numa was among the primary causes of the prosperity of that city, for it gave rise to good institutions, good institutions brought it good fortune, and from its good fortune came the happy, successful results of its undertakings. And as the observance of divine worship is the cause of the greatness of republics, similarly, disregard for it is the cause of their ruin. For where the fear of God is wanting, either the state will come to ruin, or it will be held together by the fear of a prince which will compensate for the lack of religion. But because the lives of princes are short, that state will, of necessity, fail quickly, declining along with the virtue [*virtù*] of the prince. Thus, states that depend entirely on the virtue [*virtù*] of one man do not last long, because that virtue [*virtù*] comes to an end with his life, and it rarely happens that it is revived by his successor, as Dante wisely declares:

5. For Numa's relationship with the nymph Egeria, see Livy, *History of Rome*, 7.4–5.

Rade volte discende per li rami
l'umana probitate, e questo vuole
quei che la dà, perché da lui si chiami.[6]

Therefore, the well-being[7] of a republic or a kingdom does not depend on having a prince who governs it prudently during his life, but in having one who gives it such a constitution that even after he dies, it will survive on its own. And although it is easier to persuade uncultured men to adopt a new institution or viewpoint, it is not, for all that, impossible to persuade even civilized men who presume they are not among the uncultured.[8] It does not seem to the people of Florence that they are either ignorant or uncultured, yet they were persuaded by Frate Girolamo Savonarola[9] that he talked with God. I do not propose to judge whether it was true or not, because one should speak with reverence of so great a man, but I do say that countless people believed it without having seen anything extraordinary to make them do so, for his life, his teaching, and the topic[1] he chose were sufficient to make them have faith in him. Therefore, let no one be dismayed if he is unable to accomplish what has been accomplished by others, for men, as we said in our preface, are born, live, and die, always in the same manner.

Chapter 12

On the Importance of Taking Religion into Account, and How Italy Has Been Ruined for Lack of It, Thanks to the Church of Rome

Those princes and republics that want to avoid becoming corrupt must, above all, preserve the purity of their religious observances and always treat them with reverence, for there is no greater indication of the ruin of a country than to see divine worship despised there. This is easy to understand once one knows on what basis the religion of a man's birthplace is founded, for every religion has some one of its

6. *Purgatorio,* 7.121–23: "Rarely does human worth descend through the branches, and He wills this who gives it, so that it should be asked for from Him." The "branches" are those of one's family tree. Dante believes that God prevents people from passing their virtues on to their descendants, so that they will recognize that those things come from Him.
7. Here Machiavelli uses *la salute,* a noun I have translated as "well-being," although "welfare" might also work. But Machiavelli's noun means, more literally, "health" or "salvation." Both of these meanings fit Machiavelli's conception of the prince as a doctor throughout *The Prince* and his conception of the prince as redeemer in its last chapter.
8. Machiavelli's word is *rozzo,* which means "rough, coarse, crude" and defines people who are not considered truly civilized (*civile*).
9. Frate (i.e., Brother) Girolamo Savonarola was a religious reformer who became the spiritual leader of Florence after the Medici were driven out in 1494. For more details on his life and death, see *The Prince,* n. 8, p. 19.
1. Here Machiavelli uses *suggetto,* which means the topic from the Bible he spoke about in his sermons.

principal institutions as the basis of its life. The religious life of the pagans was based on the responses of the oracles and on the body of its diviners and augurs. All the rest of their ceremonies, sacrifices, and rites depended on these things, for they readily believed that the god who could predict your future for you, whether it would be good or bad, was also able to bestow it on you. From this source came their temples, from this their sacrifices, from this their supplications and every other ceremony used in venerating the gods, and from this they had the oracle of Delos, the temple of Jupiter Ammon,[2] and other famous oracles which filled the world with wonder and devotion. When the oracles later began to say what was pleasing to the powerful, and this falsity was discovered by the people, men became nonbelievers and were inclined to subvert all their good institutions.

It is, therefore, the duty of the rulers of a republic or a kingdom to preserve the foundations of the religion they practice, and if this is done, it will be easy for them to keep their state religious and, in consequence, good and united. And they must support and amplify everything that favors their religion, even if they might think it is false, and they should do this all the more, the more prudent they are and the better they understand natural phenomena. And because this method has been followed by wise men, it has given rise to a belief in miracles which are celebrated even in false religions, for prudent men will amplify them, no matter what their origin, and their authority will then make everyone believe in them. Rome had many such miracles, among them one that occurred when Roman soldiers were sacking the city of Veii.[3] When some of them entered the temple of Juno, and approaching her image, said to her, "Do you want to come to Rome?" some imagined that they saw her nod in assent, and others believed that she said yes.[4] For those men were deeply imbued with religion, something which Titus Livy shows us, in that, as they entered the temple, they did not create a disturbance, but all were devout and filled with reverence, and so it seemed to them that they heard the response to their question that they had perhaps anticipated. This belief and this credulity were fully favored and magnified by Camillus and by the other leaders of the city.[5]

2. Ammon, or Amun, was an Egyptian deity who was the king of their pantheon and was later identified with the Greek Zeus and the Roman Jupiter. The oracle of Delos was located in a temple dedicated to Apollo on the island of Delos that was itself sacred to the gods Apollo, Artemis, and Leto.
3. An important Etruscan city about sixteen miles northeast of Rome, Veii was captured in 396 BCE.
4. On this episode, see Livy, *History of Rome,* 5.22. Machiavelli cites the men's question in Latin: *"Vis venire Romam?"*
5. Marcus Furius Camillus (d. 365? BCE) was a Roman politician and general who Livy says was considered a second Romulus—that is, a second founder of Rome—because he commanded the army that defeated the Gauls after they had sacked Rome in 390 BCE. For more on Camillus, see n. 2, pp. 132–33.

If such religiosity had been maintained by the princes of Christendom just as its founder ordained it, Christian states and republics would be much more united and prosperous than they are. Nor can any better conjecture be made about its decline than to note that those peoples who live closest to the Church of Rome, the head of our religion, are the least religious. And whoever examines its foundational principles and sees how different its present practices are from them, would undoubtedly conclude that its ruin or its scourging is near.

And because many people are of the opinion that the well-being of the cities of Italy is due to the Church of Rome, I want to present such arguments against that opinion as occur to me. Indeed, I will present two of them that are extremely powerful and cannot, as I see it, be refuted. The first is that because of the wicked examples of that court, this country has lost all its piety and religion, and this has brought in its train countless improprieties and disorders, for just as one takes it for granted that all is good where one finds religion, so, where it is lacking, one takes the contrary for granted. The first debt, therefore, that we Italians owe the Church and its priests is that we have become irreligious and wicked. But we also owe them a greater debt, which is the second cause of our ruin: it is that the Church has kept, and still keeps, this country divided. And in truth, no country was ever united and prosperous if the whole of it were not under the sway of one republic or one prince, as has happened in France and Spain. And the reason why Italy is not in the same situation and why it also does not have a republic or a prince to govern it, is the Church alone. For although it has been established here and has held temporal authority, it has not had enough power or ability [*virtù*] to be able to create a tyranny in Italy and make itself the ruler, nor has it been so weak, on the other hand, that, for fear of losing its dominion over temporal affairs, it could not call in another power to defend it against any state in Italy that had become too powerful. There are many examples of this in earlier times, as when, with the help of Charlemagne, the Church drove out the Lombards, who were almost kings over all of Italy; as well as in our times, when it stripped away the power of the Venetians with the help of France and then drove out the French with the aid of the Swiss.[6]

6. The Lombards, a Germanic tribe, invaded Italy between 568 and 572, eventually creating a kingdom in the northern part of the country. Pope Stephen II asked for aid against them from the Franks in 754, and in 774 Charlemagne succeeded in dislodging the Lombards from their kingdom. When speaking of his own times, Machiavelli is referring to the exploits of Pope Julius II, who formed the League of Cambrai (1508–10) with France, Spain, the Holy Roman Empire, and several Italian city-states against the Venetians, whom they defeated decisively at the battle of Agnadello on May 14, 1509. Julius then formed the Holy League with the Venetians as well as with Spain, the Holy Roman Empire, and the Swiss against the French. Although the French defeated the troops of Julius II at Ravenna on April 11, 1512, they lost many men there, including their leader Gaston de Foix, and the next month twenty thousand Swiss troops came to the aid of the pope and defeated them. The French were then expelled from Italy after the battle of Novara on June 6, 1513.

The Church, then, not having been strong enough to take possession of Italy, nor having permitted another to take possession of it, has been the reason why Italy has not been united under one head, but has been under many princes and lords, who have brought about such discord and weakness and led it to the point of becoming the prey not only of powerful barbarians, but of anyone who attacks her. For this we Italians owe a debt to the Church and nobody else. And should anyone wish to see the truth of this more directly by an actual experiment, he would have to have such power that he could send the Roman court, with all the authority it has in Italy, to reside in the territories of the Swiss, who are the only people today who live like the ancients insofar as both their religion and their military institutions are concerned. And he would see that in a little while the evil habits of that court would create more disorder in that country than any other event that could have ever occurred there.

* * *

Chapter 14

The Romans Interpreted Auspices According to Their Needs, and Prudently Made a Show of Observing Religion, Even When They Were Not Compelled to Do So; and They Punished Anyone Who Was So Foolhardy as to Disparage It

Not only were auguries in large part the basis of the ancient religion of the pagans, as we said above, but they were also the cause of the well-being of the Roman republic. Consequently, the Romans took more care of them than of any other institution, and they made use of them at the meetings of their consuls, at the beginnings of campaigns, in sending their armies into the field, when engaging in battles, and in all their important actions, whether civil or military. Nor would they have ever ventured upon an expedition unless they had persuaded their soldiers that the gods promised them victory. And among the other augurs, they had in their armies a certain order of diviners whom they called poultrymen,[7] and whenever they were preparing to engage the enemy in battle, they asked the poultrymen to take the auspices, for if the chickens pecked at their food, they considered it a good sign and would fight, but if the chickens did not peck, they would abstain from battle. Nevertheless, when reason showed them that a certain thing had to be done, they did it anyhow,

7. *Pullarii* in Machiavelli's Italian, which is his rendering of the Latin *gallinarii*. The term was used by the Romans for priests who took care of a roost of chickens that were considered sacred and that were consulted before every important decision by the senate and before every battle. The usual method of divination was what Machiavelli says here—namely to observe whether and how the chickens ate the grain that the priest gave them.

even if the auspices were adverse, but they were so clever at turning things around with their words and actions that it did not seem as though they were doing anything to disparage their religion.

This cleverness was used by the consul Papirius on the occasion of a very important battle he was fighting with the Samnites, after which the latter were left completely enfeebled and broken.[8] For when Papirius was encamped opposite the Samnites, feeling sure he would be victorious in the battle and wanting to choose the day, he ordered the poultrymen to take the auspices. But the chickens did not peck. And seeing that the army was ready and willing to fight and that the general and all the soldiers felt that they would win, the chief of the poultrymen, in order not to deprive the army of the opportunity to do their best, reported to the consul that the auspices had gone well. So, Papirius set his squadrons in order. But some of the poultrymen told certain soldiers that the chickens had not pecked; the soldiers told it to Spurius Papirius, the consul's nephew; and he reported it to the consul. The latter replied immediately that his nephew should pay attention to doing a good job of attending to his office, and that, as far as he and the army were concerned, the auspices were good, and if the poultryman had told lies, it would turn out to his disadvantage. And to make the outcome correspond to his prognostication, he ordered the legates to put the poultrymen in the first ranks of the battle. And thus it came about that when they were moving against the enemy, a Roman soldier hurled a javelin and by chance killed the head of the poultrymen. When the consul heard this, he said that all was going well and with the favor of the gods, for by the death of that liar the army had been purged of any blame and of any anger that the gods might have felt against it. And so, by knowing how to accommodate his plans effectively to the auspices, he made the decision to go into battle without his army's ever realizing that he had neglected the laws of their religion in any way.

Appius Pulcher did just the opposite in Sicily during the First Punic War.[9] Wishing to engage the Carthaginian army in battle, he had the auspices taken by the poultrymen, and when they reported that the chickens were not pecking, he said: "Let's see if they want to drink!" and he had them thrown into the sea. He then began his attack and lost the battle. For this he was condemned in Rome, whereas Papirius was honored, not so much because the one had been victorious and the other had been beaten, as because, in

8. Lucius Papirius Cursor was a Roman general who won an important victory over the Samnites in 293 BCE at the battle of Aquilonia. His father, who had the same name, preceded him as one of Rome's most distinguished generals. This is the battle Machiavelli is referring to. See Livy, *History of Rome,* 10.38–42.

9. Publius Claudius Pulcher was consul in 249 BCE and defied the auspices by attacking the Carthaginian fleet at Drepana, where he lost 93 of 123 ships. He was put on trial and publicly disgraced in Rome and died sometime before 246. Machiavelli's source here is either Polybius, *The Histories,* 1.49–52, or Cicero, *On the Nature of the Gods,* 2.3.7.

acting against the auspices, one had been prudent, and the other, rash. Nor did this system of taking the auspices have any goal other than to make the soldiers go into battle with confidence, for that confidence almost always produced victory. * * *

* * *

Chapter 27

Very Rarely Do Men Know How to Be Entirely Good or Entirely Bad

In 1505, when Pope Julius II went to Bologna[1] to expel from that state the house of the Bentivogli, which had ruled it for a hundred years, he also wanted to remove Giovampagolo Baglioni from Perugia, which he governed as a tyrant, for the pope had been plotting against all the tyrants who were occupying the territories of the Church. Having arrived at Perugia[2] with this mental framework and this purpose, which was known to everyone, he did not wait to enter the city with his army to protect him, but went in unarmed, despite the fact that Giovampagolo was inside with a substantial force he had assembled for his defense. Carried away by that impetuosity which controlled all his actions, he thus placed himself with only a small guard in the hands of his enemy, whom he then took away with him, leaving behind a governor in that city who would administer it for the Church.

The temerity of the pope and the cowardliness of Giovampagolo were noted by the prudent men who accompanied the pope,[3] and they could not understand how it came about that Giovampagolo did not acquire eternal fame by getting rid of his enemy at a single stroke and enrich himself with booty, for the pope was there with all his cardinals and all their valuables. Nor could they believe that goodness or conscience held him back, because there was no possible way for pious considerations to have entered the breast of a ruffian who had been his sister's lover and had murdered his cousins and nephews in order to become ruler. But they concluded that it must be due to the fact that men do not know how to be either gloriously bad or perfectly good, and that when a crime has a certain grandeur in it or possesses a certain magnanimity, they do not know how to commit it.

Thus, Giovampagolo, who thought nothing of incest and of being the notorious assassin of members of his family, did not know

1. Julius II (b. 1443; pope 1503–13) championed the extension of the papacy's secular control in Italy, and he sometimes led his own troops into battle, as he did against Bologna in 1506 (not 1505, as Machiavelli says). Because of the latter, he became known throughout Europe as the "Warrior Pope." Machiavelli discusses Julius extensively in Chapter 25 of *The Prince,* emphasizing his impetuosity and bellicosity (see pp. 79–80).
2. Julius entered Perugia on September 13, 1506.
3. Among those "prudent men" was Machiavelli himself.

how—or better, did not dare—to perform an act, despite having a justifiable opportunity, for which everyone would have admired his courage and which would have enabled him to leave behind him eternal fame, since he would have been the first to show prelates how little esteem is felt for men who live and govern as they do. Plus, he would have done something whose grandeur would have overcome all the infamy and all the danger that could have resulted from it.

Chapter 28

Why the Romans Were Less Ungrateful to Their Citizens Than the Athenians Were

Whoever reads about what republics have done will find in all of them examples of some sort of ingratitude toward their citizens, but they will find less of it in Rome than in Athens and perhaps in any other republic. And seeking the reason for this—to speak only of Rome and Athens—I believe it was due to the Romans' having less cause to mistrust their citizens than the Athenians did theirs. For in Rome, from the expulsion of the kings to the time of Sulla and Marius,[4] none of its citizens ever deprived his country of its liberty, so that there was no great reason to be suspicious of them and, consequently, to offend them recklessly. Quite the contrary happened in Athens. For that city, deceived by what it thought would be good for it, was deprived of its freedom by Peisistratos at the height of its prosperity,[5] but as soon as it became free again, remembering the

4. Around 509 BCE, the Romans expelled the last of their kings, Lucius Tarquinius Superbus, and turned Rome into a republic. Lucius Cornelius Sulla (c. 138–78 BCE) and Gaius Marius (157–86 BCE) were the leading rivals for power in Rome during the 90s and 80s BCE. Sulla was allied to the senate and the patricians; Marius, to the plebeians. In 89–88 BCE, they fought an open war for control of the city. Although there had been social unrest before that time, this was Rome's first true civil war. Marius's reformation of the Roman army in this period had allowed it to expand from its base of citizen-soldiers to include unpropertied urban citizens, citizens whose first allegiance was to their commander rather than the state. The result was that political opponents in Rome now led something like their own private armies, and subsequent political rivalries turned into a series of full-fledged civil wars that ended only when Octavius defeated Marc Antony at the battle of Actium and became the first Roman emperor Augustus in 27 BCE.

5. Peisistratos came to power in 561 BCE by allying himself with the numerically superior lower classes of Athens. He ruled the city as its *tyrannus* (not a tyrant, but a king who earned, rather than inherited, his position) until his death in 527 BCE, although he was sent into exile twice during this period by his aristocratic enemies. The government of Athens had essentially been in the hands of aristocrats up until the 6th century BCE, when their constant feuding among themselves led to the reforms of Solon who, among other things, in 594 BCE set up the Assembly, which consisted of all male citizens, as the key governing body. But Solon's reforms still left most of the important offices in the hands of aristocrats and opened the way for Peisistratos to come to power. After Peisistratos's death, the city became a democracy once again, although it was still dominated by the aristocracy until the government was reformed anew by Cleisthenes in 508/507 BCE, who redefined the concept of *citizen* in terms of where people lived rather than the wealth they possessed, thus definitively undermining the power that the aristocracy had wielded. Athens then generally remained a democracy in one form or another until Philip II of Macedonia conquered it in 338 BCE. Machiavelli's view that Peisistratos became the ruler of Athens when it was "at the height of its prosperity" is dubious at best, since the conventional view today is that the Golden Age of Athens occurred in the 5th century

injuries it had received and its past servitude, it became the swiftest of avengers, not only when its citizens made errors, but even when there was only the shadow of an error. It was this that gave rise to the exile and deaths of so many exceptional men, this that led to the institution of ostracism and every other form of violence used by that city at various times against its upper classes.[6] Writers about politics are telling the truth when they say that people bite more savagely when they have recovered their liberty than when they are simply acting to preserve it.

Considering, therefore, what has been said, no one will fault Athens or praise Rome for what happened; rather, he will accuse necessity alone for it, a necessity that was determined by the different sets of events that occurred in those cities. For if one looks into things with care, one will see that if Rome had been deprived of its liberty the way Athens was, it would not have been any more merciful toward its citizens than Athens. One can make an extremely accurate conjecture about how Rome would have acted if one considers what happened to Collatinus and Publius Valerius after the expulsion of the kings: although the first had helped to liberate Rome, he was sent into exile for no other reason than the fact that he bore the name of Tarquin; the other came close to being exiled as well, simply because he had aroused suspicion on account of a house he had built on the Velian Hill.[7] Consequently, seeing how suspicious and severe Rome was with these two men, one is led to the conclusion that it would have shown the same ingratitude as Athens, if, like that city, Rome had been injured by its own citizens in its early days and before its expansion. And so as not to be obliged to return to

BCE, not the 6th, specifically the period between the Persian Wars (499–469 BCE) and the Peloponnesian Wars (431–404 BCE) and particularly during the time of Pericles (c. 495–426 BCE), who led Athens between 461 and 429 BCE.

6. Some members of the Athenian aristocracy were indeed sent into exile after Peisistratos's reign, either as the result of trials or by being ostracized. Ostracism (from *ostraka,* the pottery shards used as voting tokens by the members of the Athenian Assembly) was, according to Aristotle, also instituted by Cleisthenes. It did not involve a trial. Rather, once a year the members of the Assembly wrote the names of those they wished to send into exile for a ten-year period on their voting tokens, after which they exiled the person who received the most votes, although that person needed to have at least six thousand votes against him. Those ostracized were mainly aristocrats, but there were altogether only a dozen or so between the first ostracism in 487 and the last one in 416 BCE.

7. For the expulsion of the Tarquins and the founding of the Roman Republic, see n. 7, p. 118. Lucretia's husband, Lucius Tarquinius Collatinus, and Publius Valerius Publicola were among the four men who avenged her rape and suicide, threw out the Tarquins, and helped found the republic. Because Lucretia's husband was a member of the Tarquin family, however, the people voted to exile him, despite what he had done for Rome. Publius Valerius Publicola was chosen as one of the two consuls at the head of the new republic, but when he started building a house on the Velian Hill (Machiavelli mistakenly refers to it as the Caelian Hill), which looked more like a fortress than a house, rumors circulated that he wanted to make himself the new king of Rome. To prevent being sent into exile, he appealed to the people and then had the house he had started building demolished in a single night.

this subject of ingratitude, I shall say what needs to be said about it in the following chapter.

Chapter 29

Which Is More Ungrateful, a People or a Prince?

With regard to the subject mentioned above, it seems to me appropriate to discuss whether ingratitude is exemplified better by a people or a prince. And the better to carry on a debate about this subject, let me say that this vice of ingratitude arises from either avarice or suspicion. For when a people or a prince has sent out one of their generals on an important expedition in which, if he wins, he will acquire much glory, then that prince or people is obliged to reward him for it. But if, instead of a reward, they are moved by avarice, and they either dishonor him or are offensive in the way they treat him—for this greed of theirs keeps any desire they might have to satisfy him in check—then they commit an error for which there is no excuse—on the contrary, it leaves them with endless infamy. And yet, there are many princes who make this mistake. Cornelius Tacitus tells us the cause of this in the following sentence: "It is easier to avenge an injustice than to repay a benefit, for gratitude is considered a burden and revenge, a gain."[8]

But when their motive for not giving him a reward, or rather, for offending him, is not avarice, but suspicion, then both the people and prince merit an excuse of some sort. Of ingratitude arising from this cause, there are lots of examples one can read about, because that general who, by his valor [*virtuosamente*], has defeated the enemy and extended his lord's dominions, winning glory for himself and riches for his soldiers, will necessarily acquire such a great reputation with his troops, with the enemy, and with that prince's own subjects that his victory cannot help but be distasteful to the lord whose commands he was carrying out. And since it is the nature of men to be ambitious and suspicious and to be incapable of placing any limits on their fortunes, it is impossible that the suspicion, which is suddenly aroused in the prince after his general's victory, should not be increased by the insolence that might appear in some of the things he says or does. This being the case, the prince cannot think of anything other than his own security, and to achieve it, he will consider either having the man killed or depriving him of the reputation that he gained for himself with his army and with the people by using every means to show that the general's victory was not due to his valor [*virtù*], but to Fortune or the cowardice of

8. Tacitus, *Histories,* 4.3: "*Proclivius est iniuriae, quam beneficio vicem exsolvere, quia gratia oneri, ultio in quaestu habetur.*"

the enemy or the prudence of the other officers who were with him in that action.

After Vespasian was declared emperor by his army while he was in Judea, Antonius Primus, who was in Illyria with another army, took his side and marched into Italy against Vitellius, who was ruling in Rome, and with great valor [*virtuosissimamente*] routed two of Vitellius's armies and occupied Rome, so that Mutianus, who had been sent there by Vespasian, found that through Antonius's valor [*virtù*] everything had been acquired and all difficulties overcome. The reward that Antonius received for what he had done was that Mutianus immediately deprived him of his command of the army and reduced him step by step to a position in which he had no authority in Rome. In response, Antonius went off to find Vespasian, who was still in Asia, and Vespasian received him in such a way that in a short while he was left with no rank at all and died in despair.[9]

The histories are full of such examples. In our own times, everyone now living knows how much resourcefulness and valor [*virtù*] Gonsalvo Ferrante displayed when fighting in the Kingdom of Naples against the French on behalf of King Ferdinand of Aragon; how he defeated them and conquered the kingdom; and how the reward he got for his victory was that Ferdinand left Aragon, and having arrived in Naples, first he deprived Gonsalvo of his command of the army, then took his fortresses away from him, and finally brought him to Spain with him, where shortly afterwards, he died in disgrace.[1]

9. Machiavelli gets the information in this paragraph from Tacitus, *Histories,* 3 and 4. Vespasian (b. 9 CE; ruled 69–79 CE) was the last of the emperors in the Year of the Four Emperors. In June 68, after having sent Vespasian to put down a rebellion in Judea, the emperor Nero committed suicide, plunging Rome into civil war. Servius Sulpicius Galba (3 BCE–69 CE) emerged as his successor and ruled for seven months until January 69 CE, when he was killed by Marcus Salvius Otho (32–69). Otho ruled from January to April 69, when he committed suicide after his forces were defeated by those of Aulus Vitellius (15–69), who had been declared emperor by his legions in Germany in January and ruled from April to December 69. Vespasian (Titus Flavius Caesar Vespasianus) had been declared emperor by his legions in June 69. (Machiavelli has this happening in Judea, but the first of Vespasian's legions to declare him emperor were those in Alexandria, Egypt.) Vespasian was supported by Gaius Licinius Mucianus, who lived in the 1st century and probably died during Vespasian's reign, and by Marcus Antonius Primus (30/35–after 81 CE), and the latter led an army into Italy that defeated that of Vitellius in October 69, after which Antonius entered Rome in truimph. Vitellius was killed on December 22, 69, and Mucianus arrived the next day. According to Tacitus, Antonius was arrogant and behaved as though he were the emperor because of all his military successes. Mucianus knew about it and worried that Antonius was a threat to Vespasian. Consequently, after initially seeming to favor him, Mucianus finally deprived him of any sort of position of power, upon which Antonius went off to Vespasian's court, where his status decreased even further. Tacitus does not speak of Antonius's death.

1. Gonsalvo Fernández de Córdoba (1453–1515) fought in what is known as the Reconquista, in which the Spanish finally drove the Moors out of Spain in 1492. He then fought in Italy during several periods, the last one occurring between 1501 and 1503, during which he drove the French from the Kingdom of Naples and was made the viceroy of Naples in 1504. For his military victories he became known as the Gran Capitán, but Ferdinand II of Aragon was jealous of him, accused him of spending money from the public treasury on his soldiers, and recalled him to Spain in 1507, where he was publicly honored, but was given no further military assignments and died in relative obscurity from malaria in 1515.

This suspicion comes so naturally to princes that they cannot defend themselves against it, and thus it is impossible for them to show gratitude to those who, by the victories they achieved under their princes' banners, have made important conquests for them. And if a prince cannot defend himself from such ingratitude, it is not miraculous or worthy of further consideration if a people cannot defend itself from it. For a city that enjoys freedom has two goals: one is to enlarge its dominion; the other, to preserve its freedom. And it is natural for it to err in both cases out of excessive zeal. As for the errors made in enlarging its dominion, they will be discussed in their proper place. As for the errors made in preserving its freedom, they are, among others, the following: to injure those citizens whom it should reward; to suspect those in whom it should have confidence. And although these things occasion great evils in a republic that is already corrupt, and often hasten it down the path to tyranny—which happened under Caesar in Rome, who took for himself by force what ingratitude refused him—still, in a republic that is not corrupt, they are highly beneficial and enable it to preserve its freedom, since the fear of punishment makes men better and less ambitious for a longer period of time.

It is true that of all the peoples who have ever possessed an empire, Rome was the least ungrateful for the reasons discussed above, for it may be said that there is no example of its ingratitude other than that of Scipio, whereas Coriolanus and Camillus were both exiled on account of the injuries they had inflicted on the plebeians. The one was never pardoned, because he always maintained a hatred of the people; the other was not only recalled from exile, but for the entire remainder of his life was honored like a prince. But the ingratitude with which Scipio was treated arose from a suspicion the citizens began to have of him which they had not had of the others and which was due to the greatness of the enemy Scipio had defeated, to the reputation which his victory had earned him after so long and dangerous a war, to the speed with which he had earned it, to the favors which his youth, his prudence, and his other remarkable virtues [*virtudi*] had won for him. All of these were so great that, for no other reason, the magistrates of Rome feared his authority, something which displeased the wise men as something unheard of in Rome. And his way of living seemed so extraordinary that Cato the Elder, reputed a saint, was the first to go against him and to say that a city could not call itself free in which there was a citizen who was feared by the magistrates.[2] Thus, if the people of Rome followed the

2. Scipio defeated Hannibal in the final battle of the Punic Wars at Zama in 202 BCE, was given a triumph in Rome, and enjoyed great support among the people. (For more on Scipio, see n. 3, p. 120.) Nevertheless, Scipio and his brother Lucius were attacked by their enemies in the senate, led by Marcus Porcius Cato the Elder (234–195 BCE), also known as Cato the Wise, a staunch conservative. Accused of bribery and treason,

opinion of Cato, they are entitled to that excuse, which, as I said above, those peoples and princes may claim who are ungrateful because of their suspicions. Thus, in concluding this discourse, I say that insofar as this vice of ingratitude results from either avarice or suspicion, it will be seen that the people never fall into it because of avarice, and as far as suspicion is concerned, they do so far less than princes because they have less reason for suspicion. * * *

* * *

Chapter 34

The Authority of the Dictatores Was Beneficial, Not Injurious, to the Roman Republic; It Is the Authority That Citizens Usurp for Themselves, Not That Which Is Given to Them through Free Elections, That Is Harmful to Civic Life

Those Romans who invented the practice of creating *dictatores* have been condemned by a certain writer[3] because, over time, it led to tyranny in Rome. They allege that the first tyrant in that city governed it under the title of *dictator*[4] and say that if this office had not existed, Caesar would not have been able to make his tyranny seem honest under any other public title. The person who holds this view did not examine the matter very well, and it was totally unreasonable that it should have been believed. For it was neither the name nor the rank of the *dictator* that subjected Rome to servitude, but the authority citizens acquired because of the length of their rule. And if the title of *dictator* had not existed, they would have taken another one, for it is easy for power to acquire a title, but not for a title to acquire power.

Scipio expressed his displeasure at this ingratitude by retiring to his estate in 185 BCE and having his bones buried at Liternum rather than in Rome. Gaius Marcius Coriolanus (5th century BCE) was a Roman general who defeated the Volscians at the battle of Corioli (hence his sobriquet "Coriolanus"), but when he argued against the distribution of grain to the people during a famine a few years later unless laws empowering the plebeians were revoked, he was put on trial, convicted, and fled the city. Marcus Furius Camillus (c. 446–365 BCE) was a Roman general and statesman whose defeat of many of Rome's rival city-states made it the most powerful nation in central Italy. However, as a patrician, he opposed the interests of the plebeians, such as land redistribution, and after having been accused and convicted of embezzlement by his enemies, he went into voluntary exile in 394 BCE. When the Gauls invaded Italy and captured Rome in 390 BCE, Camillus was living in Ardea, and after putting together an army, he defeated the Gauls and was brought back to Rome. This victory earned Camillus the title of the "Second Romulus"—that is, the second founder of Rome. On Scipio, see Livy, *History of Rome,* 38.50–60; on Coriolanus, 2.33–40; and on Camillus, 5.10 and 6.4.

3. This person has not been identified. I have retained the Latin *dictator* (pl. *dictatores*) in this chapter, rather than translating it as "dictator," to avoid confusing the modern concept with the Roman one. In the course of the chapter, Machiavelli will describe the carefully delimited powers of the *dictator.*
4. The reference here is presumably to Lucius Cornelius Sulla Felix (see n. 4, p. 128). What Machiavelli is referring to here is that Sulla revived the office of *dictator,* which had not been filled since 202 BCE, and had himself named *dictator* in 82 or 81 BCE, but without the traditional time limit of six months being placed on his term in office.

It is clear that as long as the *dictator* was appointed according to public laws and not on his own authority, the office was beneficial to Rome. For republics are harmed when magistracies are created and authority is granted in extraordinary ways, not in ordinary ones, as was the case with Rome, where for a long period of time, no *dictator* did anything that was not beneficial to the Republic.

The reasons for this are very clear. First, in order for a citizen to be able to do harm and to obtain extraordinary authority, he must have many qualities which he can never have in a republic that remains uncorrupted, for he will need to be extremely rich and to have many followers and partisans, something he cannot have so long as the laws are being observed. And even if he had them, men of his sort are so frightening that people would not vote freely for them. Besides this, the *dictator* was appointed for a limited term, not in perpetuity, and only in order to deal with the issues because of which he was chosen. His authority was extensive, going so far as to enable him to decide by himself the remedies for the urgent danger they faced, to do everything without consulting anyone, and to punish people without the right to appeal. But he could do nothing to diminish the state, such as taking away the authority of the senate or the people, or abolishing the old institutions of the city and making new ones. So, when we add together the brief period during which he was *dictator*, the limited authority he possessed, and the fact that the Roman people were not corrupt, it was impossible for him to overstep the bounds imposed on him and to harm the city. Indeed, experience shows that the *dictator* always helped it.

And truly, compared with all the other Roman institutions, this one deserves to be considered as numbering among those to which the greatness of its vast empire was due, because without such an institution, it will be difficult for cities to extricate themselves from extraordinary situations. For the institutions normally found in republics function slowly, since they have no council or magistrate empowered to do everything on his own. Indeed, in many cases they actually have need of one another, and it takes time to harmonize their different views. Consequently, their remedies are very dangerous when they have to be used in a situation that does not brook delay.

Republics should therefore have a mechanism like this one among their institutions. And the Republic of Venice, which ranks high among modern republics, has reserved to a small group of citizens the authority to deal with urgent matters, and to do so, if they are all of one mind, without further consultations with any other body.[5]

5. Machiavelli is referring to the Council of Ten, created in 1310 to deal with a revolt and made a permanent fixture of the state in 1355.

For when a republic lacks such a mechanism, either it will inevitably come to ruin if it sticks to its constitution, or it will have to violate it in order to avoid being destroyed. And in a republic it is not desirable that anything should occur that would have to be managed by means of extraordinary measures. For even if an extraordinary measure should work well in one instance, it will still set a bad example, since it establishes the practice of violating the constitution for a good purpose, and that pretext will be used to violate it in the future for some bad one. Thus, a republic will never be perfect if it has not provided for every eventuality by means of its laws and has established a remedy and determined the way to apply it. And therefore I say in conclusion that those republics which, facing imminent peril, do not have recourse to a *dictator* or some similar authority, will always come to ruin when serious misfortunes occur.

With regard to this new institution, it should be noted how wisely the Romans provided a method to elect the *dictator*. Since his creation reflected badly on the consuls to some degree, in that they, though the heads of the state, had to submit to him and obey him just like everyone else, and since it was assumed that this might elicit contempt for them among the people, the Romans decided that the consuls should have the power to appoint him. They were thinking that, should something happen so that Rome needed such royal power, the consuls would have to make the appointments of their own accord, and since they did so themselves, it would be less painful for them. For the wounds and all the other evils that a man inflicts on himself spontaneously and by choice hurt a great deal less than those done to you by others. In later times, however, the Romans used to give such authority to a consul instead of a *dictator*, with the words: "Let the consul see that the republic is not harmed."[6]

And I will conclude by returning to our subject matter: it was Rome's neighbors who, seeking to crush the city, caused it to create institutions not only to defend itself, but to attack them with greater force, better counsel, and more authority.

* * *

6. Machiavelli is quoting in Latin the standard language used by the senate: "*Videat Consul, ne Respublica quid detrimenti capiat.*" For examples, see Livy, *History of Rome,* 3.4 and 6.19.

Chapter 37

What Troubles the Agrarian Law Gave Birth to in Rome, and How Very Much Trouble Is Created in a Republic by Making a Law That Is Retroactive and Contravenes an Ancient Custom of the City

According to a saying of ancient writers, men are accustomed to afflict themselves in evil times and to become weary with the good, and that both of these passions produce the same effects. For whenever men are not obliged to fight out of necessity, they do so out of ambition, which is so powerful in the human breast that it never abandons them, no matter what rank they ascend to. The reason for this is that nature has created men in such a way that they are able to desire everything, but unable to attain it, so that their desire is always greater than their ability to attain things, with the result that men are discontent with what they possess and dissatisfied with their situation. From this arise the changes in their fortune: since some of them desire to have more, and others are afraid to lose what they have acquired, enmities and wars ensue, and this brings about the ruin of one province and the elevation of another.

I have made these remarks because it was not enough for the Roman plebeians to have secured themselves against the nobility through the creation of the tribunes,[7] something which necessity forced them to ask for, but once they had obtained this, they began to fight with the nobility out of ambition and to seek a share of their honors and possessions as things men value more. From this was born the disease which gave birth to the conflict over the agrarian law,[8] and that, in the end, caused the destruction of the republic. And because well-ordered republics have to keep the public rich and their citizens poor, it was evident that this law in the city of Rome was defective: either it was not made at the beginning in such a way

7. Practically from its creation in 509 BCE, the Roman Republic was characterized by a constant struggle between the aristocrats, or patricians, who ruled the city through the senate, and the lower-class plebeians. The latter forced the creation of the office of Tribune of the Plebs in 494 BCE. These tribunes were almost always plebeians, and while there were initially just two of them, their number eventually rose to ten in 457, at which figure it remained for the rest of Roman history. Only the tribunes could convene a council of all the plebeians, and by the 3rd century BCE, its laws applied to all Roman citizens and the tribunes were also permitted to propose legislation to the senate. When Rome became an empire under Augustus, he was appointed tribune, as were all the emperors after him, so that the office lost most of its authority and power.

8. A set of reforms instituted by the tribunes Tiberius Sempronius Gracchus in 133 BCE and his brother, Gaius Sempronius Gracchus, in 122 BCE. The reforms limited the amount of public land one person could control—aristocrats often possessed vast amounts of it—and made that land available to plebeians, many of whom lived in the cities, for a low rent. The reforms of the Gracchi led to a century of civil war, which generally pitted representatives of the plebeians against the patricians, and which came to an end only with the creation of the Roman Empire under Augustus in 27 BCE.

that it did not need to be revised, or its creation was deferred for so long that it was obnoxious because its application seemed anachronistic, or it was well ordered at the start, but afterwards it had become corrupt in practice. No matter how it happened, whenever this law was discussed in Rome, everything got turned topsy-turvy in that city.

The law had two main parts: the first provided that no citizen could possess more than so many acres of land; the other, that all the lands that were taken from their enemies should be divided among the Roman people. This thus gave offense to the nobility in two different ways, for those who possessed more territory than the law permitted—which was the case with the greater part of the nobility—had to deprived of it, and by dividing the enemy's goods among the plebeians, it took away the nobility's means to enrich itself. Therefore, since these offenses affected powerful men and it seemed to them that to resist the law was to defend the common good, whenever the subject was brought up, the entire city was turned topsy-turvy, as was said, and the nobles, acting patiently and resourcefully, would put it off, either by calling out an army, or by getting another tribune to oppose the one who was proposing it, or sometimes by making a partial concession, or again by sending a colony to the place where the land was to be distributed. This happened with regard to the lands about Antium which had given rise to a dispute over the law, because a colony, drawn from Rome, was sent there, and the lands were assigned to it. In reference to this, Titus Livy makes a remark worth noting, for he says that it was difficult to find those in Rome who would put down their names to go to that colony, for the plebeians were so much readier to express their desire for things in Rome than to take possession of them in Antium.[9]

This disposition toward the law went on causing trouble in Rome for a time, until the Romans began leading their armies into the farthest reaches of Italy or beyond, after which it seemed that things had calmed down. The reason for this is that the lands possessed by the enemies of Rome were far away from where the plebeians lived and in a location where it was not easy to cultivate them, so that the plebeians were less interested in having them. Moreover, the Romans were less inclined to punish their enemies in this manner, and when they did deprive a city of the lands around it, they distributed them among their colonists. Thus, for these reasons, the agrarian law lay dormant, as it were, up to the time of the Gracchi, who awoke it, and it completely ruined Roman liberty. For the city found that the

9. Machiavelli is paraphrasing Livy's *History of Rome* here: "*Cetera multitudo poscere Romae agrum malle quam alibi accipere*" (3.1.7: The rest of the people preferred to ask for lands in Rome than to accept them elsewhere).

power of the adversaries within it had doubled, and as a result, such hatred between the plebs and the senate was set ablaze that it led to armed conflict and bloodshed that went beyond all bounds and all civil customs. Thus, since the public magistrates were unable to find a remedy for the situation, and none of the factions had any confidence in them, people had recourse to private remedies, and each of the parties decided to look for a leader who would defend it. In this scandalous, disorderly situation, the plebeians staked their reputation on Marius, going so far as to make him consul four times, and as his consulship continued with only a few short interruptions, he was able to have himself made consul another three times. The nobility, having no remedy for this plague, bestowed its favor on Sulla, and when they had made him the head of their party, civil war broke out, and after much bloodshed and many changes in their fortune, the nobility came out on top.[1] These animosities were revived in the time of Caesar and Pompey. For when Caesar had made himself the leader of Marius's party, and Pompey, the leader of Sulla's,[2] they came to blows, and Caesar, having emerged victorious, became the first tyrant in Rome, with the result that afterwards the city was never free again.

Such was the beginning and the ending of the agrarian law. Elsewhere we have shown that the enmity between the senate and the people of Rome kept the city free because it gave rise to laws in favor

1. On the rivalry of Marius and Sulla, see n. 4, p. 128. Note that Marius was elected consul in 107, 104, 103, 102, 101, 100, and finally in 88 BCE. Sulla was also consul in 88 as well as in 80, and dictator in 81 BCE. In 88 BCE, the senate chose Sulla to lead an army to fight in the east, but Marius, who was then quite old, nevertheless wanted the position for himself, got a tribune to call an assembly of the plebeians, and was appointed to the position Sulla held. Sulla had not yet left Italy and returned to Rome, leading the first Roman army ever to defy custom and tradition by invading the city. He defeated Marius's forces and entered Rome. He then returned to his mission in the east where he waged a series of successful campaigns between 87 and 83 BCE. In his absence, Marius returned to Rome in 87 BCE, enacted reprisals on Sulla's followers, and was elected consul; however, he died early the following year. Sulla made a second march on the city after his return to Italy, defeating the forces of those who supported a more popular government in 82 BCE, after which he was made dictator, a position giving him virtually absolute authority. He then instituted a series of reforms to curb the power of the plebeians and ensure the ultimate control of the state by the senate. He retired from his position and from public life in general in 81 BCE, dying three years later at the age of sixty.
2. Pompey (Gnaeus Pompeius Magnus, 106–48 BCE) was an enormously successful Roman general who was elected consul at a young age and in 60 BCE entered into an alliance, known as the First Triumvirate, with Gnaeus Julius Caesar (100–44 BCE) and Marcus Licinius Crassus (c. 115–53 BCE). The alliance was sealed in part by the marriage of Caesar's daughter Julia to Pompey, but when she died in 54 BCE, and Crassus died the next year, the two remaining members of the Triumvirate fell out with one another and fought a protracted civil war in which Pompey allied himself with the Roman patricians and Caesar, with the plebeians. The war ended in 48 BCE with Pompey's defeat at the battle of Pharsalus in southern Thessaly, after which he fled to Egypt, where he was assassinated at the orders of Ptolemy XIII. Caesar spent the next four years mopping up lingering groups of Pompey's supporters until he became, in effect, the sole leader of Rome. In 44 BCE, on the Ides of March (March 15), Caesar was, of course, assassinated by Brutus, Cassius, and other senators who feared he was going to become the new king of Rome, and he was replaced by the Second Triumvirate, who defeated his assassins and then split into a rivalry between Marc Antony and Octavius. The latter eventually emerged the winner and became the first Roman emperor in 27 BCE.

of liberty.[3] And although that the results of this agrarian law may seem incompatible with such a conclusion, let me say that I am not, on this account, going to change my opinion, for the ambition of the nobility is so great that if it is not repressed by various ways and means in any city, that city will soon be brought to ruin. Hence, if the struggle over the agrarian law took three hundred years to lead Rome into a condition of servitude, it would perhaps have been brought there sooner if the plebeians had not, by means of this law and their other demands, always kept the ambition of the nobility in check.

This also shows how much more men value possessions than honors. For in matters of honor, the Roman nobility always gave way to the plebeians without causing serious difficulties, but when it was a matter of possessions, so great was its obstinacy in defending them that the plebeians, in order to satisfy their appetite, had recourse to those extraordinary measures described above. The chief promoters of this disorder were the Gracchi, whose intentions were more praiseworthy than their prudence. For to seek to remove a disorder which has grown inveterate in a republic by enacting a law that is too retrospective is a poorly thought-out way to proceed, and as has been discussed at length above, only serves to hasten your way to that evil to which that disorder is leading you, whereas by temporizing, that end will come later on, or it will, over time, be extinguished all by itself before it reaches its goal.

* * *

Chapter 58

The Masses Are Wiser and More Constant Than a Prince

Nothing is more vain and inconstant than the masses,[4] as our Titus Livy, like all the other historians, affirms. For in the stories of the actions men have performed, one often sees how the masses have condemned someone to death, and that afterwards the very same people have wept for him and ardently wished he were alive. This is what the Roman people did in the case of Manlius Capitolinus, for they condemned him to death and then ardently wished he were alive. And these are the author's words: "The people were immediately filled with desire for him as soon as he was no longer a danger to them."[5] And elsewhere, when he relates the events that occurred in Sicily

3. Machiavelli did this in the fourth chapter of this book.
4. See n. 4, p. 110.
5. Livy, *History of Rome*, 6.20: "*Populum brevi, posteaquam abeo periculum nullum erat, desiderium eius tenuit.*" In 390 (or 387) BCE, the half-legendary Marcus Manlius Capitolinus supposedly repulsed the Gauls, who had captured Rome, from the Capitoline Hill (hence his nickname "Capitolinus") after being awakened to the danger by Juno's geese. He was put to death in 384 BCE because of his tyrannical ambitions.

after the death of Hieronymus, the grandson of Hieron, he says: "It is the nature of the masses either to serve obsequiously or to rule with arrogance."[6] In undertaking to defend a position which, as I have said, all the writers attack, I do not know if I am taking on a task that is so hard and full of difficulties that I will either have to abandon it with shame or to go forward weighed down by this heavy burden. But however that may be, I do not think, nor will I ever think, that it is wrong to defend an opinion with rational arguments, as long as one has no intention of appealing to authority or employing force.

Let me say, then, that all men, and especially princes, can be blamed individually for having the same fault for which writers criticize the unbridled masses, for whoever is not controlled by the laws would make the same errors as they do. And this is easy to see, for there are, and have been, a great many princes, but of good and wise ones, there have been only a few. I am speaking of princes who have been able to break the bonds that could have held them in check. Among them I do not count those kings who were born in Egypt, when, in the most ancient period of antiquity, that country was governed by laws; or the kings who were born in Sparta; or those of our times who have been born in France, a kingdom which is regulated more by the laws than any other of which we have any knowledge at present. And those kings who were born under such constitutions should not be placed in the same group as those whose natures we have to consider individually to see if they are similar to the masses. Rather, they should be compared to a people who are controlled by the laws in the same way as those kings are, and we will find in those people the same good qualities as in those kings, and we will see that they neither rule with arrogance nor serve obsequiously.

Such were the people of Rome, who, so long as the republic remained uncorrupted, neither served obsequiously nor ruled arrogantly, but rather, having its own laws and magistrates, it honorably maintained its position in society. And when it was necessary to unite and move against some powerful man, it would do so, as it did against Manlius, the Decemvirate, and others who sought to oppress it,[7] and when, for the sake of the public good, it was necessary to

6. Livy, *History of Rome,* 24.25: "*Haec natura multitudinis est: aut humuliter servit, aut superbe dominatur.*" For Hieron, see *The Prince,* n. 1, p. 19. Hieronymus (231–214 BCE) succeeded Hieron II to the throne of Syracuse in 215 BCE when he was merely sixteen. A weak and dissolute character, he was persuaded to break the traditional alliance his city had with the Romans to support the Carthaginians and was about to lead an army into the field to assist them when he was assassinated in 214.

7. According to Roman history, in 450 BCE all regular magistracies were suspended and replaced by a group of ten men called the Decemvirate (from *decem,* "ten," and *viri,* "men"). This group was largely made up of former consuls and was charged with rewriting the Roman law code. It was appointed for one year and was succeeded by a second group in 449. That second group wanted to extend its powers and prolong its term in office, and it is that group that the Roman plebeians resisted.

obey the *dictatores* and the consuls, it would do so. And if the Roman people wanted Manlius Capitolinus back after his death, that is no wonder, for they wanted his virtues [*virtù*], which had been such that the memory of them aroused compassion in everyone, and they would have had the power to produce the same effect in a prince, for all writers agree that virtue [*virtù*] is to be praised and admired even in one's enemies. And if Manlius had been resuscitated in response to such a desire, the Roman people would have pronounced the same judgment on him that they did when they took him from prison and, a little after that, condemned him to death, although one also finds some reputedly wise princes who have had people put to death and then deeply longed for them, as Alexander did for Cleitus and other friends of his, and Herod did for Mariamne.[8] What our historian says about the nature of the masses, however, he is not saying about those who are controlled by the laws, as the Romans were, but about the undisciplined ones, such as the Syracusans, who made the kind of errors men make when they are infuriated and unrestrained, just as Alexander the Great and Herod did in the examples mentioned above. Therefore, the nature of the masses is not more reprehensible than that of princes, for all do wrong in the same way when there is nothing to prevent them from doing so. There are a great many examples of this in addition to those I have mentioned, both among the Roman emperors and among other tyrants and princes, in whom one finds as much inconstancy and changeability in behavior as would ever be found in any people.

I thus arrive at a conclusion contrary to the common opinion, which says that the people, when they are in power, are variable, unstable, and ungrateful, affirming that these defects are in no way different in them than they are in individual princes. And anyone who blames both peoples and princes alike could be speaking the truth, but by excepting princes, he deceives himself, for a people that rules and is well-ordered will be stable, prudent, and grateful in much the same way as a prince is, or it will be even better than a prince, even one who is considered wise; and on the other hand, a prince unrestrained by the laws will be ungrateful, fickle, and imprudent more than the people are. Nor does the difference in their behavior derive from a difference in their nature, for that is the same in everyone—and if there is a positive advantage here, it lies with the people—but rather, the difference between them is due to their

8. Alexander the Great (356–323 BCE) did not tolerate criticism at court. When his friend Cleitus (d. 328 BCE) criticized him at a banquet, Alexander killed him in a drunken fury, and then later regretted it. Herod the Great (c. 73–4 BCE) ruled over Judea and other areas of Palestine under the Romans. Toward the end of his life he became increasingly savage toward members of his own family, and in 7 BCE, he had his favorite wife, Mariamne, and her two sons executed.

having more or less respect for the laws under which both of them live.

Anyone who studies the Roman people will see that for four hundred years they hated the very name of king and loved the glory and the common good of their country, and he will find many examples in them that bear witness to both characteristics. And should anyone allege the ingratitude they displayed toward Scipio, I will reply with what I said earlier, and at length, about this subject, where I showed that the people are less ungrateful than princes.[9] But as regards prudence and stability, I say that the people are more prudent and more stable, and display better judgment than a prince. And not without reason is the voice of a people compared to that of God,[1] for popular opinion has been seen to prognosticate events in so wonderful a manner that it seems as if they foresee the evil and the good that may befall them by means of some occult power [*virtù*]. As for judging things, it is exceedingly rare that, when they hear two orators of equal talent [*virtù*] advocating different alternatives, we see them fail to choose the better opinion and show themselves incapable of discerning the truth in what they hear. And if they do err in matters involving questions of courage or utility, as has been said above, a prince often errs, too, where his passions are concerned, for they are much greater than those of the people. It is also evident that in the election of magistrates they make far better choices than a prince does, nor will the people ever be persuaded that it is good to put in public office a man of bad repute and corrupt habits, whereas a prince is easily persuaded to do that in a thousand different ways. When the people begin to have a horror of something, one sees that they stick to this opinion for many centuries, a thing never seen in the case of a prince. And on both of these points I will let the Roman people suffice as proof, for in so many hundreds of years and so many elections of consuls and tribunes, they did not make four choices of which they had to repent. And they had, as I have said, so much hatred for the name of king that no sense of obligation for services rendered by any citizen who was seeking that title could allow him to escape the punishment he deserved. Furthermore, we see that cities in which the people are the master vastly expand their territory in a very short time, and much more than do those which have always been under a prince, as Rome did after the

9. See Book 1, Chapter 29 (pp. 130–33).
1. Machiavelli translates here the Latin saying *Vox populi, vox Dei:* the voice of the people is the voice of God. The phrase can be traced back to the English clergyman and scholar Alcuin of York (c. 735–804), who used it in a letter to Charlemagne in 739, warning him against such a democratic idea. The phrase began circulating widely in a positive sense during the 18th century, although Machiavelli's allusion to it here anticipates that transformation just as Machiavelli's *Discourses* generally anticipates the republicanism of many 17th- and 18th-century thinkers.

expulsion of the kings, and Athens after it freed itself from Peisistratos.[2] This cannot arise from anything other than the fact that the governments of the people are better than those of princes.

Nor do I wish anyone to cite in opposition to this opinion of mine what our historian says in the text cited earlier, or in any other one, for if we consider all the disorders caused by the people and all the disorders caused by princes, all the glories of the people and all those of princes, it will be seen that the people are far superior in goodness and in glory. And if princes are superior to the people in instituting laws, forming civil societies, and establishing statutes and new institutions, the people are so superior in maintaining what has been established that they, without a doubt, add to the glory of those who established them.

And in short, to conclude this subject, I say that just as princely states have lasted a very long time, so, too, have republics, and both needed to be regulated by the laws, for a prince who can do whatever he wants is mad, and a people that can do whatever it wants is hardly wise. If we are speaking, therefore, about a prince who is bound by the laws and about a people that is chained up by them, more virtue [*virtù*] will be seen in the people than in the prince; if we are speaking about both of them released from that control, fewer errors will be seen in the people than in the prince, and they will be less serious and will be easier to remedy. For a good man can speak to a licentious and disorderly people and easily lead it back to the right road, whereas no one can speak to a wicked prince, nor is there any remedy for him except the sword. From this one can conjecture about the seriousness of the maladies of both: if words suffice to cure the malady of the people, and if the sword is necessary for that of the prince, no one will fail to conclude that where the cure is greater, there the defects are greater. When a people is truly unrestrained, one need not fear the follies it commits; nor is one afraid of present evils, but of what can arise from them, since a tyrant might appear in the midst of so much confusion. But the contrary is the case with wicked princes: one fears present evils while feeling hope for the future, since men persuade themselves that the ruler's wicked life may lead to a resurgence of freedom. Thus you see the difference between the two, which is that between what is and what is likely to be. The cruelties of the masses are directed against those they fear will take over the common good; those of a prince are against people he fears will take over his own property.[3] But the prejudice against

2. See n. 5, pp. 128–29.
3. English cannot capture the clever verbal contrast here between "take over the common good" (*occupi il bene comune*) and "take over his own property" (*occupi il bene proprio*): when *bene* is modified by *comune,* it becomes "the common good" (or, the public interest); when it is modified by *proprio,* it becomes the good that belongs to the prince—namely the property or the possessions he owns.

the people derives from the fact that everyone can speak evil of the people freely and fearlessly, even while they are ruling, but of princes one always speaks with a thousand fears and hesitations. Nor does it seem to me to be inconsistent with my purpose, since this subject leads me to it, to discuss in the following chapter which confederations can be trusted more, those made with a republic, or those made with a prince.

Chapter 59

Which Confederation or League Can Be Trusted More, One Made with a Republic, or One Made with a Prince

It happens on a daily basis that a prince will form a league or an alliance with another prince, or a republic with another republic, and similarly, that a confederation and accord will be formed by a republic and a prince, and so, it seems to me that I should examine which agreement is the more stable and the more to be relied on, the one made by a republic, or the one made by a prince. In examining the whole subject, I believe that in many instances they are similar, and in others there are certain differences. Furthermore, I believe that neither a prince nor a republic will honor agreements with you that are imposed by force; I believe that when they come to fear for their state, in order to avoid losing it, both of them will break their faith with you and treat you with ingratitude. Demetrius, the one who was called the Conqueror of Cities,[4] had conferred countless benefits on the Athenians: when he was later defeated by his enemies and sought refuge in Athens as though it were a friendly city under obligation to him, it refused to receive him, which gave him much more pain than the loss of his troops and his army. Pompey, after his defeat by Caesar in Thessaly, took refuge in Egypt with Ptolemy, whom on a former occasion he had reinstated in his kingdom, and who put him to death.[5] Such things as these had the same causes, but nevertheless, it is clear that the republic acted with more humanity and inflicted less of an injury than the prince.

Where there is fear, therefore, one will find, in fact, this same kind of loyalty. And if one discovers either a republic or a prince that would be faithful to you even at the risk of ruin, this, too, may be

4. Demetrius I (337–283 BCE) ruled Macedonia from 294 to 288 BCE. He was given the sobriquet of Poliorcetes, "the Besieger," because of the ingenious siege weapons he invented when he was fighting in Rhodes. He had freed the Athenians from the power of the Ptolemies in 307 BCE and ruled the city for a while, but when he lost a major battle in 301 BCE, the Athenians refused to let him enter the city. On his life, see Plutarch's *Life of Demetrius*.

5. On these details from Pompey's life, see n. 2, p. 138. Note that Pompey had not assisted Ptolemy XIII, but his father, Ptolemy XII, to recover his throne in Egypt. Machiavelli confuses the two figures.

due to similar causes. And as for the prince, it may well be that he is the ally of a powerful ruler who does not have an opportunity to defend him at that moment, but who, the prince may hope, will reinstate him in his principality over time; or he may truly believe that, since he has followed that ruler as his partisan, that ruler will never make treaties or enter into alliances with the prince's enemies. Such was the fate of the princes of the Kingdom of Naples who adhered to the French party.[6] And as for republics, this was the lot of Saguntum in Spain that expected its ruin for having adhered to the Roman side, as did Florence for having adhered to the French side in 1512.[7] And if everything is taken into account, I believe that in such cases, where there is imminent danger, republics will be found to be somewhat more reliable than princes.

* * *

BOOK 2

Preface

Men always praise ancient times and find fault with the present, though often without reason, and they are such partisans of things past that not only do they celebrate those ages that they know from the accounts that historians have left of them, but also those that as old men they recall having seen in their youth. And if this opinion of theirs is false, as it is most of the time, I am persuaded that there are various causes that lead them into this illusion. The first, I believe, is that we never fully understand the truth about the past and that writers very frequently conceal things that would disgrace their age, while magnifying and presenting in full detail those that would bestow glory on it. For the majority of writers follow the fortunes of the winners so obsequiously that, in order to render their victories glorious, they not only exaggerate what those men accomplished by means of their prowess [*virtuosamente*], but also embellish the actions of their enemies, so that anyone born afterward in either one of the two countries, whether that of the victors or that of the defeated, will have cause to marvel at those men and those times and be forced to praise them and admire them to the utmost.

6. In the war between France and Spain over Naples in 1503–04, a number of Neapolitan noblemen who allied themselves to the French were imprisoned by Gonsalvo da Cortona, the Spanish captain, and were left to their fate when a truce was signed later.
7. Saguntum remained loyal to Rome during the First Punic War and was captured and destroyed by Hannibal in 218 BCE. On this point, see Livy, *History of Rome*, 21.5–16. Florence had allied itself with the French, but in 1512 was captured by Spanish troops, who restored the Medici to power.

Moreover, given that men hate things out of fear or envy, two very powerful reasons for hating things in the past are eliminated, for it cannot inspire either apprehension or envy. But it is very different with the affairs of the present, in which we are either actors or spectators, and of which we have a full understanding, in that nothing about them is concealed from us, and since you see the good in them along with other things that are unattractive, you are forced to conclude that the present is inferior to the past, even though present things may be much more worthy of glory and renown. I do not speak about matters pertaining to the arts, which shine with such intrinsic merit that time can hardly take away or give them more glory than they possess in themselves. Rather, I speak about such things as pertain to the lives and customs of men about which we do not possess such clear evidence.

In response, therefore, I say that although this custom of praising and blaming, which I have written about above, does exist, it is not always the case that it is mistaken. Sometimes the judgment involved cannot help but be correct, since human affairs, being in a state of perpetual movement, are always either rising or falling. And so, we see one city or country with a government that has been well organized by some man of distinction, and for a time, thanks to the talents [*virtù*] of its founder, it progresses, getting better and better. Now, if a person who is born in such a state should praise the past more than modern world, he deceives himself, and his deception is caused by the things said above. But as for those who are born later on in that city or country, when the time has arrived for it to begin its decline, then they are not deceiving themselves.[1]

And thinking about how these things happen, it is my belief that the world has always been in the same condition and that there has always been as much good as bad in it, but the bad and the good vary from country to country, as we learn from those ancient kingdoms that differed from one another in their customs, while the world always stayed the same. The only difference is that whereas the world had first placed all its virtue [*virtù*] in Assyria, it then put it in Media, afterwards in Persia, until it finally arrived in Italy and Rome; and if, after the Roman empire, no empire succeeded it that lasted for any length of time, and there was no place in which the world kept all of its virtues [*virtù*] together, we nevertheless see that they have been scattered among many nations where people live virtuously [*virtuosamente*], as was the case with the kingdom of the French, the kingdom of the Turks, and that of the Sultan, and today

1. Machiavelli rehearses his theory of governmental cycles, based on the ancient Greek historian Polybius, in 1.2, pp. 109–11.

among the people of Germany, and earlier with that Saracen tribe[2] which, having destroyed the Eastern Roman Empire, accomplished so many great things and occupied so large a part of the world. After the Fall of Rome, then, in all of these countries and in all of these peoples, there has been, and still is in some parts of them, the virtue [*virtù*] that people long for and that is given such honest praise. Those who are born in those countries and praise times past more than the present may be deceiving themselves, but those who have been born in Italy and Greece—not someone who has become a supporter in Italy of those who have come from beyond the mountains, or turned Turk in Greece—those people have good reason to find fault with their own times and to praise others. For in those other times there are a great many things that make those countries seem marvelous, whereas in these times there is nothing that redeems them from all the extremes of misery, infamy, and reproach, for there is no observance of religion in them, or concern for the laws, or interest in military matters—instead, they are stained by filth of every sort. And these vices are all the more detestable as they are more likely to be found in those who preside over tribunals, command everyone else, and wish to be adored.

But to return to our argument, I say that if men's judgment is defective in deciding whether the present century or antiquity is better with regard to those things which, because of their antiquity, we cannot have such complete knowledge of as we do of our own times, then that ability should not be defective in old men when they are judging the times of their youth and their old age, since they have known and observed both the former and the latter equally. This would be true if men always judged in the same way and had the same appetites at all times in their lives, but since these vary, even though the times do not, things will not seem the same to men who have other appetites, other pleasures, and other concerns when they are old than they did in their youth. For as men age, they lose their vigor, while their judgment and prudence improve, so that the same things that seemed good and tolerable in their youth must, of necessity, become bad and insupportable when they are old, and where they ought to blame their judgment for this, they blame the times. Besides, as the appetites of humans are insatiable—for they get from nature the capacity and the will to desire everything, and from Fortune the ability to obtain very little—the result is a constant discontent in men's minds and a

2. The Turks who completed their conquest of the Byzantine Empire by taking Constantinople in 1453 and then continued to spread into the Balkan peninsula and elsewhere over the next three centuries. The Sultan here is the sultan of Egypt. Machiavelli is referring to the Mamelukes, a dynasty of warrior-princes who ruled Egypt as sultans from the 13th century until they were displaced by the Turks in 1517.

weariness with the things they do possess, which makes them fault the present, praise the past, and long for the future, even though they have no reasonable motive to do so.

I do not know if I deserve to be numbered among those men who deceive themselves since in these discourses of mine I praise the times of the ancient Romans too much while finding fault with our own. And truly, if the virtue [*virtù*] that ruled then and the vice that rules now were not clearer than the sun, I would be more restrained in speaking, fearful of falling into the same deception for which I blame others. But the matter being so manifest that everyone sees it, I shall be bold and say clearly what I think about ancient times as well as about the present, so that the minds of the young men who will read my writings may be able to avoid the latter and prepare themselves to imitate the former whenever Fortune may present them with the opportunity to do so. For it is the duty of a good man to teach others about the good things which you yourself have not been able to put into effect because of the malignity of the times and of Fortune, so that among so many capable people, one of them who is more beloved of Heaven will be able to make those changes. * * *

* * *

Chapter 13

That Fraud Will Serve a Man Better Than Force to Rise from a Base Condition and Achieve a Great Fortune

I believe it to be unequivocally true that men of low station rarely, if ever, happen to achieve elevated positions without having recourse to force and fraud, unless they get the position that someone else has achieved as a gift or an inheritance. Nor do I believe that force alone will ever be seen as sufficient, although it will be found that fraud is enough all by itself, as anyone will see clearly who reads the life of Philip of Macedonia, that of Agathocles of Sicily,[3] and those of many other similar men who from the lowest, or at any rate, from a low, station have acquired either a kingdom or very large empires. Xenophon shows us in his *Life of Cyrus* how necessary deception is: considering that the first expedition he has Cyrus make against the king of Armenia is replete with fraud and that he has him use deception and not force in order to take possession of that

3. Agathocles of Syracuse, here called Agathocles of Sicily (361–289 BCE), came to power in 316, thanks to a military coup; in *The Prince*, Machiavelli says he was the son of a potter, although his father was actually the wealthy owner of a pottery factory (see n. 2, p. 27). As a youth, Philip II of Macedonia (382–336 BCE) had been held as a hostage in Thebes, but he received a good education there and eventually returned to Macedonia in 364 and was the architect of its expansion into an empire.

kingdom,[4] he draws no other conclusion from such actions than that it is necessary for a prince who wants to achieve great things to use deception. Xenophon also has Cyrus practice a variety of deceptions upon Cyaxares, king of the Medes,[5] his maternal uncle, and he shows that without that fraud Cyrus could never have attained that greatness which he finally did. Nor do I believe that there was ever a man placed in a low station who acquired a great empire by the use of naked force alone and without resorting to guile, whereas there are many who have succeeded by fraud alone, as did Giovanni Galeazzo Visconti, who took the state and the sovereignty of Lombardy from his uncle, Messer Bernabò.[6]

Moreover, that which princes are obliged to do when they start expanding their realms, republics are also obliged to do until they have become powerful enough so that force alone is sufficient. And as Rome, whether by chance or by choice, used all means necessary in every instance to attain greatness, she did not fail to use this one, too. Nor could she have employed a greater kind of deception at the start than by taking the course we described above of making other peoples her allies, for under this name she made them her slaves, as she did with the Latins and the other peoples around her.[7] For first, she availed herself of their armies in order to subdue neighboring peoples and to acquire a reputation for herself as a state; then, once they were subdued, she became so great that she could beat everyone. And the Latins never realized that they were totally enslaved until they had seen Rome defeat the Samnites twice and force them to make peace.[8] As this victory greatly increased the reputation of the Romans with far-off princes, who came to know Rome by name without having had any experience of her arms, so it generated envy and apprehension in those who both heard about and felt the weight of those arms—and among them were the Latins. Indeed, this envy and this fear were so powerful that not only the Latins, but the colonies that the Romans had established in Latium, together with the Campanians, whom the Romans had defended just before then, conspired against the Roman nation. And the Latins started this war in

4. On Cyrus and the king of Armenia, see Xenophon, *Cyropaedia,* 1.6, 2.4–3.1, 4.1, and 5.5. Xenophon's work had been translated into Latin by the humanist Poggio Bracciolini in the 15th century, and that is the version Machiavelli most likely read. Here he is, perhaps deliberately, misremembering Xenophon, who says Cyrus engaged in deception only when on military campaigns.
5. See *Cyropaedia,* 4.5.8–34.
6. Giovanni (Gian) Galeazzo Visconti (1351–1402) inherited Pavia in 1378 from his father; in 1385, assassinated his uncle, with whom he had been the joint ruler of Milan; and in 1395 was made duke of Milan by the Holy Roman Emperor.
7. In 2.4, Machiavelli praises Rome for contracting alliances with various peoples in the Italian peninsula, using them in its wars of expansion, but always making sure that it controlled its "allies."
8. The Samnites were defeated twice during 343 BCE in Campania, first at Mount Gaurus and then near the town of Suessala; see Livy, *History of Rome,* 7.32–33, 37–38.

the way most wars are begun, as we have shown above, not by attacking the Romans, but by defending the Sidicini from the Samnites who were waging war against them with the permission of the Romans. And the truth is that the Latins started this war because they had become aware of the Romans' deception, as Titus Livy shows us, when, at the Latins' council, he puts these words into the mouth of the Praetor Annius Setinus: "For if even now we can endure servitude under the cover of a treaty of equals," etc.[9] Thus we see that in their initial expansion the Romans did not fail to use fraud, which those who wish to climb from humble beginnings to sublime heights must always employ, and which is less to be condemned the more it is concealed, as this was by the Romans.

* * *

Chapter 29

Fortune Blinds Men's Minds When She Does Not Wish Them to Oppose Her Designs

If one observes carefully the course of human affairs, one will often notice that events and accidents occur for which the heavens did not wish us to make any provision at all. And if the kind of events to which I am referring happened in Rome, where there was so much virtue [*virtù*], so much religion, and such order, it is no wonder that similar things occur much more frequently in a city or a province that lacks the positive attributes I just mentioned. And because the case in point is quite remarkable for demonstrating the power heaven has over human affairs, Titus Livy relates it at length and most effectively.[1] He says that since heaven wanted the Romans, for whatever reason, to know its power, first it caused the Fabii, when they were sent as ambassadors to the Gauls, to make a serious error, so that what they did excited the Gauls to wage war on Rome. Then it ordained that nothing worthy of the Roman people should be done in Rome to oppose that war, for it earlier arranged things so that Camillus, who might have been the sole remedy for so great an evil, should have been sent into exile in Ardea. And afterwards, although

9. Livy, *History of Rome,* 8.4.2: "*Nam si etiam nunc sub umbra foederis aequi servitutem pati possumus,* etc." Machiavelli discussed the way that the Latins brought about this war in 2.9.

1. See Livy, *History of Rome,* 5.35–37, 48–55. Machiavelli goes on to rehearse Livy's account of how the Gauls, having been invited into Italy, were in the town of Clusium in the northeastern part of the peninsula when, in 391 BCE, Quintus Fabius Ambustus and two of his brothers were sent to negotiate their withdrawal. Instead, the brothers violated protocol by fighting the Gauls. Upon returning to Rome, they were elected to lead Rome's army, but at the river Allia they were defeated by the Gauls who then proceeded to sack the city. On Camillus and his subsequent defeat of the Gauls, see n. 2, pp. 132–33.

the Romans had often created *dictatores* as a remedy to check the assaults of their enemies, including the Volscians and other neighboring peoples, they failed to do so when the Gauls were marching on Rome. Moreover, in levying soldiers, they displayed such a lack of zeal and diligence, and were so slow in taking up arms that they barely arrived in time to encounter the Gauls at the river Allia, ten miles outside of Rome. Here the tribunes set up their camp without any of their usual diligence, not inspecting the site first, not surrounding it with a ditch and a stockade, and not availing themselves of any remedy, human or divine, for the situation. And in setting things up for the battle, they spread their ranks thin, weakening them so that neither the soldiers nor their captains were doing anything worthy of Roman discipline. Then they fought without loss of blood because they fled before they were attacked, and the greater part of the army went off to Veii, while the rest retreated to Rome, where, without stopping at their homes, they made straight for the Capitol. And they did it in such a way that the senate, without giving a thought to defending Rome, did not even close its gates, and part of them fled and part of them entered the Capitol with the others. Still, in defending the Capitol, their methods were not entirely disorderly, for they did not crowd it with useless people, and they stored all the grain there that they could in order to be able to survive a siege. And as for the useless crowd of old people, women, and children, the majority fled to neighboring towns, while the remainder stayed in Rome, a prey to the Gauls. Thus, anyone who had read about what that people had done so many years before and then read about them in this period could not possibly have believed that they were the same people. And after describing all the disorders noted above, Titus Livy concludes by saying: "Fortune blinds men's minds to such an extent when she does not want them to check her growing power."[2]

Nothing could be truer than this conclusion: men who ordinarily experience either great adversity or great prosperity deserve less praise or less blame, for one generally sees that they have been brought to ruin or were enabled to achieve greatness through some significant advantage that the heavens have provided them, thereby either giving them the opportunity to act effectively [*virtuosamente*], or taking it away from them. Fortune does this well: when she wants to accomplish great things, she selects a man who has so much courage and so much ability [*virtù*] that he will recognize the opportunities she places before him. And in the same way, when she wishes to bring about some great ruin, she puts forward men who will

2. Livy, *History of Rome*, 5.37.1: "*Adeo obcaecat animos fortuna, cum vim suam ingruentem refringi non vult.*"

contribute to it. And if there is anyone who is capable of opposing her, she either kills him or deprives him of the means to do anything of worth.

We certainly see from this passage how, in order to enhance Rome's power and lead it to the greatness it achieved, Fortune deemed it necessary to beat it down (as we will discuss at length at the start of the next book). She did not want to ruin it entirely, however, and for this purpose we see that she had Camillus exiled but not killed; had Rome captured but not the Capitol; prevented the Romans from thinking of anything worthwhile for the protection of the city, but then made sure they did not overlook anything of value for the sake of defending the Capitol. In order to ensure that Rome would be taken, she caused the majority of the soldiers who were defeated at Allia to go to Veii, thus cutting off any way to defend the city of Rome. And in arranging all this, she was preparing everything for Rome's recovery, for she had led an entire Roman army to Veii and brought Camillus to Ardea, so that they could put a great force in the field under a captain who had not been stained with ignominy because of the defeat and had kept his reputation intact for the sake of recapturing his fatherland.

In order to confirm what I have said, it would be possible to cite some modern examples, but we will omit them because we do not think they are necessary since the one we have given here should satisfy everyone. Indeed, let me affirm once again the incontrovertible truth that is apparent in all the histories, namely that men can second Fortune, but not oppose her; they can weave their threads into her warp, but not break it. They should certainly never abandon their struggle, for they do not know her purpose, and since she goes down crooked and unknown paths, they should always remain hopeful, and if they have hope, they should never give up, no matter what happens and no matter what difficulty they might find themselves in.

* * *

BOOK 3

Chapter 1

For a Religious Sect or a Republic to Survive for Long, It Is Necessary to Restore It with Some Frequency to Its Original Principles

It is indisputable that all the things in this world have limits to their lives, and that only those will run the entire course generally ordained for them by heaven whose bodies do not fall into disarray, but maintain themselves in an orderly condition, and who do not change, or if they do, that change helps to preserve, rather than to harm, them. And because I am talking about mixed bodies, such as republics and religious sects,[1] let me say that those alterations are healthy that bring them back to their origins. And therefore, the bodies that have the best constitutions and will have the longest lives are those whose institutions make frequent renovations possible, or that achieve renovation thanks to some sort of accident which has nothing to do with their constitution. And it is clearer than daylight that, without such renovations, these bodies will not last.

The way to renew them is, as I have said, to lead them back to their origins. For at their start, all religious sects and republics and kingdoms must have some good in them, by means of which they obtain their initial reputation and growth. But since that goodness becomes corrupt over the course of time, that body will inevitably die, unless something intervenes to lead it back to its original condition. Thus, our doctors of medicine say, in speaking of the human body: "every day it absorbs something that requires a cure sooner or later."[2]

In the case of a republic, this return to its origins is brought about either by some external accident or by the prudent judgment of those living within it. As for the first, we see how it was necessary for Rome to be taken by the Gauls[3] in order for it to be reborn and through that rebirth to acquire new life and new vitality [*virtù*], and also to take up again the observance of religion and justice which were beginning to decay. This is quite apparent in Livy's history, for at the time when the Romans led their army out against the Gauls and created tribunes with the power of consuls, they were observing no religious ceremonies at all. In the same way, not only did they punish the three Fabius brothers, who fought against the Gauls, "contrary to the laws of nations," but they also made them tribunes.[4] And we may readily presume that they were also beginning to treat all those institutions that had been so well established by Romulus and those other wise princes

1. Machiavelli's word here is *sètte,* which meant any group of people who believed in a particular opinion or accepted a doctrine or formed a faction or were members of a religious order. However, later in the chapter (see p. 155 for a summary), because he talks about the way that the Franciscans and the Dominicans were "sects" that revived the Church, the addition of "religious" in the translation seems justified.
2. The quotation is in Latin: "*Quod quotidie aggregatur aliquid, quod quandoque indiget curatione.*" Its source is not known, although it may come from a medieval translation of Avicenna (Ibn Sīnā, 980–1037). He was a Persian polymath whom some credit as being the father of modern medicine.
3. I have translated Machiavelli's *Franciosi* (literally "Frenchmen") as "Gauls" because he is clearly referring to the sacking of Rome by the Gauls in 390 (or 387) BCE.
4. In 390 BCE, when the Gauls had entered Italy and were besieging the Tuscan town of Clusium, Quintus Fabius Ambustus and his brothers, Numerius and Caeso, were sent to negotiate with them. Instead of doing so, they gathered the people from the town together and attacked the Gauls. The latter then demanded that the Romans hand over the three brothers because they had acted "against the law of nations" (*contra ius gentium*) by violating a truce in order to negotiate. Instead, the brothers were rewarded by being made consular tribunes. In response, the Gauls attacked Rome and sacked the city.

with less respect than was reasonable and necessary for the preservation of their freedom. Their being beaten by outsiders was needed so that all the institutions of the city would be renewed and the people would be shown that it was not only essential to continue to support religion and justice, but also to hold good citizens in high esteem and to value their virtues [*virtù*] more than any discomforts they felt they had experienced because of what those three men had done. This, one sees, is exactly what happened, because as soon as Rome was taken back from the Gauls, they renewed all the ordinances of their ancient religion, they punished the Fabius brothers who had fought contrary to the law of nations, and now they valued the virtue [*virtù*] and goodness of Camillus so highly that the senate and the rest of the people set aside all the envy they felt toward him and placed the entire weight of the republic on his shoulders once again.

It is necessary, therefore, as I have said, for men who are living together in some sort of organized state to undergo frequent self-examinations, whether they are the result of external events or the product of internal ones. And as far as the latter are concerned, they normally occur because of a law that requires the members of this body politic to give an account of themselves quite often, or indeed because a good man arises among them who, by his example and his virtuous [*virtuose*] deeds, produces the same effect as the law.

This benefit is thus conferred on republics either because of the virtue [*virtù*] of a man or because of the virtue [*virtù*] of an institution. And as for the latter, the institutions that brought the Roman Republic back to its beginnings were the tribunes of the people, the censors, and all the other laws that countered men's ambition and insolence. But such institutions also have to be brought to life by the virtue [*virtù*] of a citizen who vigorously assists in putting them into effect against the power of those who transgress them.

[Machiavelli proceeds to identify a series of events before and after the invasion of the Gauls when individuals who broke the laws were severely punished, usually by death. He notes that when those punishments grew less frequent, the republic became corrupt.]

It would therefore be desirable that no more than ten years should pass between such executions, because by that time men begin to change their customary behavior and to transgress the laws, and if nothing happens to bring back the memory of those punishments to their minds and to revive their fear in their hearts, soon so many delinquents will have come together that it will not be possible to punish them without danger. * * *

Such a return to the origins also comes about in republics through the simple virtue [*virtù*] of a single man, independently of any law that calls for you to have people executed. For that individual will have such a reputation and be so exemplary that good men will desire to imitate him and bad ones will be ashamed to lead lives contrary to his. * * *

And if the executions, together with the appearance of such exemplary figures, had occurred in that city [i.e., Rome] every ten years, it necessarily follows that it would never have become corrupt. But as these two things began to occur less frequently, corruption began to spread wider and wider. For after Marcus Regulus, there was no exemplary figure like him, and although the two Catos did appear,[5] there was so great a temporal distance between him and them, and between the two of them, and they remained so isolated, that they could not produce any good effects by means of their good examples—and especially the younger Cato who found the greater part of the city so corrupt that he could do nothing by means of his example to bring about any improvement among the citizens. * * *

* * *

[Machiavelli devotes the next section of this chapter to the way the Franciscans and the Dominicans have brought the Church back to its origins by calling for the clergy to embrace poverty and Christ-like compassion as virtues. He sees them as the only things keeping the Church from becoming totally corrupt. After that, Machiavelli turns his attention to the way the French kingdom has renewed itself thanks to its *parlements*, judicial bodies that are the conservators of the originary laws of the kingdom and have prevented the ambitious aristocracy from undermining them and the state.]

I therefore conclude that there is nothing more necessary for a community, whether it be a sect, a kingdom, or a republic, than to restore to it the reputation that it had at its beginning and to do everything possible to ensure that it has either good institutions or good men who will produce such a restoration, rather than having to have an external force bring it about. For although sometimes

5. Marcus Porcius Cato, also known as Cato the Elder and Cato the Censor (234–149 BCE) was a Roman statesman and orator who disliked luxury and ostentation and opposed what he saw as decadent Greek influences on Rome. He was celebrated for his austerity and moral probity. Marcus Porcius Cato, also referred to as Cato the Younger (95–46 BCE), was, like his great-grandfather of the same name, similarly celebrated for his moral rectitude. He joined Pompey in opposing Julius Caesar, and when Pompey was defeated, he went to Utica in North Africa, and after he saw the last of his army safely evacuated by sea, committed suicide rather than fall into Caesar's hands. Marcus Atilius Regulus (c. 307–250 BCE) was a Roman consul and general. His career has been embellished by legend, but nevertheless, according to various accounts, he was captured by the Carthaginians in 255 BCE, but released to return to Rome and negotiate a peace treaty. Instead, he advised his countrymen to reject the terms being offered, and then, over their protests, returned to Carthage, where he was supposedly tortured to death, thus becoming an exemplary figure for the Romans.

that is the best remedy, as it was in Rome, it is so dangerous that it is in no way to be desired. * * *

* * *

Chapter 3

How It Is Necessary to Kill the Sons of Brutus in Order to Preserve a Newly Acquired Freedom

The severity of Brutus was no less necessary than useful for the maintenance of that liberty in Rome that he had acquired for her. It is a rare example in all of history to see a father sit in judgment and not only condemn his sons to death, but to be present at their execution.[6] And everyone who reads ancient history will always recognize that after a change of government, whether from a republic to a tyranny or from a tyranny to a republic, there must be a memorable execution of those who are the enemies of the present state of affairs. And whoever makes himself a tyrant and does not kill Brutus, and whoever liberates a state and does not kill the sons of Brutus, does not last long. And since I discussed this subject at length above,[7] I refer to what was said there and limit myself here to citing just one memorable example from our times and our fatherland. And this is that of Piero Soderini,[8] who believed that he would be able, with his patience and his goodness, to overcome the desire of the sons of Brutus to put themselves back again under another form of government—and in this he deceived himself. Although he, being prudent, recognized what was necessary, and although chance and the ambition of those who fought against him gave him the opportunity to wipe them out, nevertheless, he could never make up his mind to do

6. See Livy, *History of Rome,* 2.5. In Livy's account, Lucius Junius Brutus was the republican hero responsible for the expulsion of Tarquinus Superbus and the ending of the Roman monarchy in 509 BCE. Admired for his rigor, he supposedly had two of his sons killed for plotting to bring back the kings. The more famous Brutus, Marcus Junius Brutus, who participated in the assassination of Julius Caesar, stressed his connection to this figure who was his ancestor.
7. Machiavelli may be referring to 1.16, but he covers some of the same material in *The Prince,* Chapters 5–8 (see pp. 15–30).
8. Piero di Tommaso Soderini (1450–1522) was a Florentine statesman who was elected *Gonfaloniere a vita* of Florence in 1502 in an attempt to provide some sort of stability for the Florentines' republican government. He was responsible for creating a citizen militia and was recognized for the mildness of his rule. However, he was forced to flee Florence in 1512 when papal troops restored the Medici to power, and although he was later reconciled with the Medici pope Leo X and served him in Rome, he was never allowed to return to Florence. A *gonfaloniere* was a "standard-bearer," someone who held the banner or flag (*gonfalo*) when leading troops into battle. In 1289, the Florentines created the *Gonfaloniere del popolo,* also called the *Gonfaloniere della repubblica* and the *Gonfaloniere di giustizia,* who headed a force of a thousand armed men that protected the civil magistrates of the city. By the 15th century, the term had lost its military meaning and identified instead the person who was elected as the executive head of the civil government, something like a chief magistrate or a mayor. This was the position that Soderini held.

so. For, in addition to believing that with patience and goodness he could eliminate those bad humors[9] and that with rewards he could extinguish others' hostility, he thought (and often acknowledged it to his friends) that in order to take vigorous action against the opposition and beat his adversaries, he would have to assume extraordinary authority and destroy civil equality along with the laws. And he felt that such authority, even if he did not use it tyrannically afterwards, would have so dismayed the masses that after his death they would never again agree to elect a *Gonfaloniere* for life, an office he thought it a good idea to strengthen and preserve.

This respect of his was wise and virtuous. Nevertheless, one should never allow an evil to continue out of concern for the good when that good might easily be overwhelmed by that evil. And Soderini should have borne in mind that since his deeds and his motives would have had to be judged by their outcome—if he had been fortunate and lived that long—he could have convinced everyone then that what he had done had been done for the safety of the fatherland and not because of his ambition. Moreover, he would have been able to arrange things so that his successor could not use for an evil end what he had used for a good one. But he was deceived in his first opinion, not recognizing that malice is not mastered by time or placated by any sort of gift. Thus, because he did not know how to imitate Brutus, he lost, together with his fatherland, his government and his reputation. * * *

* * *

Chapter 8

Whoever Wishes to Change a Republic Should Consider Its Existing Condition

We have already shown that a wicked citizen cannot do evil in a republic that is not already corrupt.[1] Besides the reasons given elsewhere, this conclusion is reinforced by the example of Spurius Cassius and Manlius Capitolinus. This Spurius was an ambitious man and sought to obtain extraordinary authority in Rome and win over the people to support him by conferring many gifts on them, such as dividing up among them the lands which the Romans had taken from the Hernici.[2] His ambition was uncovered by the senators and

9. Here Machiavelli means the different classes or political factions in state. For a more detailed discussion of this metaphor, see *The Prince,* n. 1, p. 31.
1. Machiavelli discussed this topic in 1.34 and 3.6.
2. The Hernici, an Italic tribe in Latium, concluded a peace treaty with the Romans in 486 BCE, ceding two-thirds of their land to Rome. For the story of Spurius Cassius, see Livy, *History of Rome,* 2.41. Spurius Cassius Viscellinus (d. 485 BCE) was a distinguished Roman leader, but after his final consulship, he was accused of seeking regal power and was put to death by the senate.

brought him under such suspicion that when he spoke to the people and offered to give them the money from the sale of grain that the government had arranged to be brought in from Sicily, they refused it altogether, for it seemed to them that Spurius was offering it as the price for their freedom.

The example of Manlius Capitolinus[3] is even more striking, because in him one can see how the best qualities (*virtù*) of mind and body and how many good deeds done in support of the fatherland are later canceled by his evil ambition to rule, an ambition that, we see, arose in him because of the envy he felt over the honors bestowed on Camillus.[4] And his mind was so blinded by this that without reflecting on the customs of the city or examining the condition it was in—it was not yet ready to receive a bad form of government—he set about stirring up disturbances in Rome against the senate and the laws of the fatherland. Here one sees the perfection of that city and the goodness of the people who inhabited it, for in his case, not one of the nobility, despite being the fiercest defenders of their collective interests, undertook to defend him, none of his relatives engaged in any effort on his behalf, and although people were accustomed to appear, dressed in black and thoroughly grief-stricken as though in deep mourning, in order to beg for mercy for the accused, no one like that was seen with Manlius. The tribunes of the people, who were always accustomed to favor what appeared to benefit the people—and the more so as it was opposed to the interests of the nobility—in this instance united with the nobles to overcome a common pestilence. The people of Rome, most concerned about its own interests and backing whatever went against the nobility, nevertheless, even though it had bestowed many favors on Manlius, when the tribunes cited him and brought his case before the judgment of the people, that same people, having become judges instead of defendants, condemned him to death without showing any respect for what he had accomplished.

I therefore think that there is no more suitable example in this history that demonstrates the excellence of the entire constitution of that republic than this one, seeing as how no one in the whole city was moved to defend a citizen possessing every virtue [*virtù*] who both publicly and privately had performed a great many praiseworthy deeds. For the love of the fatherland had more power over them than any other consideration, and they paid more attention to the

3. Marcus Manlius Capitolinus (d. 384 BCE) famously held the Capitoline Hill against the Gauls when they sacked Rome in 390 BCE. After the Gauls retreated, he supported the plebeians, who had been left impoverished after the sack. He was consequently accused of seeking to become king, condemned to death in 385 BCE, and executed a year later.

4. Camillus was Marcus Manlius's rival, but supported the patricians. For more on him, see n. 2, pp. 132–33.

present dangers to which he exposed them than to his past merits. And Titus Livy says: "Thus ended the career of this man who would have been memorable except that he was born in a free city."[5]

From this there are two points to be taken into consideration: first, that there are different means for attaining glory in a corrupt city than in one that still preserves its civic institutions; the second, which is almost the same as the first, that men, in their conduct, and especially in their greatest actions, should consider the times and accommodate themselves to them. And those who do not conform to the times, either because they make bad choices or because of their natural inclination, will in most cases have unhappy lives, and their actions will produce negative results, whereas it will be just the opposite for those who are in harmony with the times. And doubtless one may conclude from the words of the historian who has just been cited that if Manlius had been born in the times of Marius and Sulla, when the people were already corrupt, and when he could have molded them according to his ambition, he would have achieved the same results and successes as Marius and Sulla[6] and the others who, after them, aspired to become tyrants. And in the same way, if Marius and Sulla had lived in the times of Manlius, they would have been crushed in their first undertakings. For a man may well begin, by means of his deeds and his use of evil means, to corrupt a people, but it is impossible for him to live long enough to corrupt them in such a way that he himself may enjoy the fruits of it. And even if it were possible that over a long period of time he should manage to accomplish his end, such success would still be impossible for him because of the way men behave, for they are impatient and cannot brook any delay in the gratification of their passions, and they wind up deceiving themselves about their own concerns and especially about what they desire the most, so that because of too little patience or because of self-deception they would begin an undertaking at the wrong time and see it end badly for them.

Therefore, in order to acquire supreme authority in a republic and establish a bad form of government there, it is necessary to find that the people in it have been corrupted over time and that they have been led, little by little, from one generation to the next, to this condition, to which they will necessarily be led unless, as we have shown above, they are often reinvigorated by good examples or brought back by means of good laws to their first principles.[7] Manlius thus would have been regarded as a rare and memorable man if he had been born in a corrupt city. And therefore, citizens in

5. Livy, *History of Rome*, 6.20.14: *"Hunc exitum habuit vir, nisi in libera civitate natus esset, memorabilis."*
6. On Marius and Sulla, see n. 4, p. 128 and n. 1, p. 138.
7. Machiavelli discussed this topic in 3.1, pp. 152–56.

republics who want to engage in an undertaking either in favor of liberty or in favor of tyranny ought to consider the current condition of the state and judge from that how difficult their undertaking will be. For it is as difficult and dangerous to seek to free a people who are resolved to live in servitude as it is to subject a people to servitude who desire to live in freedom. And because we argued earlier that men, when they act, must take the nature of the times into consideration and proceed accordingly, we will speak at length on this subject in the following chapter.

Chapter 9

How People Must Change with the Times if They Always Want to Have Good Luck

I have often thought that men's having good luck[8] and bad is a matter of their adapting their mode of proceeding to the times, for one sees how some men act impetuously in their affairs, while others proceed with diffidence and caution, and because they always go beyond the proper limits when acting in either way, they make errors in both cases and cannot stay on the true path. By contrast, that man turns out to err less and to have better luck who adapts his methods to the times, as I have said, and always proceeds in the direction nature compels you to go. Everyone knows how Fabius Maximus proceeded in a cautious, hesitant manner with his army,[9] very distant from any sort of Roman impetuosity and audacity, and it was his good fortune that made his method sort well with the times. For since Hannibal, a young man with a fresh fortune, had come into Italy and had already routed the Roman people twice, and since that republic was deprived of almost all of its best troops and was discouraged, it could not have had better luck than to have a captain who, with his slow pace and his caution, kept the enemy at bay. Fabius could not have found times more suitable for his methods, as a result of which everything redounded to his glory. And that Fabius acted thus because of his nature and not by choice is revealed by the fact that when Scipio[1] wanted to cross over into Africa with those same troops in order to put an end to the war, Fabius vigorously disagreed—just like a man who could not detach himself from his methods and his habits—so that if it had been up to him, Hannibal would have still been in Italy, for Fabius failed to perceive that the times had changed

8. Here Machiavelli's word is *fortuna;* I used "luck" because it is more idiomatic.
9. Quintus Fabius Maximus (d. 203 BCE) was Hannibal's principal opponent in the first, defensive phases of the Second Punic War (218–201 BCE). His policy of cautiously refusing to engage in battles he knew he would lose earned him the sobriquet of "Cunctator," "the Hesitator" or "the Delayer."
1. See n. 3, p. 120.

and that it was necessary to change the method of waging war. And if Fabius had been the king of Rome, he could easily have lost that war, for he would not have known how to change his methods to suit the changing times. But he had been born in a republic where there were different kinds of citizens and different kinds of humors, like Fabius himself, who was best suited for times when a war had to be protracted, just as Rome later had Scipio when the time was ripe for winning it.

It is this that leads to a republic's having a longer life and enjoying good fortune longer than a principality does, for the diversity of the citizens who live in it enables it to adapt itself better to changing circumstances than a prince is able to do. For a man who is used to acting in one way will never change, as has been said, and when the times change and no longer harmonize with his methods, he will come to ruin.

Piero Soderini, whom we have mentioned on other occasions,[2] acted in all his affairs with humanity and patience. He and his country prospered as long as the times were in conformity with his mode of proceeding, but afterwards, when the moment arrived for him to put aside his patience and humility, he did not know how to do it, with the result that he, together with his country, was ruined. Pope Julius II[3] acted throughout the entire period of his pontificate impetuously and passionately, and because the times suited him well, he was successful in all of his undertakings. But if other times had come that had required a different approach, he would necessarily have come to ruin, for he would not have changed either his methods or his way of acting. And there are two reasons why we cannot change ourselves: first, we cannot resist the way in which nature inclines us to go; second, if a man has had great success by using a certain mode of proceeding, it is impossible to persuade him that he can do well by proceeding differently. This is why a man's luck will vary, since Fortune causes circumstances to change, but he does not vary his methods. The ruin of cities also comes about in this way, as we have fully shown above, for republics do not modify their institutions to suit the times, but rather, move ahead quite slowly, since it is more difficult for them to change. For if they are going to change, it is necessary for a time to come that shakes up the entire state, at which point it will require more than having one man change the way he acts.[4]

* * *

2. Soderini is mentioned in 1.7, 1.52, and 3.3, pp. 156–57.
3. For a fuller discussion of Julius II, see *The Prince,* Chapter 25, pp. 79–80.
4. Machiavelli discusses what is required of republics to adapt swiftly to changing circumstances in 3.1, pp. 152–56.

Chapter 19

Whether Indulgence[5] or Punishment Is More Necessary in Order to Govern the Masses

The Roman republic was disturbed by the hostility between the nobles and the plebeians, yet when they were faced with a war, they sent out Quintius and Appius Claudius with their armies.[6] Cruel and harsh as a commander, Appius could hardly get his men to obey him, so that he fled from the province to which he had been sent as though he were defeated; Quintius, because of his kind and humane disposition, had obedient soldiers and returned victorious from his. It thus seems that to govern the masses[7] it would be better to be humane than haughty, compassionate than cruel. Nevertheless, Cornelius Tacitus, with whom many other writers agree, comes to the opposite conclusion in one of his aphoristic statements, when he says: "In ruling the masses punishment is worth more than indulgence."[8] I have been considering how these two opinions can be reconciled, so let me say this: you will either be ruling over men who are normally your equals, or over those who will always be your subjects. If they are your equals, you cannot depend entirely upon punishments or upon that severity of which Cornelius speaks. And because the plebeians in Rome shared political power with the nobility, anyone who became their temporary leader, that is, someone who ruled over them for just a limited amount of time, could not treat them with cruelty and harshness. Moreover, we have frequently seen that Roman captains who got their armies to love them and were indulgent in leading them often obtained better results than did those who made their troops extraordinarily fearful, unless those

5. Here Machiavelli uses *ossequio,* which comes from the Latin *obsequium,* a word that is frequently used by Tacitus and appears in a quotation later in the first paragraph. *Obsequium,* a noun based on the verb *obsequor,* means "to accommodate oneself to, to gratify, to show considerateness toward." I have thus translated *ossequio* as "indulgence," because it strikes me as capturing many of these meanings.
6. Titus Quintius (or Quinctius) Barbatus Capitolinus (513–after 423 BCE) and Appius Claudius Sabinus (fl. 482–470 BCE) were consuls in 471 BCE. Although both men were hostile to the interests of the plebeians, Titus Quintius was more conciliatory than his fellow consul and sought peace between the factions. In 471, Titus Quintius was put in charge of an army sent to fight the Aequi, who had raided Roman territory. He treated his men mildly and returned a victor. By contrast, in the same year Appius Claudius was put in charge of an army sent to fight the Volscians; he imposed harsh discipline on his soldiers, and when they fled from a battle, he had them brutally punished. Needless to say, he did not return to Rome a victor. The next year, according to Livy, accusations were brought against him by the tribunes, but he died before going to trial. Machiavelli's point in this sentence is that the Roman army, which was composed of plebeians, was being led by patricians despite the civil discord between the two groups. On this episode, see Livy, *History of Rome,* 2.55–60.
7. See n. 4, p. 110.
8. Tacitus, *Annals,* 3.55.4: "*In multitudine regenda plus poena quam obsequium valet.*"

captains were also endowed with exceptional virtue [*virtù*], as was the case with Manlius Torquatus.[9] But the man who is governing his subjects, the man of whom Cornelius is speaking, must incline toward severity rather than indulgence lest those subjects become insolent and trample all over you because you take it too easy on them. Still, this severity should also be used in moderation so as to avoid arousing hatred, for things have never turned out well for any prince who has made himself hated. The way to avoid hatred is to leave your subjects' property alone, for, except when greed is his hidden motive, no prince wants to shed blood unless he is driven to it, and that is something that seldom occurs. But when greed gets involved, blood will inevitably be spilled, and neither the desire to shed it, nor causes for shedding it, will ever be wanting, as I explain in detail in another treatise on this subject.[1] Thus, Quintius was entitled to more praise than Appius, and the judgment of Cornelius also deserves to be approved, but only within limits, nor can it be applied in the case of Appius.

* * *

Chapter 49

If It Wishes to Preserve Its Freedom, a Republic Needs to Make New Provisions for That Freedom Every Day; and Why Quintus Fabius Deserved to Be Called Maximus

As I have said at other times, in a great city emergencies occur every day that require a physician, and the more serious they are, the wiser the physician needs to be. And if such emergencies ever occurred in any city, they occurred in Rome, both strange and unexpected ones, as, for example, the plot which all the Roman women seemed to have formed together to murder their husbands, for many were found who had poisoned them, and many others who had prepared the poison to do so.[2] There was also the conspiracy of the Bacchanals,[3] discovered at the time of the Macedonian war, in which many thousands of men and women were implicated, and had it not been discovered, and had the Romans not been accustomed to punishing large groups of wrongdoers, it would have represented a danger for that city. For if the greatness of that republic were not made

9. On Manlius Torquatus, see n. 3, p. 120.
1. Machiavelli is referring to *The Prince*, Chapter 17, pp. 52–54.
2. These events took place in 331 BCE; see Livy, *History of Rome*, 8.18.
3. Bacchanals, also know as Bacchants, were priests, priestesses, and followers of the god Bacchus and were known for their wild revelries and orgies. Livy describes the discovery of such cults in Rome around the year 186 BCE; see his *History of Rome*, 39.8–9, 41.

apparent by countless other signs, as well as by the way its laws were administered, one sees it in the character of the punishments she inflicted on the guilty. Rome did not hesitate to pronounce a sentence of death on an entire legion at a time, as well as on a city, and to send eight or ten thousand men into exile, imposing extraordinary conditions on them which had to be observed not just by one man, but by so very many—as happened to those soldiers who had fought unsuccessfully at Cannae: she banished them to Sicily, imposing the condition on them that they should not live in town and should eat standing up.[4]

Of all the procedures she employed as punishments, however, the most terrible was the decimation of her armies, in which, by lot, one soldier out of every ten was put to death. Nor could they find a more terrifying punishment than this to chastise a multitude, for when a great number of people commit a crime and it is not certain who its authors are, it is impossible to punish them all, there being too many of them. To punish part of them and to let another part remain unscathed would wrong those who were punished while those who got off would be encouraged to do wrong at some other time. But by putting every tenth man to death by lot, when all deserve it, then the one who is punished grieves over his fate, while the one who gets off is afraid that it will be his turn on some other occasion and will be careful to avoid committing a crime.

Thus, the poisoners and the Bacchanals were punished as their crimes deserved. And although the consequences of these diseases in a republic are bad, they are not fatal, because there is almost always time to correct them. But there is no time to do so with those that affect the state itself, for unless they are corrected by some prudent man, they will cause its ruin. Thanks to the liberality with which the Romans used to grant citizenship to foreigners, the city came to have so many newcomers who started controlling such a large percentage of the votes that the government began to change, turning away from the traditions and the men it used to follow. Quintus Fabius[5] noticed this when he was censor, and put all of these newcomers, who were the source of this disorder, into four Tribes, so that, their activities being confined within such small

4. See Livy, *History of Rome*, 23.25, 25.5–7. During the Second Punic War, the Roman army was defeated by the Carthaginian general Hannibal on August 2, 216 BCE, in the battle of Cannae, a town in Apulia in southern Italy. Although the Romans significantly outnumbered the Carthaginians, they were outmaneuvered by Hannibal, and according to Livy—whose figures are generally accepted—around fifty thousand of the seventy-thousand-man-strong Roman army were killed or captured.

5. Quintus Fabius Maximus Rullianus (fl. 325–295 BCE) was a Roman statesman and general who served as a consul five times and was made *dictator* in 315 BCE. For this episode, see Livy, *History of Rome*, 9.46.

spaces, they could not corrupt the whole of Rome. Fabius grasped just what the problem was, and without making any alteration in the government, he found an appropriate remedy for it, a remedy so well received by that state that he truly deserved to be called Maximus.[6]

6. An honorific meaning "the Great." This is the final word in the *Discourses,* and it allows Machiavelli not just to end his work by celebrating the prudence of Quintus Fabius and the good judgment of the Roman people, but to praise the city itself one last time because of its republican form of government, the kind of government that could produce worthy citizens and a great leader whom they rewarded with an honorific addition to his name. By bringing his work to a close with the word *Maximus,* Machiavelli seems to be implying that if Quintus Fabius deserved to be called "the Great," the Roman Republic itself does so as well.

Machiavelli the Correspondent

Machiavelli wrote hundreds, possibly thousands, of letters—after all, as a secretary, that was his job. The letters vary according to the addressee, and even within them the tone oscillates from paragraph to paragraph, even sentence to sentence. We have included two of them. The first is famous, because in it Machiavelli reveals for the first time that he is writing *The Prince,* but it is also astonishing for its description of Machiavelli's daily routine during the period when the Medici, who had resumed control of Florence in 1512, had exiled him to his modest country estate. The second comes from 1521, after the Medici decided to allow Machiavelli back into Florence. It is wonderfully, though poignantly, comic. He was sent to the provincial town of Carpi to deal with a business matter for the Medici, and to find a friar in a Dominican monastery there to come to Florence and preach during Lent. Neither mission was very important, and thus the trip must have felt at least slightly degrading to a man who had served as Florence's envoy to such figures as the king of France and the Holy Roman Emperor. So, Machiavelli decides to play a kind of confidence trick on the friars: he asks his correspondent, Francesco Guicciardini, to send lots of messengers to him as though he were a person of great importance and his mission to Carpi were truly serious. The irreverent Machiavelli obviously derived great pleasure from making fun of the credulous friars. More important, the trick he was playing also enabled him to compensate, vicariously to be sure, for any feelings of degradation he may have had about his mission specifically and his exile to the country more generally. Playing this confidence game, Machiavelli is able to put himself in the position of his prince: he happily manufactures fictions for a bunch of dupes who are too dense to see what is really going on, thereby giving him back a small sense of the power and importance that he had lost in 1512.

NICCOLÒ MACHIAVELLI

From The Private Letters†

To Francesco Vettori

10 December 1513, Florence

To the Magnificent Francesco Vettori, His Benefactor, Florentine Ambassador to the Supreme Pontiff, in Rome[1]

Magnificent Ambassador:

Divine favors were never late.[2] I say this, because it seemed to me that I had lost—no, rather strayed away from—your favor, since it's been so long since you've written to me, and I was uncertain what the reason could be. And I paid little attention to all the explanations that came to mind except for this one: I feared you'd stopped writing to me because someone had written to you that I was not a good steward of your letters, and I knew that, aside from Filippo and Pagolo,[3] no one has seen them because of anything I've done. I've found your favor again thanks to your recent letter of the twenty-third of the past month. I'm extremely pleased to have learned from it in how orderly a manner and how calmly you are carrying out your public duties, and I encourage you to continue doing that, because whoever forgoes his own interests for those of others, only sacrifices what's his own and gets no thanks from them. And since Fortune aims to shape everything, she wants us to let her do so, and to be quiet and not give her any trouble, and to await the time when she will let men do something. And that will be the moment for you to work harder and pay closer attention to things, and for me to leave my farm and say: "Here I am." Since I want to bestow an equal favor on you, there's nothing I can tell you about in this letter

† From Niccolò Machiavelli, *Lettere familiari,* edited by Edoardo Alvisi, 305–10, 422–26 (Firenze: G. C. Sansoni Editrice, 1883). Translated and annotated by the editor of this Norton Critical Edition.

1. Machiavelli's close friend Francesco Vettori (1474–1539) came from an old Florentine family and was a writer, politician, and diplomat. He was elected to the Signoria in 1503 when Florence was a republic, but then served the Medici when they were restored to power in 1512. He had been on a diplomatic mission to Germany with Machiavelli in 1507, and from 1513 to 1515 he was the Florentine ambassador to the Papal See.
2. Machiavelli is citing, inexactly, line 13 from Petrarch's *Trionfo dell'eternità* (*Triumph of Eternity*), which means that God's *grazie,* here rendered as "favors," can never come too late.
3. Two of Machiavelli's close friends: Filippo Casavecchia (1472–after 1520), and Pagolo (or Paolo) Vettori (1477–1526), Francesco's younger brother. The former played an active role in the political life of Florence and was one of Machiavelli's greatest admirers; the latter was also politically active and helped the Medici return to power in 1512, for which he was later named the head of the papal fleet by Leo X.

except what my life is like, and if you decide that you'd like to swap it for yours, I'll be happy to make the exchange.

I'm living on my farm, and since my last run of bad luck,[4] I have not spent twenty days, if you add them all together, in Florence. Up to now, I've been snaring thrushes with my own hands. I'd get up before daybreak, prepare the birdlime, and go out with such a bundle of cages on my back that I looked like Geta when he was coming back from the harbor with Amphitryon's books.[5] I would catch at least two, at most six, thrushes. And so I passed all of September.[6] Then this pastime, though contemptible and alien to me, petered out—to my regret.

I shall tell you about my daily routine. I get up in the morning with the sun and go into one of my woods which I'm having cut down. There I spend a couple of hours reviewing the work of the previous day and passing time with the wood-cutters, who always have some dispute on their hands either among themselves or with their neighbors. And I could tell you a thousand good stories about those woods and the things that have happened to me there, and about both Frosino da Panzano and others who wanted some of the firewood. And Frosino, in particular, sent for several loads of wood without saying a word to me, and when it came time for payment, he wanted to withhold ten *lire* that he says he should have gotten from me four years ago when he beat me at *cricca*[7] at Antonio Guicciardini's house. I began to raise hell and was going to accuse the wagoner who had come for the wood of being a thief, but finally Giovanni Machiavelli came in between us and got us to make peace. Battista Guicciardini, Filippo Ginori, Tommaso del Bene, and some other citizens all ordered a load of wood from me when that north wind was blowing.[8] I promised some of it to each of them, and I sent a load to Tommaso, which became half its size in Florence, because he, his wife, his servants, and his children

4. I.e., his imprisonment in the Bargello on February 12, 1513, because his name was found on a list of conspirators, headed by Pietropaolo Boscoli and Agostino Capponi, to lead a rebellion against the Medici. Machiavelli was subjected to torture (six drops on the strappado, as he recalls in a poem), although had nothing to confess. Still, he would have languished in prison, had he not been released on March 13, 1513, when Giovanni de' Medici became Pope Leo X and granted amnesty to all such political prisoners.
5. This is an allusion to a farcical episode in *Geta e Birria,* a popular tale from the 15th century based on Plautus's comedy *Amphitruo* (*Amphitrion*). In the story, the protagonist, Anfitrione, has just returned from a sea voyage, and in order to let his wife know he has arrived in the port, he has his servant Geta carry a heavy load of books to her.
6. This may be a mistake for November, although it is uncertain if this is Machiavelli's mistake or that of the copyist, Giuliano de' Ricci, who is the source for this text.
7. A card game like rummy in which the object is to get three of a kind.
8. Although Machiavelli's reference to the north wind here may well be literal, some editors have interpreted it as a veiled allusion to the difficulties he experienced after the return of the Medici to Florence in 1512.

were there to stack it up: they looked like Gabbura on Thursdays when he and his boys are pounding out the meat of an ox.[9] Consequently, once I saw who was profiting here, I told the others that I had no more wood, and all of them got really angry about it, and especially Battista, who puts this alongside his other calamities in Prato.[1]

Leaving the woods, I go off to a spring, and from there to one of the places where I hang up my birdnets. I have a book under my arm, either Dante or Petrarch or one of the minor poets, such as Tibullus, Ovid, and the like. I read about their amorous passions and their loves, remember my own, and for a while these thoughts make me happy. Then I make my way along the road to the inn, speak with passersby, ask for news about their towns, learn various things, and note the diverse tastes and the different fancies of men. In the midst of all this, the hour for dinner arrives, and then I eat with my family[2] such food as this poor farm of mine and my minuscule patrimony grant me. Once I've eaten, I return to the inn, where there is, ordinarily, the innkeeper, as well as a butcher, a miller, and two kiln-tenders. With these men I lower myself and become a yokel[3] for the entire day, playing at *cricca* and backgammon. These games give birth to thousands of squabbles and endless insults and offensive words, and most of the time we are fighting over a penny. Be that as it may, people can hear us yelling from as far away as San Casciano. Cooped up this way among these lice, I wipe off the mold from my brain and vent my feelings about the malice of my fate, content that she should trample on me like this just to see if she will ever feel ashamed of doing so.

9. Gabbura was probably a well-known butcher, although his exact identity has not been determined. Machiavelli is comparing the way that Gabbura and his assistants pounded meat to make it thinner with the way that Tommaso del Bene and his family stacked the wood so tightly that it seemed only half a load.
1. Battista Guicciardini was the *podestà* (chief magistrate) of Prato, which is just north of Florence, when it was stormed by Spanish troops on August 29, 1512. They took Guicciardini prisoner as the city was brutally sacked, and thousands of its inhabitants were tortured, mutilated, or slain. The Spanish troops had been sent into Tuscany by Pope Julius II and King Ferdinand II of Aragon to restore Medici rule in Florence, and they were accompanied by Giovanni de' Medici, who would become Pope Leo X in 1513. Because about 40 percent of the Florentine troops who were routed when defending Prato came from Machiavelli's citizen militia, the Signoria felt it could not count on the rest of them and quickly agreed to the restoration of the Medici in September of 1512.
2. Machiavelli's word here is *brigata,* which normally refers to a group of people, not necessarily related, who have come together to enjoy one another's company. Boccaccio uses the word in his *Decameron* (written 1349–51 or –52) for the company of ten young men and women who have escaped from the plague in Florence and tell one another stories during two weeks in the country. Machiavelli's use of this word may thus suggest jocularity and conviviality. His "family" would have included, potentially, servants in addition to his wife, children, and relations.
3. Machiavelli's Italian is *io m'ingaglioffo,* which means that he becomes a *gaglioffo*—that is, a rascal, rogue, or knave. Since Machiavelli is playing games here with a bunch of people he no doubt considered country bumpkins, "yokel" seems as apt a translation as any.

When evening comes, I return home and enter my study, and at the threshold, I take off my everyday clothes, full of mud and filth, and put on regal and courtly garments; and now, dressed appropriately, I enter the ancient courts of ancient men where, received by them with affection, I feed on that food which is mine alone and for which I was born, where I am not ashamed to speak with them and ask them about the reasons for their actions, and they, in their humanity, answer me. And for four hours at a time, I do not feel boredom, I forget all my troubles, I do not dread poverty, I am not terrified at death: I transfer myself into them completely.[4] And because Dante says that one does not have knowledge unless one retains what one has understood, I've noted down what I've profited from in their conversation, and I've composed a little work *On Principalities,* where I delve as deeply as I can into ideas on this subject, discussing what a principality is, what species there are of them, how they are acquired, how they are maintained, why they are lost.[5] And if you've ever enjoyed any whimsy of mine, this one should not displease you; and by a prince, and especially by a new prince, it ought to be welcomed. Therefore, I'm dedicating it to his Magnificence Giuliano.[6] Filippo Casavecchia has seen it; he'll be able to give you some account of it, both of the thing itself and of the discussions I've had with him about it, although I'm still fattening it up and polishing it.

You would like me, Magnificent Ambassador, to leave this life behind and come to enjoy yours with you. I shall do it in any case, but what keeps me here now are certain affairs of mine that I'll have taken care of in the next six weeks. What gives me pause is that the Soderini are there,[7] and were I to come, I'd be obliged to

4. Machiavelli's words here, *tutto mi trasferisco in loro,* echo what he said in the previous paragraph, *trasferiscomi poi in su la strada* (Then I make my way along the road [to the inn]), thus inviting us to compare his physical traveling around his estate and down the road to the inn with his psychological traveling back in time, by way of reading, as he happily engages in dialogues with the ancients.
5. Machiavelli had been working on what would become his *Discourses on the First Ten Books of Titus Livy* when he took time off to write *The Prince,* so the ancient with whom he was primarily having a conversation was the Roman historian Livy. For the citation from Dante, see *Paradiso* 5.41–42. Machiavelli refers to his most famous work with a Latin title: *De principatibus.*
6. Initially, Machiavelli intended to dedicate *The Prince* to Giuliano de' Medici, duke of Nemours (b. 1479; ruled 1512–16), who was residing in Florence in 1512–13, but after his death on March 17, 1516, Machiavelli dedicated it to Lorenzo de' Medici, duke of Urbino (b. 1492; ruled Florence 1516–19). His description of his work here suggests he may have completed only the first ten chapters or so of it by this time, but this is by no means certain.
7. There were two members of the Soderini family in Rome: Piero, formerly the head of the Florentine Republic, under whom Machiavelli had served in the Second Chancery; and Piero's brother Francesco, who was a cardinal and the bishop of Volterra. Both had been given permission by Pope Leo X, a member of the Medici family, to reside in Rome. Machiavelli's concern is that if he came to Rome to visit Vettori, he would feel obligated to visited the Soderini brothers, too, and that might expose him to new reprisals from the Medici in Florence.

visit and talk with them. I would fear that on my return I could not count on dismounting at home, but would do so at the Bargello,[8] for although this regime has very substantial foundations and great security, nevertheless, it is new and therefore suspicious, and there is no lack of rogues who, to cut a figure like Pagolo Bertini, would put others on the dinner bill and leave the reckoning to me.[9] I beg you to make this fear disappear, and then, no matter what, I'll come to visit you within the time frame I mentioned.

I've discussed this little work of mine with Filippo and whether or not it would be a good idea to give it [to Giuliano de' Medici], and if it were a good idea to give it, whether it would be better for me to bring it myself or send it to you. Not giving it myself would make me worry that it would not be read, to say the least, by Giuliano, and that this Ardinghelli would take the credit for this latest work of mine.[1] Giving it is something I am being driven to by the necessity that hounds me, for I'm wasting away and cannot remain as I am for long without becoming contemptible because of my poverty.[2] Besides, I really want these Medici lords to begin making use of me, even if they'd start out by making me roll a stone around.[3] For then, if I couldn't win them over, I'd have only myself to blame. And by means of this treatise, were it to be read, it would be clear that during the fifteen years I've been studying statecraft, I have not been sleeping or playing around, and anyone should be happy to have the service of someone who has gained so much experience at the expense of others. Nor should there be any worry about my loyalty, for, having always kept my word, it would be hard for me to learn how to break it now, and whoever has been good and faithful for forty-three years,[4] as I have been, cannot change his nature, and to my loyalty and honesty my poverty bears witness.

8. Here Machiavelli worries that after an encounter with the Soderini family, he might return home only to be thrown into prison, the Bargello, where he had been held before.
9. This allusion to Pagolo Bertini is unclear, but Machiavelli may be referring to one of the conspirators against the Medici, since Machiavelli's name was found on an incriminating list ("the bill"), for which he was arrested and tortured (paid "the reckoning").
1. Piero, or Pietro, Ardinghelli (1470–1526) was a Medici partisan and was made one of Leo X's secretaries in 1514. Following the advice of Giulio de' Medici (1478–1534), who would become Pope Clement VII in 1523, Ardinghelli advised Giuliano to have nothing to do with Machiavelli.
2. The idea that poverty is contemptible was a classical commonplace.
3. Here Machiavelli underscores the desperation of his desire to return to Florence and to reenter political life there; his phrase may be an allusion to the punishment inflicted in hell on sinners such as Sisyphus (see Vergil, *Aeneid,* 6.616, on Sisyphus, and Dante, *Inferno,* 7.16–66, where this eternal punishment is meted out to the avaricious and the prodigal).
4. Machiavelli was born in 1469, so he was actually forty-four when he wrote this letter, although his service to the city of Florence ended a year earlier.

I'd appreciate it, then, if you'd write to me and tell me what you think about this matter. I commend myself to you. Be happy.[5]

On the tenth day of December, 1513.
Niccolò Machiavelli, in Florence

To Francesco Guicciardini

17 May 1521, Carpi[1]

To His Magnificent Master Francesco Guicciardini, J. U. D.,[2] Governor of Modena and Reggio, most worthy and greatly to be honored.

Magnificent Sir, Ruler Most Worthy of Respect,

I was seated on the crapper when your messenger arrived, and just then I was thinking about all the absurdities of this world, and devoting all my attention to imagining the kind of preacher I'd like for the position in Florence, and that he should be precisely the kind that would please me, because in this matter I want to be just as stubborn as I am about all my other opinions. And since, when I've been able to assist that republic, I've never failed her—something I've never done, if not with deeds, then with words, if not with words, then with gestures—I don't intend to fail her in this matter either. It's true that I know I'm opposed, as I am in many other things, to the opinion of the citizens there. They'd like a preacher who'd teach them the road to Paradise, and I'd find one who'd teach them the way to the Devil's house. And then they'd like him to be a man who's prudent, blameless, and true, whereas I'd like to find one who is crazier than Ponzo, craftier than Fra Girolamo, more hypocritical than Frate Alberto,[3] for that would seem to me to be a fine thing, and worthy of these good times, that everything

5. Machiavelli's final words in Latin are *Sis felix,* and can mean either "May you be happy" or "May you be prosperous."

1. On May 14, Machiavelli was sent to Carpi to transact business on behalf of the Medici with the *Capitolo,* or General Assembly, of the Franciscan order, which was meeting there at that time. He had also been asked by the masters of the Wool Merchants Guild in Florence to go there and arrange for Brother Giovanni Gualberto, known as *il Rovaio* (The North Wind) to come to the city and preach during Lent. Guicciardini had written to Machiavelli on May 17 that sending him to find a preacher would be like commissioning one or another of two well-known sodomites to find a beautiful wife for a friend. Continuing in this jocular vein, Guicciardini told Machiavelli that he would be sacrificing his honor if he suddenly converted and became pious, since he had always professed a contrary religious attitude, and that if he did convert, people would think he had become senile. Machiavelli's reply in this letter is equally jocular.
2. I.e., *Juris Utriusque Doctor,* "Doctor of Both Laws" (canon and civil). The lofty titles Machiavelli uses for Guicciardini are part of the joke in this comic letter that almost immediately descends, quite literally, to the level of the potty.
3. Possibly the trickster who is the main figure in the second tale on Day 2 of Boccaccio's *Decameron,* although he may also be a historical figure, Frate Alberto da Orvieto, who was sent to Florence in 1495 by Pope Alexander VI in an attempt to trick Savonarola into coming to Rome where the pope would have had him imprisoned and eventually executed. Ponzo's identity is obscure, but it is possible that he was an adversary of Savonarola ("Fra Girolamo").

we've experienced in the case of many friars should now be experienced in a single one, because I believe that this would be the true way of going to Paradise, namely to learn the way to Hell in order to avoid it. Besides, when one sees how much credit a bad man has who hides himself under the cloak of religion, it's easy to conjecture how much a good one would have who would truly—rather than just pretend to—walk through the mud in the footsteps of Saint Francis. So, since my fantasy seems good to me, I've planned to take il Rovaio,[4] and if he's like his brothers and sisters, that choice will be a good one. I'd appreciate it if, the next time you write to me, you'll let me know your opinion about this.

I continue in idleness here because I can't complete my commission until the friars have selected their leader and the assessors[5] are chosen, and I keep thinking about how I could sow so much discord among them, that here or elsewhere, they'll start going at one another with their wooden clogs.[6] And if I keep my wits about me, I think I'll certainly succeed, and I believe that Your Lordship's advice and assistance would be of great service to me. In fact, it would not be a bad idea if you were to come all the way here under the pretext that you were just going out on some excursion, or at least if you were to write to me, giving me some master stroke to use on them, because if you send me a servant once a day just for this purpose, as you did today, you would accomplish several good things. For one, you'll shed light on several pertinent matters for me; for another, you'll enhance my reputation among the members of this house when they see the dispatches coming thick and fast. And I can tell you that when the crossbowman arrived with your letter, and he said, bowing down to the ground, that he'd been sent to me expressly and in haste, all of them got up, bowing so much and making so much noise that everything was turned topsy-turvy. Several of them asked me for news, and in order to enhance my reputation, I said that the emperor was expected in Trento, that the Swiss had convened new assemblies, and that the king of France wanted to go and confer with that king, but that his counselors were advising him not to do so—and the result was that they all stood around with their mouths agape and their caps in their hands. And while I'm writing, I have a circle of them around me, and as they watch me writing at length, they marvel and look at me as if I were possessed by a spirit, and to make them marvel all the more, I sometimes stop moving my pen and hold my breath, and then they open their mouths as wide as though they were going to yawn. And if they knew what I'm writing to you, they would marvel even more.

4. See n. 1, p. 173.
5. Machiavelli's word for "leader" is *il generale,* which is short for *il ministro generale,* the "general minister" who headed the chapter and *ministered* to the needs of the brothers in it. "Assessors" are of a lower rank and manage the affairs of the chapter.
6. The typical footwear of friars.

Your Lordship knows what these friars say, that when one is confirmed as being in a state of grace, the devil no longer has the power to tempt him. So, I have no fear that they will hang their hypocrisy on me since I think I am really well confirmed.

As for the lies of the Carpigiani, I'd like to have a contest with all of them about that, because it's been a while since I got my doctorate in that subject, so I don't need to have Francesco Martelli[7] as my servant. For I've never said anything I believe for some time now, nor do I ever believe what I'm saying, and if at times I do indeed happen to tell the truth, I hide it among so many lies that it's difficult to find it.

I didn't speak with the ruler, because, having found lodgings,[8] I thought it was unnecessary for me to speak with him. It's certainly true that I observed him closely in church this morning for a little while as he stood looking at some paintings. To me he seemed a man who was well put together, and one should believe that the whole should correspond to the part and that he would be just the way he looked: for the hump on his back would not lie.[9] So, if I had your letter with me, I would've made a good try at drawing a bucketful out of him.[1] Still, no damage has been done, and tomorrow I'm expecting some advice from you about these affairs of mine and for you to send me one of those crossbowmen. But let him hurry and arrive covered in sweat so that the whole gang here will be amazed, for by doing that, you'll bring me honor and at the same time your crossbowmen will get a little exercise, which is very healthy for the horses on these spring days.

I'd write yet more to you now if I wanted to tire out my imagination, but I want to keep it as fresh as possible for tomorrow. I send my regards to your Lordship, and may you ever prosper as you desire.

In Carpi, 17 May 1521.
Your faithful Niccolò Machiavelli

Ambassador to the Friars Minor

7. His identity is unknown, but he must have been quite the storyteller.
8. Machiavelli was staying with Sigismondo Santi, the chancellor of Alberto III Pio (b. 1475; ruled 1477–1531), the prince of Carpi ("the ruler").
9. Machiavelli is implying that if Pio's body was deformed (he was a hunchback), then his mind and character were as well.
1. Machiavelli means he would have played a bunch of tricks on the man.

INTERPRETATIONS

ISAIAH BERLIN

Berlin opens his essay by noting how many varied interpretations there have been of Machiavelli's *The Prince* and *Discourses* since they appeared in the sixteenth century and also how much of a moral shock they have produced in their readers. He then devotes the first portion of his essay to a review of these diverse reactions. Some readers, he notes, operating on the basis of Machiavelli's republican sympathies, which are expressed directly in the *Discourses,* have seen *The Prince* as a warning against just such a ruler, a masterpiece of irony, an exposé, even a satire. Others have styled it a tough-minded version of the "Mirror for Princes," a genre of advice books written throughout the Middle Ages and the Renaissance usually recommending that the ruler be taught to follow Christian principles. There is a debate over whether, and to what extent, Machiavelli was a believing Christian, but despite the possibility that he was, many have treated his work as an attack on Christianity or the Catholic Church (as well as on the feudal system of the late Middle Ages). An important group of critics, especially in the last two centuries, have characterized Machiavelli as an anguished moralist, anguished precisely because he feels compelled to describe with such accuracy the real ways of the world of politics. Yet others dismiss the idea of anguish and present him simply as the ultimate political realist for whom morality is irrelevant. Many of these groups are opposed by those who take issue with the idea of Machiavelli the realist, faulting him instead as being unscientific, inspired by a fictional view of antiquity, and offering readers nothing more than a fantasy about princely success, especially in the last chapter of his work, in which he exhorts the Medici to unite Italy and drive out the "barbarian" invaders (namely, the French and the Spanish). This exhortation actually led many, especially Italian, readers in the eighteenth and nineteenth centuries to celebrate Machiavelli as a patriot whose dream of a united Italy finally came to fruition in 1871. According to Berlin, one of the most influential views that has held sway in the twentieth century is that Machiavelli is to be credited for having separated (amoral) politics from ethics. Berlin finally ends his summary by noting that the most common view of Machiavelli and his prince nowadays actually dates back to the Renaissance itself, the view that he is a teacher of evil, someone in league with the devil (if not the devil himself), and that his prince, who became the "murderous Machiavel" on the Elizabethan stage, is a brutal, immoral, ruthless figure who pursues power at any price, more Mafia Don than public servant.

From The Question of Machiavelli†

* * *

There is prima facie something strange about so violent a disparity of judgments. What other thinker has presented so many facets to the students of his ideas? What other writer—and he not even a recognized philosopher—has caused his readers to disagree about his purposes so deeply and so widely? Yet, I must repeat, Machiavelli does not write obscurely; nearly all his interpreters praise him for his terse, dry, clear prose.

What is it that has proved so arresting to so many?

Machiavelli, we are often told, was not concerned with morals. The most influential of all modern interpretations—that of Benedetto Croce[1] * * *—is that Machiavelli, in E. W. Cochrane's words, "did not deny the validity of Christian morality, and he did not pretend that a crime required by political necessity was any less a crime. Rather he discovered * * * that this morality simply did not hold in political affairs and that any policy based on the assumption that it did would end in disaster. His factual, objective description of contemporary political practices, then, is a sign not of cynicism or detachment but of anguish."[2]

This account, it seems to me, contains two basic misinterpretations. The first is that the clash is one between "Christian morality" and "political necessity." The implication is that there is an incompatibility between, on the one hand, morality—the region of ultimate values sought after for their own sakes, values recognition of which alone enables us to speak of "crimes" or morally to justify and condemn anything; and, on the other, politics—the art of adapting means to ends, the region of technical skills. * * * This is the heart of the divorce of politics from ethics which Croce and many others attribute to Machiavelli. But this seems to me to rest on a mistake.

If ethics is confined to, let us say, Stoic, or Christian or Kantian, or even some types of utilitarian ethics, where the source and criterion of value are the word of God, or eternal reason, or some inner

† From *New York Review of Books* (November 4, 1971): 20–32. That essay is itself an abbreviated version of "The Originality of Machiavelli" in *Studies on Machiavelli*, ed. Myron P. Gilmore (Florence: Sansoni, 1972), pp. 149–206. The full essay is included in revised form in Berlin's *Against the Current: Essays in the History of Ideas*, ed. Henry Hardy, 2nd ed. (Princeton, NJ: Princeton UP, 2013), and our excerpts have been collated with this text by Berlin's editor, who has sometimes preferred its readings. Notes are Berlin's unless otherwise indicated.

1. Benedetto Croce is the father of the view that Machiavelli separated politics from ethics as two separate but equal systems of values; see his *Etica e politica* (Bari: Laterza, 1931) [editor's note].
2. Eric W. Cochrane, "Machiavelli 1940–1960," *The Journal of Modern History*, 33 (1961): 115.

sense or knowledge of good and evil, of right or wrong, voices which speak directly to the individual consciousness with absolute authority, this might have been tenable. But there exists an equally time-honored ethics, that of the Greek *polis*, of which Aristotle provided the clearest exposition. Since men are beings made by nature to live in communities, their communal purposes are the ultimate values from which the rest are derived, or with which their ends as individuals are identified. * * *

Ethics so conceived—the code of conduct of, or the ideal to be pursued by, the individual—cannot be known save by understanding the purpose and character of his *polis;* still less be capable of being divorced from it, even in thought. This is the kind of pre-Christian morality that Machiavelli takes for granted. "It is well known," says Benedetto Croce, "that Machiavelli discovered the necessity and the autonomy of politics, politics which is beyond moral good and evil, which has its own laws against which it is futile to rebel, which cannot be exorcised and banished from the world with holy water." Beyond good and evil in some non-Aristotelian, religious or liberal-Kantian sense; but not beyond the good and evil of those communities, ancient or modern, whose sacred values are social through and through. * * *

But if Aristotle and Machiavelli are right about what men are (and should be—and Machiavelli's ideal is, particularly in the *Discourses*, drawn in vivid colors), political activity is intrinsic to human nature, and while individuals here and there may opt out, the mass of mankind cannot do so; and its communal life determines the moral duties of its members. Hence in opposing the "laws of politics" to "good and evil" Machiavelli is not contrasting two "autonomous" spheres of acting—the "political" and the "moral": he is contrasting his own "political" ethics with another ethical conception which governs the lives of persons who are of no interest to him. * * *

He is indeed rejecting Christian ethics, but in favor of another system, another moral universe—the world of Pericles or of Scipio, or even of the Duke Valentino, a society geared to ends just as ultimate as the Christian faith, a society in which men fight and are ready to die for (public) ends which they pursue for their own sakes. They are choosing not a realm of means (called politics) as opposed to a realm of ends (called morals), but opt for a rival (Roman or classical) morality, an alternative realm of ends. In other words the conflict is between two moralities, Christian and pagan (or, as some wish to call it, aesthetic), not between autonomous realms of morals and politics. * * *

The second thesis in this connection which seems to me mistaken is the idea that Machiavelli viewed the crimes of his society with anguish. * * * There is no evidence for this: there is no trace of agony in his political works, any more than in his plays or letters.

The pagan world that Machiavelli prefers is built on recognition of the need for systematic guile and force by rulers, and he seems to think it natural and not at all exceptional or morally agonizing that they should employ these weapons wherever they are needed. Nor is the distinction he draws that between the rulers and the ruled. The subjects or citizens must be Romans too: they do not need the *virtù* of the rulers, but if they also cheat, Machiavelli's maxims will not work; they must be poor, militarized, honest and obedient; if they lead Christian lives, they will accept too uncomplainingly the rule of mere bullies and scoundrels. No sound republic can be built of such materials as these. Theseus and Romulus, Moses and Cyrus did not preach humility to their subjects, or a view of this world as but a temporary resting-place.

But it is the first misinterpretation that goes deepest, that which represents Machiavelli as caring little or nothing for moral issues. This is surely not borne out by his own language. Anyone whose thought revolves round central concepts such as the good and the bad, the corrupt and the pure, has an ethical scale in mind in terms of which he gives moral praise and blame. Machiavelli's values are not Christian, but they are moral values. * * *

It does not, of course, follow that he was not often fascinated by the techniques of political life as such. The advice given equally to conspirators and their enemies, the professional appraisal of the methods of Oliverotto or Sforza or Baglioni spring from typical humanist curiosity, the search for an applied science of politics, fascination by knowledge for its own sake, whatever the implications. But the moral ideal, that of the citizen of the Roman Republic, is never far away. * * *

This leaves still with us the thorny problem of the relation of *The Prince* to the *Discourses*. But whatever the disparities, the central strain which runs through both is one and the same. The vision, the dream—typical of many writers who see themselves as tough-minded realists—of the strong, united, effective, morally regenerated, splendid and victorious *patria*, whether it is saved by the *virtù* of one man or many, remains central and constant. * * *

His vision is social and political. Hence the traditional view of him as simply a specialist on how to get the better of others, a vulgar cynic who says that Sunday-school precepts are all very well, but in a world full of evil men you too must lie, kill and betray if you are to get somewhere, is incorrect. * * * Machiavelli is not specially concerned with the opportunism of ambitious individuals; the ideal before his eyes is a shining vision of Florence or of Italy. In this respect he is a typically impassioned humanist of the Renaissance, save that his ideal is not artistic or cultural but political. * * *

Machiavelli's values, I should like to repeat, are not instrumental but moral and ultimate, and he calls for great sacrifices in their name. For them he rejects the rival scale—the Christian principles of *ozio*[3] and meekness—not, indeed, as being defective in themselves, but as inapplicable to the conditions of real life. * * *

If you object to the political methods recommended because they seem to you morally detestable, if you refuse to embark upon them because they are * * * too frightening, Machiavelli has no answer, no argument. In that case you are perfectly entitled to lead a morally good life, be a private citizen (or a monk), seek some corner of your own. But, in that event, you must not make yourself responsible for the lives of others or expect good fortune; in a material sense you must expect to be ignored or destroyed. * * *

There are two worlds, that of personal morality and that of public organization. There are two ethical codes, both ultimate; not two "autonomous" regions, one of "ethics," another of "politics," but two (for him) exhaustive alternatives between two conflicting systems of value. If a man chooses the "first good way," he must, presumably, give up all hope of Athens and Rome, of a noble and glorious society in which human beings can thrive and grow strong, proud, wise and productive. Indeed, they must abandon all hope of a tolerable life on earth: for men cannot live outside society; they will not survive collectively if they are led by men who (like Soderini) are influenced by the first, "private" morality; they will not be able to realize their minimal goals as men; they will end in a state of moral, not merely political, degradation. But if a man chooses, as Machiavelli himself has done, the second course, then he must suppress his private qualms, if he has any, for it is certain that those who are too squeamish during the remaking of a society, or even during the pursuit and maintenance of its power and glory, will go to the wall. Whoever has chosen to make an omelette cannot do so without breaking eggs. * * *

There is more than one world, and more than one set of virtues: confusion between them is disastrous. One of the chief illusions caused by ignoring this is the Platonic-Hebraic-Christian view that virtuous rulers create virtuous men. This, according to Machiavelli, is not true. Generosity is a virtue, but not in princes. A generous prince will ruin the citizens by taxing them too heavily, a mean prince (and Machiavelli does not say that meanness is a good quality in private men) will save the purses of the citizens and so add to public welfare. A kind ruler—and kindness is a virtue—may let intriguers and stronger characters dominate him, and so cause chaos and corruption.

3. Idleness (Italian); often used in a negative sense such as "laziness" or "indolence." Traditionally, *ozio* (*otium* in Latin) was valued by Christians throughout the Middle Ages and beyond as a time of spiritual contemplation, as opposed to the active life most people normally lived. Machiavelli is decidedly hostile to *ozio* in every sense of the word [editor's note].

Other writers of "mirrors for princes" are also rich in such maxims, but they do not draw the implications; Machiavelli's use of such generalizations is not theirs; he is not moralizing at large, but illustrating a specific thesis: that the nature of men dictates a public morality that is different from, and may come into collision with, the virtues of men who profess to believe in, and try to act by, Christian precepts. These may not be wholly unrealizable in quiet times, in private life, but they lead to ruin outside this. The analogy between a state and people and an individual is a fallacy: "a state and a people are governed in a different way from an individual"; "not individual good but common good is what makes cities great."

One may disagree with this. One may argue that the greatness, glory and wealth of a state are hollow ideals, or detestable, if the citizens are oppressed and treated as mere means to the grandeur of the whole. * * * If so, one is simply contradicting Machiavelli's thesis. * * * He is convinced that states which have lost the appetite for power are doomed to decadence and are likely to be destroyed by their more vigorous and better-armed neighbors; and Vico and modern "realistic" thinkers have echoed this.

Machiavelli is possessed by a clear, intense, narrow vision of a society in which human talents can be made to contribute to a powerful and splendid whole. He prefers republican rule, in which the interests of the rulers do not conflict with those of the ruled. But * * * he prefers a well-governed principate to a decadent republic; and the qualities he admires and thinks capable of being welded into—indeed, indispensable to—a durable society are not different in *The Prince* and the *Discourses:* energy, boldness, practical skill, imagination, vitality, self-discipline, shrewdness, public spirit, good fortune, *antiqua virtus, virtù*—firmness in adversity, strength of character, as celebrated by Xenophon or Livy. All his more shocking maxims—those responsible for the "murderous Machiavel" of the Elizabethan stage—are descriptions of methods of realizing this single end: the classical, humanistic and patriotic vision that dominates him.

Let me cite the best known of his most notoriously wicked pieces of advice to princes. You must employ terrorism or kindness, as the case dictates. Severity is usually more effective, but humanity, in some situations, brings better fruit. You may excite fear but not hatred, for hatred will destroy you in the end. It is best to keep men poor and on a permanent war footing, for this will be an antidote to the two great enemies of active obedience—ambition and boredom—and the ruled will then feel in constant need of great men to lead them (the twentieth century offers us only too much evidence for this sharp insight). Competition—divisions between classes—in a society is desirable, for it generates energy and ambition in the right degree.

Religion must be promoted even though it may be false, provided it is of a kind that preserves social solidarity and promotes manly virtues, as Christianity has historically failed to do. When you confer benefits (he says, following Aristotle), do so yourself; but if dirty work is to be done, let others do it, for then they, not the prince, will be blamed, and the prince can gain favor by duly cutting off their heads; for men prefer vengeance and security to liberty. * * * Men will be false to you unless you compel them to be true by creating circumstances in which falsehood will not pay. And so on.

These examples are typical of "the devil's partner." Now and then doubts assail our author: he wonders whether a man high-minded enough to labor to create a state admirable by Roman standards will be tough enough to use the violent and wicked means prescribed; and, conversely, whether a sufficiently ruthless and brutal man will be disinterested enough to compass the public good which alone justifies the evil means. Yet Moses and Theseus, Romulus and Cyrus combined these properties. What has been once, can be again: the implication is optimistic.

These maxims have one property in common: they are designed to create or resurrect or maintain an order that will satisfy what the author conceives as men's most permanent interests. Machiavelli's values may be erroneous, dangerous, odious; but he is in earnest. He is not cynical. The end is always the same: a state conceived after the analogy of Periclean Athens, or Sparta, but above all the Roman Republic. Such an end, for which men naturally crave (of this he thinks that history and observation provide conclusive evidence), "excuses" any means. In judging means, look only to the end: if the state goes under, all is lost. * * * Romulus could not have founded Rome without killing Remus. Brutus would not have preserved the republic if he had not killed his sons. Moses and Theseus, Romulus, Cyrus and the liberators of Athens had to destroy in order to build. Such conduct, so far from being condemned, is held up to admiration by the classical historians and the Bible. Machiavelli is their admirer and faithful spokesman.

What is there, then, about his words, about his tone, which has caused such tremors among his readers? * * * It is evident that the effect of the shock that he administered was not a temporary one: it has lasted almost to our own day.

Leaving aside the historical problem of why there was no immediate contemporary criticism, let us consider the continuous discomfort caused to its readers during the four centuries that have passed since *The Prince* was placed upon the Index. The great originality, the tragic implications of Machiavelli's theses seem to me to reside in their relation to a Christian civilization. It was all very well to live by the light of pagan ideals in pagan times; but to preach paganism more than a thousand years after the triumph of Christianity was to do so after the loss of innocence—and to be forcing men to make a conscious choice. The choice is painful because it is a choice between two entire worlds. * * *

In killing, deceiving, betraying, Machiavelli's princes and republicans are doing evil things, not condonable in terms of common morality. It is Machiavelli's great merit that he does not deny this. Marsilio, Hobbes, Spinoza, and, in their own fashion, Hegel and Marx did try to deny it. So did many a defender of the *raison d'état,* imperialist and populist, Catholic and Protestant. These thinkers argue for a single moral system: and seek to show that the morality which justifies, and indeed demands, such deeds is continuous with, and a more rational form of, the confused ethical beliefs of the uninstructed morality which forbids them absolutely. * * *

Machiavelli is not a defender of any such abstract theory. It does not occur to him to employ such casuistry. He is transparently honest and clear. In choosing the life of a statesman, or even the life of a citizen with enough civic sense to want his state to be as successful and splendid as possible, you commit yourself to rejection of Christian behavior. * * *

Compromise with current morality leads to bungling, which is always despicable, and when practiced by statesmen involves men in ruin. The end "excuses" the means, however horrible these may be in terms of even pagan ethics, if it is (in terms of the ideals of Thucydides or Polybius, Cicero or Livy) lofty enough. * * * If one can produce the right results by using the devotion and affection of men, let this be done by all means. There is no value in causing suffering as such. But if one cannot, then Moses, Romulus, Theseus, Cyrus are the exemplars, and fear must be employed. * * *

This position has not been properly understood by some of those who claim to be not unsympathetic to Machiavelli. * * * Perhaps the majority of his interpreters * * * look on him as the originator, or at least a defender, of what later came to be called "raison d'état," "Staatsraison," "Ragion di Stato"—the justification of immoral acts when undertaken on behalf of the state in exceptional circumstances. * * * These parallels seem to me to rest on a deep but characteristic misunderstanding of Machiavelli's thesis. He is not saying that while in normal situations current morality—that is, the Christian or semi-Christian code of ethics—should prevail, yet abnormal conditions can occur such that the entire social structure in which alone this code can function becomes jeopardized, and in emergencies of this kind acts that are usually regarded as wicked, and rightly forbidden, are justified. * * *

For the defenders of the *raison d'état,* the sole justification of these measures is that they are exceptional—that they are needed to preserve a system the purpose of which is precisely to preclude the need for such odious measures, so that such steps are justified only because they will end the situations that render them necessary. But for Machiavelli these measures are, in a sense, themselves quite normal. No doubt they are called for only by extreme need; yet political life tends to generate a good many such needs. * * *

The notion of *raison d'état* entails a conflict of values which may be agonizing to morally good and sensitive men. For Machiavelli there is no conflict. Public life has its own morality, to which Christian principles (or any absolute personal values) tend to be a gratuitous obstacle. This life has its own standards: it does not require perpetual terror, but it approves, or at least permits, the use of force where it is needed to promote the ends of political society.

Sheldon Wolin[4] seems to me right in insisting that Machiavelli believes in a permanent "economy of violence"—the need for a consistent reserve of force always in the background to keep things going in such a way that the virtues admired by him, and by the classical thinkers to whom he appeals, can be protected and allowed to flower. Men brought up within a community in which such force, or its possibility, is used rightly will live the happy lives of Greeks or Romans during their finest hours. They will be characterized by vitality, genius, variety, pride, power, success (Machiavelli scarcely ever speaks of arts or sciences); but it will not, in any clear sense, be a Christian commonwealth. The moral conflict which this situation raises will trouble only those who are not prepared to abandon either course: those who assume that the two incompatible lives are, in fact, reconcilable. * * *

One of the deepest assumptions of Western political thought is the doctrine, scarcely questioned during its long ascendancy, that there exists some single principle that not only regulates the course of the sun and the stars, but prescribes their proper behavior to all animate creatures. Animals and sub-rational beings of all kinds follow it by instinct; higher beings attain to consciousness of it, and are free to abandon it, but only to their doom. This doctrine, in one version or another, has dominated European thought since Plato; it has appeared in many forms, and has generated many similes and allegories. At its center is the vision of an impersonal nature or reason or cosmic purpose, or of a divine creator whose power has endowed all things and creatures each with a specific function; these functions are elements in a single harmonious whole, and are intelligible in terms of it alone. * * *

This unifying monistic pattern is at the very heart of the traditional rationalism, religious and atheistic, metaphysical and

4. In his book *Politics and Vision* (Little, Brown, 1960).

scientific, transcendental and naturalistic, that has been characteristic of Western civilization. It is this rock, upon which Western beliefs and lives had been founded, that Machiavelli seems, in effect, to have split open. So great a reversal cannot, of course, be due to the acts of a single individual. It could scarcely have taken place in a stable social and moral order; many beside him, ancient skeptics, medieval nominalists and secularists, Renaissance humanists, doubtless supplied their share of the dynamite. The purpose of this essay is to suggest that it was Machiavelli who lit the fatal fuse. * * *

When such solutions were discussed in earlier periods, it was normally assumed that the perfect society could be conceived, at least in outline; for otherwise what standard could one use to condemn existing arrangements as imperfect? It might not be realizable here, below. Men were too ignorant or too weak or too vicious to create it. Or it was said (by some materialistic thinkers in the centuries following *The Prince*) that it was technical means that were lacking, that no one had yet discovered methods of overcoming the material obstacles to the golden age; that we were not technologically or educationally or morally sufficiently advanced. But it was never said that there was something incoherent in the very notion itself.

Plato and the Stoics, the Hebrew prophets and Christian medieval thinkers, and the writers of Utopias from More onward had a vision of what it was that men fell short of; they claimed, as it were, to be able to measure the gap between the reality and the ideal. But if Machiavelli is right, this entire tradition—the central current of Western thought—is fallacious. If his position is valid then it is impossible to construct even the notion of such a perfect society, for there exist at least two sets of virtues—let us call them the Christian and the pagan—which are not merely in practice, but in principle, incompatible. * * *

This was indeed a profoundly upsetting conclusion. It entailed that if men wished to live and act consistently, and understand what goals they were pursuing, they were obliged to examine their moral values. What if they found that they were compelled to make a choice between two incommensurable systems? To choose as they did without the aid of an infallible measuring rod which certified one form of life as being superior to all others, and could be used to demonstrate this to the satisfaction of all rational men? Is it, perhaps, this awful truth, implicit in Machiavelli's exposition, that has upset the moral consciousness of men, and has haunted their minds so permanently and obsessively ever since?

Machiavelli did not himself propound it. There was no problem and no agony for him; he shows no trace of skepticism or relativism; he chose his side, and took little interest in the values that this choice ignored or flouted. The conflict between his scale of values and that of conventional morality clearly did not (*pace* Croce and the other defenders of the "anguished humanist" interpretation) seem to worry Machiavelli himself. It upset only those who came after him, and were not prepared, on the one hand, to abandon their own moral values (Christian or humanist) together with the entire way of thought and action of which these were a part; nor, on the other, to deny the validity of, at any rate, much of Machiavelli's analysis of the political facts, and the (largely pagan) values and outlook that went with it, embodied in the social structure which he painted so brilliantly and convincingly. * * *

I should like to suggest that it is Machiavelli's juxtaposition of the two outlooks—the two incompatible moral worlds, as it were—in the minds of his readers, and the collision and acute moral discomfort that follow, which, over the years, has been responsible for the desperate efforts to interpret his doctrines away, to represent him as a cynical and therefore ultimately shallow defender of power politics; or as a diabolist; or as a patriot prescribing for particularly desperate situations which seldom arise; or as a mere time server; or as an embittered political failure; or as nothing more than a mouthpiece of truths we have always known but did not like to utter; or again as the enlightened translator of universally accepted ancient social principles into empirical terms; or as a crypto-republican satirist (a descendant of Juvenal, a forerunner of Orwell); or as a cold scientist, a mere political technologist free from moral implications; or as a typical Renaissance publicist practicing a now obsolete genre; or in any of the numerous other roles that have been and are still being cast for him.

Machiavelli may have possessed some, at any rate, of these attributes, but concentration on one or other of them as constituting his essential, "true" character seems to me to stem from reluctance to face, still more discuss, the uncomfortable truth that Machiavelli had, unintentionally, almost casually, uncovered: namely that not all ultimate values are necessarily compatible with one another—that there might be a conceptual (what used to be called "philosophical"), and not merely a material, obstacle to the notion of the single ultimate solution which, if it were only realized, would establish the perfect society.

Yet if no such solution can, even in principle, be formulated, then all political and, indeed, moral problems are thereby transformed. This is not a division of politics from ethics. It is the uncovering of the possibility of more than one system of values, with no criterion common to the systems whereby a rational choice can be made between them. This is not the rejection of Christianity for paganism (although Machiavelli clearly prefers the latter), nor of paganism for Christianity (which, at least in its historical form, he thought incompatible with the basic needs of normal men), but the setting of them side by side, with the implicit invitation to men to choose either a good, virtuous private life or a good, successful social existence, but not both. * * *

Croce has rightly insisted that Machiavelli is not detached or cynical or irresponsible. His patriotism, his republicanism, his commitment are not in doubt. He suffered for his convictions. He thought continually about Florence and Italy, and of how to save them. Yet it is not his character, nor his plays, his poetry, his histories, his diplomatic or political activities that have gained him his unique fame. Nor can this be due only to his psychological or sociological imagination. His psychology is often excessively primitive. He scarcely seems to allow for the bare possibility of sustained and genuine altruism; he refuses to consider the motives of men who are prepared to fight against enormous odds, who ignore *necessità* and are prepared to lose their lives in a hopeless cause. * * *

Few would deny that Machiavelli's writings, more particularly *The Prince,* have scandalized mankind more deeply and continuously than any other political treatise. The reason for this, let me say again, is not the discovery that politics is the play of power—that political relationships between and within independent communities involve the use of force and fraud, and are unrelated to the principles professed by the players. That knowledge is as old as conscious thought about politics—certainly as old as Thucydides and Plato. Nor is it merely caused by the examples that he offers of success in acquiring or holding power—the descriptions of the massacre at Sinigaglia or the behavior of Agathocles or Oliverotto da Fermo are no more or less horrifying than similar stories in Tacitus or Guicciardini. The proposition that crime can pay is nothing new in Western historiography. * * *

Machiavelli's cardinal achievement is his uncovering of an insoluble dilemma, the planting of a permanent question mark in the path of posterity. It stems from his *de facto* recognition that ends equally ultimate, equally sacred, may contradict each other, that entire systems of value may come into collision without possibility of rational arbitration, and that this happens not merely in exceptional circumstances, as a result of abnormality or accident or error—the clash of Antigone and Creon or in the story of Tristan—but (this was surely new) as part of the normal human situation.

For those who look on such collisions as rare, exceptional and disastrous, the choice to be made is necessarily an agonizing experience for which, as a rational being, one cannot prepare (since no rules apply). But for Machiavelli, at least of *The Prince,* the *Discourses, Mandragola,* there is no agony. One chooses as one chooses because one knows what one wants, and is ready to pay the price. * * *

I do not mean that Machiavelli explicitly asserts that there is a pluralism or even a dualism of values between which conscious choices must be made. But this follows from the contrasts he draws between the conduct he admires and that which he condemns. He seems to take for granted the obvious superiority of classical civic virtue and brushes aside Christian values, as well as conventional morality, with a disparaging or patronizing sentence or two, or smooth words about the misinterpretation of Christianity. * * *

If what Machiavelli believed is true, this undermines one major assumption of Western thought: namely that somewhere in the past or the future, in this world or the next, in the church or the laboratory, in the speculations of the metaphysician or the findings of the social scientist, or in the uncorrupted heart of the simple good man, there is to be found the final solution of the question of how men should live. If this is false (and if more than one equally valid answer to the question can be returned, then it is false), the idea of the sole true, objective, universal human ideal crumbles. The very search for it becomes not merely utopian in practice, but conceptually incoherent. * * *

One can surely see how this might seem unfaceable to men, believers or atheists, empiricists or apriorists, brought up on the opposite assumption. Nothing could well be more upsetting to those brought up in a monistic religious or, at any rate, moral, social or political system than a breach in it. This is the dagger of which Meinecke speaks,[5] with which Machiavelli inflicted the wound that has never healed; even though Felix Gilbert[6] is right in thinking that he did not bear the scars of it himself. For he remained a monist, albeit a pagan one.

Machiavelli was doubtless guilty of much confusion and exaggeration. He confused the proposition that ultimate ideals may be incompatible with the very different proposition that the more conventional human ideals—founded on ideas of natural law, brotherly love and human goodness—were unrealizable, and that those who acted on the opposite assumption were fools, and at times dangerous ones; and he attributed this dubious proposition to antiquity, and believed that it was verified by history.

The first of these assertions strikes at the root of all doctrines which entail the possibility of attaining, or at least formulating, final solutions; the second is empirical, commonplace and not self-evident. The two propositions are not, in any case, identical or logically connected.

5. In the omitted first part of the essay Berlin speaks of "Meinecke, for whom he is the father of *Staatsräson,* with which he plunged a dagger into the body politic of the West" [Hardy's note].
6. Gilbert wrote *Machiavelli and Guicciardini: Politics and History in Sixteenth Century Florence* (Princeton, NJ: Princeton University Press, 1965). Friedrich Meinecke wrote *Die Idee der Staatsräson in der neueren Geschichte,* which was published in Germany in 1924 and was first translated into English by Douglas Scott as *Machiavellism: The Doctríne of Raison d'État and Its Place in Modern History* (London, 1947) [editor's note].

Moreover he exaggerated wildly: the idealized types of the Periclean Greek or the Roman of the old Republic may be irreconcilable with the ideal citizen of a Christian commonwealth (supposing such were conceivable), but in practice—above all in history, to which our author went for illustrations if not for evidence—pure types seldom obtain. * * * Still, to attack and inflict lasting damage on a central assumption of an entire civilization is an achievement of the first order.

Machiavelli does not affirm this dualism. He merely takes for granted the superiority of Roman *antiqua virtus* (which may be maddening to those who do not) over the Christian life as taught by the Church. He utters a few casual words about what Christianity might have become, but does not expect it to change its actual character. There he leaves the matter. Anyone who believes in Christian morality, and regards the Christian commonwealth as its embodiment, but at the same time largely accepts the validity of Machiavelli's political and psychological analysis and does not reject the secular heritage of Rome—a man in this predicament is faced with a dilemma which, if Machiavelli is right, is not merely unsolved, but insoluble. * * *

This is the negative implication. There is also one that is positive, and might have surprised and perhaps displeased Machiavelli. So long as only one ideal is the true goal, it will always seem to men that no means can be too difficult, no price too high, to do whatever is required to realize the ultimate goal. Such certainty is one of the great justifications of fanaticism, compulsion, persecution. But if not all values are compatible with one another, and choices must be made for no better reason than that each value is what it is, and we choose it for what it is, and not because it can be shown on some single scale to be higher than another, * * * then a picture emerges different from that constructed round the ancient principle that there is only one good for men.

If there is only one solution to the puzzle, then the only problems are, first, how to find it, then how to realize it, and finally how to convert others to the solution by persuasion or by force. But if this is not so (Machiavelli contrasts two ways of life, but there could be, and, save for fanatical monists, there obviously are, more than two), then the path is open to empiricism, pluralism, toleration, compromise. Toleration is historically the product of the realization of the irreconcilability of equally dogmatic faiths, and the practical improbability of complete victory of one over the other. Those who wished to survive realized that they had to tolerate error. They gradually came to see merits in diversity, and so became skeptical about definitive solutions in human affairs.

But it is one thing to accept something in practice, another to justify it rationally. Machiavelli's "scandalous" writings begin the latter process. This was a major turning-point, and its intellectual consequences, wholly unintended by its originator, were, by a fortunate irony of history (which some call its dialectic), the bases of the very liberalism that Machiavelli would surely have condemned as feeble and characterless, lacking in single-minded pursuit of power, in splendor, in organization, in *virtù,* in power to discipline unruly men against huge odds into one energetic whole. Yet he is, in spite of himself, one of the makers of pluralism, and of its—to him—perilous acceptance of toleration.

By breaking the original unity, he helped to cause men to become aware of the necessity of making agonizing choices between incompatible alternatives, incompatible in practice or, worse still, for logical reasons, in public and in private life (for the two could not, it became obvious, be genuinely kept distinct). His achievement is of the first order, if only because the dilemma has never given men peace since it came to light (it remains unsolved, but we have learned to live with it). Men had, no doubt, in practice, often enough experienced the conflict that Machiavelli made explicit. He converted its expression from a paradox into something approaching a commonplace. * * *

To know the worst is not always to be liberated from its consequences; nevertheless it is preferable to ignorance. It is this painful truth that Machiavelli forced on our attention, not by formulating it explicitly, but perhaps the more effectively by relegating much uncriticized traditional morality to the realm of Utopia. This is what, at any rate, I should like to suggest. Where more than twenty interpretations hold the field, the addition of one more cannot be deemed an impertinence. At worst it will be no more than yet another attempt to solve the problem, now more than four centuries old, of which Croce at the end of his long life spoke as "Una questione che forse non si chiuderà mai: la questione del Machiavelli."[7]

J. G. A. POCOCK

In his groundbreaking book, *The Machiavellian Moment,* Pocock is concerned with the development of republican political philosophy in Renaissance Italy and with the impact it had on English thought during and after their civil war (1642–60) and on America at the time of their revolution. The "moment" he refers to is the period when a republic must confront the problem of legitimacy that is needed to maintain the stability of its institutions and the allegiance of its citizens. This moment is defined as "Machiavellian" because Machiavelli and his friends and associates were concerned precisely with that problem. In Pocock's reading of *The Prince,* he argues that the work presents the prince as an innovator, the creator of a new state, but that does not

7. "A question that may never be settled: the question of Machiavelli."

solve the problem of how to make that state stable and secure. According to Pocock, that is the solution Machiavelli offers in his *Discourses:* he attempts to show how a modern republic can legitimize itself by imitating the Roman one, and the bulk of Pocock's book is consequently devoted to the *Discourses* and the influence the work had on contemporary and subsequent republican thought.

From Machiavelli's *Il Principe*†

* * * *Il Principe* is not a work of ideology, in the sense that it cannot be identified as expressing the outlook of a group. It is rather an analytic study of innovation and its consequences; but within that character, it proceeds straight to the analysis of the ultimate problem raised by both innovation and the decay of citizenship. This was the problem of *fortuna,* to which Guicciardini and the lesser *ottimati*[1] had not yet addressed themselves, perhaps because the assumption that they belonged to an elite was still strong enough to carry the implication that they were relatively secure. Machiavelli led too vulnerable an existence to make any such assumptions concerning himself; but the theoretical exploration into which he was led was not inconsistent with the optimate intellectual position. If politics be thought of as the art of dealing with the contingent event, it is the art of dealing with *fortuna* as the force which directs such events and thus symbolizes pure, uncontrolled, and unlegitimated contingency. * * *

[Pocock goes on to note how civic humanists of fifteenth-century Italy, such as Leonardo Bruni, followed a tradition stretching back to Boethius in late antiquity that saw the ruler as a man whose *virtus* or *virtù* was identical with what we would normally refer to as virtue. The civic humanists claimed that the prince could rely on that *virtù* to defeat Fortune and that if the other citizens of the state also possessed some version of the ruler's virtue, then the state as a whole was legitimized by its people's collective morality. Machiavelli is thus seen as grappling with the problems that arise when his ideal prince acts as an innovator who establishes a new state by means of his *virtù,* which cannot be equated with virtue, and who lacks the kind of legitimacy enjoyed by hereditary rulers.

† From *The Machiavellian Moment: Florentine Political Thought and the Atlantic Republican Tradition* (Princeton, NJ: Princeton University Press, 1975), pp. 156, 160–71, 173, 175–81. Notes are Pocock's unless otherwise indicated, with full bibliographical information supplied by the editor.

1. Optimates; members of the elite class of Florentine citizens, some more powerful and important than others, who were the equivalent of the nobility in states such as France and England. They included many of Machiavelli's friends, such as Francesco Guicciardini, but not Machiavelli himself [editor's note].

Simply put, Machiavelli's problem is that princely innovation is morally problematic and necessarily destabilizing.]

* * *

Innovation, the overthrow of an established system, opens the door to fortune because it offends some and disturbs all, creating a situation in which they have not yet had time to grow accustomed to the new order. * * * The new prince, therefore, required exceptional and extraordinary qualities, standing outside the norm defined by the case of the *principe naturale.* These qualities might be termed *virtù,* that by which form was imposed on the matter of *fortuna,* but since form and matter must be appropriate to one another it followed that the innovator's exposure to fortune, being extraordinary, must be met by extraordinary *virtù.* * * * The prince might have acquired his position through his own arms or those of supporters; he might owe it to his own abilities or to sheer good luck. When Machiavelli uses *virtù* and *fortuna* to denote the second of these antitheses, he is not using them with absolute precision. Since it was almost unthinkable that a man should acquire power without displaying some *virtù* of his own, there was always a sense in which *virtù* was the instrument of the innovation which exposed him to *fortuna;* but on the other hand *virtù* continued to mean that by which fortune was controlled, and the essential distinction lay between an innovator having means of his own to stay where he was and one continuing in dependence on whatever had put him there. At this point the second antithesis opened to include the first, and *virtù* took on the double meaning of the instruments of power, such as arms, and the personal qualities needed to wield those instruments.

In two ways, therefore, the nature and circumstances of the innovation operated to vary the problem which the innovator confronted. The more he could transfer to himself the habitual legitimacy enjoyed by his predecessor, the less he was exposed to the naked confrontation of *virtù* and *fortuna,* and the less urgent his need of *virtù* (in either of its meanings) became. The more his innovation had rendered him dependent on circumstances and people outside his immediate control, the greater his exposure to *fortuna* and his need of *virtù* to emancipate him. * * *

* * *

The insecurity of political innovation * * * springs from the fact that it injures some and unsettles all, while creating a situation to which they have not yet had time to grow accustomed. Perhaps the key to the thought of *Il Principe* is Machiavelli's perception that behavior in such situations is partly predictable, so that strategies for acting in them may be devised; his great originality is that of a student of delegitimized politics. But to the extent that structures of accustomed behavior survive the prince's acquisition of the territory, the discussion of human behavior outside such structures must be postponed and the question is how these will affect the prince's power and authority. In chapters III to V, Machiavelli examines aspects of this question, and the emphasis throughout is on the idea of the accustomed. * * *

In all this it is noteworthy that Machiavelli seems to be presupposing an entirely traditional form of society, one based upon custom to the exclusion of the relations between citizens that formed the groundwork of the Aristotelian polis. In chapter V, however, he proceeds to say that just as a territory with customs of its own is harder to hold than one whose customs are easily assimilable, so a city accustomed to liberty and the use of its own laws is hardest to hold of all. It may be held by the establishment of an oligarchy dependent on external support, but the only certain method is to destroy it; and the reason is that the memory of its former liberties, which can never serve to legitimize the new prince, is extraordinarily tenacious. Once again Machiavelli's emphasis is on usage; nothing else seems capable of providing legitimacy, and the innovator's problem is always that his subjects are not used to him and are used to something of which he has deprived them. * * * But the real question is why the usage of liberty is so hard to shake off, so impossible to forget. The answer seems to be that when men are used to obeying a ruler, they do not have to alter their natures in order to obey someone else; but the experience of citizenship, especially if prolonged over several generations, sets an indelible mark upon their natures, so that they must indeed become new men if they are to learn willing obedience to a prince. * * * Machiavelli does not seem to think this transformation can be effected; indeed, it is essential to his whole theory of fortune that men cannot change their natures, except perhaps at the infinitely slow rate indicated by the concept of custom. * * *

By now the new prince has entered the domain of contingency; the time he is living in is shaped by human behavior as it is when men are no longer guided by structures of habitual legitimacy. He is therefore vulnerable to fortune, but it is perhaps the central assertion of *Il Principe* that the time-realm he now inhabits is not wholly unpredictable or unmanageable. It is a Hobbesian world in which men pursue their own ends without regard to any structure of law; that they do so is partly the innovator's own doing, that he inhabits this world is almost wholly so; and that by which they pursue their ends is power, so defined that each man's power constitutes a threat to every other's. The second half of chapter III is the first essay in that strategic analysis of the delegitimized world of the power-seekers which, as has always been recognized, brings Machiavelli's thought into sharpest focus; and it is here that we hear for the first time the assertion that the prime necessity of strategic behavior is action. The alternative to action is delay and temporization, and once time has become the domain of pure contingency it is impossible to temporize because there can be no secure assumptions about what time will bring; or rather, the only assumption must be that, unless acted upon, it will bring change to one's disadvantage. * * *

* * * Chapter VI and its successors are dedicated to the role of *virtù* in acquiring and holding new dominions, and Machiavelli enters the realm of moral ambiguity by the single step of defining *virtù* as an innovative force. It is not merely that by which men control their fortunes in a delegitimized world; it may also be that by which men innovate and so delegitimize their worlds, and we shall see in a moment that it may even be that which imposes legitimacy on a world which has never known it. * * *

In chapter VI the prince is internal rather than external to the society over which he acquires power; we are not now concerned with a prince adding to his dominions, but with a private individual who becomes a prince. This, says Machiavelli, presupposes either *virtù* or *fortuna;* but it is clear that the relation between the two is more than simply antithetical. On the one hand *virtù* is that by which we innovate, and so let loose sequences of contingency beyond our prediction or control so that we become prey to *fortuna;* on the other hand, *virtù* is that internal to ourselves by which we resist *fortuna* and impose upon her patterns of order, which may even become patterns of moral order. This seems to be the heart of the Machiavellian ambiguities. It explains why innovation is supremely difficult, being formally self-destructive; and it explains why there is incompatibility between action—and so between politics defined in terms of action rather than tradition—and moral order. The politicization of virtue had arrived at the discovery of a politicized version of original sin.

Within the central ambiguity, it was possible to isolate the antithetical relation between *virtù* and *fortuna;* and Machiavelli's thought was now concentrated upon it. The more the individual relies upon his *virtù* the less he need rely upon his *fortuna* and—since *fortuna* is by definition unreliable—the safer he is. But if *virtù* is that by which we acquire power, the ideal type we are now seeking is the individual who acquires it wholly by the exercise of his personal qualities and not at all as the result of contingencies and circumstances outside himself. This explains why we must examine the acquisition of power by one who is a private individual and not a power-wielder at the moment of acquiring it; but to do so does not exhaust the difficulties. The career of any individual in a given society is conditioned by the particular circumstances of that society, which, not being of his making, are part of his *fortuna.* But to find an individual unconditioned by social membership is next to impossible. * * * The quasi-solution is given by Machiavelli's declaration that the ideal type (*li piú eccellenti*) of those who have become princes through their own *virtù* and not by *fortuna* is to be found in "Moses, Cyrus, Romulus, Theseus and their like."[2] These are the classical legislators in the strictest possible sense of state-founders, * * * the divine or divinely aided beings who could create societies because their *virtù* was such that it did not need the social frame which was the precondition of virtue in ordinary men. * * *

* * * It is the function of the legislator to impose the form of *politeia*—the constitution—upon the matter of *politeuma,* the citizen body; and it is the function of *virtù* to impose form upon *fortuna.* But when the subject is innovation, there is a pressing danger that *virtù* may deliver itself into *fortuna*'s power, and therefore the ideal type of innovator is he who depends as little as possible on circumstances beyond his control. * * * To attain the ideal type, therefore, we must suppose a situation in which the matter has no form, and above all no previously existing form, but what the innovator gives it; and the innovator must be a legislator. It was therefore a logical necessity that each hero should find his people in a condition of total anomie; since if the matter had had any vestige of form, that would have detracted from his *virtù*'s total independence of *fortuna.*

It is difficult to imagine so ideal a situation in concrete terms. Apart from the problem of envisaging a specific society in a totally anomic condition, the more we insist that there is nothing for the legislator to replace the less can there be anything for him to build upon; and we face the problem of finding any terms in which to describe what he does or how he does it. The legislator has such *virtù* that his command of *occasione* is absolute and he has unconditioned ability to dictate form to matter; but he has now become a species of demiurge, able to actualize all potentialities by a single creative command, and very much above the level of ordinary humanity. * * *

* * * Our analysis of chapter VI of *Il Principe* is approaching Machiavelli's allusion to Savonarola as typifying the "unarmed prophet" who invariably fails where the "armed prophets" succeed;[3] but this observation has to be studied in the light of Machiavelli's identification of the prophet and the legislator. Both are attempting a task beyond normal human powers, and both require more than normal *virtù;* we must not say that divine inspiration is being lowered to the level of *realpolitik* without adding that *realpolitik* is being

2. Niccolò Machiavelli, *Opere,* ed. Mario Bonfantini (Milan and Naples: Riccardo Ricciardi Editore; vol. 29 in the series *La Letteratura Italiana: Storia e Testi,* undated but 1954), pp. 18–19.
3. *Opere,* p. 20.

raised to the level of divine inspiration, and that Machiavelli may have been a pagan but was not a *philosophe.* Moses was an armed prophet, but need have been no less a prophet for his use of the sword. The prophet requires arms because, as an innovator, he must not be dependent on the contingent goodwill of others, and must therefore possess the means of compelling men when they cease to believe in him. * * *

* * *

Chapters VII to IX, it may be said, constitute an exploration of the category "innovator," still in terms of the *virtù-fortuna* polarity, with attention to those new princes who lack the superhuman *virtù* of legislators and prophets. Since the last-named are considered independent of *fortuna,* chapter VII opens by positing the case of the new prince who owes his position wholly to it. * * *

This is the context in which we are introduced to Cesare Borgia. Machiavelli was notoriously fascinated by this figure; and so much has been written on the assumption that he is the hero of *Il Principe,* and that its main themes are all to be understood by reference to his role, that it is desirable to define the exact status which he occupies in the book. If we apply the *virtù-fortuna* criterion, it defines his position as that of one among a number of ideal types, all located along a spectrum of degrees to which *virtù* is independent of *fortuna.* The legislator's *virtù* endows him with almost complete independence, but in Cesare we see combined the maximum *virtù* with the maximum dependence on fortune. * * *

* * *

If Cesare is not a legislator, it may be that—as Machiavelli indeed avers—he is the ideal type which every new prince in his (carefully defined) category should follow.[4] But from this we should have to deduce, contrary to some interpreters of Machiavelli, that the new prince is not a potential legislator, and that the legislator is an ideal type situated at one extreme of the category of innovators, of which genus the new prince is a species. Not only is the legislator's *virtù* related to *fortuna* in a way utterly different from that of the new prince; he is performing an innovation of a different order. He finds his *materia*—the people he is to mold—in a condition so anomic that his *virtù* needs only a sword to impose form upon it; very little is said of the previous structure of accustomed behavior which other innovators displace. Moreover, in imposing form upon matter he is the founder of a political order: Cyrus, Theseus and Romulus founded kingdoms, Lycurgus a polity and Moses a nation in

4. *Opere,* p. 27.

covenant with God. The word *stato*—normally employed by Machiavelli and Guicciardini to mean "rule by some over others"—does not appear to denote what the legislator brings into being, a highly viable political community, stabilized by his *virtù* and (at least if it is a republic) by the *virtù* of its citizens; a kingdom is stabilized by use and inheritance. By contrast, the new prince does not find matter lacking all form; he takes possession of a society already stabilized by customs of its own, and his task—relatively hard or easy according as it is used to liberty or obedience—is * * * to disturb old forms and change them into new. The old form being rooted in custom and "second nature," his innovation disorients men's behavior patterns and this exposes him to *fortuna.* What he is seen to establish is *stato,* a limited form of government only partly legitimized, only partly rooted in customs and "second nature" new to the people; and to get past this stage would require *virtù* of a kind the more extraordinary because it would not be identical with the *virtù* of the legislator.

J. H. Hexter has pointed out[5] that the phrase most frequently used by Machiavelli to describe the purposes of the new prince is *mantenere lo stato,* and that this carries short-term implications; it seems to mean little more than to maintain himself in the position of power and insecurity which innovation has brought him. On this view, the prince is not to look so far ahead as to hope to achieve for his *stato* either the near-immortality achieved by the creation of the legislator or the legitimacy achieved by use and inheritance in the hereditary principality. *Stato* means that one's eye is always upon immediate dangers; *virtù* is that by which one resists them, not that by which one is emancipated from the need to fear them. The new prince does not hope to transform the conditions of his political existence, or look to a time when he will be anything but a parvenu. * * *

This interpretation seems to be borne out if we consider the perceptive as opposed to the analytical chapters of *Il Principe:* after those which explore the category of innovators, those which isolate the new prince and tell him what to do. The transition from one to the other comes about two chapters after the profile of Cesare Borgia. The dominant themes do indeed appear concerned with the prince's techniques for rendering himself safe against immediate threats. He inhabits a world of competitors, and so we return to the theme of inter-princely relationships in which his chief need is an army and the skill to use it. * * *

If the military chapters on the whole depict arms as a weapon against short-term dangers, the famous chapters (XV-XIX) on the morality of princely behavior adopt a similar perspective. Here it is

5. "*Il Principe* and *lo stato,*" *Studies in the Renaissance* 4 (1957), 113–38.

simply assumed that by the fact of his own innovation, the prince inhabits a context in which human behavior is only partly legitimized and only partly subjected to the rules of morality. Consequently, the intelligence of the prince—his *virtù*—includes the skill necessary to know when it is possible to act as if the rules of morality (whose validity in itself is nowhere denied) were in force and to be relied on as governing the behavior of others, and when it is not. Formally, this has reference to a specific political context, that which is the result of innovation; if it is possible to detect moments at which Machiavelli speaks as if it had reference to all political contexts whatsoever, the reason may be that he had adopted a short-term perspective in which the consequences of innovation were not expected to be lived down, and that this had enabled him to see that all political situations were in part the products of innovation and contest for power, and that the short-term perspective never ceased altogether to be valid. * * * Discussion of whether the prince should obey moral law therefore becomes discussion of when he should obey it, and this in turn blends into discussion of whether it is better to be loved or feared, to be audacious or prudent. The answer is always the same. The essence of *virtù* is to know which of these paired courses is appropriate to the moment; but other things being equal, the better course is always the more aggressive and dramatic—to be audacious, to act so as to be feared. To be loved takes time.

We know that it is in the long-term context—the eternity of reason, the antiquity of custom—that legitimation resides. Since by his own act the innovator inhabits a delegitimized context, where *fortuna* rules and human behavior is not to be relied on, he is obliged to take the short view and continue to act—and in that sense, to innovate. In a very precise sense, then, action is *virtù;* when the world is unstabilized and the unexpected a constant threat, to act—to do things not contained within the structures of legitimacy—was to impose form upon *fortuna.* Aggression was the better part of value.[6] It is this, and not the erotic fantasies to which Machiavelli was admittedly given, that lies behind his repeated descriptions of *fortuna* as a woman who could be taken by force but would destroy you if you did not—the words should be weighed carefully—act in time.

But the *virtù* of action did not legitimate its environment. The forms it imposed existed only for a short time, whereas those of the legislator aimed at secular immortality. * * *

* * * [M]en in the world of innovation live in the present. Given a world which they see and experience as action and fluctuation

6. Pocock's "value" here is possibly a misprint for *valor,* for he is clearly playing on the expression "discretion is the better part of valor" [editor's note].

rather than as tradition and legitimacy, their feelings about the present are bound to be the stronger; action is more exciting than custom, it holds the attention and stirs up the emotions. In the present, the new prince can outshine the hereditary and evoke more loyalty; his *virtù*—functioning where rational and traditional authority are both absent—is a kind of charisma. But if we ask whether the charisma has been institutionalized, we must move from the short view to the long, and Machiavelli will not be moving with us; just as *Il Principe* does not inform us what is meant by "good laws, good arms and good examples," for which we must wait till the *Discorsi.* * * * As for the spectacular *virtuosi* of the new principates, if there is one thing certain about them it is that they continue to exist in fortune's world. In chapter xxv Machiavelli returns to the themes of how far men may hope to resist *fortuna,* and whether audacity or caution is the best means of dealing with her. In a crucial passage he lays down that sometimes one and sometimes the other is appropriate strategy; but men are audacious or cautious by nature, and so succeed or fail according to the times they have the fortune to live in. * * *

Machiavelli is saying that our second nature, the product of use and wont * * * is acquired as we become habituated to acting audaciously or cautiously. No *virtù* can so completely dominate *fortuna* as to ensure that the same strategy remains always appropriate; and what is more important still, no *virtù* of this order gives men power to change their own natures, or consequently to act "in time." If the prince cannot change his own acquired second nature, it does not seem that he can change those of his subjects. The legislator and prophet impose something of the kind on the anomic personalities they come to rule; but the new prince finds men habituated to a certain *vivere* and must, if he is to legitimize his power, habituate them to another. This his *virtù* does not seem capable of doing, least of all when they have been habituated to the usages of civic liberty which Machiavelli describes as ineradicable. * * * Since legislators established highly stable republics, we must turn to Machiavelli's republican theory to know what he thought about the stabilization of political life; and, it should seem, we are forced in the same direction by the effort to solve the riddle of chapter xxvi. *Il Principe* concludes with a passionate "exhortation to liberate Italy from the barbarians." This is addressed to a "new prince," and the question has consequently been how far the preceding chapters are to be seen as leading up to and progressively delineating the portrait of this liberating hero. But on the assumption used here—that *Il Principe* does not present a single rounded portrait, but a gallery of specimen types of innovator—the question must rather be to which subcategory, or combination of them, the liberator belongs. Rhetorically, it seems that he is a legislator: Moses, Cyrus, and Theseus are invoked once more, and we are told that the Italians are as prostrate as the Hebrews, Persians, and Athenians were in their generations, so that the *virtù d'uno spirito italiano* can be displayed in the imposition of form upon matter, as fully as were those of the ancient liberators.[7] But are we to understand that the anomie of Italians has reached the point where the *virtù* of a legislator will owe nothing to *fortuna* except *occasione?* Machiavelli was a Florentine, and knew perfectly well that there were republics and *principi naturali* to be met with, the acquired or natural characteristics of whose subjects would complicate the liberator's task. Italy was not inert matter to be organized into form, though he says it is; he had himself worked against Cesare Borgia's intended *regno* in the Romagna. The other thing we are told about the hero of chapter XXVI is that he is to be a military organizer, whose tactical principles will revive *virtù militare* and (in Petrarch's phrase) *antico valore.*[8] It has been hinted that there are ways in which military *virtù* can be associated with—can perhaps be the foundation of—civic *virtù,* but we have not yet learned what they are; and the language of this chapter seems to preclude the possibility that the liberator can stop short of restoring both kinds of virtue to Italy. If he does less he will be a "new prince" at a low level, a victim of *fortuna* obliged to live in the present; if he is to be a figure of the magnitude of Moses, Romulus, and Theseus, the army he trains must evolve into a people. Machiavelli admired military leaders—Borgia early in his career, Giovanni delle Bande Nere in his later years—and in the idealized Fabrizio Colonna of the *Arte della Guerra* he hinted that a *condottiere* might in theory become a legislator. But a mere hegemon does not reach men's civic personalities. In the *Discorsi sopra . . . Tito Livio* we meet both the military leader who founds a republic, and the republic itself as hegemon.

QUENTIN SKINNER

In his extremely influential study, *The Foundations of Modern Political Thought,* in which he stresses the necessity of placing books such as *The Prince* in the context of their contemporary political language, Skinner examines the role that major political statements, such as Machiavelli's *Prince,* played in the formation of the modern state. Before the Renaissance, political theorists saw the state as a hierarchical entity that the ruler possessed and maintained by virtue of his superior position within it. By contrast, from about the fifteenth century on, the state came to be seen as an entity separate from its ruler and possessing its own distinctive government. According to Skinner, the only way to understand texts

7. *Opere,* p. 83.
8. *Opere,* pp. 84–85.

such as Machiavelli's is to reconstruct the political discourse or discourses of the period in which it was written. Texts, in other words, speak, but they do so through the political "vocabulary" available to them, so that to understand what distinguishes them, one must look for their differences within that context. Skinner begins by arguing that the humanist political thought of the Renaissance was usually quite moralistic. It developed out of ancient Stoicism together with Christianity and stressed the need for rulers and governments to behave virtuously. By the end of the fifteenth century, however, most republics that made up Italy were replaced by states ruled by princes, and the humanists who wrote on politics, often referred to as civic humanists, had to address their works to a prince whom they nevertheless continued to conceive of in traditional terms as a moral figure, a *vir virtutis,* or "man of virtue."

[Machiavelli and the Triumph of Princely Government]†

* * *

Their hero was still the *vir virtutis,*[1] and they continued to insist that the right ambition for this heroic character should be that of winning for himself the greatest possible degree of honour, glory and fame. * * * The later humanists even placed an increasing emphasis on these already familiar beliefs, since they typically viewed the prince as a man capable of achieving *virtus* to an unsurpassable extent. * * *

These values are no less clearly endorsed by Machiavelli in *The Prince.* He insists that princely conduct must be *onesto* as well as *utile,* and accordingly demands that all princes must take as their model 'some historical figure who has been praised and honoured', keeping 'his deeds and actions before them' at all times.[2] He points to Ferdinand of Aragon as a contemporary ruler worthy of imitation, singling him out at the start of his Chapter on 'How a prince must act to win honour' on the grounds that 'from being a weak king he has risen to being, for fame and glory, the first king of Christendom' (p. 119). Conversely, he expresses contempt for Agathocles of Sicily, in spite of his remarkable achievements, on the grounds that the criminal methods he invariably employed 'can win a prince power but not glory' (p. 63). And when he turns at the end of *The Prince* to address himself directly

† From *The Foundations of Modern Political Thought,* vol. 1: *The Renaissance* (Cambridge: Cambridge University Press, 1978, rpt. 2004), pp. 118–38. © Cambridge University Press 1998. Reproduced by permission of the publisher. Notes are Skinner's unless otherwise indicated, with full bibliographical information supplied by the editor.

1. Virtuous man or man of virtue (Latin) [editor's note].
2. Niccolò Machiavelli, *The Prince,* trans. George Bull (Harmondsworth: Penguin, 1961), p. 90. [All Skinner's citations of *The Prince* come from this edition—editor's note.]

to the Medici, his main concern is still to offer them the assurance that 'nothing brings a man greater honour' than the founding of a new principality—thus reminding them that if they succeed in bringing 'new laws and new institutions' to Italy, they will also gain for themselves the richest prize in political life (pp. 133–6).

A second element of continuity between the mirror-for-princes theorists and their predecessors lay in their analysis of the forces opposing the *vir virtutis* in his quest for honour, glory and fame. They all agree that the chief responsibility for the collapse of our best-laid plans must be attributed to the capricious and potentially overwhelming power of fortune. * * *

The same belief is again repeated—and with characteristic vehemence—in Machiavelli's *Prince.* * * * He begins * * * by conceding that it is possible to attract the favourable attentions of fortune, and acknowledges that men are sometimes permitted to 'achieve great things' in this way. He lays it down as an axiom in his opening chapter that there are two main ways of gaining a principality, either by the exercise of *virtù* or by the gift of fortune (p. 33). And later he includes a special section on 'new principalities acquired with the help of fortune' in which he takes the case of Cesare Borgia as the most instructive example of a man who 'acquired his state' entirely through 'good fortune' (pp. 53–4). Machiavelli's main emphasis, however, is always on the goddess's unstable character, and the consequent folly of relying for any length of time on her support. * * *

Having emphasised the role of fortune in human affairs, the mirror-for-princes writers go on to ask what qualities a ruler needs to possess in order to ensure that fortune's power is controlled and minimised. The answer they suggest again reveals their dependence on the scheme of concepts already outlined by the earlier *quattrocento* humanists. They all agree that, as Patrizi declares, 'it is only by means of *virtus*' that a prince can hope to overcome the malice of fortune and achieve the goals of 'honour, glory and fame'.[3] * * * As in the case of the earlier humanists, Patrizi has two main claims in mind at this point. One is that a prince who acquires true *virtus* 'will never be dominated in his affairs by fortune' since he will always be able to remain steadfast even in the most adverse circumstances (p. 280). The other is that, since 'good fortune is always the companion of bravery', a prince who possesses *virtus* will also have the best chance of enlisting the support of the capricious goddess in the conduct of his affairs (p. 280). * * *

Once again we find Machiavelli reiterating the same doctrines in *The Prince.* He insists first of all that a man of true *virtù* can never be totally overwhelmed even by the most evil fortune. Although he

3. Francesco Patrizi, *The Kingdom and the Education of the King* [*De Regno et Regis Institutione*] (Prato, 1531), p. 228.

concedes in his chapter on 'How far human affairs are governed by fortune' that the goddess may well be 'the arbiter of half the things we do', he still contends that this leaves 'the other half or so to be controlled by ourselves' (p. 130). He is also a firm believer in the adage that *Fortes Fortuna Adiuvat*—that fortune favours the brave. * * *

For Machiavelli, as for the other humanists, the concept of *virtù* is thus used to denote the indispensable quality which enables a ruler to deflect the slings and arrows of outrageous fortune, and to aspire in consequence to the attainment of honour, glory and fame. This emerges very clearly in his chapter on 'Why the Italian Princes have lost their states' (p. 128). He issues a warning to all new princes that, if they wish to achieve the 'two-fold glory' which comes from establishing a new principality and securing it, they need above all to recognise that 'the only sound, sure and enduring methods' to employ are 'those based on your own actions and *virtù*' (p. 129). The same commitment recurs even more strongly in the final chapter of *The Prince,* in which Machiavelli issues his 'Exhortation' to the Medici 'to liberate Italy from the barbarians' (p. 133). * * *

Finally, most of the mirror-for-princes writers continue to endorse the familiar humanist assumption that, since the right kind of education is of crucial importance in shaping the character of the *vir virtutis,* there must be a close connection between the provision of the best educational and the best political advice. Machiavelli constitutes something of an exception to this rule, since he only glancingly mentions the question of the ruler's 'intellectual training'—perhaps because he genuinely believed (as he sometimes seems to imply) that the best education for a prince would simply consist of memorising *The Prince* (cf. p. 89). But in most of the other advice-books for rulers and courtiers there is a continuing emphasis on both the central claims we have already seen to be characteristic of humanist educational treatises. First of all, there is a strong endorsement of the belief that no absolute distinction should be drawn between the type of education suitable for gentlemen or princes and the type of education suitable for 'clerks'.[4] * * * The other familiar issue these writers discuss is the nature of the curriculum to be followed by aspiring princes and courtiers alike. The fullest account is given by Patrizi in the second Book of *The Kingdom and the Education of the King.* He begins by stressing the importance of acquiring suitable tutors for young princes, and goes on to outline a detailed course of instruction of a typically humanist kind. * * * The outcome is to make it the strenuous duty of the prince to offer himself as a model of 'the Renaissance man' to the rest of his subjects.

4. From the Latin *clericus.* In the Middle Ages and early Renaissance, those who were educated (in Latin) as opposed to a member of the secular elite, who was defined primarily by his skills as a warrior [editor's note].

So far we have considered the extent to which the mirror-for-princes writers of the later Renaissance continued to endorse the values and concepts already articulated by the earlier *quattrocento* humanists. It remains to analyse the ways in which the changing character of their audience prompted them to introduce a number of new elements into their moral and political thought.

They tended in the first place to differ sharply from most of their predecessors in their views about the purposes of government. The 'civic' humanists, as well as the authors of advice-books for * * * city magistrates, had all committed themselves to the claim that the preservation of liberty and justice must be taken to constitute the main values in political life. By contrast, the mirror-for-princes theorists developed an argument which * * * had already been canvassed by the earliest defenders of 'despotic' and 'tyrannical' regimes. They contended that the essential business of government consists of maintaining the people not so much in a state of liberty as in security and peace. * * *

The same shift in priorities is no less clearly marked in Machiavelli's *Prince*. He mentions the 'ancient liberty' of Republics only to remark that this tends to make them less amenable to princely government (p. 49). He repeatedly asserts that the chief duty of a ruler must be to attend to his own 'security and strength', while ensuring at the same time that his subjects are 'stabilised and made secure' (pp. 113, 114). And he even characterises his own aim in writing *The Prince* as an attempt to draw up a set of rules such that anyone who follows them 'will appear to have been long-established and will quickly become more safe and secure in his government than if he had been ruling his state for a long time' (p. 128).

The mirror-for-princes writers generally go on to argue that, since these values can be secured most readily under the rule of a prince, it follows that monarchy must be regarded as the best form of government. It is true that Machiavelli and Patrizi both refuse to draw this alleged corollary. Machiavelli in particular prefers to hold in tension two contrasting views about the rival merits of princely and popular regimes. On the one hand he stresses, both in *The Prince* and later in *The Discourses*, that in conditions of advanced political corruption it will always be necessary—in a Republic no less than a principality—to rely on the strong rule of a single man in order to restore the pristine *virtù* of a commonwealth. But on the other hand he implies in *The Prince*, and later states as explicitly as possible in *The Discourses*, that his own personal preference will always be for a life of political liberty, and hence for a Republican form of government.

* * *

The other major change introduced by the mirror-for-princes theorists into their inherited political vocabulary centred on their analysis of the key concept of *virtus*. * * * [T]hey agreed with their humanist predecessors in defining the concept heuristically as the quality which enables a man to combat the power of fortune and attain the goals of honour, glory and fame. If we now turn, however, to investigate the nature of the qualities they had in mind in applying the term, we find that their interest in the *virtus* of rulers rather than ordinary citizens prompted them to incorporate two significant new emphases into their accounts.

The first of these was the suggestion—adapted from Aristotle's *Politics*—that the qualities which deserve admiration in a prince may be different from those which deserve admiration in a private citizen. * * *

The same dichotomy is even more sharply drawn by Machiavelli in *The Prince*. The *virtù* of the ruler is treated as an astonishingly creative force, the key to 'maintaining his state' and enabling him to fight off his enemies. The chief merit of the people is taken by contrast to lie in their characteristic tendency to benign passivity. Machiavelli assumes throughout that 'the people ask only not to be oppressed', and scarcely troubles in consequence to assign them a speaking part in the drama of political life. He insists that as long as their ruler 'does not rob the great majority of their property or their honour', they will 'remain content' and largely pliable (p. 102). And he counsels the 'wise prince' to strengthen these habits of loyalty by devising 'ways by which his citizens are always and in all circumstances dependent on him', the aim being to ensure that 'they will always be faithful to him' in times of necessity (p. 71). The prince is invariably portrayed by Machiavelli as a figure in movement, but the activity of the people is said to be confined to 'the restlessness of a few', who 'can be dealt with easily and in a variety of ways' (p. 102).

The second new element which the later humanists introduce into their discussions of *virtus* is a tendency to explain the meaning of the term by reference to an increasingly heroic list of individual moral qualities. Although Machiavelli dissociates himself as sharply as possible from this move, it is generally assumed in the more conventional advice-books that the possession of *virtus* can be equated with the possession of two particular groups of the conventional virtues.

It is first of all claimed that no one can be accounted a man of true *virtus* unless he displays all the leading Christian virtues as well as the 'cardinal' virtues singled out by the moralists of antiquity.[5] * * *

5. In the Middle Ages and the Renaissance, there were seven principal virtues (which differed to some degree from writer to writer). The three Christian or theological virtues were faith, hope, and charity; the four cardinal or secular virtues were prudence, temperance, fortitude or courage, and justice [editor's note].

The other virtues these writers emphasise are those which they take to be especially appropriate for kings and princes to cultivate. * * *

They begin by declaring that all rulers must seek to acquire the related virtues of liberality and magnificence. * * *

The second princely virtue was said to be clemency. This contention led the mirror-for-princes theorists to take up a question which * * * had invariably been debated by the authors of advice-books for * * * city-magistrates: whether it is better for a ruler to seek to be feared or loved. As in the case of their predecessors, all these writers answer that, as Castiglione puts it, the prince must always aim to be 'not only loved but almost adored by his subjects'.[6] It is true that there was an element of disagreement at this point, for it was sometimes suggested—for example by Patrizi—that it may occasionally be appropriate and impressive for a ruler to behave with marked severity (p. 325). But even Patrizi concedes that this is a dangerous course to adopt, since severity 'readily degenerates into savagery', and 'there is no vice more shameful, detestable or inhuman' than cruelty in a prince (p. 325). * * *

Finally, the prince was exhorted to remain at all times the soul of honour, always giving his word freely and never breaking his promises. * * *

MACHIAVELLI'S CRITIQUE OF HUMANISM

So far, in considering Machiavelli's *Prince,* we have concentrated on the extent to which it can be shown to embody the values and preoccupations characteristic of the mirror-for-princes *genre* as a whole. It seems essential to begin by adopting this perspective. This makes it possible in the first place to identify a common misunderstanding of the relationship between *The Prince* and the more conventional political literature of its age. It is often claimed that Machiavelli's book is entirely *sui generis,* that it is 'not to be placed in any category', and even that it 'completely ignores the concepts and categories' in terms of which other political theorists of his generation were accustomed to express themselves. It will by now be evident, however, that the format, the presuppositions and many of the central arguments of *The Prince* make it a recognisable contribution to a well-established tradition of later *quattrocento* political thought. A second reason for adopting this perspective is that, in setting out the main assumptions of the mirror-for-princes writers, we are also placing ourselves in the best position to observe how far Machiavelli may have had the further intention to question or even to ridicule some of their values. It is of course evident—and we have

6. Baldesar Castiglione, *The Book of the Courtier,* trans. Charles S. Singleton (Garden City, NY: Doubleday, 1959), p. 317.

Machiavelli's own assurance on the point—that he saw himself as a self-conscious critic of several key elements in the existing literature of advice-books for princes (cf. p. 90). But it is only when we have grasped the precise intellectual context within which he was writing that we can hope to recognise the points at which, and the extent to which, he was in fact concerned to challenge and repudiate his own humanist heritage.

There are two main sections of *The Prince* in which Machiavelli is clearly concerned to mount a direct attack on the political theories of his contemporaries. He first denounces them for failing to emphasise the significance of sheer power in political life. * * * [I]t had generally been assumed that, as long as the prince devotes himself whole-heartedly to a life of virtue, this will enable him to attain the highest goals of honour, glory and fame. Machiavelli insists by contrast that this naively overlooks the extent to which the maintenance of a successful government depends on an unflinching willingness to supplement the arts of persuasion with the employment of effective military force. * * *

It is necessary, however, to exercise a certain caution in making this point. It is sometimes suggested that, with the publication of Machiavelli's political theory, 'it is possible to date the beginning of a new view of warfare'.[7] This arguably overestimates the novelty of Machiavelli's insistence on the need to construe the concept of *virtù* in part as a military quality. It would certainly be mistaken to think of him as the first writer to introduce this doctrine into humanist political thought. For the willingness to fight on behalf of one's *patria,* the readiness to employ violence in its cause, had always been treated by the earlier 'civic' humanists as an indispensable aspect of the *virtus* of the true citizen. * * *

There is no doubt, however, that Machiavelli places an exceptionally strong emphasis on the role of sheer force in the conduct of government. He devotes three central chapters of *The Prince* to discussing military affairs, arguing that 'the main foundations of every state' are constituted by 'good laws and good arms' (p. 77). He begins with the very strong contention that 'where there are good arms, good laws inevitably follow' (p. 77). And he summarises his advice by insisting, with characteristic exaggeration, that the prince 'should have no other object or thought, nor acquire skill in anything, except war, its organisation and its discipline' (p. 87). He also discusses a related topic which * * * had always been stressed by the earlier *quattrocento* humanists: the folly and danger of employing mercenary troops. * * *

7. Michael Walzer, *The Revolution of the Saints* (London: Weidenfeld & Nicolson, 1966), p. 273.

The other point at which Machiavelli challenges the prevailing assumptions of the mirror-for-princes writers is in discussing the role of *virtù* in political life. As we have seen, two main contentions about the idea of *virtù* had arisen out of the humanist tradition of moral and political thought: first, that *virtù* is the quality which enables a ruler to attain his noblest ends; and secondly, that the possession of *virtù* can be equated with the possession of all the major virtues. As a result, the leading theorists of princely government had all gone on to furnish the same fundamental piece of political advice: that if a ruler wishes to 'maintain his state' and achieve the goals of honour, glory and fame, he needs above all to cultivate the full range of Christian as well as moral virtues. It is precisely this central conclusion that Machiavelli denies. * * *

While it is clear what position Machiavelli is attacking at this pivotal point in his argument, the exact nature of the position he wishes to defend is a little obscured by his love of paradox. Sometimes he seems to be saying that, while princes have a duty to act virtuously, they must recognise that in order to act as virtuously as possible they should not attempt to act virtuously all the time. * * * Machiavelli first gestures at this line of thought in discussing the virtue of liberality. He points out that since the desire to appear generous often leads princes to impose gratuitous burdens on their people, a prince who is not afraid to act parsimoniously may discover that 'in time he will be recognised as being essentially a generous man' (p. 93). The same paradox is even more clearly invoked in his ensuing discussion of clemency. He begins by observing that 'Cesare Borgia was accounted cruel', but he immediately adds that 'this cruelty of his reformed the Romagna, brought it to unity, and restored order and obedience' (p. 95). The moral of the story is said to be that a prince who is confident enough to start out by 'making an example or two' will eventually 'prove more compassionate' than a ruler who fails to put down 'disorders which lead to murder and rapine' simply in order 'to escape being called cruel' (p. 95).

The heart of Machiavelli's message, however, consists of two somewhat different—though scarcely less paradoxical—claims about the role of the conventional virtues in relation to the attainment of princely honour, glory and fame. The first is that nothing matters so much as the keeping up of appearances. * * * The indispensable talent is the ability to counterfeit virtue: the prince 'need not necessarily have all the good qualities', but he must 'certainly appear to have them' at all times (p. 100).

* * *

Machiavelli's reason for attaching so much importance to the arts of dissimulation and concealment becomes clear as soon as he moves on to his other claim about the role of the virtues in political life. He argues that while it is always essential for princes to appear conventionally virtuous, it is often impossible for them to behave in a conventionally virtuous way. * * *

Machiavelli makes this self-consciously level announcement of his most heterodox claim in Chapter 15 of *The Prince,* in the course of discussing 'the things for which men, and especially princes, are praised or blamed' (p. 90). The working-out of this doctrine and its implications then occupies him for the next four chapters—the notorious section on 'how a prince should govern his conduct towards his subjects or his friends' (p. 90). Machiavelli begins by stating the conclusion he is concerned to establish: that 'the gulf between how one should live and how one does live is so wide that a man who neglects what is actually done for what should be done learns the way to self-destruction rather than self-preservation' (p. 91). He then proceeds to illustrate this argument by launching an attack on precisely those virtues which the writers of advice-books for princes had always held to be particularly appropriate for rulers to cultivate.

* * *

Conversely, Machiavelli insists in these chapters that if a prince wishes to 'maintain his state' he will often find it essential, and positively advantageous, 'to act in defiance of good faith, of charity, of kindness, of religion' (p. 101). He illustrates this claim in a similarly polemical vein by enlarging on the usefulness of precisely those vices which the mirror-for-princes writers had always counselled the prince to avoid at all costs. * * *

It is often claimed that the originality of Machiavelli's argument in these chapters lies in the fact that he divorces politics from morality, and in consequence emphasises 'the autonomy of politics'.[8] But this interpretation appears to embody a misunderstanding of the relationship between his outlook and that of his contemporaries. Machiavelli and the more conventional writers on princely government are in complete agreement, as we have seen, about the nature of the goals which princes ought to pursue. As Machiavelli repeatedly affirms, their aim should be to 'maintain their state', to 'achieve great things' and to seek for the highest goals of honour, glory and fame (pp. 99, 101). The crucial difference between Machiavelli and his contemporaries lies in the nature of the methods they took to be appropriate for the attainment of these ends. The basic assumption of the more conventional theorists was that, if the prince wishes to

8. For a discussion of the origins and widespread acceptance of this interpretation, see Eric W. Cochrane, "Machiavelli: 1940–1960," *The Journal of Modern History* 33 (1961): 115. Cochrane sees Croce as the most influential source of the opinion that Machiavelli's fundamental aim was to vindicate "the autonomy of politics"; cf. Benedetto Croce, *Politics and Morals,* trans. Salvatore J. Castiglione (New York: Philosophical Library, 1945), esp. p. 59.

achieve these goals, he must ensure that he follows the dictates of Christian morality at all times. Machiavelli's basic assumption is that a prince who 'acts virtuously in every way' will rapidly discover that he 'comes to grief among so many who are not virtuous' (p. 91). His fundamental criticism of his contemporaries is thus that they are insensitive to what he sees as the characteristic dilemma of the prince. As he observes with more than a touch of asperity, they want to be able to express their admiration for a great leader like Hannibal, but at the same time to 'condemn what made his achievements possible', especially the 'inhuman cruelty' which Machiavelli frankly sees as the key to Hannibal's glorious success (pp. 97–8). The only way out of this dilemma, he insists, is to accept unflinchingly that, if a ruler is genuinely concerned to 'maintain his state', he will have to shake off the demands of Christian virtue, wholeheartedly embracing the very different morality which his situation dictates. Thus the difference between Machiavelli and his contemporaries cannot adequately be characterised as a difference between a moral view of politics and a view of politics as divorced from morality. The essential contrast is rather between two different moralities—two rival and incompatible accounts of what ought ultimately to be done.[9]

After demolishing the usual scale of values underlying the mirror-for-princes literature, Machiavelli recognises that the next step he needs to take—as he notes without undue modesty—is to 'draw up an original set of rules' for the guidance of new princes (p. 90). The advice this leads him to offer is not presented with complete consistency. Sometimes he seems to be saying that, although the princely virtues may be good in themselves, there is no place for them in political life (p. 100). This leads him to assert that, while the ruler should attempt as far as possible to keep up an appearance of possessing these qualities, he should at the same time abandon them altogether in the actual conduct of his government. * * *

This highly subversive line of thought culminates in Chapter 17, in which Machiavelli raises a question which * * * had been prominently debated in the literature of advice-books for * * * city-magistrates: 'whether it is better to be loved than feared, or the reverse' (p. 96). Hitherto this dilemma had invariably been resolved in the same way. Since the inculcation of fear was taken to involve cruelty, and since cruelty was regarded as an inhuman vice, the ruler was always enjoined to make himself loved rather than feared. But Machiavelli insists on the opposite point of view. Counselling a

9. For a recent and extremely eloquent statement of this interpretation of Machiavelli's originality, see the important essay by Isaiah Berlin, "The Originality of Machiavelli," in *Studies on Machiavelli*, ed. Myron P. Gilmore (Florence: Sansoni, 1972), esp. p. 183 [p. 181 of this Norton Critical Edition].

straightforward avoidance of the conventional virtues at this point, he argues that 'it is far better to be feared than loved if you cannot be both' (p. 96). For the bond of love, he contends, is one which men 'will break when it is to their advantage', whereas 'fear is strengthened by a dread of punishment which is always effective' (pp. 96–7).

The main thrust of Machiavelli's advice, however, does not generally involve him in abandoning the conventional moral norms with so much readiness. He begins his discussion of the princely virtues by acknowledging that 'everyone will agree that it would be most laudable' if a ruler actually possessed and acted on all those qualities which are usually 'deemed to be good' (p. 91). * * * So the most accurate summary of his advice, as he himself intimates towards the end of Chapter 18, is that the prince 'should not deviate from what is good, if that is possible, but he should know how to do evil, if that is necessary' (p. 101). There is a clear allusion at this point to the conventional humanist assumption that the true *vir virtutis* must never engage in such underhand tricks, since he must never depart from the conduct befitting a man of true manliness. Machiavelli begins by observing that, because this frank and manly way of proceeding 'often proves inadequate', it is in fact indispensable for the ruler to become 'half beast and half man', since 'he cannot survive otherwise' (p. 99). He then adds that because it is essential for a prince to know how to make 'a nice use of the beast and the man', it is also essential that he should know which beasts to imitate (p. 99). So the essence of Machiavelli's advice comes to be embodied in the image of the ruler who, being 'forced to know how to act like a beast', learns to model his conduct on both the lion and the fox (p. 99).

This startling conclusion quickly won Machiavelli the reputation amongst Christian moralists of being a man of satanic wickedness. * * * The figure of 'the murderous Machiavel' soon became a stock caricature in sixteenth-century drama, and the tendency to strike a note of horrified denunciation in discussing his works—first popularised by Gentillet in his *Anti-Machiavel* of 1576—can still be found even in a number of contributions to modern scholarship. * * *

It must of course be conceded to these traditional interpretations that Machiavelli sometimes likes to affect a self-consciously cool and amoral tone. This is partly a reflection of his own sense of himself as a political expert, capable of offering maxims and reflections suitable for each and every occasion. * * * But the main reason for the shocking tone Machiavelli tends to employ lies in his deeply pessimistic view of human nature. He declares that 'one can make this generalisation about men: they are ungrateful, fickle, liars and deceivers, they shun danger and are greedy for profit' (p. 96). So it is hardly surprising that he feels a special obligation to warn the prince that, since men are commonly such 'wretched creatures', he will have to be ready to act in defiance of the conventional pieties if he wishes to remain secure (pp. 96, 101).

Despite his enjoyment of paradox, however, and his undoubted fondness for throwing off shocking asides, it seems something of a vulgarisation of Machiavelli's outlook to label him a preacher of evil. * * * His main concern is of course with the unfortunate fact that, if a prince possesses 'all the good qualities' and 'always behaves accordingly', he 'will find them ruinous' (p. 100). But he also speaks with disapproval of those princes who never make the least attempt to behave virtuously even in favourable circumstances. His main example is that of Agathocles, the tyrant of Sicily, who 'behaved like a criminal' at 'every stage of his career' (p. 62). * * *

It will by now be evident that the whole of Machiavelli's advice is governed by a highly original sense of what should be taken to constitute true *virtù* in a prince. Hitherto, as we have seen, it had generally been assumed that the possession of *virtù* could be equated with the possession of all the major virtues. With Machiavelli, by contrast, the concept of *virtù* is simply used to refer to *whatever* range of qualities the prince may find it necessary to acquire in order to 'maintain his state' and 'achieve great things'. It is then made brutally clear that, while these qualities may sometimes overlap with the conventional virtues, the idea of any necessary or even approximate equivalence between *virtù* and the virtues is a disastrous mistake. * * *

* * *

MARK HULLIUNG

Hulliung's main argument in his book *Citizen Machiavelli,* from which these extracts have been taken, is that the worldview Machiavelli espouses in his works was derived from classical, and especially Roman, sources. In his "conversations" with the ancients, he embraced their "pagan" notion of heroism. He separated it, however, from attempts by Cicero, Virgil, and others to reconcile it with ethical ideals such as service to the state, so that for Machiavelli, classical heroism became a matter not just of displaying valor on the battlefield but also of using both force and fraud to triumph over others, triumph being the only thing that was important. Thus, for Hulliung, modern scholars get it wrong when they attempt to "save" Machiavelli from a popular vision of him as endorsing an amoral, knife-in-the-back prince who would stop at nothing to gain power. The scholars, says Hulliung, argue that princely violence can be justified as a (bad) means leading to a (good) end, or that it was a necessary concession to "realism" in the political realm, or that if Machiavelli endorsed it, he did so only because he saw it as a temporary measure that would be followed by a return to morally acceptable activities. The scholars want a Machiavelli who is acceptable to modern liberalism and socialism, as Hulliung sees it, but what they miss is that Machiavelli fully endorsed the use of force and fraud, had no qualms about the need for violence, and was committed to what we would call power politics—in a word, to Machiavellism. The actions involved, no matter how shocking, no matter how morally depraved, enabled both Machiavellian princes, such as Cesare Borgia, and Machiavellian states, such as Rome, to achieve what really mattered: greatness, glory, and grandeur.

Hulliung's book also argues that Machiavelli's works were indebted to the specific genres Roman literature had more or less codified. Because they saw history and epic as high genres that taught one how to be a good citizen and to perform public duties, Machiavelli wrote histories and something approaching epic in *The Prince* and the *Discourses*. And because the Romans considered comedy a low genre that taught one how to be a good father, mother, servant, and so on, Machiavelli also wrote comedies, some just translations from the Latin as well. All of those genres offered ethical instruction, and Hulliung argues that Machiavelli thought so too, although he did so only because he could cast aside the Romans' moralizing and remake what they were teaching into different forms of Machiavellism. Consequently, Hulliung rejects the widespread scholarly argument that can be traced back to the work of Benedetto Croce in the early part of the twentieth century, the notion that what distinguishes Machiavelli's *Prince* from all the other political treatises before his is his vision of politics as an autonomous realm separated absolutely from ethics. In his "conversations" with the ancients, Machiavelli embraced the "pagan" classics, but only because he could remake individuals as well as the Roman Republic itself into Machiavellians who pursued political greatness any way they could. The following extracts from Hulliung's book come from the chapter after the one about Machiavelli's conversations with the ancients.

From Conversations with the Moderns†

Machiavellism and the Classics

Machiavelli's method of conversing with his contemporaries, of persuading, cajoling, and winning them over to his point of view, was to insinuate his message into their conversations with the ancients. Thus the dialogues of the Renaissance humanists with the classical authors would become a dialogue with Machiavelli, and the more the humanists read the classics, the more humanism would become Machiavellism. The constant effort of Machiavelli was to underscore, intensify, and dramatize what was Machiavellian in Latin literature, ancient and modern, Roman and humanist.

† From *Citizen Machiavelli* (New Brunswick, NJ: Transaction Publishers, 2015), pp. 170–88, 190–97. Originally published in 1983 by Princeton University Press. Copyright 2015 by Transaction Publishers. Reproduced by permission of Taylor and Francis Group, LLC, a division of Informa plc. Notes are Hulliung's, with full bibliographical information supplied by the editor.

Happily for Machiavelli, the Roman and humanist theme of grandeur, glory, and greatness had done much preparatory work for his message. Machiavelli the typical humanist was therefore already well along the way to a doctrine of power politics, and when he infiltrated his most strikingly atypical thoughts into the tradition of Italian humanism, he did so with a deftness inviting the erroneous but not implausible conclusion that some two centuries of humanist scholarship had been struggling to make Machiavelli possible. Machiavelli's teaching was not that humanism must face up to its opposite, Machiavellism; it was that humanism is Machiavellism. * * *

When offering a literary representation of the private sphere, Machiavelli followed the humanists, who combined Roman comic form with Boccaccian content. But he also went beyond the humanists as he turned the moralistic and didactic comic theory of the Renaissance upside down. If comedy preaches the duties of fatherhood, it also teaches the methods of seduction, and may thus be said to be a training in the Machiavellism of the household. From such a conclusion the humanists had retreated to an idealizing theory of comedy, Ciceronian in origin, which was contradicted time and again by their literary practice in the comic genre. As usual, Machiavelli did not retreat, and it was perhaps from the strict moralist Cicero's reluctant concession in *De Officiis* that, alas, though born for grave affairs, a citizen does need his occasional amusements, that Machiavelli derived his notion of a variable nature best served by daytime seriousness and nighttime folly. * * *

In historiography, too, Machiavelli followed the humanists, the better to lead them. Other histories of Florence, notably Leonardo Bruni's and Poggio Bracciolini's, had been written before his by authors who took their theory of historical writing from the ancient Roman authors. * * *

* * * Bruni and the republicans had taken pride in countering the traditional monarchical genealogy of Florence, the child of Caesar, with a republican genealogy tracing the beginnings of Florence to an earlier date, preceding the downfall of the Republic. A disenchanted republican, Machiavelli located Florentine origins in the era of transition from the corrupt Roman Republic to the monarchical Roman Empire, and argued that Florence suffered both from a despicably corrupt parentage and from an unfree beginning, quite unlike the beginning of the Roman Republic, a city born of itself and hence free to do great deeds.[1] * * *

1. [On the decadence of Florence, see] *Discorsi,* I, 1, 49; *Istorie fiorentine,* II, 2. [On the beginnings of Rome, see] *Discorsi,* I, 1. All quotations from Machiavelli's works refer to *Niccolò Machiavelli: Tutte le opere,* ed. Mario Martelli (Florence: Sansoni, 1971). Translations are from *Machiavelli: The Chief Works and Others,* ed. and trans. Allan H. Gilbert, 3 vols. (Durham, NC: Duke University Press, 1965).

* * * Whereas Roman virtue could be traditional and limit its violence to acts committed against other cities, Machiavellian virtue had to be radical and willing to resort to violence within the city. His brand of *virtù* could hardly be credible and persuasive to humanists unless an argument for it could be squeezed out of classical thought. That was precisely what Machiavelli set about doing. He called upon the classics for assistance as he depicted a man of *virtù,* expert in the use of internal violence—a "new" prince, a usurper who ideally would exercise his illegitimate power to reinvigorate a fading republic. Cesare Borgia is the name this man bears in *Il Principe,* but in truth he is an abstraction Machiavelli created by taking elements from both Greek and Roman thought and compounding them into a creation all his own. * * *

* * *

No strategy of persuasion is more common in Machiavelli's writings than that of imposing a Machiavellian reading upon Roman history and Roman ideals. Occasionally, as for instance in the notion that politicians invented and manipulated pagan religion, a mere repetition of the words spoken by Polybius or some Roman author sufficed to achieve a Machiavellian Rome. At the other end of the spectrum he sometimes dared build his case for a Machiavellian Rome by explicitly disagreeing with classical authors, as when he argued against Plutarch that Rome's conquest of the world had little to do with *fortuna.*[2] But his favorite method of turning Romans into Machiavellians was to invert the idealizing and moralizing mentality that was congenital to Latin literature. * * * Machiavelli's so-called "realism" is simply this Roman moralism turned upside down. No more than his classical forebears did Machiavelli paint portraits of individuals in all their complexity, individuality, and self-contradiction. His individuals are as much types, abstractions, and exemplars as were those of the Romans, the single difference being that Machiavelli's heroes are good at being bad. * * *

The greatest hero-villain to appear in Machiavelli's works is not Cesare Borgia or Romulus; it is not a person but a collectivity, republican Rome, which rose from humble beginnings to grandiose finale by using—so Machiavelli argued—the methods of force and fraud. * * *

Just how radically Machiavelli altered the Renaissance image of Rome cannot be appreciated unless we recall that the thought of the classical authors to whom the humanists were indebted for their image of Rome was deeply imbued with Stoicism. Challenging all of classical and neoclassical Latin literature, Machiavelli boldly

2. *Discorsi,* II, 1.

substituted Machiavellism for Stoicism as the inner meaning of Roman history. Despite their imperialism, Virgil and Livy felt the need to justify their politics by appeals to the destiny of Rome, taking their notion of destiny from Stoic philosophy. * * * Livy was a Stoic humanitarian and yet he could without inconsistency rejoice in the Roman takeover of Greece, because he understood that episode as a war of liberation fought by republican Rome for the sake of freeing her fellow republics. Machiavelli's determination to reverse Livy is nowhere more evident than in his reinterpretation of Rome's actions in Greece, which he cited as an example of the willingness of the Romans to expand their empire by destroying free, republican cities:

> They were forced to destroy many cities of that province in order to hold her, because in truth there is no certain way for holding such [free] states except destruction; and he who becomes master of a city used to being free and does not destroy her can expect to be destroyed by her.[3]

Stoic, too, in Livy's *History* was the frequent antithesis of the expedient (*utile*) with the honorable (*honestum*) and the claim that the virtuous Romans never sacrificed the latter to the former. In Cicero's *De Officiis*, a work familiar to all humanists, the Stoic preference for the honorable over the expedient is used to stop Machiavellian thoughts before they start. * * * Machiavelli, then, is Stoicism inverted; grandeur and nobility, he proclaims, are impossible without fraud practiced on a grand scale, and he calls the history of republican Rome, as interpreted in the *Discourses on Livy*, to bear witness to the truth of his testimony.[4] * * *

"In praise of deception" is a leitmotif in Machiavelli's writings because "in denunciation of deception" is in Roman and humanist writings. Fraud and deception figure in Livy's history as the methods of the enemies of Rome, particularly Hannibal, and any evidence of Roman deceitfulness is accounted for by terming it un-Roman.[5] Sallust frequently speaks of Roman fraud and deception,[6] but does so because he is forced to by his task of recording the increasing corruption of once virtuous Rome. * * * During the Italian Renaissance Latini argued, in imitation of the classical texts, that the ruler "must actually be as he wishes to seem"; and Alberti never doubted that "a noble spirit prefers to be virtuous rather than just give that impression." "To gain fame," Alberti adds, "we must have virtue; to obtain virtue we must wish to be, not appear to be, what we want

3. *Il Principe*, 5.
4. *Discorsi*, II, 4, 13.
5. See Livy, *History*, trans. Henry Bettenson (Baltimore: Penguin, 1976), I, 53 on Roman deceit as un-Roman.
6. Sallust, *The War with Catiline*, XI; *The War with Jugurtha*, IV, in *Sallust*, trans. J. C. Rolfe (Cambridge: Harvard University Press, 1965).

others to think we are."[7] Against this backdrop of classical and neoclassical quotations, Machiavelli wrote the celebrated eighteenth chapter of *The Prince* which promotes *parere* (to appear) to inclusion in the list of virtues and ranks it higher than *essere* (to be). * * *

* * *

Still more striking was Machiavelli's transformation of Roman history into a showcase of masterful fraud and conspiracy, planned in the earliest days of the republic and so effectively carried out as to culminate in the greatest empire ever known. * * *

* * *

Machiavelli's Rome was a republic that devoured all other republics by making full use of the methods of force and fraud. Before Machiavelli arrived on the scene of Italian humanism, Livy had been a humanist and Rome an embodiment of humanism; after the *Discourses on Livy* was written, Livy was a Machiavellian and Rome an embodiment of Machiavellism.

Tradition and Innovation

Machiavelli's work was innovative and destructive of tradition precisely insofar as it belonged to an intellectual tradition, that of classical and humanist thought. Myths, symbols, vocabulary—these and more were furnished him by an established tradition of thought, and upon this tradition he incessantly drew even as he rebelled against it, knowing full well that his classically educated audience was ideally prepared to appreciate his provocative and disturbing performance. * * *

The classical tradition against and through which Machiavelli rebelled was both pagan and Christian. It was a tradition begun by the Greeks, revised by the Romans, and then selectively absorbed into Christian doctrine. In the largest sense Machiavelli's originality can only be appreciated when his thought is studied in terms of the contending varieties of paganism—Greek and Roman—and of the conflict between pagan and Christian viewpoints, all contained within the classical tradition.

While Machiavelli's fusion of the hero with the immoralist would not have been striking had he been working within the Greek tradition, it was remarkably subversive given that he asserted his views through Roman materials. * * *

7. [For the quotation from Brunetto Latini, see] Quentin Skinner, *The Foundations of Modern Political Thought: The Renaissance* (Cambridge: Cambridge University Press, 1978), p. 47; [for the quotation from Leon Battista Alberti, see] *I libri della famiglia*, trans. Guido A. Guarino as *The Albertis of Florence* (Lewisburg, PA: Bucknell University Press, 1971), p. 305.

* * * Virgil, spokesman for Roman tradition, castigates Ulysses as cruel, merciless, and even blasphemous, much as Livy treated Hannibal. Rome was built, Virgil proclaims, by the survivors of once great Troy, that noble city finally sacked after ten years of glorious defense when tricked by Ulysses, perpetrator of the despicable deceit of the horse. * * * Aeneas is as upright as Ulysses is underhanded, which was Virgil's way of communicating that Greece is ignoble, Rome noble, and that the heroic ethic has no room for craft, guile, and deception. Rome deserves to rule Greece as surely as nobility deserves to rule ignobility.

* * *

Machiavelli went far beyond declaring the political necessity of sometimes engaging in acts of ignoble fraud for the sake of survival. He proclaimed fraud essential to nobility, greatness, and heroism, making his argument not by recovering Greek ideals but by taking the standard Roman literary materials and reshaping them in the image and likeness of Machiavellism. * * *

* * *

* * * *Virtus* in Roman literature implied prowess in most any activity, particularly arms and ruling, but did not, before Machiavelli, imply virtuosity in the use of political violence. *Virtù* did imply skill in violence for many modern Italians who, in their un-Christian moments, could designate almost any activity effectively pursued a proof of the *virtù* of its doer, including the violent activities of a usurping prince. In effect Machiavelli took this meaning of *virtù*, attributed it to the word *virtus* in Latin literature, and then used the rewritten Roman classics to judge his contemporaries wanting in excellence. * * *

Stoicism, by separating virtues from their results, made Machiavelli possible and necessary, and the Christian belief in a pure good, a good indifferent to results, greatly increased his necessity. Unlike Christians, Roman Stoics had at least attempted, however feebly, to reintegrate the good and the useful with the claim that virtue succeeds, an assumption Renaissance humanists added to the Christian "mirror-of-princes" genre, which before their time had spoken of virtue but not of utility.[8] Machiavelli shattered both Christian and humanist outlooks in one deft blow with the argument of *The Prince* that success is mandatory, and virtue, Stoic and Christian, its nemesis. All his life Machiavelli spoke in the vocabulary of Stoicism and Christianity turned inside out and upside down. * * *

8. F[elix] Gilbert, "The Humanist Concept of the Prince and *The Prince* of Machiavelli," *The Journal of Modern History* 11 (December 1939), 449–83.

* * *

Machiavelli's absorption of Christian symbols into his unchristian philosophy was much more than simply a rhetorical device. It was nothing less than an attempt to displace and supplant the Christian world-view with an alternative world-view, one reminiscent of ancient paganism. Parceling out one's life, as the humanists did, between immersion in the pagan past and loyal adherence to the Christian present was not Machiavelli's way. Rather, he attacked Christianity, sometimes quite openly, as in his devastating contrast of the greatness of pagan *virtù* with the smallness of womanish Christianity; sometimes more covertly, as in his claim that a truthful "interpretation" of Christian doctrine would yield a modern religion sharing the ancient pagan contempt for humility. * * *

* * *

* * * In truth, Machiavelli was less interested in Christianity interpreted according to *virtù* than in Christianity the slave of *virtù*. The corruption, in Christian terms, of the papacy, its frequent subservience to worldly and dynastic ambitions, might be the opportunity Italy needed to regain her *virtù*. Had Cesare Borgia, the dark hero of *The Prince,* lived to unite his empire in the Romagna with the papal chair held by his corrupt father, advantages might have accrued to all Italy. Were Leo X, son of Lorenzo the Magnificent, to pool his resources with the younger Lorenzo de' Medici, the arbiter of Florentine affairs to whom *The Prince* was dedicated, a great empire might be the upshot. * * *

Virtù could be injected into modern Italy by either Julius II and his militant Christianity or by Alexander VI and his corrupt Christianity, one pope being the servant of the Church, the other its master, both being ecclesiastical princes answering to the worldly standards of greatness and success. Only the Christianity of the reforming orders, forever striving to restore Christianity to its original, antiworldly, pacifistic, and enervating values, was flawed beyond hope of redemption. * * *

* * *

* * * No greater rhetorical offensive against the Christian stronghold was ever undertaken by Machiavelli than when he substituted "fame" and "immortality" for "eternity." Many another figure of his day had sung the praises of fame, of course—indeed, so many did that Burckhardt cited the clamoring for enduring reputation as a

distinguishing characteristic of the Italian Renaissance.[9] Machiavelli did not create but he did alter the craving for fame, making it more anti-Christian, more pagan, more Machiavellian. * * * Machiavelli's innovation was that he underscored how a name can be gained by committing evil acts as well as good ones; he showed, moreover, how evil sometimes rises to a plane of greatness beyond good and evil; and he not only refused to back down, in cowardly humanist fashion, from a sometime ideal of fame to an all-the-time fear of eternity—he actually took the symbols of eternity and put them to work promulgating the ideal of immortality.

* * *

* * * The heaven and hell that matter are located on this side of eternity, as the greatest of founders and rulers have always known, and as even the feeble Florentines once knew in the past when they challenged the religious sanctions Pope Gregory XI had imposed upon them. "They were called saints, even though they had little regard for the Censures, stripped the churches of their property, and forced the clergy to celebrate the offices. So much higher did those citizens then value their city than their souls!"[1]

Max Weber, in his memorable essay "Politics as a Vocation," cites the preceding quotation from the *Florentine History* as a "beautiful"[2] recognition of the enormous torment any politician must suffer who is responsible enough to accept his calling of mediating between idealism and power politics: hands forever stained, a soul permanently soiled, and a cross of exceptional heaviness to bear are the wages of the sins that are necessarily committed by a responsible political leader. To this reading it must be objected that Weber's Machiavelli was more Machiavelli as Weber wanted him than as he was. The image of losing one's soul is used several times by Machiavelli, but he never means it; he simply means to restate his very un-Christian thought in Christian imagery. Whoever recalls Machiavelli's statement, "I love my native city more than my own soul,"[3] would do well to remember that his Hell is hardly an undesirable place in which to take up residence. Certainly Callimaco finds Hell so little terrifying that neither he nor any other seducer in his right mind has cause to reconsider his wrongdoing:

9. Jacob Burckhardt, *The Civilization of the Renaissance in Italy,* trans. S. G. C. Middlemore (New York: Macmillan, 1958), Pt. 2, Ch. 3.
1. *Istorie Fiorentine,* III, 7.
2. Max Weber, "Politics as a Vocation," in *From Max Weber: Essays in Sociology,* ed. H. H. Gerth and C. Wright Mills (New York: Oxford University Press, 1958), p. 126.
3. Machiavelli to Francesco Guicciardini, 16 April 1527, no. 321 in *Tutte le opere.*

> The worst you can get from it is that you'll die and go to Hell. But how many others have died! And in Hell how many worthy men there are! Are you ashamed to go there?[4]

Callimaco's vision of an agreeable Hell was later Machiavelli's on his deathbed, where he is said to have told the last of those tall tales that had always delighted him and the telling of which was not the least of the joys he took in everyday existence. He said he had had a dream in which, first, a group of poor, miserable, and humble people appeared, formerly the salt of the earth and now the blessed souls of Paradise. Then, on the spot where the humble had stood a moment before, a second group of men appeared, wearing regal robes and discussing affairs of state, and among them were numbered Plato, Plutarch, Tacitus, and many other famous ancients, who despite their greatness on earth had been condemned to Hell by Dante. Asked with which group he wished to spend eternity, he chose the second.[5] * * *

Machiavelli loved the poetry of the *Divine Comedy,* knew much of it by heart, and quoted it frequently. Every time he took Dante's meaning and changed it to his own, it was as a deliberate act of subversion and one that his contemporaries, who shared his familiarity with Dante's masterpiece, were certain to appreciate. The use and abuse to which we have seen Machiavelli subject the image of Hell was not lost on his fellow Florentines; nor could they fail to understand his hilarious and yet serious misappropriation of Dante's canto on Limbo. Souls consigned to Limbo, suggests Dante, are those which on earth had known how difficult and demanding are both the good and the evil life, and knowing this, were unable to commit themselves to either choice or to do anything other than be indecisive. For such as these, too weak to be evil, not even the devils have any use. * * *

So we read in the *Divine Comedy,* and it is as a mischievous footnote to Dante that Machiavelli's rhyme of "Soderini" with "bambini" must be read.

> The night when Piero Soderini died, his spirit went to the mouth of Hell. Pluto roared: "Why to Hell? Silly spirit, go up into Limbo, with all the rest of the babies."[6]

Piero Soderini, formerly head of the Florentine republic and Machiavelli's boss, was the epitome of indecision. Too weak to purge his enemies, too given to a wait-and-see foreign policy, Soderini was as undeserving of either praise or infamy as a child. Upon entering Hell, his insignificant soul was therefore decisively rejected by Pluto

4. *Mandragola,* IV, 1.
5. Roberto Ridolfi, *The Life of Niccolò Machiavelli,* trans. Cecil Grayson (Chicago: University of Chicago Press, 1963), pp. 249–50.
6. *Tutte le opere,* p. 1005.

and rerouted to Limbo. Machiavelli's joke is far more than a joke; it tells the truth about Soderini (and about Florence in general, the indecisive republic)[7] and exemplifies one of Machiavelli's favorite intellectual strategies, that of politicizing Christian imagery and pressing it into the service of ideals anything but Christian.

However often the reader travels forward and backward across Machiavelli's writings, there is one location in *Tutte le opere* that is privileged. To it we return time after time, necessarily and inescapably, and that is the eighteenth chapter of *Il Principe,* which takes the virtues as its subject matter and proceeds to argue for virtuosity in seeming and dissembling. This same chapter also contains Machiavelli's single most brilliant exercise in the fine art of innovation through inverting and subverting the images of his intellectual targets, Stoicism and Christianity. There is in Machiavelli no passage more quoted than his insistence, in this chapter, that the prince must avail himself of the force of the lion and the fraud of the fox. Not a single humanist had excuse to miss the significance of Machiavelli's words, which were taken from Cicero's *De Officiis*—a work known to all students of the classics—and turned upside down.

> Wrong doing [writes Cicero] originates in one of two ways: either by force or by fraud; fraud is like a little fox, force like the lion. Both are most uncharacteristic of man, but fraud should arouse greater contempt.[8] * * *

Machiavelli's image of the lion and the fox is, then, Cicero's Stoicism stood on its head.

* * *

By no means was Machiavelli's image of a Rome that conquered because it was a lion in its force and a fox in its fraud sanctioned by Latin literature read literally. Nevertheless, Livy's endless descriptions of battles abound in predatory verbs of slaughter and butchery that give the lie to his Stoic morality and beckon a Machiavellian revision. Furthermore, it is not impossible that Machiavelli took some of his inspiration for a revised estimate of Rome from the figures of speech of the *Aeneid,* Virgil's eulogy of Roman foundation and expansion, a poem Machiavelli loved. Images of animals stalking their prey, of jaws tearing and shredding their victims, are common in Virgil. * * * [T]he Romans toned down the competitive and violent heroic ethos, especially by yoking it to the cooperative and law-abiding standards of justice. Feasibly Machiavelli's predatory Roman republic is Virgil's Rome shorn of its moralistic veneer and reinterpreted through the poetic

7. *Discorsi,* I, 38; II, 15, 23; III, 27.
8. *De Officiis,* I, 13, 41.

images of the *Aeneid*. If so, power politics may be the covert message of that very Latin literature which overtly, and even in its most jingoistic moments, understands Roman expansion as the divinely ordained extension of law and civilization across the known world.

In general, however, Machiavelli's ploy was not to discover a hidden meaning in Latin literature, but to take its outspokenly idealistic and Stoical message and invert it, changing it to power politics, to Machiavellism; he then idealized that Machiavellism through incorporating its methods of force and fraud into the heroic code. The force and fraud Cicero hated were, in Machiavelli's judgment, the heart and soul of Roman greatness.

* * *

After the Roman classics had been inverted, Machiavelli had one other task to accomplish before his radically innovative thought had spent its force. He had to annex Christianity to his world-view by acts of intellectual imperialism. This, as we have seen, he did in fact do, using every rhetorical trick available to him, notably the transformation of Christian images and the restatement of his thought in Christian terms. * * *

Machiavelli's thought could hardly be more frightening. It takes humanism and turns it into the all-devouring power politics of a people forever on the march, its energies directed by a ruling class willing to use any means promising success. Such limitations to violence as are enjoined by Machiavelli are fundamentally those flowing from the heroic code, which forbids meaningless slaughter but finds slaughter frequently meaningful as a proof of greatness. No man is great because he says he is but because others say he is, and they will not say so unless they witness great and manly deeds, which more than anything else are acts of domination.

* * *

HANNA FENICHEL PITKIN

[Machiavelli's Gendered Politics]†

Though his explicit concerns are overwhelmingly political and public, Machiavelli's writings show a persistent preoccupation with manhood. What matters for both security and glory, for both

† From *Fortune Is a Woman: Gender and Politics in the Thought of Niccolò Machiavelli* (Berkeley: University of California Press, 1984), pp. 25–26, 34–35, 45, 48–52, 54, 80–81, 90, 105, 230–40. Reprinted by permission of the author. Notes are Pitkin's unless otherwise indicated, with full bibliographical information supplied by the editor.

individuals and states, is autonomy; and autonomy constantly refers back to psychic and personal concerns. Beginning with the obvious, Machiavelli's most characteristic, central, and frequently invoked concept is that of *virtù*, a term by no means regularly translatable by "virtue," and certainly not equivalent to virtue in the Christian sense. Though it can sometimes mean virtue, *virtù* tends mostly to connote energy, effectiveness, virtuosity. * * * The word derives from the Latin *virtus,* and thus from *vir,* which means "man." *Virtù* is thus manliness, those qualities found in a "real man." Furthermore, if *virtù* is Machiavelli's favorite quality, *effeminato* (effeminate) is one of his most frequent and scathing epithets. Nothing is more contemptible or more dangerous for a man than to be like a woman or, for that matter, a baby or an animal—that is, passive and dependent.

The themes are political and public, yet the imagery in which they are expressed is often personal and sexual. Political, military, and sexual achievement are somehow merged. Political power and military conquest are eroticized, and eros is treated as a matter of conquest and domination. * * * Commentators often see Italy, in the famous last chapter of *The Prince,* as a woman "beaten, despoiled, lacerated, devastated, subject to every sort of barbarous cruelty and arrogance," who will welcome a rescuing prince as "her redeemer," but also as her lover, "with what gratitude, with what tears!"[1] And of course fortune is explicitly called "a woman," favoring the young, bold, and manly, to be confronted with whatever *virtù* a man can muster.

But what does being a man really mean, and how does one go about it? Machiavelli's writings are deeply divided on these questions, presenting conflicting images of manly autonomy. I shall begin by delineating two such images, one founded mainly in his own political experience, the other in his reading and fantasy about the ancient world: "the fox" and "the forefathers."

* * * Machiavelli was a public servant, for fifteen years second chancellor to the city of Florence, and thus secretary and factotum to those who governed the city, particularly with respect to foreign affairs. This meant both that he did their paperwork, drafted decrees and documents, and kept records, and that he traveled as a diplomat—observing, negotiating, making arrangements, and sending home dispatches and reports. Machiavelli's own experience of political life was not of election campaigns, or of budgeting negotiations, legislative

1. *Prince,* ch. 26 (G 96): cf. G 93. Machiavelli does not, however, explicitly call Italy a woman; use of the feminine pronoun in English is of course the translator's choice. [Pitkin's references to "G" are to Niccolò Machiavelli, *The Chief Works and Others,* trans. Allan Gilbert, 3 vols. (Durham, NC: Duke University Press, 1965); she refers to page number rather than to volume and page number—editor's note.]

committee work, or deliberation in the *polis* marketplace. He was a counselor and servant to those in power at home, an observer and negotiator at the courts of the powerful abroad.

Thus Machiavelli was always in but not of the world of power, an insider and yet an underling. This was his professional world. He did what could and had to be done under the circumstances, and he did it well, but the circumstances were difficult. He was a low-ranking diplomat, never an ambassador. * * *

* * *

Call him the fox, then, after Renard—this *furbo*[2] who runs the show from behind the scenes through his cleverness; who never himself wins the girl or the glory but takes his pleasure in the secret knowledge of his own surpassing foxiness; and whose pride and skill lie in the ability to deceive without being deceived. Cynic and doubter, nobody's fool, inside dopester, master of maneuver, the fox struggles to survive and even to do good in a world where no one can be trusted. The metaphor of the fox is not central in Machiavelli's writing, though it does appear occasionally. * * * Writing to a friend, Machiavelli cites the parable of the fox who sees a lion for the first time and is "ready to die for fear" but gradually overcomes his initial awe at the beast's overwhelming appearance: "Encountering him a second time he stopped behind a bush to look at him; the third time he spoke to him."[3] And in *The Prince,* the fox appears in the famous passage asserting that a successful prince must know how to fight corrupt men with the weapons of corruption, to fight animals like an animal when necessary. Since a prince must sometimes

> play the animal well, he chooses among the beasts the fox and the lion, because the lion does not protect himself from traps; the fox does not protect himself from the wolves. The prince must be a fox, therefore, to recognize the traps and a lion to frighten the wolves.[4]

Despite this unequivocal recommendation, much of the rest of the book suggests that Machiavelli intends not for the prince to be a fox himself but for him to employ a foxy counselor (Machiavelli himself is available). The fox is the clever one without overt power or glory. He remains inconspicuous.

But images of foxes are not frequent in Machiavelli's writing; let the fox serve simply as *our* metaphor for * * * a pattern esteemed and

2. Cunning, crafty, shrewd individual (Italian) [editor's note].
3. Letter to Vettori, 26 August 1513 (G 922).
4. *Prince,* ch. 18 (G 65). See also Niccolò Machiavelli, "First Decennale," lines 448–50 (G 1455).

admired in Machiavelli's time and place, and central to his professional activity. That Machiavelli valued his own foxiness, though no doubt ambivalently, is evident in all of his works. Above all, he does not want to be, or to be thought of as, gullible. He is an unmasker and demystifier, one who knows the ways of the world and is not taken in by the surfaces that fool others. He is an inverter of conventions and assumptions, a realist often to the point of cynicism. Never will he be like that "generality of men" who "feed themselves as much on what seems to be as on what is" and are often moved "more by the things that seem than by the things that are."[5]

Against this widespread gullibility, Machiavelli relies on those weapons of the intellect that had sustained him in his career. As an insider, he had come to know the reality of power from up close. * * * Machiavelli cultivated against gullibility "the eyes of Argus": he would see not merely through his own eyes but through the "truly many eyes that from Christian princes everywhere I have extracted."[6] That is, he brought to his wide experience among the great an insatiable curiosity and a passion for observation as a way of appropriating their power. Yet it was a matter not merely of external observation but of identification, the capacity to put himself in the place of another and regard the world from that location. He must become the other yet remain himself.

* * *

If a person, an action, or a pattern of character seems contemptible, that implies the existence of some standard against which it has been measured and found wanting. By what standard might Machiavelli have judged his best skill, his pride and delight, as also a source of shame, a sign of degeneracy or a lack of manhood? That standard is found in Machiavelli's second great source of knowledge, his reading, and particularly his reading in ancient works. * * *

* * *

* * * [A]ncient Rome * * * supplies the standard by which modern times and modern people are measured and found wanting. Rome was the culture that invented the concept of *virtus* and best exemplified its pursuit. It was the very model of masculinity and autonomy. As a state, Rome kept itself strong, independent, and healthy; it grew and prospered among states and won its battles. And the Roman citizenry exemplified *virtù* as well, being courageous and public-spirited, and serving in a citizen militia that was sufficiently disciplined and effective to protect their collective autonomy. Here was an

5. *Discourses* 1: 25 (G 252).
6. "Epigrams" (G 1463). Note the grisly metaphor: the fox takes, he does not receive.

uncorrupted community of real men, competent to take care of themselves without being dependent on anyone else, sharing in a fraternal, participatory civic life that made them self-governing. Nor was their public-spiritedness a spineless, deferential uniformity; in their domestic politics, as in their relations abroad, they were strong and manly: fighters. Political conflict—that "fighting by laws" of which only true men are capable—was what made and kept Rome free, healthy, and honorable.

In this respect, Rome stands in marked contrast to modern Florence, where all is weakness and cowardice, privatization and corruption. There is plenty of domestic political conflict, but it is factional, divisive, destructive of power and manliness; it is fighting in the manner of beasts. A world of foxes and their victims is incapable of true manliness or virtuous citizenship, for its members cannot trust each other and cannot genuinely subscribe to any standards or ideals. * * *

Is there any way to transform such corrupt men into citizens? Where does *virtù* come from? Who can generate manhood? It begins to seem that there is one thing even more admirable and manly than the *virtù* of the Roman Republic and its citizens: the extraordinary generative authority that could create such a state, transforming a world of foxes into one of men of *virtù*. Surely he who can father manhood is the manliest of all. As the Roman citizen out-mans the fox and shows him up as a mere beast, so the creator of Roman citizen manhood out-mans his creatures. A real man is neither an animal nor a child. Thus the fox is doubly disparaged: he can neither be a citizen nor make citizens. And the ultimate measure of manhood seems to be generative authority: the patriarchal power to create manhood.

It will help to recall the special significance that ancient Rome had for Machiavelli's time, and the distinctive character of ancient Roman society, since both are intimately bound up with paternity. The Romans, after all, were not an ideal that Renaissance Italians picked arbitrarily from the catalogue of past greatness. For Machiavelli and his audience, the Romans were literally forefathers. * * *

Moreover, the character and culture of the ancient Romans were such as to invite this imagery; Rome was the very essence of patriarchy, a society of fathers par excellence. As Hannah Arendt argued, the Romans invented the concept of authority, and that concept can bear its full meaning only in a context like that of ancient Rome, where origins, forefathers, and tradition form the basis of legitimacy. "At the heart of Roman politics . . . stands the conviction of the sacredness of foundation, in the sense that once something has been founded it remains binding for all future generations."[7] But it was

7. Hannah Arendt, "What Is Authority?" in *Between Past and Future* (Cleveland: World Publishing, 1963), 120.

not just any founding that the Romans considered sacred, as the Greeks had founded new *poleis* here and there. For Rome, what mattered was the one, unique, unrepeatable founding, the special beginning of the sacred tradition. * * * The concept of authority originates in that Roman context, from the Latin verb *augere*, to augment. What is augmented by those in authority is the original, sacred foundation; one becomes an authority by merging with and furthering that traditional authority. An authority is someone who is the author of other men's deeds and is himself authored by still earlier forefathers.

* * * With their strongly patriarchal households and ancestor-oriented religion, this society of soldiers, builders, lawyers, and administrators provides the very model of significant (fore)fatherhood. Often on the verge of being pompous but never frivolous, perhaps stolid but never petty, they were always a little larger than life. Add to this Roman self-conception the Renaissance glorification of all things ancient, and one begins to see how Rome and the ancients might serve as an alternative model of manhood that puts the fox to shame. By comparison with a forefather, a fox is impotent and contemptible; a forefather need not stoop to the weapons of a fox, for he can put his imprint on the world openly and directly.

Yet the model of the forefather is not really a single, coherent image but is deeply divided into two visions of manhood, as much in conflict with each other as with the image of the fox. On the one hand, there is a singular forefather as founder, whose potent generativity transforms beasts into men; on the other hand, there are the forefathers of Roman republican citizenship, the members of a self-governing community who fight by laws. The images differ as much as paternity differs from fraternity, as uniqueness differs from mutuality, as unanimity differs from conflict. It is necessary, then, to look more closely at each of the two models of manhood conflated in the concept of the forefather: the Founder and the Citizen.

* * *

Machiavelli reserves his greatest praise for * * * the manhood of the Founder, using the capital letter to distinguish this image from historical human beings who have founded actual institutions or states. A Founder, as Machiavelli pictures him, is a male figure of superhuman or mythical proportions, who introduces among men something new, good, and sufficiently powerful so that it continues beyond his lifetime on the course he has set. The point is never just getting others to do what you want, but changing them, introducing new patterns of action and of relationship. Such redirection of human affairs is the most challenging task a man can undertake, for nothing is "more difficult to plan or more uncertain of success or more dangerous to carry out than an attempt to introduce new institutions."[8] And to the difficulty and danger of innovation there must be added the problem of making that innovation last. A Founder does not just "rule prudently while he lives" but must "so organize" the institution he rules "that even after he dies it can be maintained."[9] * * *

* * *

Like the Romans generally, then, the Founder is the forefather par excellence, embodiment of a generative paternity so potent that it can create lasting masculinity in other men, even in a sense overcoming death. Machiavelli repeatedly employs metaphors of birth and paternity in this connection. He calls the founding of Rome a birth (*nasciamento*); for a corrupt society to be renovated means for it "to be born again" with "many perils and much blood."[1] Despite the imagery of birth in blood, however, no mother appears; it seems the issue is a purely masculine generation, singular paternity.

By itself that odd fact seems insignificant, but it is one in a series of paradoxes connected with the Founder image. That image is problematic in ways that the image of the fox is not. The foxy ideal can also be a real character type, a way of life; but the Founder is a fantasy projected by Machiavelli's imagination from his reading about ancient Rome. Though stimulated by the practical problems of Florentine politics, that fantasy was never lived, nor was it meant to be. So the difficulties of the Founder image are logical problems for the interpreter, by contrast with the psychological and practical life problems faced by a fox himself.

* * *

As a standard of manhood, the image of the Founder puts that of the fox to shame because of the Founder's capacity to father. Yet that implies that the Founder himself is only a means to Machiavelli's real goal: the new, uncorrupted society to be created. The vision of *that* society provides yet a third model of true manhood for Machiavelli, different from the manliness of both fox and Founder. Call it the image of the fraternal Citizen, and let the capitalization of the word mark the image as an ideal type distinct from actual citizenship in this or that historical society.

The Citizen is Machiavelli's most profound and promising vision and the most political of his images of manhood. It has the

8. *Prince,* ch. 6 (G 26). See also *Art of War,* bk. 7 (G 721).
9. *Discourses* 1: 11 (G 226).
1. Niccolò Machiavelli, *Opere,* 8 vols. (Milano: Feltrinelli Editore, 1960–65), 1: 125; *Discourses* 1: 17 (G 240).

potential for synthesizing what is best in his conflicting ideas about autonomy. Yet it is also the most elusive and difficult to reconstruct from the texts. * * * It has to be constructed from scattered sections and passages, often by implication or contrast with what Machiavelli calls "corruption" or "degeneracy." Yet the edifying vision of the Founder also contrasts with corruption and degeneracy and must nevertheless be distinguished from that of the Citizen.

The manhood of Citizenship is clearly tied to Machiavelli's republicanism, his deep commitment to politics, and his passionate love of Florence. Yet it is an image drawn at least as much from his reading as from his experience, for it concerns a free and healthy collective life such as Florence never experienced in his time, a way of life to which he refers variously as civic, political, and free: a *governo politico* or *governo libero*, a *vivere libero, vivere politico*, or *vivere civile*.[2]

Although the Citizen is, like the fox and the Founder, an image of manhood, it embodies *virtù* in a fundamentally different way. For both fox and Founder have *virtù* through their personal, individual autonomy, understood as needing no others, having ties to no others, acting without being acted upon. For the Citizen, by contrast, *virtù* is sharing in a collective autonomy, a collective freedom and glory, yet without loss of individuality. *Virtù* is systemic or relational. Thus it not merely is compatible with, but logically requires, interaction in mutuality with others like oneself. It lies not in isolation from or domination over others, but in the shared taking charge of one's objective connections with them. "Each Man by Himself is Weak," as a chapter title in the *Discourses* announces, but "The Populace [*la plebe*] United is Strong."[3] When individuals realize this, they act together to pursue the shared public good and thereby sustain it. When they perceive as (if they were) isolated individuals, their actions become both selfish and cowardly, for "as soon as each man gets to thinking about his personal danger, he becomes worthless and weak," his *virtù* vanishes; his actions begin to undermine the community and produce his isolation.[4] Citizen *virtù* is thus a matter both of objective activity and of outlook or attitude, each affecting the other. And in both respects, such individual *virtù* is available only in a republic; it presupposes an ethos and an institutional framework. * * * In the Citizen vision, this is the only way to achieve strength and *virtù*, for "only authority freely given is durable."[5]

2. The great frequency with which Machiavelli employs these terms, like the frequency of his use of *virtù*, is inevitably hidden by even the best translation.
3. *Discourses* 1: 57 (G 312); Machiavelli, *Opere* 1: 260.
4. *Discourses* 1: 57 (G 313).
5. *Florentine Histories* 2: 34 (G 1125). Public freedom may even be a source of strength beyond *virtù*, as in *Discourses* 1: 43 (G 286).

* * *

A plurality of classes and interests is necessary to the Citizen vision not merely because each has its unique perspective and spirit to contribute to the community, but also because internal conflict is an essential and healthy phenomenon in its own right. If relations among real men in this vision are those of peer mutuality, fraternal rather than paternal and filial, Machiavelli is not one of those romantics for whom fraternity implies a natural or automatic harmony. He never forgets that brothers hate as well as love one another. Thus, whereas the vision of the fox involves a preference for indirect methods and manipulative means, for fraud over force and both over "fighting by laws," and whereas the vision of the Founder involves a complex combination of fierce ruthlessness directed outward at the enemy with a courtly, idealized internal harmony in which no conflict can arise, the vision of manly Citizenship differs from both in the value it places on internal, political conflict and particularly on open conflict that spurns the means of deceit or indirection.

Internal conflict, aggression, ambition, directed and used in the right way, are the sources of strength, health, and growth. Roman republican political life is again the prime example. * * * The "perfection" of her government was achieved through "discord," and "disunion between the plebians and the Senate."[6] Indeed, if Rome "had become quieter . . . it would also have been weaker," deprived of the opportunity for "greatness" and for "growth."[7]

* * *

In terms of manhood, the relationships among the three images we have examined are extraordinarily complex and ultimately unresolvable because they are nontransitive. Each image is in certain respects superior to, more manly than, the other two; each is in significant ways unsatisfactory, inadequate, or unmanly. And so Machiavelli's thought in effect circles over them endlessly in various juxtapositions and transformations, the contemplation of any one of the three leading him eventually back to a reconsideration of the others. The image of the fox, though an ideal of manhood in its own right and a source of pride for Machiavelli, is also somehow despicable and unmanly, for the fox acts only by indirection and shuns direct encounter. He is put to shame by the Citizen's fearless engagement in open conflict and accusation; and a world of foxes and their victims in a world incapable of free civic life. He is put to shame by the

6. Ibid., 1: 2 (G 200). See also 1: 4 (G 202-3); 1: 17 (G 239).
7. Ibid., 1: 6 (G 209).

Founder's generative power; and a fox cannot father Citizens—indeed, foxiness undermines Citizen *virtù*. Thus, by comparison with both Citizen and Founder he is not a real man, but only an animal.

The Citizen is an ideal of *virtù,* "fighting by laws" like a man, rather than in the way of beasts. Yet citizenship seems incapable of generating itself; the Citizen is good at maintenance, but can he father himself? How is a corrupt world to be transformed into one of civic virtue? One who cannot fight by the way of beasts is bound to fail in a world of lions, wolves, and foxes. Only someone who can generate a virtuous world is a *real* man. By comparison with either the Founder's generativity or the fox's cynical knowledge, the Citizen is revealed as a dependent child not yet capable of manhood.

The Founder is the ultimate man in terms of paternity, yet, being only a means to the real goal, Citizens of *virtù,* he must be overthrown. And besides, he is a myth; the fox, or perhaps even the Citizen, can show him up as a mere fantasy, incompatible with the *verità effettuale della cosa.* The Founder image is thus an escape from reality and from effective action in the world, hence bound up with unmanliness. * * *

And so the endless circles continue. What is it that traps Machiavelli, that so divides and confounds his understanding of manhood?

* * *

Psychological theory and the peculiarities of Renaissance Florentine social life help to illuminate what one might call the family drama implicit in Machiavelli's thought. Centrally concerned about autonomy, Machiavelli frequently conflates the various senses of "being a man," so that he equates humanness not just with adulthood but, even more important, with masculinity. Civilization, liberty, law, politics, history, culture, the whole *vivere civile* that constitutes the world of adult human autonomy are then understood as male enterprises won from and sustained against female power—the engulfing mother, the captivating maiden, the vindictive wife—woman as the "other," symbolizing all that man is not, or wishes not to be. The struggle to sustain civilization and republican liberty thus reflects the struggle of boys to become men.

Machiavelli explores many different versions of this family drama, and many alternative strategies for the embattled male, each of them ultimately unsatisfactory, so that manhood remains fragmented among them. They are all unsatisfactory because being human and adult is not in fact equivalent to being male; and although the realization of autonomy may be partly stimulated, it is ultimately undermined by men's fear of women. The misogynist striving for autonomy may be energetic, even frantic, but it is self-defeating. Yet

Machiavelli also offers a different vision: an understanding of humanness that is not tied to gender, an understanding of autonomy as mutuality, which could apply as much to sexual as to political relations, an understanding of maturity not as an escape from the mythical engulfing mother (nor from the mythical rescuing father) but as a transcendence of these mythologizing distortions themselves—distortions of parents, of authority, of self. Machiavelli offers that vision, yet he is not able to sustain it. Again and again *machismo* and misogyny, invoked in the name of autonomy, win out against it.

As it has emerged so far from Machiavelli's texts, the family drama begins somewhat as follows: once upon a time there may have been a good and nurturing mother with whom one lived in blissful unity, but that was so long ago and ended so badly that she is now at most a distant dream. There are hardly any images of such a benevolent mother in the texts; at most she can be inferred, for instance from the relations between animals and nature. "In the beginning," Machiavelli says, following Polybius, "men [*uomini*] . . . lived . . . in the fashion of beasts," and "The [Golden] Ass" reveals something of what that means: beasts live in perfect harmony with nature. She teaches them what is healthful for them to do and eat and spontaneously supplies them with "all her good things."[8] They are "content" with what she has to offer, "happy," and free of "anxiety." Yet even in Circe's world that blissful absorption is fraught with ambiguity. The praise of the animals' condition comes from a pig, after all; and is expressed in terms approximating the animal to the human world, even including *virtù*. Yet the animals' condition clearly is not a desirable option for man; a life "on all fours" in Circe's palace is captivity.[9] It means a loss of "liberty," a forgetting of "human things," a "vanquishing" of human "vigor [*virtù*]."[1] It is a dependent, and not a human, life.

Even more important, the initial blissful unity proves to be unreliable. The fickle nature of the nurturing mother is soon revealed. * * * She disappears, leaving man to begin his (human) life "in weeping" and "devoid of all protection." Being human means having to provide for oneself through "art," by the power of one's own "hands and speech."[2] The initial unity, if it ever existed, is permanently lost, so that the only real possibility is to struggle forward, toward autonomy.

It is, however, a struggle. To be devoid of protection is not to be autonomous; and though the child may be abandoned, it is neither

8. *Discourses* 1: 2 (G 197); Machiavelli, *Opere,* 1: 131; "[Golden] Ass," ch. 8, lines 46–108 (G 770–72).
9. "[Golden] Ass," ch. 2, line 147 (G 756).
1. Ibid., lines 24–36 (G 753); ch. 4, lines 112–38 (G 761).
2. Ibid., ch. 8, lines 95, 130 (G 771–72).

alone nor free. The nurturing matrix has vanished, but another mother has taken her place. Less dreamlike and more definite in outline, she is not merely unreliable but downright malevolent. Though she does not nourish, this second mother is no more willing to permit autonomy than the first; she wants to infantilize and emasculate men, to keep them forever in her power. She is therefore the enemy of all things man-made; and the world created by men's "hands and speech" is their refuge from her. * * * This civic, human world is what is at stake in the battle of the sexes, men's shared struggle not merely against the real women whom they encounter, but even more against the larger feminine force: nature, fortune, or whatever her name.

It is, on the whole, an unequal struggle, for the feminine force has powerful weapons that she has implanted in the men. Natural appetite and entropy draw men back toward reabsorption into the womb and dissolution of the separate self. Men grow weary of the effort and anxiety of maintaining civilization. They yearn for the pig's mud-wallow and the infant's regular feeding. Even worse, the very impulses that stimulate men's quest for autonomy can turn into limitless, destructive cravings that defeat the quest. Sexuality, for instance, draws men out of childhood toward adulthood and masculinity; yet in the form of excessive lust it pits them against each other, enervates them, and returns them to feminine domination. Ambition and acquisitiveness, too, draw men out of nature's power. Able to foresee future needs, men use their hands and speech to construct an artificial order and to seize what is not naturally supplied. Being discontent in dependence, they seek autonomy. Yet avarice and ambition, pursued excessively or in the wrong way, are also the weapons of nature and fortune in men. They are the multilimbed "furies" sent by that "hidden power . . . in the heaven" that is "to man's being by no means friendly." They are the "appetites" that "destroy our states," so that "one goes down and another goes up" on fortune's wheel.[3]

Not only are natural need, sexuality, ambition, and avarice all ambiguous in this way, both stimulating and undermining autonomy, but the whole opposition between nature and culture as respectively feminine and masculine is still too simple to capture Machiavelli's vision. For though the *vivere civile* is continually threatened by female forces, it also presupposes an underlying connection with them; it must provide for natural needs and enlist natural energy. * * * Civilization, politics, history are human enterprises built in opposition to natural impulse and entropy; yet they must

3. "Tercets on Ambition," lines 25–42, 64 (G 735–36).

acknowledge, use, and transform rather than reject or deny the forces they oppose.

In the first place, men's animal passions must be enlisted in the cause of the *vivere civile,* or they will destroy it. * * * Machiavelli wants to understand the real foundation of the actual civilization human beings have sometimes achieved, not some fancied utopia for angels; he seeks the "*verità effettuale della cosa.*" It is "very natural and normal" for men to want possessions, to have sexual desires, and to be ambitious.[4] "Since no man has power to drive [these impulses] out of himself," the task of civilization is precisely to channel such needs and impulses. * * *

* * *

* * * Machiavelli obviously thinks that while the enormous power of feminine agencies like nature and fortune threatens human autonomy, it can also be tapped and used for the human enterprise. Though inimical to human *virtù,* these forces themselves have a kind of power, perhaps even *virtù,* of their own. That is the point of Machiavelli's famous invocation of the centaur in conjunction with the passage on the lion and the fox. Ancient writers, he says, taught that Achilles and other ancient princes were brought up by Chiron the Centaur; they were given a teacher who was "half animal and half man," so that they might learn to "adopt the nature of either animal or man," as needed. For the way of fighting "according to the laws" that is "suited to man" is "often not sufficient."[5] Similarly, the Founder should be a foundling, reared by bees or wolves.

* * * Political leaders need to be educated by centaurs because in politics and history people fashion the *vivere civile* both out of nature and against it, both by fortune and against it. Politics is a border-zone of continual interchange and frequent combat. Insofar as we begin as animals, only animal instinct and need can supply the energy for transforming the animal into the human. There is no other source. Machiavelli tends to associate these natural roots of our humanity with the feminine, the human with the masculine. So he perceives the feminine as the source and the ultimate conclusion, stronger than the entire masculine enterprise; yet it remains for him less "honorable," because it is incompatible with individuation and freedom.

Passages like that about the centaur, no doubt, are what lead Felix Gilbert to argue that Machiavelli teaches "a return to life according to man's inherent natural instincts."[6] The imitation of ancient Rome, he says, signifies a return to nature; and man can become strong only by

4. *Prince,* ch. 15 (Machiavelli, *Opere* 1: 65); ch. 3 (G 18); letter to Vettori, 31 January 1514–[1515] (G 961).
5. *Prince,* ch. 18 (G 64–65).
6. Felix Gilbert, *Machiavelli and Guicciardini: Politics and History in Sixteenth-Century Florence* (Princeton: Princeton University Press, 1965), 192.

accepting his membership in nature as his "fate." Animals have a "pristine genuineness" that in man has been "weakened by reason." To achieve "control" of his world, therefore, man must return to an animallike state, "to a level of instinctiveness where he becomes part of the forces surrounding him."[7] Yet though there is some textual support for such a reading, it cannot be fully correct. There is nothing in Machiavelli about the "weakening of instinct by reason," nor is there much hope for "control" of the world. And, above all, nature and instinct are no simple, unambiguous sources of regeneration. Most of the time they signify the opposite of human *virtù* and autonomy; they are dangerous and seductive and men must struggle against them. Far from being identified with them, moreover, ancient Rome may be Machiavelli's most powerful resource against their threat.

Acceptance of our animal nature and continued contact with it are indeed of central value to Machiavelli, a source of energy and perhaps even of *virtù,* but they are also fraught with danger. Contact with these feminine powers is essential, but it can be safely achieved only under the most stringent masculine safeguards. The mother cannot be left behind, for her powers are inside men. The struggle to use those powers without succumbing to them is thus continual, requiring the utmost resources of masculinity.

By greed, developing sexuality, and above all, ambition, the boy-child is motivated to seek escape from maternal domination, to move toward the masculine and human world, away from dependence. But, on the whole, he cannot hope to succeed in this quest by himself. The feminine powers he faces are too strong, too insidiously allied with his own desires. If he is to succeed, he will require one or another form of external masculine support. * * * Indeed, it often seems that only a patriarchal father of superhuman strength and authority would be any match for the mother's terrible power.

Yet once the rescue from matriarchy has been effected, so powerful a father turns out himself to be a new threat to the boy's developing manhood. The father's fierceness, essential to his function as rescuer, also endangers the boy himself and constrains his independence as severely as the mother did. Once having matured to sufficient strength in the shelter of the father's masculinity, the boy will have to escape or remove this patriarchal power, too, if he is to attain autonomy. What is supposed to follow patriarchal rule, of course, is the fraternal band of citizens in the *vivere civile,* each of them no more than human but by their pooled masculinity jointly able to sustain civilization. But the vision is fragile. Connected with the transition from patriarchal to fraternal power are not only serious problems—political, logical, and psychological—but also something like an inversion of Freud's

7. Ibid., 197.

"return of the repressed." While the rescuing father may be mortal, the dangerous mother is apparently eternal, and as soon as he is removed from the scene, she is once more a threat. * * *

The goal is autonomy; autonomy means adulthood; adulthood requires getting away from mother; and so autonomy comes to be identified with masculinity and misogynistically defined. But defined in that way, it becomes humanly unattainable. The goal is mutuality in the *vivere civile,* but so long as it is pursued in terms of gender, the chosen means instead reproduce domination and dependence. Every avenue of masculine defense against feminine power in Machiavelli's thought turns out to be a dead end; manhood remains split into fragments that cannot be reconciled or even ordered. Consider a summary catalogue of man's various hopes and weapons in the struggle against femininity, keeping in mind that such a list is bound to impose an artificial neatness that distorts the texts. What are the masculine resources in Machiavelli's family drama?

First, doing without a mother. This idea occurs in several forms, the first of which is a mother who is from the outset nonnurturant, so that one is never deceived about her character nor rendered dependent. As nurturance makes men vulnerable, early deprivation might strengthen them. Fortune "afflicts" those whose *virtù* she wants to develop, and necessity is such a rejecting (and therefore beneficent) mother. By preventing sensuality and laziness, "necessity makes *virtù.*"[8]

Second, parthenogenesis. If one could do without parents altogether, though unprotected, one would also be free of domination. The image of the foundling Founder expresses this possibility. Lacking both maternal nurturance and paternal sponsorship, he must in effect generate himself and be from the outset wholly autonomous. That is what qualifies him to make a break in the causal chain of history and launch genuine novelty among men.

Third, nurturance from a male. Since autonomy sorts with masculinity, it might be achieved if one could avoid women altogether, if one could be born from a father and nurtured by him alone. Cities and other human institutions have such a purely masculine birth. From a male source, nurturance seems less dangerous. Although almost no nurturant mothers appear in Machiavelli's texts, kind and nurturant fathers are not unusual, nor are they presented as engulfing.[9] They are nevertheless a problem. For the father who nurtures so that feminine power need never appear is hard to distinguish from the weak father unable to protect his sons against that power when it does appear.

Fourth, failing such avoidance of the early, nurturing mother, the growing boy may try to struggle against her power on his own, playing

8. Machiavelli, *Opere* 1: 309; this is my translation.
9. Fathers may nurture with masculine, that is, symbolic food, as the ancients "feed" Machiavelli in his study; letter to Vettori, 10 December 1513 (G 929).

out the Oedipal relationship in the father's absence. Here the protagonist is no longer a helpless infant, and the issue no longer nurturance; he must try to please or conquer her sexually by his budding manhood. Here one finds the classic confrontation between *virtù* and fortune of *The Prince*: the winning of fortune's favor, perhaps by cuffing and mauling her; the seizing of her daughter by the hair; the effort to please her by going limp when she wants to do all, becoming audacious when she is in a mood to be mastered. Such employment of sexuality can save man from his regressive wishes for nurturance, yet it is likely to leave him still enmeshed in feminine power. For sexual conquest is likely to entail sensual pleasure or even affection, which weaken men and cast them into a new dependence. Fortune's favors, moreover, are always only temporary; the ultimate power remains hers.

Fifth, a kind of sublimated conquest—sexual or nutritive—the retreat into the mind and intellectual life. By withdrawing from the bodily self that requires nurturance and desires sexual gratification, one might become invulnerable to feminine power or even able to outwit it. This is the way of the fox, prudently discerning fortune's "designs" in order to "assist in weaving" them, but only in thought. This alternative again seems to offer man a kind of autonomy yet leaves him really still in feminine power.

If early maternal nurturance is unavoidable, and sexual or intellectual confrontation of feminine power on one's own proves impossible, some form of external masculine support will be required. Thus there is *sixth,* discipline, a category that overlaps with others in the list to some extent. *Disciplina* is a kind of man-made functional equivalent of the rejecting mother. By the imposition of external controls, man may be protected against his own cravings for passivity and nurturance, making it safe for him to take what women have to offer. Roman discipline saved that city's soldiers from succumbing to the pleasures of conquered Capua; and fictionalized Castruccio defends his womanizing by saying "I have taken her, not she me."[1] Similarly, in founding a city, discipline can make safe a fertile site, securing access to nurturance without feminization. Discipline also controls the divisive effects of lust, greed, and ambition, imposing limits on the "nature of men."[2] Discipline, moreover, is more reliable than mere natural ardor or spirit. Inquiring why the French seem "more than men" at the beginning of a battle but "become less than women" as the fighting continues, Machiavelli answers that the French army lacks *virtù* because it depends on natural ardor (*furore*) without the reliable order that discipline would introduce.[3] Often, indeed, it seems that the

1. *Discourses* 1: 19 (G 381); "Life of Castruccio" (G 556).
2. *Prince,* ch. 29 (G 257). See also "Tercets on Ambition," lines 94–117 (G 737).
3. *Discourses* 3: 36 (G 510). See also *Art of War,* bk. 1 (G 581); bk. 2 (G 608, 611); bk. 6 (G 679, 694); bk. 7 (G 718).

more severe the discipline, the better secured masculine autonomy will be, as in Machiavelli's praise of pagan religion for strengthening men by its "blood and ferocity" while Christianity makes them "weak and effeminate"; or in the remarkable last chapter of the *Discourses* in which Rome is saved from the conspiracy of wives by its readiness "to punish" even large numbers in "terrible" ways.[4]

Discipline, however, is not self-generating, and Machiavelli pictures it in two rather different ways, depending on the agency by which it is imposed. The two possibilities correspond, roughly, to the images of Founder and Citizen. There is thus, *seventh,* the saving father. His discipline is the discipline of armies, allowing no internal conflict, eliminating all sensual gratification, directing punitive rage against internal deserters as well as external enemies. The saving father appears as a deus ex machina to rescue men by his ferocity, which he uses both to control their regressive and divisive passions and to defeat the mother.

In an important sense for Machiavelli, if men fail to escape the suffocating maternal embrace, it is the fault of weak or absent fathers "who do not protect us."[5] Again and again he says that if men lack *virtù,* their leaders are to blame: "The sins of the people are caused by the princes."[6] Yet Machiavelli is always an activist: if no saving father seems to be around, men who want autonomy must seek one out. If suitable guardians and models are lacking in their own time, they must seek among the great forefathers of the ancient world. Renewing contact with the ancient supply of *virtù* can strengthen contemporary men in their struggles.

External support and discipline can also come from a different source, however. Instead of the rescuing father there is, *eighth,* membership in a fraternal community. Here each relatively weak individual is aided by the pooled masculinity of his peers, and discipline is mutually imposed. To the cyclical, entropic power of nature and the capricious power of fortune, men counterpose human institutions multiplying their individual *virtù* and extending it through time in a network of mutually supportive relationships, each citizen both assisted and restrained by the others. Through such institutions suited to a "truly free and law-abiding" order, men can "overcome" the "malice" of fortune, for "good laws make good fortune."[7] The shared discipline of republican Citizenship, then, is the final male resource against feminine power. Yet its origins are a mystery, and

4. *Discourses* 2: 2 (G 331); 3: 49 (G 527–29).
5. *Prince,* ch. 26 (G 493); letter to Vettori, 26 August 1513 (G 926).
6. *Discourses,* 3: 29 (G 493). Cf. 1: 21 (G 246–47); *Art of War,* bk. 7 (G 723–24); letter to Guicciardini, after 21 October 1525 (G 987). Machiavelli obviously does not mean "sin" in the Christian sense; cf. *Prince,* ch. 12 (G 48); *Discourses* 2: 18 (G 374); 3: 38 (G 516).
7. *Florentine Histories* 3: 5 (G 1148); *Discourses* 1: 11 (G 225). See also *Florentine Histories* 5: 1 (G 1232).

its continued maintenance against internal corruption and external attack is highly problematic. Even fraternal Citizens fail to escape nature's and fortune's power for long.

The Citizen vision of manhood, however, is not merely one in a catalogue of male defenses against the feminine, although Machiavelli often presents it in these terms. It also contains an altogether different understanding of autonomy, no longer defined in terms of masculinity and the threat of female power. It offers the elements of a radically distinct way of coming to terms with sexual and generational relations. Stressing mutuality, that vision suggests ways of conceiving human adulthood that are independent of gender, in which parents are no longer mythologized but recognized as simply human, like the self. It suggests the possibility of genuine internal conflict that nevertheless observes civil limits, of genuine gratification that is nevertheless human rather than merely animal, that is safe without punitive discipline. Instead of being harshly repressed, passion and need are to be transformed, enlisted in the civic enterprise, enlarged by ties to others and to principle. Instead of the barren site, the untouched apple tree, the exclusion of women, there is a vision of autonomous mutual nurturance. Animals and infants must be fed, by nature, by a mother, or by a master; adult human beings are those capable of caring for themselves and for others. More than once Machiavelli equates public freedom with the capacity to feed oneself.[8] Political, like personal, autonomy must be rooted in the natural and requires relationships with others, but these need not imply dependence if all are providers and responsible agents, jointly free. That vision is an alternative to the entire family drama.

* * *

MAURIZIO VIROLI

In his important book, *From Politics to Reason of State*, Viroli focuses on the change in the language of politics from the thirteenth century to the end of the sixteenth. At the start of this period, *politico* was associated with politics and was concerned with preserving the state, which was conceived as a republic—that is, a community of good individuals who lived together, controlled the basic institutions of the state, and pursued justice. By the end of the period, that key idea had been replaced in political discourse by the notion of the *stato*—that is, the state as an entity ruled by someone or by a particular group of people who controlled its public institutions and handed out offices to "friends." "Reason of state" was a doctrine formulated in the course of the sixteenth

8. *Discourses* 1: 16 (G 235); "[Golden] Ass," ch. 8, lines 94–96, 130 (G 771–72).

century that justified the use of harsh means by such rulers, when necessary to preserve the state, thus allowing them to maintain their control of it. Viroli sees Machiavelli as a key figure in this transition, although he insists that Machiavelli never justified the evil that the prince has to perpetrate by appealing to the principle of "reason of state."

From Machiavelli and the Republican Concept of Politics†

In the story of the transition from politics to reason of state the central place belongs to Niccolò Machiavelli. Over the centuries, Machiavelli has been regarded as being mainly responsible for the dismissal of the notion of politics as the art of the republic, and the spiritual father of the doctrine of reason of state.

Be it his sin or his greatest contribution to modern culture, what seems to be above dispute is that Machiavelli rejected the republican language and provided us with a new account of the goals and the means of politics. Against the view that politics is the art of establishing and preserving a good community, Machiavelli, it has been argued, stressed that the goal of politics is the pursuit of power. * * *

This agreement among contemporary scholars could be further corroborated by the opinions of the political writers of the sixteenth and seventeenth centuries, who called Machiavelli the corrupter of the true (Aristotelian) idea of politics and pointed to him as the thinker who transformed the most noble of humane arts into the art of tyrannical rule. * * *

However, one political writer in Early-Modern Europe turned upside down the predominant view of Machiavelli, and claimed that his great accomplishment was the recovery of the republican view of politics. I am referring to James Harrington, who made this point forcefully in the "Preliminaries" of *Oceana,* issued in 1656. The premise of his argument is the distinction between "ancient" and "modern" prudence. "Ancient prudence" was revealed to mankind by God himself and was followed by the Greeks and the Romans. The government which was instituted according to the ancient prudence was the government *de jure,* that is, "the civil society instituted and preserved upon the common right and interest." Modern prudence, on the contrary, "is the art whereby some man or some few men, subject a city or a nation and rule it according unto his or their private interest." * * *

† From *From Politics to Reason of State: The Acquisition and Transformation of the Language of Politics 1250–1600* (Cambridge: Cambridge University Press, 1992), pp. 126–29, 131–32, 145–62, 164–65, 173–74, 176–77. Notes are Viroli's unless otherwise indicated, with full bibliographical information supplied by the editor.

> The former kind is that which Machiavel (whose books are neglected) is the only politician that hath gone about to retrieve and that Leviathan (who would have his book imposed upon the universities) goes about to destroy.[1]

The two conflicting views of Machiavelli as the subverter or restorer of the republican idea of politics have been discussed also in terms of compatibility between the content of *The Prince* and the *Discourses.* * * * Hence, if we want to clarify Machiavelli's role in the story of the transition from politics to reason of state, as well as to gain a better insight concerning his intellectual and political biography, we should reopen the question and ask: What did Machiavelli do with the conventional language of politics of his times? Did he dismantle or recover the view of politics as the art of instituting and preserving the good political community? Or did he, in fact, advocate a combination of some sort between the art of politics and the art of the state?

* * * I shall begin by remarking that in *The Prince,* Machiavelli never uses the word *"politico"* or its equivalent. For a book that has been celebrated or attacked as the keystone of the new science of politics this is surprising. * * * The vocabulary of politics is appropriate within a discourse on the city, but since *The Prince* is not a discourse on the city, there is no reason for Machiavelli to use that language. The subject matter of his treatise is the state *of* the prince and how a state can be governed and preserved.

* * *

As Quentin Skinner has correctly shown, to understand *The Prince*'s subversive meaning we have to read it in the context of the Quattrocento advice-books for princes. In this way we can see that Machiavelli's book was a devastating critique of contemporary humanism and its classical Ciceronian sources.[2] If we consider also another ideological context, namely the literature on the art of the state, we may be able to identify other important sets of meanings, and to see that *The Prince* was intended to be at the same time a critique and an endorsement of the beliefs on the art of the state that were circulating in early fifteenth-century Florence.

When Machiavelli sat in Sant'Andrea in Percussina to write *The Prince,* the art of the state was a well-established body of conventions, though not as refined as the rival language of civil

1. J. Harrington, "The Commonwealth of Oceana," in J. G. A. Pocock (ed.), *The Political Works of James Harrington* (Cambridge: Cambridge University Press, 1977), p. 161.
2. See Quentin Skinner, *The Foundations of Modern Political Thought,* 2 vols. (Cambridge: Cambridge University Press, 1978), vol. 1, pp. 128–38. Of the same author see also *Machiavelli* (Oxford: Oxford University Press, 1981), pp. 31–47.

philosophy. In Florentine discussions on government, the conventions and the vocabulary of the language of politics coexisted with those of the art of the state. Politics, however, enjoyed a much nobler public status than the art of the state. * * *

* * *

By the time Machiavelli's *Prince* was delivered to Lorenzo de' Medici in 1516, if it was delivered at all, his desk was probably covered by many other discourses or letters advising him what to do to maintain his *stato.* To have some chances to be recognized as a reliable master of the art, and considered for appointment to a government post, Machiavelli had to show that he knew the art of the state better than anyone else and that his expertise was safer than the traditional wisdom that had inspired Medicean rule since the days of Cosimo.

Machiavelli firmly believed himself to be up to the task and perfectly well trained and competent in the art of the state. For Machiavelli the art of the state was his true calling, the only art to which he felt himself inclined and attracted. His friends, too, considered him a person who possessed an outstanding talent for the "arte dello stato." * * *

The Prince was his effort to convince the Medici too. * * *

* * *

In *The Prince,* Machiavelli takes positions on all the key issues of the art of the state. When he writes that "a prudent ruler [*signore*] cannot keep his word, nor should he, when such fidelity would damage him," Machiavelli was upholding and reinforcing a line of attack against the republican–Ciceronian language of politics that was already rooted in the Florentine political language. * * * His critique of the conventional view of politics was not uncommon or unheard of. He spoke just like other Florentines did. Like them he criticized politics on behalf of the necessary rules of the art of the state, which compel the prince to behave against the principles of integrity and rectitude.

* * *

* * * [O]ne of the issues that preoccupied the theorists of the state most was the exceptional difficulty of securing the state of the Medici, because the new regime had been imposed upon the republic by means of foreign armies, with the support of the majority of the *grandi.*[3] Machiavelli, as is well known, takes the issue of the new principalities as the main focus of *The Prince.* As he baldly states

3. A reference to the members of the elite upper class in Florentine society. They were not nobles, but were treated as such by European powers such as France and Spain [editor's note].

toward the end of the book, if the measures that he has recommended are skillfully put into practice, "they will make a new ruler seem very well established, and will quickly make his power more secure and stable ['*più sicuro e più fermo nello stato*'] than if he had always been a ruler."[4]

If the prince has seized power abruptly by means of somebody else's armies, as was largely the case with the Medici, the task of securing the state is immensely difficult. Even more arduous, is to introduce new institutions and laws in order to establish his power. The undertaking is unlikely to succeed because the partisans of the old order will oppose the innovations with the utmost determination, whereas all those who might benefit from the new institutions are tepid, partly because they fear the partisans of the old order, partly because men are generally hesitant toward novelties. The only way to succeed is to be strong enough to be able to force the issue and impose the desired plan. The message that Machiavelli seems to be addressing to the Medici is, then, to be extremely prudent in dismantling the institutions of the city and replacing them with new ones more fit to sustain the new state, and to focus, first, on creating their own militia.

The traditional Medicean practice of ruling behind the scene with civility, remarks Machiavelli in the chapter on "civil principality," guarantees a poor foundation of the state. Ruling indirectly through public officials is a safe practice only in peaceful times, when the citizens need, and seek, the help of the regime ("*hanno bisogno dello stato*"). But when the regime needs the support of the citizens, very few of them are to be found. A prudent prince must then establish his power in such a way that the citizens will need him and his state ("*abbino bisogno dello stato e di lui*") both in times of peace and times of civil strife.[5]

The art that a prince must master cannot be the subtle skill of controlling public institutions through his own friends, nor is that of dissimulating power under the habiliments of civility. It must instead be the art of creating and disciplining the militia. * * * [O]ne of the most debated questions was whether the Medici should rule through civility and industry ("*industria*"), following the example of Cosimo, or rely more on force. Machiavelli confronts the issue directly and gives his own answer: the prince must apply his industriousness to create and strengthen the militia, instead of ruling behind the scene pretending to be just a citizen like everybody else.

Machiavelli adopts an equally unconventional view on the question of securing the state by means of a policy designed to create

4. *The Prince,* ch. 24. [All of Viroli's references to this work are to *Il Principe e i Discorsi,* ed. Sergio Bertelli (Milan: Feltrinelli, 1983)—editor's note.]

5. *The Prince,* ch. 9.

partisans of the state through favors and the distribution of honors and benefits. The issue is discussed in various sections of *The Prince.* In ch. 19 he stresses that a prudent prince has nothing to fear from conspiracies as long as he has been careful to satisfy the people and please the nobles. Listing the good things that a virtuous new prince can do, he mentions, in addition to good armies, good laws, and good examples—good friends ("*buoni amici*").[6] * * *

In the chapter dealing with the utility of fortresses, however, Machiavelli comes out with a much more subversive piece of advice: it is easier for a new prince to find reliable partisans among those who were hostile in the early stages of the regime than among those who have been friends of the state from the beginning. The most common advice was, conversely, to count on the time-honored friends of the state and the house. The argument that Machiavelli advances to sustain his position is that since prominent citizens always need the support of the prince, he can easily incorporate them within the state. * * *

Machiavelli's disagreement with the politics of partisanship is actually more substantial. It involves not only the ways of implementing it, but also its validity for the preservation of the state. In questioning this basic tenet of the conventional interpretation of the art of the state, Machiavelli employed an argument based on self-interest and fear, as were the arguments of the theorists of the state. From the same assumption that interest and fear are the sovereign forces that govern men's behavior, he derived the heterodox conclusion that friends gained through favors are a poor foundation of the state.

The issue is debated in ch. 17 on cruelty and mercifulness, where Machiavelli engages in the famous discussion as to whether it is better to be loved than to be feared. As in several other passages, the polemical target was the principle, directly derived from Cicero and Seneca, that a prince is more secure when he is loved by his subjects, than when he is feared. In addition to Humanist political philosophy, another ideological context seems to be relevant here, namely the debates on how to secure the *stato* of the Medici. * * * Whereas the current view was that the sort of friends gained through money and favors can be a secure bastion of the state, Machiavelli argues that a prince who relies primarily on such partisans grounds his state upon sand. Favors and honors generate a sort of love based on gratitude. But men easily break the bonds of gratitude whenever they think they have interest in doing so ("*da ogni occasione di utilità è rotto*").[7] Fear is much more effective, since it is sustained by the dread of punishment. * * * This means that the true art of the

6. *The Prince,* ch. 24.
7. *The Prince,* ch. 17. My italics.

state must be that of creating a reliable militia, rather than of buying friendship for the state.

* * *

Machiavelli also believed that the favor of the *grandi* was unquestionably less important than the support of the common citizens. A prince should respect the nobles,[8] but it is necessary to have the people as his friend ("*è necessario avere el populo amico*").[9] The friendship of the ordinary citizens is not too difficult to attain. It is enough, as he strongly recommends in ch. 21 ("*How a ruler should act in order to gain reputation*") to guarantee them security so that they can attend to their ordinary occupations in peace without fear of being dispossessed or oppressed. The nobles demand power, a much more difficult claim to satisfy. * * *

Machiavelli's insistence that the support of the people is more important than that of the *grandi* was another attack against the canonic view that the Medici's most irreducible enemy in Florence was the people, because they do not forget the republic. For him precisely the opposite was true. In addition to the arguments that we have already mentioned, he offered two more considerations, both astonishingly heterodox, against the view that those who were content with the previous regime are to be regarded as the decided enemies of the new state. Those who were discontented with the previous regime and welcomed the new one, stresses Machiavelli, are to be regarded with suspicion. They were disaffected with the former regime because it was not capable of satisfying them. * * * It is much easier to gain the friendship of those who were content with the past regime and were against him when he seized power. Machiavelli wanted to persuade the Medici that the friends of the republic were not to be considered the first enemies of the *stato,* and that the *grandi* who were the enemies of the republic because the republic was not capable of satisfying their immoderate pretentions were not, as everybody else said, the friends of the new regime.

* * *

Machiavelli wrote *The Prince* to convince the dedicatee of the book that he knew well the art of the state, even if he had served the republic. The challenge was not only to convince the prince that he was knowledgeable about the art, but also that he knew the art better than the Humanist rhetoricians and the contemporary practitioneers. Placed in the context of early sixteenth-century discussions that accompanied the restoration of the Medici in 1512, *The Prince*

8. *The Prince,* ch. 19.
9. *The Prince,* ch. 9.

reveals itself to be both a continuation and a reinterpretation of the Quattrocento art of the state. Machiavelli was fighting at the same time two ideological and political opponents: the Humanist masters of civil philosophy and the pragmatic advisers of the Medici. To the former he opposed, like others before him, the compelling rules of the art of the state; to the latter his own interpretation of the art designed to instruct a prince aiming at great things.

Yet, innovative as he was, Machiavelli never described the art of the state as politics, nor the prince concerned with preserving or imposing his state as a political man. If we want to see Machiavelli using the language of politics and understand what he did with it, we have to turn to the works where he focuses on republics, particularly, the *Discorsi*. * * *

For Machiavelli the word *"politico"* is always joined with the familiar vocabulary of the *civitas* and never used in a different sense. The only amendment that Machiavelli introduces in the conventional vocabulary of politics concerns the assessment of the value of concord versus the enlargement of the social basis of the city in view of the necessity of expanding. As we shall see, Machiavelli's innovation does not amount to a dismissal of the republican concept of politics.

The literature available to Machiavelli conventionally employed the word "*politico*" in order to contrast the authority restrained by laws with the authority *"legibus soluta,"*[1] that is, tyrannical rule. The *Discorsi* I, 25, offers an appropriate example of Machiavelli's full endorsement of current linguistic conventions. He who desires or proposes abolishing an ancient form of constitution in a city ("*un antico vivere*") and setting up a new and free form (*"uno vivere nuovo e libero"*), writes Machiavelli, must retain "as much as possible of what is old," and if changes are made in the number, the authority and the period of office of the magistrates, they should retain the traditional names. * * * To have supreme authority *legibus restricta*[2] is the best guarantee for the city being ruled justly and in moderation. The rule of law is recommended for princely rule and for popular government. * * *

* * *

Along with the rule of law, Machiavelli's use of the word *politico* reiterates another distinctive feature of the republican vocabulary of politics, namely the concept of civic equality. * * * In connecting *politico* with civic equality, Machiavelli followed a convention of the republican political language of his time and restored a principle that

1. Freed from the constraint of the laws [editor's note].
2. Constrained by the laws [editor's note].

Cicero and Livy recommended as the necessary foundation of the *respublica.* In the republican vocabulary civic equality meant above all the equality of the citizens before the law. * * *

Along with civic equality, the republican writers and their Humanist disciples also insisted on the *aequa libertas,* that is, equal access to the highest offices on the basis of virtue. In his history, Livy presented most of the quarrels between the Plebs and the Senate as conflicts concerning the access to the magistracies. The political moral that Livy always tried to convey to the reader was that the highest offices are to be open to the most virtuous citizens independently of their social position or their birth. * * *

Machiavelli repeats these republican ideas: the good political order requires that the most wise and honored citizens sit in the highest magistracies. He stresses this point in the *Discursus florentinarum rerum,* a text intended to propose constitutional reforms for Florence. Having explained that the major institutions of the city, the Signoria and the Collegi, should be reformed so that the most wise and honored citizens might be appointed to them, Machiavelli argues that if the reform is not carried out, the best citizens, who personify the majesty of the state, will be confined to a purely private status or to only the less important public institutions. * * *

As we have seen, in the ideological context of the time the word *politico* was used to denote not only the political constitution of the city in the strict sense, but also its concrete collective life: the customs, the habits and the passions of the citizens. The *vivere politico* demands that citizens be willing to give priority to the interest of the city over their particular interests. * * * In a corrupt city, where citizens give priority to their particular interests, no "vivere politico" can exist.

* * *

Along with civic virtue, another recurrent convention of the vocabulary of politics was the recommendation to preserve concord as one of the necessary foundations of the "vivere politico." In this respect Machiavelli parts company with the Humanist and the Ciceronian tradition. The point has been convincingly discussed by Quentin Skinner,[3] and here I confine myself to showing that the revision of the traditional advice implied a revision of the classical image of the "*vivere politico.*" While the classical advice stated that in order to enjoy the "*vivere politico*" we must devote our best efforts to preserve concord and peace, Machiavelli stressed that social conflicts are unavoidable and beneficial for the preservation of political liberty, if they do not degenerate into civil war. * * *

3. Q. Skinner, *The Foundations of Modern Political Thought,* I, pp. 113–15.

* * *

If the cost of having a city capable of fighting and, if necessary, expanding, is civil conflict, then the city must be prepared to deal with it. In recommending the tumultuous but powerful Roman republic over the peaceful but weak republics of Venice and Sparta, Machiavelli was not dismissing the republican ideal of politics as the art of establishing and preserving a free city. He was simply pointing out to his contemporaries that politics must face the additional task of handling civic discord as a fact of life in the city. * * *

* * *

Of the three possible methods of expansion adopted by republics, the best is for Machiavelli the Roman way, namely forming alliances in which you reserve leadership, and thus the whole authority, for yourself, and granting citizenship to conquered people. The worst is to treat the peoples of the conquered territories merely as subjects, as Sparta and Athens, and Florence, did. However, since the Roman model appears to be too difficult, the most recommendable policy for Florence would be to follow the example of the ancient Tuscans, that is to form leagues or federations on fair terms. Even if they did not become a large empire like Rome, the ancient Tuscans attained enough power to live securely for a long time, with the greatest glory and the most praiseworthy customs and religion.[4]

* * *

The point that Machiavelli stresses again and again is that a city must be in a position to fight to protect its liberty, and that one must go to war in order to have peace. They should not, however, put at stake peace in order to have war. The fundamental obligation of the good ruler must be to seek peace and the security of his subjects: it is for the sake of peace and the protection of his subjects, not for the sake of war and conquest, that he has to know how to make war. * * *

In Machiavelli's language, politics is still the art of the city. But the city must be established and preserved in an insecure world where liberty can be sustained only through virtue. Politics must order all other arts which are cultivated in the city in view of the common good. Only republican politics can succeed in building a city where virtue is honored and rewarded, poverty is not despised, military valor is esteemed and the citizens love each other and are

4. Niccolò Machiavelli, *Discorsi sopra la prima deca di Tito Livio,* ed. Corrado Vivanti (Turin: Einaudi, 1983), Bk. II, ch. 4. [All quotations of this in English are from *The Discourses of Niccolò Machiavelli,* trans. Leslie J. Walker (New Haven, CT: Yale University Press, 1950)—editor's note.]

attached to the public good. Whoever achieves such a city creates the conditions under which men can live a happier life.

* * *

Machiavelli never rejects the conventional image of the political man as a good man who benefits the "vivere politico." His hero is, as it was for the republican writers, the good man. Even if they were great conquerors and military commanders Caesar and Pompey attained fame ("*fama*"), but not glory. To attain glory it is not enough to be a great captain; one must also be a good man who devotes his talents to preserving the liberty of the republic and not to destroying it, as Caesar and Pompey did. * * * The conventional idea of the good man plays a central role in Machiavelli's language and it may help us to grasp the meaning of those passages in *The Prince* which have always been quoted to prove that Machiavelli rejected the republican idea of politics.

A man who wants to be good under all circumstances, Machiavelli writes in the famous fifteenth chapter of *The Prince,* will certainly come to ruin among the many who are not good. Therefore "a ruler who wishes to maintain his power must be prepared to act immorally ["*imparare a poter essere non buono*"] when this becomes necessary".[5] What Machiavelli seeks to accomplish, in writing that the prince must learn to be "*non buono,*" is to stress that civil philosophers were in fact teaching the prince to behave in a way that would cause him his ruin.

* * *

In writing the *Discorsi,* Machiavelli's purpose was to excite in the young the desire to emulate ancient virtue and follow the precepts of republican politics. * * * This was the message he wanted to convey to future generations: if you want to acquire perennial glory, you must devote yourself to the establishment and the preservation of the "*vivere politico*" following the example of the heroes of republican politics. * * * Though he admired the princes and the captains who knew how to use the art of the state, Machiavelli never presented any of them as true heroes of politics. * * *

To go back to the question whether Machiavelli rejected or maintained the view of politics as civil philosophy or whether he advocated a combination between politics and art of the state, I believe that the answer is that he perpetuated the republican language of politics, and contrived to keep alive the republican ideal of the political man. He recommended the necessity of integrating civil philosophy with the art of the state, but he did not reduce or equate

5. *The Prince,* ch. 15.

the former to the latter. He maintained the distinction and assigned politics a superior rank. Even when he wrote of the art of the state, as he did in *The Prince*, he never called it "politics" and always regarded it as a subordinate and transitory component of politics. Machiavelli did not contrive to change the meaning of politics. Rather, he reworked civil philosophy to make it apt to face the historical tasks of the restoration of the republic and the liberation of Italy. Both of them required the arrival of a true political man capable of using also the art of the state, if necessary. The purpose of Machiavelli was to educate the great political man that a future republic and Italy needed.

* * *

JOHN M. NAJEMY

From Language and *The Prince*†

The Prince has a reputation, one that Machiavelli himself did his best to promote, for successfully escaping the ambiguities and superfluous ornaments of language, or rhetoric, and thus making possible, and bringing to the centre of its purposes, direct contact with things themselves. Machiavelli announces this as a fundamental aim and feature of the book in the dedicatory letter where he claims to distance himself from the classical traditions of rhetorical *amplificatio:* 'I have not embellished or inflated this work with abundant rhythmical cadences or with turgid and grandiloquent words; neither are there any other blandishments and irrelevant decorations with which many authors usually describe and bedeck their writings.'[1] * * *

* * * [I]n this passage from the dedicatory letter of *The Prince* he quite deliberately and polemically shares in, and contributes to * * * the modern misunderstanding of *ornamentum* as a purely decorative and thus dispensable aspect of language. Machiavelli's assumption is precisely that *ornamento* is 'estrinseco'—on the outside, marginal, and, in one sense of the Latin word from which this usage derives, irrelevant. * * *

† From *Texts in Culture: Niccolò Machiavelli's* The Prince: *New Interdisciplinary Essays*, ed. Martin Coyle (Manchester, UK: Manchester University Press, 1995), pp. 89–109, 111–14. Reprinted by permission of Manchester University Press. Notes are Najemy's, with full bibliographical information supplied by the editor.

1. For the text of *The Prince* and Machiavelli's other works, I quote from Niccolò Machiavelli, *Tutte le opere*, ed. Mario Martelli (Florence: Sansoni, 1971), henceforth cited as *Opere*. Where none is specified, English translations are my own. However, for the passage quoted above from the dedicatory letter, I have used the translation of James M. Atkinson in Niccolò Machiavelli, *The Prince* (Indianapolis: Bobbs-Merrill, 1976).

In the dedicatory letter Machiavelli implicitly repudiates the entire tradition, central to Renaissance humanism, that had accepted the beneficent power and the utility of language and eloquence in politics and political discourse. * * *

The mistrust of rhetoric and its meretricious ornament that Machiavelli displays in the dedicatory letter reflects a still more fundamental worry about language itself. * * * The locus of this worry is an awareness of a certain indeterminacy or inexactness of language, which Machiavelli only occasionally acknowledges and never openly theorises in the letters or in *The Prince*. One notable expression of this worry is the letter to Vettori of 9 April 1513, in which Machiavelli (responding to similar doubts expressed by Vettori himself) asserts that 'if it has become bothersome to you to discuss things [i.e. politics], because many times you see events taking place apart from the discourses and concepts that one forms about them, * * * you are right, for a similar thing has happened to me'.[2] * * * The letter of 9 April 1513 shows Machiavelli in some doubt and anxiety about the nature, or even the possibility, of this correspondence of 'cose' and 'discorsi'. Things, he now admits, have happened apart from (literally 'outside of'—*fuora*) the 'discourses and concepts' one forms about them. This admission brought close to the surface some troubling, though unspoken, questions. Do 'things' always go their own way, oblivious of the efforts of language to understand them? Is the desired 'riscontro' ever possible, and, if so, how? Or is it frequently, or always, merely an illusion? Is language always missing the mark? And what relationship actually exists, or can exist, between 'discourses and concepts' and 'things' outside language?

The Prince wants to provide answers to these questions, and it does so, as I shall try to suggest, in practice if not in theory and in a way that aims to subordinate language, with all its potential indeterminacies and ambiguities, to the discipline and purposes of a discourse that does not depend on common usage. Before we examine passages that place this aim in evidence and seek to implement it, it is essential to realise that the aim itself of liberating discourse from the pitfalls of common usage implicitly rejects another notion central to Renaissance theorising about language, a notion that may be the most important and revolutionary development in the philosophy of language in the century before Machiavelli. * * * [T]he historically grounded linguistics of Lorenzo Valla (d. 1457) was the spearhead of an attack on the prevailing theory of language that had assumed its essentially representational, or referential, function. In that traditional view, words represent, or stand for, things because

2. *Opere*, p. 1131.

of some connection or identity that is necessary and inherent in the relationship between word and thing, and which is thus neither random nor contingent. * * *

Valla sought to overturn this whole way of thinking about language. Two principal notions governed his approach: first, that any language changes with time, as his studies of the history of the Latin language revealed, with the addition not only of new words but of new meanings for old words; and, second, almost as a corollary to the first point, that the meanings of terms are thus determined by usage and convention. * * * Within the framework of these assumptions, apparently obvious and simple but in fact far-reaching in their implications, 'knowledge and truth are functions of the "common use" of language.'[3] 'Knowledge' of the world is a consequence of how humans use language and can never be independent of it. * * *

Machiavelli's response to this dilemma ignored or contradicted the crucial ideas that emerged from Valla's linguistic revolution: the historical and social processes by which words become invested with meaning. *The Prince*'s mistrust of the temporal and collective dimensions of language is especially evident in passages in which Machiavelli attempts to stabilise and control the meaning of words. Wherever the text encounters a potential slipperiness or uncertainty in the terms it employs, Machiavelli intervenes swiftly to contain and stabilise this polysemous tendency—what we might call the 'spill-over' effect that produces a multiplicity of meanings for any term. This strategy is implicit in one of *The Prince*'s best-known features: its almost obsessive reliance on differential pairs, or binary oppositions, whose appeal for Machiavelli must have been their capacity to generate the impression that the meaning of each term is determined and stabilised by its apparently necessary oppositional relationship to its paired other. * * *

If the strategy of preemptive stabilisation of language is implicit and taken for granted in the first half of *The Prince,* it becomes explicit and a more open locus of worry beginning with chapter XV, 'Concerning matters for which men, and particularly princes, are praised or blamed' (p. 280). This is the first time in the book that a chapter title openly refers to things predicated of princes by others. The chief purpose of the chapter is to assess the way people use language to make judgments about princes, and it is no coincidence that a more direct concern with controlling and containing the threat posed by the slipperiness of language should appear at the point where the text takes up the problem of how people look at, evaluate and say things about princes. But why, we might ask, does

3. Richard Waswo, *Language and Meaning in the Renaissance* (Princeton: Princeton University Press, 1987), p. 102.

a chapter that proposes to examine the criteria for praising and blaming princes—a topic that will quickly translate itself into a discussion of linguistic usage and meaning—begin with Machiavelli's bold pronouncement that, because it is his 'intention to write something useful to those who can understand it' ('sendo l'intento mio scrivere cosa utile a chi la intende'), he believes it (I give a clumsily literal translation for the purposes of the analysis that follows) 'more worthwhile to go behind to the effectual truth of the thing than to the imagination of it' ('più conveniente andare drieto alla verità effettuale della cosa, che alla imaginazione di essa') (chapter XV, p. 280)? One reason for this beginning is that the ensuing discussion will claim that accurate and true judgements about princes are indeed possible. The ability to write 'useful' and 'true' things about princes requires the notions of utility and truth to be themselves stabilised. Machiavelli is evidently not satisfied to say, simply and tautologically, that he will write truth where others have written falsehood. Instead he combines 'truth' and 'utility' into 'effectual truth', and, according to his usual method of defining terms by differentiating them from their paired others, he opposes this 'effectual truth' to 'imaginazione'.

But why did Machiavelli choose 'imaginazione' as the assumed opposite of 'effectual truth'? And what indeed is the sense of 'imaginazione' in this passage? Typically, the text pretends that the opposition is both self-evident and reflective of relationships outside the linguistic realm. But a reading of the letters that Machiavelli and Vettori exchanged during the summer of 1513—just months or even weeks before the composition of *The Prince*—reveals that it was Vettori who introduced into their dialogue the verb 'immaginare' as part of his critique of Machiavelli's claims to be able to interpret, accurately and effectively, the words, purposes and actions of princes. Vettori had suggested that such interpretation was inevitably a matter of approximation and guesswork. * * * Vettori's scepticism is grounded in the idea that any discourse about princes is necessarily a matter of reading and interpreting * * * the words and actions that stand between the purposes and secrets of princes and those who would know these secrets. * * * [T]he relationship established between a prince's words and actions and his secrets and purposes is, as far as one can ever tell, little more than an approximate and imperfect correspondence inferred but never known for certain. And whenever even this risky process of reading the signs proves unsatisfactory, the alternative, says Vettori, is to 'immaginare' what cannot be interpreted.

* * * Chapter XV of *The Prince* shows Machiavelli wrestling with Vettori's notion of an inevitable structural indeterminacy in any discourse about princes. The first step in containing this threat is to

oppose 'verità effettuale' to 'imaginazione', which allows Machiavelli to assert that 'true' knowledge about princes is indeed possible. * * *

But there is another and more subtle step contained in Machiavelli's declaration that he has found it more profitable to 'go behind to the effectual truth of the thing *than to the imagination of it*'. * * * What this sentence implies is that the 'cosa' (events, princes, their actions, policies, etc.) is there in any case, and that one can either get 'behind' it and seize its 'effectual truth' or—such would seem to be the logic of the sentence—remain in front of it and see only *its* 'imaginazione'. * * *

But this was not at all the meaning of 'immaginare' for Vettori. * * * For Vettori all political discourse begins with the interpretation of appearances; and when this fails or falters, as he seems to assume it must, we can only 'immaginare'. Machiavelli redefines 'imaginazione' to mean precisely those sometimes misleading appearances which, for Vettori, are in most cases the only material available for interpretation. * * * But did he notice that in the next sentence he uses the same word in a very different sense in saying that 'many have imagined ["si sono imaginati"] republics and principalities that have never been seen or known to exist in reality ["essere in vero"]' (chapter XV, p. 280)? This 'imaginazione' seems to be the pure invention of worlds that exist only in the mind, not the perception of appearances suggested by the phrase 'imaginazione di essa'.

The opposition between appearances and essences directs the rest of chapter XV to the issue of language and generates the long list of paired 'qualities' that Machiavelli says are generally used to praise or blame princes. The crux of the matter is the necessity of distinguishing between, on the one hand, the inevitably misleading impressions created by the everyday, ordinary use of language and, on the other, what Machiavelli believes he can identify as the *actual* consequences of the 'modi e governi', the methods and conduct, of princes. His attention goes first to the structure of common speech about princes: 'I say that all people, when they are spoken of ["quando se ne parla"], and especially princes because they are in a higher position, are designated ["notati"] by some or the other of those qualities that bring them either blame or praise' (chapter XV, p. 280). This is the continuation of the sentence that begins with Machiavelli's declaration that he will 'leave aside things *imaginate* about princes', and his point is surely that the habits of everyday speech that result in the attribution to princes of these qualities, thus producing their blameworthy or praiseworthy reputations, are themselves among the 'things *imaginate* about princes'. They belong, in other words, to the realm of misleading appearances. But Machiavelli's next sentence reveals his entrapment in the fundamental contradiction of *The Prince*'s notions of language. Wishing simultaneously to give his first example of this structure of common speech and to explain and justify his own choice of terms with which to provide this example, Machiavelli writes: 'Thus it is that one person is held to be *liberale* [generous], and another *misero* (to use the Tuscan term, since "avaro" in our language is more one who desires to possess by means of theft, and we call "misero" the person who refrains excessively from using what is his own)' (chapter XV, p. 280). Machiavelli's larger argument asserts the imprecise and misleading quality of the habits of speech involved in the conventional use of the pairs of terms he is about to list, and the *liberale/misero* pair is presumably the first bit of evidence adduced in support of this contention. But his parenthetical aside concerning the choice of *misero* over *avaro*—his belief that *misero* is the 'correct' opposite for *liberale*—reveals his own need to stabilise language, to make each term mean this and not that, and thus his conviction that in *his* use of language terms can indeed stand for the correct things. * * *

[Najemy goes on to list a number of paired opposites that appear in Chapter 15, noting how Machiavelli's love of binaries leads him not just to define one term by its opposite, but also to isolate a specific meaning of that term, a meaning that he seems convinced is its *real* meaning. He assumes too easily, according to Najemy, that this meaning is also inevitably opposed to the more conventional one for the word.]

Apparently not noticing this difficulty, Machiavelli continues chapter XV by saying that he 'knows' that 'everyone professes that it would be a most praiseworthy thing for a prince to have, of all the qualities listed above, those that are held to be good ones' (p. 280). But he insists that this entire way of speaking about princes is flawed. The first of the two reasons he gives is about human nature: 'the human condition does not permit' anyone to have or be all those good things. And, because a prince must choose for which of these 'good' qualities he wishes to be known, the criterion governing his choice should be that of survival in power. * * *

The second reason why this common usage is so flawed, according to Machiavelli, concerns language itself. He contends that the meanings and judgments normally attaching to these terms simply do not correspond to the *real* effects or results of the modes of conduct that the terms presume to represent and evaluate. * * * Common speech is ignorant of what Machiavelli claims to know: namely, that some modes of conduct usually called virtues are in fact damaging to a prince, while others commonly called vices strengthen him. Implicitly, Machiavelli faults common speech for not knowing, or obscuring, the real meanings of these qualities, which he claims to know by seeing, and speaking, beyond the misleading appearances of conventional speech to the actual effects of a given mode of conduct—to what he takes to be the thing itself and its consequences. * * *

The Prince that Machiavelli invents is a master of this distinction between conventional speech, trapped in its ambiguities, imprecision and misleading appearances, and the higher and purified discourse hypothesised by Machiavelli, in which words mean only what they ought to mean, language faithfully reflects and represents an extralinguistic reality, and the 'effectual truth' of things luminously emerges. * * *

Chapters XVI to XIX are devoted to explicating the difference between the conventional usage surrounding the pairs of terms listed in chapter XV and the meanings, judgements and truths that come to light if the habits of everyday speech are replaced by a different set of practices. In each case Machiavelli shows the inadequacy of the commonly accepted understanding of the 'qualities' used to judge princes, and the heart of these demonstrations is, in the words of chapter XVIII, that whereas 'everyone sees what you [the prince] appear to be, few feel what you are' ('Ognuno vede quello che tu pari, pochi sentono quello che tu se') (p. 284). The Prince, unlike the people he rules, speaks and acts in a linguistic realm of pure and exact signification in which words can convey precisely what things 'are' and not what they seem to be.

The mistrust and rejection of ordinary speech implicit in these chapters become explicit in the advice Machiavelli offers in chapters XXII and XXIII concerning the Prince's choice of ministers and the need to avoid flatterers. * * * [B]ecause the discourses of others in *The Prince* always belong to the lower order of language dominated by indeterminacy, imprecision and mere appearance, counsellors inevitably represent the dangerous intrusion of an extraneous discourse that the Prince must control. * * *

In chapter XXIII Machiavelli attempts to translate this radical distinction between the Prince's own discourse and that of the world around him into a set of coherent recommendations for dealing with advisers and avoiding flatterers. About the latter, he says that the only way to 'guard oneself against flattery' is to make people understand that they do not offend you in telling you the truth', except that 'if everyone can tell you the truth, you lose respect' * * * (chapter XXIII, p. 293). * * *

So Machiavelli recommends * * * limiting the speech that reaches the Prince to that of certain 'wise men' ('uomini savi') to whom 'alone he must give free rein to speak the truth to him, and only on those things about which he asks and not about anything else' * * * (chapter XXIII, p. 293). Machiavelli must have noticed the gap between the 'libero arbitrio' that the Prince should give to his wise men and the simultaneous restriction of that freedom to 'only those things about which he asks', since he immediately closes the gap by recommending that the Prince must of course 'ask them about everything and hear their opinions', generally conducting himself with his advisers in such a way that each may understand that 'the more freely they speak, the more it will please him' * * * (chapter XXIII, pp. 293–4).

* * *

The origin of the difficulties Machiavelli encounters in chapter XXIII lies in the presupposition that the truth sought by his Prince must be distinct from, even opposed to and threatened by, ordinary speech and language. The problem of advising the Prince becomes one of isolating him from this common speech, and thus of controlling language and speakers, in a word, a matter of censorship. The Prince must prevent most people even from speaking to him, and he must allow the chosen few to speak only when he so authorises them. Only by knowing already and on his own where and on what subjects he is likely to hear the truth should a prince permit even his selected wise men to speak, which brings Machiavelli close to saying that the Prince himself is the arbiter of truth, the guarantor of the necessary demarcation between the misleading conventions of common language and the truth of his own uncontaminated discourse. The Prince's greatest power is his extraordinary (literally, beyond the ordinary and conventional) ability to use, hear and interpret language in such a way as to filter out appearances and ambiguities, to define and control a superior form of language use on the basis of that ability, and thus to know and speak a truth inaccessible to other forms of speech. It was, to use the terms Hanna Pitkin has applied to other aspects of Machiavelli's thought,[4] a fantasy of autonomy. * * *

The Prince's notions of language betray a pervasive theoretical contradiction that the text pretends not to notice by assigning one sense of how language works (and one side of the contradiction) to people in general and the other to the Prince (and his inventor). In this book, quite unlike much of what he wrote in subsequent years, Machiavelli simultaneously acknowledges and rejects what Renaissance reflections on language had taught him: that language is continuously made, constructed, revised, refashioned, unsettled and destabilised by collective usage. In *The Prince* he wants to believe that, although this was *generally* so, for certain purposes and in

4. Hanna Fenichel Pitkin, *Fortune Is a Woman: Gender and Politics in the Thought of Niccolò Machiavelli* (Berkeley: University of California Press, 1984), especially chapters 1 and 12, pp. 3–22, 307–27.

certain hands—those of the Prince and of the few who touch, perceive and feel what he really is—another kind of language practice is both possible and necessary for survival in power.

But, as always, *The Prince* is not the whole of Machiavelli. Very different ideas about language inform the works that came later, and what separates *The Prince* from them may be, more than anything else, the process by which Machiavelli dismantled the linguistic fantasy contained in the work for which he is (rightly or wrongly) best known to us. * * *

This different approach to language is already apparent in the opening pages of the *Discourses on Livy.* One example must suffice here. In the second paragraph of the second chapter of the first book,[5] 'wishing to discuss what the *ordini* of the city of Rome were and what events led to its perfection', Machiavelli addresses the question of the classification of constitutional systems. 'I say', he begins, 'that some who have written about republics say that in [each of] them is [found] one of the three kinds of regime, which they call Principate, Aristocracy and Popular [government]'. * * * In this sentence it is worth noting that, whatever Machiavelli means by 'republiche', the term represents a genus one of whose three species, called 'stati', is the 'Principato'. This is not the same relationship established among these terms in the opening sentence of the first chapter of *The Prince.* * * * But, of course, in *Discourses,* I.2 Machiavelli does not claim to be giving his own view of the matter. * * *

The second opinion reported by Machiavelli in *Discourses,* I.2 is that there are six, instead of three, kinds of government, three of which are very bad ('pessimi') and three 'good in themselves, but so easily corrupted that even they turn out to be pernicious'. The three good ones are those already mentioned in his summary of the first view. The other three are described as follows:

> The bad ['rei'] ones are three others which depend on the first three; and each of them is so similar to the one that is closest to it that they easily jump from the one to the other: thus a Principate easily becomes tyrannical; Aristocracy easily becomes an oligarchic regime; Popular government converts itself without difficulty into anarchy. Thus if the founder of a republic establishes one of the three [good] regimes in a city, he does so for a brief time only, because he is unable to apply any remedy to prevent it from slipping into its contrary, on account of the similarity of the virtue and the vice in such cases.[6]

5. The text of *Discourses,* I.2, discussed in the rest of this chapter, is quoted from *Opere,* p. 79. The translation is mine.
6. *Opere,* p. 79; my translation.

Machiavelli here mocks the very notion, so crucial to *The Prince,* of the stability of categories, terms and definitions. * * * [W]hen Machiavelli * * * comments about the similarity and proximity of the opposing terms of the differential pairs that structure the argument ('Principato'/'tirannico'; 'Ottimati'/'stato di pochi'; 'Popolare'/'licenzioso'), and how this similarity causes the 'good' kinds of government to 'jump' and 'slide' into the opposing but corresponding 'bad' kinds, he is quite deliberately (even if playfully) signalling his abandonment of the assumptions about language that underlie *The Prince.* Here he no longer assumes that differential pairs generate stable meanings or even that they define oppositions. * * *

* * *

* * * The structure of *Discourses,* I.2 points to the extent to which any discourse of politics—including that most authoritative of discourses, the words of one who founds a republic ('uno ordinatore di republica')—is inevitably implicated in the ambiguities and instability, not only of conventional speech but of all the categories and definitions on which any discourse of politics needs to be based, and thus dependent on the whole community of discourse in which the knowledge of anything must consist. In *Discourses,* I.2 it is not at all clear what distinction remains between words and things, between history and politics as objects of knowledge and as 'discourses and concepts' invented and transmitted by one's predecessors. * * * Even the best theories are approximate and leave much unexplained. The next paragraph begins in fact with the assertion that 'these variations of governments occur by chance'—which is to say that * * * it is impossible to know actually why these changes happen. There are no claims here to a realm of perception and speech transcending usage, context and tradition. The language of this book depends on, and is part of, social and historical communities of discourse from which there is no appeal to the kind of higher tribunal that Machiavelli had imagined in *The Prince.*

MIKAEL HÖRNQVIST

Hörnqvist sees Machiavelli's texts as rhetorical in the sense that are designed to affect readers and move them to act in the world. He also follows political scientists, such as Quentin Skinner, by insisting that those texts can be understood only in their historical context, which means, for Machiavelli, Italian—and more specifically Florentine—political thought in the fifteenth and early sixteenth centuries. In that period, Italian thinkers saw Rome as a model republic that pursued internal freedom for its citizens and dominion over other states. Florentines went further in claiming that Florence was the actual successor to Rome. In *Discourses* 1.29, Machiavelli identifies the two goals of the city-state to be internal freedom (allowing the most talented to rise to the top) and external conquest. But he sees these goals as the results of human nature, thereby demoting Rome from its position as *the* model state one had to imitate to that of *a* model state which should be imitated in certain ways, but not in others, such as its civil wars that eventually led to the autocratic rule of Augustus. Machiavelli thus advocates that Florence should imitate Rome because it gave its citizens liberty and engaged in wars to expand the state, but he especially liked the mixed constitution of Rome that allowed for the state to be run by a *dictator* for a limited amount of time when the state was in peril. For him, true grandeur (*grandezza*) is attached to the state, to the republic, and not to its ruler, as would be the case in a despotism. Hörnqvist sees Chapter 19 of *The Prince* as the key to understanding the entire work: on the surface it reassures the prince that he can easily avoid hatred and contempt, but at the same time, the chapter keeps reminding him of just how uncertain his future will be because of external threats, conspiracies among the *grandi* (i.e., the nobility), and the potential dissatisfaction of the commoners. These last two threats are treated as the most important.

[Machiavelli's Republican Rhetoric]†

As an example of a well-ordered and well-governed modern kingdom, Machiavelli singles out the French monarchy, in which, according to him, countless good institutions guarantee the liberty and the security of the king. Foremost among these is the Parlement of Paris, which Machiavelli also describes as a third judicial body, *uno iudice terzo*. * * * The essence of the French model * * * is a form of mixed government based on a certain, if yet limited, division of power. By allowing conflicts between the two classes making up society—the great and the people—to be settled by independent judicial bodies, this constitutional arrangement has the virtue of diverting the resentment of the few and the hatred of the many away from the prince. Being able to withdraw from the ignominious bickerings of internal affairs, Machiavelli implies, the prince will be free to devote himself to more glorious enterprises. Indications of wherein these activities would consist, we have already been given in chapters 14 and 16, where the prince was exhorted to dedicate all his time to the art of war and its orders and discipline, and was encouraged to enrich his state and to enhance his own reputation by waging wars of conquest. * * *

† From *Machiavelli and Empire* (Cambridge: Cambridge University Press, 2004), pp. 219–25, 227, 266–69, 271–72, 274–75, 277–85. © Mikael Hörnqvist 2004. Reproduced by permission of the publisher. Notes are Hörnqvist's unless otherwise indicated, with full bibliographical information supplied by the editor.

The rest of chapter 19 consists of a brief—or in the context of *The Prince,* not so brief—account of Roman imperial history from Marcus Aurelius to Maximinus, that is, from AD 161 to 238. Of the ten emperors who held power during this 77-year period, we learn that only Marcus and Septimus Severus died natural deaths. All the rest were killed . . . in conspiracies! At the end of this digression, Machiavelli recommends his princely reader to imitate the two successful emperors, Marcus and Severus. According to this advice, which can be read as a summary of Machiavelli's teaching in chapters 17 through 19, the prince "should take from Severus those qualities (*parti*) which are necessary to found his state and from Marcus those which are appropriate and glorious to conserve a state that is already established and stable."[1] While to imitate Severus means to use the lion and the fox, cruelty and fraud, along the lines already established in chapters 17 and 18, the counsel to imitate Marcus brings us back to the constitutional solution put forward earlier in the chapter, based on a rudimentary mixed regime. * * *

* * *

To appreciate how radically Machiavelli's advice in chapter 19 breaks with the Aristotelian tradition, we need to consider it in relation to the former Secretary's general thought on the mixed regime. Machiavelli's most elaborate treatment of this constitutional ideal is to be found in *Discourses* 1.2 and 1.5–6, where he discusses the relative merits of the Roman, the Spartan, and the Athenian constitutions. Dismissing the popular regime Solon introduced in Athens in the sixth century BC as a misguided and short-lived experiment in democracy that ended in failure, because it neglected to provide for the interests of the great, or the aristocratic few, Machiavelli follows Polybius's lead in concentrating on the Roman and the Spartan alternatives. When he first presents the Spartan constitution in *Discourses* 1.2, Machiavelli claims that Lycurgus, the lawgiver, had "ordered his laws so as to give their roles to the kings, the aristocrats, and the people."[2] * * * However, when Machiavelli returns to the Spartan example in *Discourses* 1.5–6, he makes clear that the state Lycurgus founded was only partially mixed, combining elements of monarchy and aristocracy, being "governed by a king and by a narrow Senate," but giving no representation to the people.[3]

1. Niccolò Machiavelli, *Il principe* 19, in *Opere,* ed. C. Vivanti, 3 vols. (Turin: Einaudi, 1997–), p. 175. [All Hörnqvist's citations of Machiavelli's works come from this edition, unless otherwise specified. The translations of Machiavelli's Italian are by Hörnqvist—editor's note.]
2. *Discorsi* I.2, p. 206.
3. Ibid., I.6, p. 214.

The ancient Roman republic offers a sharp contrast in this regard. * * * Rome began as a monarchy, but Romulus, its founder, had from the very beginning, by reserving to himself only the right to command the armies and to convoke the Senate, imposed strict limits on the authority of the royal office.[4] Although Rome remained a monarchy for centuries, Romulus's orders proved so conformable to "a civil and free way of life" (*uno vivere civile e libero*) that when the city later became a republic, the only innovation needed was the replacement of the king by two annually elected consuls.[5] Later, the Tribunes of the Plebs were introduced to check the power of the Senate and to safeguard the interests of the people, a function previously performed by the king. Since this open and processual approach to constitutional development allowed Rome to increase her population, to arm her citizens, to expand her borders, and to conquer the world, it is to be preferred, Machiavelli argues, to the Spartan policy of isolation, stability, and self-chosen weakness.

* * *

How does the constitutional argument of *The Prince* fit into this line of reasoning? As we have begun to see, the mixed regime Machiavelli insinuates in chapter 19, centered on a strong, acquisitive monarchic element and a broad popular base, bears an intriguing likeness to the constitution of the ancient Roman republic. When we arrive at *The Prince* 19, the role Machiavelli is fashioning for his princely reader has also begun to resemble that of Romulus, the founder of the Roman state, as Machiavelli later was to describe it in the *Discourses.* * * * And as we recall, Romulus founded a monarchy that conformed so well to *uno vivere civile e libero* that it later was able to evolve into a full-fledged, and perfect, mixed republic, *una republica perfetta.*

* * *

The fact that Machiavelli in *The Prince* chooses to present the mixed regime from a monarchic perspective, and in the *Discourses* from a republican one, need not surprise us. By doing so, students of classical rhetoric can tell us, he is simply heeding Aristotle's advice and adapting his argument and his rhetorical performance to the circumstances, the audience, and the constitutional context: appealing to security before the tyrant and to liberty in the popular assembly. In keeping silent about the republican intent of his political project in *The Prince*—a work addressed to a princely ruler, or to a Medici ruler with princely aspirations—it could be argued,

4. Cf. *Discorsi* I.9, p. 224.
5. Ibid.

Machiavelli was not only being prudent, but playing by the book as well.

It should now be obvious that Machiavelli's conception of the mixed regime represented a radical break with the traditional understanding, which had conceived of this constitutional ideal as a system of checks and balances. For the Florentine, it was instead an instrument for mobilizing the three orders of society, their contrasting viewpoints, and their desire for domination, within a constitutional framework designed for expansion and territorial growth. In Machiavelli's scheme, mobilizing the princely element means stimulating his lust for power and his tyrannical impulse, and turning it outward towards the republic's external end—growth, acquisition, and glory. What we witness in *The Prince* 19, and the work at large, is how Machiavelli transforms tyranny from being a destructive force that turns against and threatens to dissolve the other constitutional elements, into a dynamic, creative, and expansive power. * * *

* * *

In reworking Aristotle's theory Machiavelli also reveals his intention in writing *The Prince*. By fashioning his princely reader as a tyrant in the classical sense of the term, and by creating a series of scenarios that play on the tyrant's desire for glory and greatness and his fear of assassination and loss of power, the Florentine creates a new prince who will unwittingly serve as an instrument for a Roman-inspired republican development, acting as founder and embodying the acquisitive spirit that will promote and fuel the future growth of the republic. * * *

* * *

In commenting on his native Florence, his beloved *patria*, Machiavelli states time and again that her current plight is due to her failure to follow the Roman path, or to be more precise, her refusal to enter the cycle of development inscribed in the Roman model. * * *

* * * Machiavelli conceives of Florence as an unfounded, or at least insufficiently founded, city or state. This reading is supported by the opening of his *Discursus Florentinarum Rerum* of 1520, where the former Secretary claims that Florence, as a result of her many and frequent changes of government, never has been either a republic or a principality worthy of the name.[6]

The thwarted quest for a Florentine foundation is a recurrent theme in *The Prince* as well. Here Machiavelli treats in turn

6. In *Opere,* I, p. 733.

Girolamo Savonarola, Cesare Borgia, and Piero Soderini as failed founders of a Florentine or Tuscan state. * * *

While illustrating the inherent dangers of weak and ambiguous policies, the Florentine examples in *The Prince* take on added importance from the fact that the treatise is addressed to the Medici, the new rulers of Florence and the successors of Savonarola and Soderini, who in the final chapter also are exhorted to found a new principality in Italy. * * *

When Machiavelli returns to the foundation theme in the *Discourses,* he claims that a city of Florence's type, where there are no feudal lords (*signori di castella*) and where an extreme degree of equality reigns, can easily be given a free, republican form of government (*uno vivere civile*) by "a prudent man having knowledge of the ancient civilization."[7] * * *

The difference in emphasis between the *Discourses* and *The Prince* on this point should not be mistaken for a sudden reversal of values or ideological allegiance. The fact that Machiavelli in the *Discourses* comments on the possibility of founding a republic (*uno vivere civile*) in Florence, and in *The Prince* gives general advice on how to found a new principality (*un principato nuovo*), does not contradict this reading. On the contrary, since according to the Roman example, as described in the *Discourses,* Rome's constitutional development and territorial expansion began with Romulus's founding of the city as a monarchy capable of developing in the direction of *uno vivere civile.* If Florence is to follow in the footsteps of her ancient forebear, Machiavelli teaches, she needs to be founded, or refounded, by "a prudent man" as *uno vivere civile* (the *Discourses*), or as a principality capable of developing in this direction (*The Prince*).

* * *

Machiavelli's contrasting of ancient Rome and contemporary Florence on the level of general principles needs to be complemented by a more detailed discussion of how this dichotomy is played out on the ideological level. The ideological aspects of Machiavelli's work, which in recent years have attracted increasing attention from scholars, raise the question of the Florentine's place within the Western tradition and of the puzzling relationship between the monarchic teaching of *The Prince* and the republican theory of the *Discourses.* In separate studies, Quentin Skinner and Maurizio Viroli have, by situating *The Prince* in the genres of Quattrocento advice-books for princes and early Cinquecento Florentine treatises on *arte dello stato,* and the *Discourses* in that of classical and medieval republicanist theories of political liberty, given authoritative accounts of ideological conventions and vocabularies in which Machiavelli's work

7. *Discorsi* I.55, p. 312.

participates.[8] According to their interpretation, the alleged conflict between *The Prince* and the *Discourses* can be understood largely in terms of the two works belonging to, or depending on, different ideological traditions. The current study has taken issue with this view by arguing that the primary context of Machiavelli's work is not the mirror-for-princes genre or medieval and Renaissance republicanism in general, but the ideological writings of the Florentine civic humanists and the Florentine tradition at large. In this tradition * * * Florence was seen as an elect city, designated to become alternately the new Rome and the new Jerusalem. Celebrating their city's ancient origins and using her Roman heritage to bolster her republican form of government and her claim to territorial rule, Florentine propagandists and humanists created a powerful ideology based on the twin notions of liberty at home and empire abroad. Throughout his chancery career and later in his theoretical works, Machiavelli shared this patriotic outlook and sought out ways to promote Florence's longstanding aspirations to become a great and expanding empire, modeled on the example of the ancient Roman republic.

* * *

* * * While Machiavelli shared his predecessors' Roman-inspired view of the Republic as having two aims or ends—to preserve its liberty internally and to expand its empire externally—he did not, in contrast to them, regard the republican and imperial legacy of the ancient Roman republic as an exclusive Florentine birthright. To him, the Roman heritage was instead to be seen as a political and strategic model, which any state, or any ruler, could adopt and use as a blueprint for success. * * *

The fact that Florence had no hereditary right to the title of the new Rome, or to the pragmatic Roman model, in Machiavelli's view did not diminish the importance of the Roman example for his native city. On the contrary, it merely meant that the ideological language of the Florentine tradition had to be recast into a rhetorical mold, and given a more practical and process-oriented articulation. The centrality of the Florentine context for Machiavelli's work is evident from how he on the ideological level labored to influence, and to change, the ways in which the Florentine elites, present and future, not men in general, thought and talked about politics. * * * [T]he main target of criticism in his theoretical writings, *The Prince* and the *Discourses* included, are the *savi,* the wise men of Florence, whom he reproaches for having elevated their weak policy of half-measures and

8. The principal studies on the ideological aspects of Machiavelli's work are Skinner, *The Foundations of Modern Political Thought* (2 vols., Cambridge: Cambridge University Press, 1978), I, pp. 113–89; Maurizio Viroli, *From Politics to Reason of State: The Acquisition and Transformation of the Language of Politics 1250–1600* (Cambridge: Cambridge University Press, 1992), pp. 126–77.

compromise to the level of political wisdom. To win acceptance for his own radical views, and to pave the way for a policy based on the Roman model in Florence, Machiavelli found it necessary to expose the ideological nature of this received wisdom, and to contest the ideological foundation of the Florentine republican tradition and the established Florentine foreign policy doctrine, based on notions such as the middle way, temporization, and neutrality.

Machiavelli's attack on the ideological conventions of Florentine political culture took added historical importance from the fact that the middle way (*via del mezzo*) was not only a central tenet of Florentine foreign policy, but also a key element in Aristotelian ethics. As is well known, Aristotle had defined virtue as a mean, or a middle way, between extremes. By turning Aristotle's notion on its head and by redefining virtue as the ability to encompass and to make complementary use of the extremes, Machiavelli, inspired by the Roman imperial strategy, came to effect a minor revolution in the history of ethics. To repeat Roman success and to achieve republican liberty and imperial greatness, Machiavelli implies, the modern Florentines would have to break with the Aristotelian and the Christian definitions of virtue. For him, to be "good" or to be "virtuous" includes displaying the conventional virtues, but also being able to make calculated and dispassionate use of vice, or to "enter into evil," as he puts it in *The Prince*. * * *

* * *

There were * * * two sides to Rome's successful imperialism. On the one hand, it involved a policy of destruction that included the razing of cities, mass executions, and the deportation of peoples; on the other hand, it included a policy of benefits, such as the granting of citizenship, spectacular displays of mercy, and the resettlement of the vanquished in Rome. * * *

The modern Florentines, with their parochial assumptions, their insistence on the policy of the middle way, and their inability to encompass and to combine the extremes, had never been able to achieve this reshaping of political identities. Whereas the rulers of the Roman monarchy and the early Roman republic had cultivated and developed the complex strategy of destroying *and* benefiting into a veritable imperialist art, the wise men of contemporary Florence had, because of "their weak education and their slight knowledge of things," failed to transcend the suffocating limits of the city-state.[9] * * *

To achieve their longstanding aims of liberty and empire, and to found a true republic, Machiavelli contends, his compatriots would have to gain a better understanding of the dynamics of the ancient Roman republic, rethink their foreign policy doctrine based on

9. *Discorsi,* III.27, p. 487.

appeasement and containment, and subject Aristotelian and Christian virtue to a radical redefinition. But Machiavelli's aim in *The Prince* and the *Discourses,* as elsewhere, is not merely to challenge and to manipulate the ideological conventions and the political language of his day, but also to influence policy-making and political action in a more concrete sense. To remain within the realm of political discourse would in his view be a sign of the very weakness and the corruption, political as well as intellectual and moral, that his work was intended to combat and remedy. The theoretical insights and the historical lessons it contains would remain ineffective and immaterial, he would have argued, if they were not implemented or applied to the *here and now,* where political decisions are made and the fates of nations decided. This observation leads us to address the rhetorical level of Machiavelli's work.

In this study, we have explored the meaning of Machiavelli's work mainly on two of the three levels of interpretation outlined above: on the one hand, the ideological level, focusing on how it draws on, challenges, and seeks to reshape a number of entrenched ideological and intellectual conventions, beliefs, and practices at the heart of Florentine political culture; on the other hand, the rhetorical level, inquiring into how Machiavelli in his principal works, *The Prince* and the *Discourses,* rhetorically addresses and interacts with his intended, or original, audiences with regard to the particularities of time, place, and circumstances. * * *

This type of rhetorical reading requires a broad and multi-faceted contextual approach. To achieve this aim, we have situated our interpretations of *The Prince* and the *Discourses* in a great variety of political and cultural contexts. * * * We have also argued that Machiavelli's intellectual development and political project need to be understood in relation to the general ideological climate and the changing attitudes to the ancient Romans in early Cinquecento Florence. As we have seen, Machiavelli's overt and covert use of the Roman model and his repeated adaptations to the changing ideological, political, and moral landscape of contemporary Florence go a long way to explain his perplexing mixture of studied silences, insinuating remarks, and outspoken advice on subjects such as the connection between contemporary Florence and ancient Rome, and the republic's dual aim of liberty and empire. Our focus on how Machiavelli fitted his Roman example and his rhetorical strategies to suit the time, place, and circumstances has contributed to shedding new light on some of the major interpretative difficulties surrounding his work, and most importantly, offered a plausible explanation for the much-debated difference between *The Prince* and the *Discourses.*

* * *

* * * [T]he ancient Romans had in early Cinquecento Florence, for ideological, moral, and religious reasons, come to be viewed with suspicion, if not outright hostility. * * *

After the return of the Medici in 1512, the ideological climate of Florence underwent a profound change and the ancient Romans regained their former symbolic role within the artistic, ritual, and political culture of the city. During St. John's Day of 1513, the new regime staged four triumphs with Roman imperial motifs—featuring Julius Caesar, Pompey, Caesar Augustus, and Trajan—accompanied by scrolls and tablets. * * * Machiavelli's references to ancient Roman examples in *The Prince,* which was begun around this time, reflect, comment on, and obliquely subvert the political message of these Medicean manifestations. In chapters 3 to 5 of the treatise, ancient Rome is explicitly cited as the prime model for expansionist warfare and imperialist strategy. * * * The internal, liberty-oriented implications of the Roman model are insinuated into *The Prince* 19 and 25, where Machiavelli, by intimating the necessity of the mixed constitution and the republican principle of rotation in office, advocates modes and orders that we have reason to believe were inspired by the processual view of the Roman development described above.[1]

In our analysis of *The Prince,* we have come to witness how the former Secretary, by shaping his *principe nuovo* into part-classical tyrant and part-Roman triumphator, creates a vehicle for the foundation of a strong and expansive republic. Having freed his self-interest and his thirst for reputation, honor, glory, and greatness from conventional constraints, Machiavelli goes on to cut away the ground under his princely reader's feet to make him susceptible to rhetorical manipulation and to the advice that he has no other remedy at his disposal than to introduce an embryonic form of civil government. The strategy of exploiting the self-serving and power-seeking character of a tyrannically inclined ruler for a good end * * * follows naturally from Aristotle's assumptions that a tyrant, who primarily sees to his own utility, is more likely to let himself be persuaded and moved if exhorted to do so for the sake of his own security, or personal gain, than for some other, more noble end. It also seems to stem from Machiavelli's general view of human nature. According to the Florentine most men are wicked, shortsighted, selfish, governed by appearances, fears, and hopes of short-term gains. Such persons, it could be argued, can only be persuaded to serve a good end, or to

1. Hörnqvist argued that in Chapter 25 of *Il principe,* Machiavelli states that men will succeed in overcoming Fortune only if they adapt their behavior to the times, being diffident when that is required and impetuous when that is required. He expresses his pessimism that any man can be so adaptable, but Hörnqvist says that Machiavelli's real purpose here is to suggest the superiority of republics to principalities, since the former, with their mixed constitutions and rotation of offices, can adapt better to the changes of Fortune [editor's note].

pursue good effects, unwittingly, and in spite of themselves, through appeals to their selfish desires or aspirations.

* * *

The absolute, or next to absolute, silence Machiavelli in *The Prince* observes on the Florentine and republican dimensions of his project needs little explanation. For openly to advocate a program of Florentine expansionism in a manuscript set to circulate at the Roman curia would have been naïve in the extreme, and to speak frankly about republican motives in a treatise addressed to a family aspiring to princely power equally imprudent. * * *

Addressing his republican friends of the Orti Oricellari later in the *Discourses* and *The Art of War* (begun in 1518 and published in 1521), Machiavelli cast off the courtier's mask to offer extensive analysis of the political and military system of the ancient Roman republic, and the love of liberty and the acquisitive mentality which he regarded as the driving forces behind Rome's unprecedented territorial expansion and empire-building. * * * In the *Discourses,* the reader is invited to participate in Machiavelli's own investigations into Roman history, ancient and modern republicanism, the general principles of power politics, the instrumental use of religion, the causes of political and moral corruption and decay, and so forth. * * * Machiavelli's primary concern in this work, it would seem, is to promote his readers' understanding and judgment of statesmanship and worldly things in general. Instead of presenting his advice in a candid and straightforward manner, Machiavelli takes his readers on a long quest for the secrets behind Rome's rise to greatness, assigning them a role as co-participants in the text, leaving many things to be inferred and many conclusions precariously suspended along the way. * * *

But as we have seen, the Florentine and the republican reader of the *Discourses* is addressed in *The Prince* as well, where he, in various subtexts beneath the princely discourse of the work, is conjured into being through a series of conspiratorial winks and subtle innuendos. By reading between the lines, an ability Machiavelli's text actively encourages us to develop, and by investigating purposeful irregularities and intentional ambiguities, the analytical reader of *The Prince* is led to discover the work's Florentine bias and the embryonic stages of the republican development, described more fully and openly in the *Discourses.* * * * Machiavelli's irony and the tongue-in-cheek tone of his text can in large part be explained as an effect of his double-layered form of discourse, which allows two conflicting perspectives to coexist without loss of textual integrity: on the one hand, the limited understanding of the princely reader; on the other, the more farsighted and synoptic point of view of the republican counselor or political analyst. Since the former perspective is contained within the latter, the ideologies and the constitutional ideals they represent cannot be considered to be of equal or comparable value. As we have been able to conclude, there is in *The Prince,* as well as in the *Discourses,* internal textual evidence to support the notion that the republic is superior to the principality, and that the latter is to be seen as nothing more than a preparatory, or preliminary, stage in a constitutional development based on the Roman model. This is also to say that the contrast between *The Prince* and the *Discourses* should be understood as a difference in audience, strategy, and emphasis, but not in aim.

How, then, is Machiavelli's subtle and elaborate way of writing to be explained? While it is easy to see the reasons for him engaging in secret writing in *The Prince,* where he speaks directly to the hostile, or potentially hostile, audience of a tyrannical ruler, and only indirectly to the good, it is more difficult to see why he should continue to write in this guarded, or indirect, manner also in the *Discourses,* where he explicitly addresses good men, who for "their infinite good parts" deserve to be princes.[2] The intricate form of discourse that Machiavelli develops in the latter work, we may speculate, stems not from external constraints, but from the insight that a teaching based on implicatures and implied meanings is more effective, and more congenial to the cultivation of political prudence, than the open and direct form of education contained in the traditional mirror-for-princes and the humanist treatises on republican government. In any case, through this rhetorical invention, Machiavelli took political discourse to new, unprecedented heights, and developed a radically new form of strategic thinking that was later to find its way on to the Elizabethan stage, as well as into the secret chambers of Whitehall, Quay d'Orsay, and Washington.

* * *

WAYNE A. REBHORN

Machiavelli's *Prince* in the Epic Tradition[†]

"He who builds on the people builds on mud": Machiavelli cites this saying in *The Prince* (9.272)[1] only to refute it by arguing that the people, if properly managed, will provide a more secure foundation

2. *Discorsi,* dedication, p. 196.

† From *The Cambridge Companion to Machiavelli,* ed. John M. Najemy (Cambridge: Cambridge University Press, 2010), pp. 80–93. © Cambridge University Press 2010. Reproduced by permission of the publisher.

1. Citations of Machiavelli's works are from Niccolò Machiavelli, *Tutte le opere,* ed. Mario Martelli (Florence: Sansoni, 1971); all translations are my own. Citations of *The Prince* provide chapter and page from Martelli's edition.

for the Prince's state than fortresses or allies or mercenaries. This important moment in Machiavelli's work does more than elevate the people as well as the Prince who rules them; it also focuses on what must be considered perhaps the key metaphor in the book defining the Prince's activities: he "makes foundations [*fare fondamenti*]." Machiavelli repeats some version of this notion dozens of times in the relatively short text of *The Prince,* encouraging the reader to see the Prince as a cross between an architect and a mason, and illustrating the thesis, argued long ago by Jacob Burckhardt in his classic *Civilization of the Renaissance in Italy* (1860), namely, that people in the period saw the state as a work of art. That Machiavelli should focus on foundations is not surprising since the Prince he describes is "new": he does not inherit a state, but is faced with the challenge of creating one. Machiavelli is thinking of such "new" princes as Hieron of Syracuse, who rose up through the ranks of the army to seize control of Syracuse; the mythical Theseus, who founded Athens; and, perhaps the most memorable of them all, Cesare Borgia, who attempted, but failed, to create an enduring state in Italy. Even established rulers who already possess states, such as Ferdinand of Aragon, can be "new" (21.291), in this case because he is new to those portions of his realm he acquired after his marriage to Isabella of Castile. "New" princes must, of course, begin at the beginning: before they can build a state, they must make its foundations.

Fittingly, *The Prince* is dedicated to Lorenzo de' Medici, a potential new prince, and ends with a clarion call to that prince and his house to apply the political wisdom Machiavelli has offered them and to save Italy from the "barbarians," that is, from the French, the Spanish, and the Swiss, who have overrun the peninsula. Machiavelli's treatise does not begin by discussing the new prince directly, however. In keeping with what may have been his original title, *De principatibus* (*On Principalities*), the first eleven chapters offer a taxonomy of different kinds of princely states, including hereditary, mixed, civil, and ecclesiastical ones as well as those ruled by new princes. Many of the states he discusses nevertheless are, or include, newly acquired realms, and in most of the chapters Machiavelli discusses princely rulers rather than, say, political structures, constitutions, and the like. After two chapters (12 and 13) condemning mercenary armies, the rest of the book is focused on the new Prince, on how he must have real expertise in military affairs, avoid dependence on fortresses for his security, and make sure he controls his subordinates. In the most "scandalous" section of the work, chapters 15–19, Machiavelli discusses the Prince's relationship to conventional virtues such as liberality, mercy, trustworthiness, and piety, arguing that he need only *appear* to have these qualities, since his actual embracing of them might cost him his state. Finally, after devoting his twenty-fourth chapter to explaining that contemporary princes have lost their states because of their indolence and lack of foresight, Machiavelli focuses the twenty-fifth on Fortune, insisting that the new Prince can indeed defeat her through a combination of prudence and force, thus setting the stage for his calling upon the Medici in the last chapter to begin laying the foundations for a new Italy.

To say that Machiavelli's Prince makes foundations is to describe how he intervenes in the world of history. In this context, Machiavelli's metaphor is, however, somewhat unexpected, since he typically describes the movement of history using organic metaphors of birth and growth. Thus, one might think he would imagine the Prince as a farmer who plants seeds or a father who engenders and then cares for a child. Such notions do, in fact, appear fleetingly in *The Prince,* but they are not central to Machiavelli's thinking the way laying foundations is. This chapter will explain why Machiavelli would prefer to think in such terms, why the vision of the Prince as an architect and mason had such a hold on him. As we shall see, this vision is about freedom and power, and it connects the Prince to the tradition of the epic and to one important ancient epic hero in particular, Virgil's Aeneas. As we shall also see, however, Machiavelli's Prince is very different from his epic prototype: a hero like Aeneas, he is an Aeneas without a Rome.

To understand the meaning of Machiavelli's insistence on the metaphor of "laying foundations," it is necessary to examine first the way in which he imagines the movement of history. Occasionally, Machiavelli chooses fairly neutral, colorless verbs to describe what "happens" or "occurs," verbs such as *avvenire* (once), *occorrere* (twice), and *succedere* (four times). More frequently, however, and more suggestively, as he imagines historical events as going through a cycle, as being born, growing, and—although he hesitates to say so—dying, he rehearses a conceptual vocabulary that went back to the ancient Greek historian Polybius (d. 118 BCE).[2] Thus, Machiavelli uses forms of the verb *nascere,* "to be born," no fewer than twenty-seven times in *The Prince.* For example, in chapter 23, he says the Prince should avoid flatterers and never vacillate, because from such things there "arises [*nasce*] the low opinion others have of him" (294). At one point Machiavelli replaces this metaphor with a similar one when he worries that, if the Prince is miserly, it "will give birth to [*partorisce*] infamy" (16.281). Machiavelli may be using such verbs because he wishes to stress the logical, cause-and-effect

2. On Machiavelli's knowledge of Polybius' cyclical view of history, see, among others, Felix Gilbert, *Machiavelli and Guicciardini: Politics and History in Sixteenth-Century Florence* (Princeton University Press, 1965), pp. 320–1; and Gennaro Sasso, *Studi su Machiavelli* (Naples: Morano, 1967), chap. 5.

nature of events, especially since his project in *The Prince* is to offer rational explanations for history and then to formulate general rules to guide princely action. Thus, in the seventeenth chapter, Machiavelli writes that the good discipline Hannibal preserved in the huge army he led into Italy should not be seen as one of his "miraculous actions," that is, as something inexplicable, but rather as resulting from (*nascere*) the "inhuman cruelty" (282) he used to discipline his troops. However, as Machiavelli explains effects by supplying causes for them, the verb *nascere* that he uses to tie the two together never stops having its literal meaning: events as effects, in other words, are always "born" out of events as causes.

If Machiavelli's *nascere* makes history an organic process, so do the verbs *crescere* (to grow) and *accrescere* (to cause to grow), each of which appears six times in *The Prince*. For instance, Machiavelli talks at one point of how the Florentines and Venetians had "increased [*cresciuto*]" their states by employing mercenaries (12.276). Using the verb *accrescere* in chapter 11, he says that Pope Julius II did everything he could "to cause the Church to grow" (274), and in chapter 3 he praises the Romans for not allowing the states of the Achaeans or the Aetolians "to grow" (260). Moreover, although Machiavelli does not apply the verb *morire* (to die) to states, reserving it for individuals, he does think of the state as succumbing to potentially fatal illnesses, faulting rulers, for instance, who do not spot those illnesses when they "arise [*nascono*]," because they will then "grow [*crescere*]" and will be "incurable" (3.260).

If one ponders Machiavelli's Polybian conception of the state as an entity that is born, grows, and may finally die, then one might expect he would conceive of it either as a plant or as an animate being. In one striking passage, Machiavelli does indeed talk about its being like "all the other things in nature that are born and grow [*nascono e crescono*]" (7.266). Moreover, as the last example in the previous paragraph indicates, he does sometimes talk of how the Prince finds "remedies" for illnesses afflicting the state, as if it were human. In fact, on two occasions the Prince creates the state by "introducing form into matter" (6.264, 26.296–7), a conception harking back to the Scholastics and Aristotle that was used to describe, among other things, procreation. Considering the fact that Machiavelli repeatedly sums up the unpredictable, contingent nature of history in the personified, female figure of Fortune, it is not surprising that he would represent the Prince's introduction of the form of the state into the matter of history in such sexual terms—which is just what he does suggest at the end of chapter 25. If the Prince is to master Fortune, Machiavelli writes, he must "beat her and knock her about" and make her into his "amica," his "friend," ally, and lover (296). Nevertheless, neither conception—of the state growing like a plant or being produced through the Prince's sexual union with *Fortuna*—is as central to Machiavelli's thinking about the Prince as is the notion of his making foundations.

How can we account for such a preference? The best answer may be that, whether the Prince is planting the seed of the state in the ground or inseminating Fortune with his own seed, he effectively loses control over the process. By contrast, if the creation of the state involves the laying of foundations, then the Prince-as-architect has full responsibility over its design just as the Prince-as-mason does over its actual construction. Through this metaphor, in other words, the Prince takes charge of the world of history. Machiavelli might, of course, acknowledge that the making of foundations must be adapted to the nature of the terrain, depends on the availability of building materials, and involves a host of subordinate workers who may have very different agendas than the Prince does. Indeed, Machiavelli's consistent preoccupation with what the Prince must do in order to make his people loyal and obedient subjects might lead one to conclude that the foundations metaphor is an oversimplification. Nevertheless, Machiavelli does insist on it, and this insistence, coupled with the disconnect between the metaphor and reality, suggests that what we are dealing with here comes close to myth or fantasy despite Machiavelli's claim that he is writing about the "effectual truth" of things rather than "imaginary republics and principalities" (15.280). In fact, we can specify one particular myth that his metaphors suggest. As Machiavelli's imagination turns the people into inert blocks of stone and makes the Prince himself immensely powerful as he puts them in place by flexing his will, the Prince becomes something like a version of Amphion, the legendary founder of Thebes, whose eloquence, according to the Roman poet Horace, was so powerful that he was able to build the city, "moving the rocks and putting them where he wanted by means of the sound of his lyre."[3] Particularly relevant to what the Prince is doing is the fact that writers on rhetoric throughout the Renaissance identified Amphion's magical power with eloquence, with the orator's ability to move his listeners.

Machiavelli's Prince is an epic hero as well as a figure out of myth. His defining attribute, his *virtù*, means "valor," "cunning," "prowess," and "manliness"—all attributes of the hero—and his primary activity, waging war, drives the action of almost all ancient and Renaissance epics. I have argued elsewhere that one epic prototype for the Prince is Homer's Odysseus, a hero who unites in himself both cunning and martial prowess, eloquence and violence, the fox and the

3. Horace, *Ars poetica* 394–6. Although Machiavelli does not refer to Amphion, he no doubt knew the myth from Horace or Dante (*Inferno* 32.11).

lion.[4] However, a good case can be made for a very different epic hero as the inspiration for the Prince, a hero whose story Machiavelli certainly knew very well. While uniting some aspects of both Odysseus and Achilles, this hero was seen as transcending both of them in virtue and was especially admired as the founder of the state that Machiavelli and the rest of the Renaissance took as the model for their own. That hero was, of course, Virgil's Aeneas.

Before examining the ways in which Machiavelli's Prince resembles—and, more importantly, differs from—Virgil's Aeneas, it is important to see that, in shaping his Prince as a hero, Machiavelli also followed Virgil's lead in setting up an implicit generic opposition in *The Prince,* contrasting the Prince's epic action with the idleness of pastoral. Virgil himself was not merely aware of this generic opposition, but transmitted it to posterity through his Sixth Eclogue by having the singer of the poem begin in the epic vein with kings and battles, and then having the god Apollo rebuke him for attempting to go beyond the "slender" poetry of pastoral. In fact, the generic opposition between pastoral and epic structured Virgil's career, for he began with the low genre of pastoral and ascended to the heights of epic in *The Aeneid* during the last decade of his life. In general, pastoral—including Virgilian pastoral—embraces pleasure, assumes a benevolent, even protective, natural world that exists apart from the world of time and history, and presents characters who play and sing rather than work. It celebrates happiness as they take their ease, enjoying the *otium,* the idleness and lack of striving, that is, perhaps, the defining feature of the genre. This pastoral *otium* stands at the opposite extreme from the *negotium*—the "work," "business," "trouble," or "labor"—that defines the life of the epic hero. Unlike pastoral swains who never worry about tomorrow, the heroes of epic dwell in a potentially hostile universe and live lives of unremitting effort and constant strife; they are obsessed with time, often looking back to the past with nostalgia, but driven forward in a quest for the future. And if any epic hero embodies these traits, that hero is Virgil's Aeneas.

Machiavelli structures his thought in *The Prince* in terms of this Virgilian opposition between pastoral *otium* and epic *negotium.* Just as Aeneas' life is one of ceaseless toil in pursuit of future goals, so is that of Machiavelli's Prince. He may create spectacles to satisfy his people, but he cannot stop to enjoy them himself. Never idle, he is always busy founding the state, working to maintain it, striving desperately to avoid its collapse. In chapter 14, Machiavelli offers a vision of the Prince that explicitly defines him in epic terms: he is a

4. Wayne A. Rebhorn, *Foxes and Lions: Machiavelli's Confidence Men* (Ithaca, N.Y.: Cornell University Press, 1988), chap. 4.

warrior who commits every moment of his life to "training [*esercizio*] for war" (279). Machiavelli ends the chapter by placing his Prince in the company of such epic conquerors as Cyrus the Persian and Alexander the Great, whose lives were characterized by "industriousness" and who rejected the defining feature of pastoral by refusing to be "idle [*ozioso*]," even "in times of peace" (280).

If the Prince's commitment to *negotium* connects him to Aeneas, so, as we have noted, does his laying the foundations of his state. The creation of Rome is, of course, central to *The Aeneid*, although the actual founding of the city occurs well after Aeneas' death and is not described in the poem. In fact, Virgil actually pays more attention to the *fall* of cities. That of Troy preoccupies Aeneas throughout the first half of the poem and is described in detail in book 2, at whose climax Venus grants Aeneas a vision in which he sees "Neptune with his great trident shak[ing] the walls, dislodg[ing] them from their base, and tear[ing] the entire city down off of its foundations" (*Aeneid* 2.610–12). Moreover, there is another city in Virgil's poem whose destruction is at issue, although that destruction, like the building of Rome, is merely anticipated in the poem. That city is Carthage, whose "walls" are "rising" (1.437) when Aeneas comes upon it, and whose ultimate destruction is foreshadowed by Dido's tragic death. As her body burns, her people wail "as if all of Carthage had fallen to an invading enemy" and the furious flames were already burning through the "roofs of houses . . . and temples" (4.671). Dido's sister, Anna, says it directly: with her suicide, Dido has destroyed herself, her people, and her "city" (4.683).

Although the actual building of Rome, like the burning of Carthage, does not occur in Virgil's narrative, Aeneas does have glimpses of what is to come. When he meets his father in the underworld, he is allowed to view his descendants, including Romulus, who is identified with a Rome not merely imagined as extending its "empire" over the earth but as a city that "will have seven hilltop citadels surrounded by a wall" (*Aeneid* 6.782–3). Later, in book 8, when Aeneas' shield is described, he can see Augustus on it, "borne in triumph through the walls of Rome" (8.714–15). This is the Rome, of course, for which and in which Virgil is writing his poem. Looking forward to a glorious future, Aeneas' son declares that the spot where they make their first camp in Italy is the "home," the *patria* or "fatherland," they were destined to reach (7.122), and shortly thereafter they identify a site to build their "city" (7.149), a city Aeneas himself designs (7.157–9). In all the examples just cited, Virgil clearly links Aeneas and the Trojans to the imperial city their descendants will found. What is more, he identifies that city with its walls at least as much as its buildings. The brief opening paragraph of Virgil's poem covers the entire arc of this history:

beginning with Aeneas, an "exile because of fate" (1.2), who suffers and fights until he can found his "city" (1.5), it ends by anticipating what Aeneas' descendants will build one day, the "altae moenia Romae [the walls of lofty Rome]" (1.7).

If Machiavelli's Prince resembles Aeneas as a builder, he also resembles his Roman model as the potential creator of a powerful, independent Italian state that will expel the "barbarian" invaders from the north, showing, in the words of Petrarch with which *The Prince* ends, that "ancient valor is not yet dead in Italian hearts" (26.298). Machiavelli's Prince will thus create anew the Roman Empire in the modern world. There are, however, many differences between the Prince and his Roman predecessor. One of the primary ones involves Aeneas' concern for morality and religion, a concern summed up in the concept with which he is associated throughout Virgil's poem, his *pietas,* which meant piety toward the gods, toward ancestors and family, and toward the state in general, and duty, the duty Aeneas displays, for example, by fighting for his people and their future. The medieval Christian tradition later identified *pietas* with love of God, and the word eventually came to mean not just religious piety, but mercy and even pity, so that being pious finally became incompatible with warfare. Writing at the end of this historical transformation, Machiavelli considers *pietas* in chapter 17 of *The Prince,* using the Latin word in its title, "De crudelitate et pietate," "On Cruelty and Piety [or Mercy]" (281). In fact, since this chapter also contains *The Prince's* only citation from *The Aeneid*—and one of the rare mentions of Virgil in all of his writings—it seems clear that he is here inviting readers to think back to Virgil's poem and to compare and contrast his Prince with Aeneas.

Machiavelli's conception of princely *pietas* is an inversion of Virgil's as well as a rejection of the Christian identification of it with piety, mercy, and pity. Although Machiavelli does say the Prince should be pious, a show of religiosity is all that is required. In fact, Machiavelli is convinced that princes who are truly pious will, like the unarmed prophet Savonarola (6.265), come to a bad end. Thus Machiavelli argues that, since "it is much safer to be feared than to be loved" (17.282), "cruelty" is by far a greater virtue than "piety." Moreover, the model princes who appear in Machiavelli's book also display little or none of Aeneas' loyalty to family, let alone his concern for retainers, friends, and allies. Nevertheless, Virgil's hero and Machiavelli's Prince do seem similar in one way: both are dedicated to the states they found. Aeneas' Rome, however, is an impersonal, transhistorical entity to which he subordinates himself and his desires—he is the agent of a community larger than himself—whereas the Prince treats his state as his personal possession and rules it with an iron fist. As princes and leaders, then, both men may be, in Virgil's words, "renowned for piety" (1.10), since both feel a keen sense of duty to the state. Each is, however, pious in his own way.

Machiavelli's Prince differs even more fundamentally from Aeneas in terms of what he is imagined as building. Aeneas, as we have noted, builds walls and even designs a city that points toward the ultimate *urbs,* Rome itself. The Prince, by contrast, is seen as a maker of foundations. Indeed, at virtually no point in *The Prince* does Machiavelli talk about the *walls* of the Prince's city, let alone imagine him building a castle or residing in a palace. Rather than think of him as an Aeneas *redivivus,* then, it might be better to style him an Aeneas *manqué*—for he seems unable to imagine the building constructed on the foundations he is laying. For example, although words such as *fondare* and *fondamenti* sound from one end of *The Prince* to the other, words related to edifices and buildings make themselves scarce. *Casa* (house), for instance, appears only twelve times, but four of these involve the houses of the people, not of the Prince, and seven are metaphorical, identifying the "ruling house" of a family. Only once, when Oliverotto da Fermo has been "fuori di casa," "away from home" (8.270), is the word used in reference to a prince's abode, although here it is not a structure this would-be Prince is building so much as one he hopes to usurp from the uncle who raised him. Significantly, while Machiavelli celebrates Romulus, the *founder* of Rome, as a model prince (6.264–5), in *The Prince* he never mentions Augustus, who brought peace to the Roman world and was responsible for building the city of which Virgil sings.

Ironically, nowhere is the absence of princely buildings from Machiavelli's vision more noticeable than in the twentieth chapter, which asks whether princes ought to "build fortresses" (289). Although Machiavelli presents this question at the start, he spends the bulk of the chapter reviewing the relationship the Prince has with his subjects, returning to the issue of building fortresses only in the last paragraph. There he begins by endorsing the building of fortresses because it has been done from ancient times. However, he immediately supplies no fewer than three examples of princes whom he praises for having wisely torn down fortresses in order to ensure their hold on their states. He then generalizes that fortresses are useful, or not, depending on circumstances: if the Prince has more fear of his own people than of foreigners, he should build fortresses, but if the situation is reversed, he should not. Having thus presented a seemingly "balanced" judgment of the matter, Machiavelli again criticizes fortress building, speaking of how the Sforzas' huge "castle" (291) in the center of Milan has done them more harm than good. Finally, only at the end of the paragraph does Machiavelli seem to offer a positive example of a fortress, that of the Countess of Forlì (Caterina Sforza), who was able to take refuge in hers when her people rebelled, waiting there until aid arrived from Milan. Machiavelli quickly takes back this last example, however, noting that her fortress was useless to her later when Cesare Borgia attacked her, for her people, who hated her, joined with Borgia and drove her away. When, in the very last sentence of the chapter, therefore, Machiavelli restates his earlier "balanced" opinion of fortresses, he must be speaking ironically: the conclusion he wants the reader to reach is that the best fortress is not a fortress, but the people. Revealingly, although the people implicitly constitute the Prince's fortress, Machiavelli never says that explicitly. An earlier passage reveals what he really thinks: if the Prince manages the people correctly, they will be the "good foundation" of his state (9.272).

To say that Machiavelli cannot imagine the palace or the city his Prince will build is not to say that he does not imagine specific political goals for him. Fundamentally, his goal is to create and maintain *lo stato* (the state), a word which in Machiavelli's lexicon designated both a geographical and a political entity. To accomplish this goal, he will act to establish a citizen army, institute laws and *ordini*, enforce a sometimes brutal form of justice, create a system of rewards for his citizens to increase their loyalty to the state, and put on spectacles to entertain them. Clearly, in addition to the Prince's own energy and acumen, what is crucial for the state that Machiavelli would establish is the people on whom it will be built. And yet, despite his insistence that they are not to be thought of as mud but as the stone blocks moved by a Prince with Amphion-like abilities, it may well be that he cannot envisage a house or castle or city actually being erected on the foundation they supply precisely because his work also contains a very different vision of them.

This vision appears intermittently in the text whenever Machiavelli stresses the people's egocentric pursuit of their own interests, their undependability, their cowardice, their resistance to innovation. Machiavelli sums it up in chapter 17 of *The Prince:*

> This can be said of men in general: that they are ungrateful, fickle, hypocrites and dissemblers, avoiders of dangers, greedy for gain; and while you benefit them, they are entirely yours, offering you their blood, their goods, their life, their children, as I said above, when need is far away, but when you actually become needy, they turn away. (17.282)

Although the good Prince hopes to be able to shape such beings to serve his ends, they are by their nature an unstable, rather slippery lot—so slippery, in fact, that from this angle they actually do seem more like yielding mud than solid stones. To put the matter less metaphorically: since the Prince cannot truly depend on the people to remain faithful to him, to love him no matter what, he can never rest secure with the foundations he has laid down. Those foundations only seem to be solid; in reality they are always threatening to disintegrate, forcing the Prince to build and rebuild them over and over again.

If Machiavelli, unlike Virgil, cannot imagine the state his hero would create as a city with walls and buildings, he does share with his great forebear a fear that that state, like Aeneas' Troy, can be destroyed. Not surprisingly, to talk about that destruction, Machiavelli consistently uses the verbs *rovinare* and *ruinare* and the noun *ruina,* which appear more than forty times in *The Prince.* All these words derive from the Latin *ruere,* which means "to fall or tumble or rush down," the result of which is, of course, *ruins.* Occasionally, Machiavelli applies one of the verbs to actual buildings, as when he speaks of how people who have taken refuge in a fortified city might find that their possessions outside have been "destroyed [*ruinate*]" (10.273) by their besiegers. Even more strikingly, he uses the two alternate forms of the verb in the same sentence when he compares Fortune to "one of these destructive [*rovinosi*] rivers" that "destroy [*ruinano*] trees and buildings" (25.295). Machiavelli also thinks of ruins on a grander scale, as when he refers to the hiring of Goths as soldiers as the "first cause of the fall [*ruina*] of the Roman Empire" (13.278). Although Machiavelli does not write here or elsewhere of physical ruins, his use of *rovinare, ruinare,* and *ruina* cannot help but suggest them.

Normally, when Machiavelli uses some form of these words, he is talking about the fall, that is, the failure or death, of people, and in particular, of princes. Thus, in chapter 15, he says that anyone who assumes human beings will be good will only achieve "his ruin [*ruina*] rather than his preservation" (280). Similarly, at the end of the long chapter 19, Machiavelli sums up what he has been saying about a host of Roman emperors, most of whom failed and were murdered, by explaining how either hatred or scorn was the cause of their "ruina" (289). And in chapter 26 he speaks of how the seemingly invincible Swiss were "defeated [*rovinati*]" by the Spanish infantry (298). However, the literal, architectural sense of those words, though often buried, is never too deep that it cannot be brought into the light, as when Machiavelli says, "It is necessary for a prince to lay good foundations; otherwise, he is certain to come to ruin [*che ruini*]" (12.275). In these two short clauses Machiavelli identifies the fundamental opposition that defines the Prince's life: he either lays foundations or crashes down in ruins. Any life he might have between these two states, a life, that is, in which he would build the walls of his house and city, and then live in them, is simply omitted.

Reinforcing this sense of an absent center between extremes is the one quotation that Machiavelli takes from *The Aeneid* and uses in his discussion of princely *pietas.* In chapter 17 he argues that cruelty is the best policy for rulers, especially new princes, because too much mercy will lead to political chaos. To underscore this point, Machiavelli cites Dido's words from Virgil's poem: "Harsh necessity and the newness of my reign force me to take such measures and to watch over my borders with a widespread guard" (17.282, quoting *Aeneid* 1.563–4). Note what Machiavelli does *not* do here: he does not cite a passage about the difficulties the Trojans have in establishing themselves in Italy, even though the second half of *The Aeneid* is devoted to that very subject. Instead, he cites the words of Dido, whose Carthage is just being built when Aeneas arrives, the sight of which is, ironically, the only glimpse Aeneas has of the building of a great city, like the Rome his descendants will create. It is, however, a Carthage that will eventually be turned into ruins. In other words, when Machiavelli seeks an analogue in Virgil's poem for his Prince's situation, he does not find it in Aeneas' successful journey from the ruined city of Troy to Italy, where the "walls of lofty Rome" will rise one day, but in Dido's Carthage, whose initial construction and final destruction, its foundations and its ruins, must have haunted Machiavelli's imagination.

The imaginary landscape of the Prince's world has very few features. There are open fields in which the Prince hunts and travels and fights; the odd castle or city; many foundations; and plenty of ruins. These last two landmarks tend to become one, for ruins, in their most extreme form, amount to little more than foundations. Machiavelli plays on this similarity when he speaks of how Duke Guidobaldo of Urbino "ruinò funditus," "razed to the ground," the fortresses his enemies used against him (20.290). *Funditus* is a Latin word that means "to the *fundus*," that is, "to the bottom," or "to the foundations." The imaginary landscape of the Prince is thus full of foundations that uncannily anticipate the ruins they will eventually become. The real landscape of Machiavelli's Italy was also filled with ruins, real ruins, the vestiges of the Roman empire whose success Machiavelli may want contemporary Italian states to imitate, but whose fall is equally present in his book. He devotes the longest chapter of *The Prince,* the nineteenth, to a description of the decadence, not the triumph, of Rome, discussing a long series of emperors who failed as rulers and were murdered. However, the clearest sign of Rome's fall in Machiavelli's work is the Italy that it has become, an Italy "without a head, without order, beaten, despoiled, torn apart, overrun . . . [which has] endured every sort of ruin" (26.297). Machiavelli's last term here, "ruina," may refer to the devastation wrought by the French, Spanish, and Swiss, but it cannot help but evoke the *ruins* of the ancient empire that perished a millennium earlier.

In Machiavelli's vision of princely activity, his Prince thus seems trapped in an endless cycle of beginnings and endings. No sooner has he made his foundations than they seem to metamorphose into the ruins that threaten the end of his state. Moreover, his ruin is, in a sense, inevitable, as inevitable as the failure of Cesare Borgia, the fall of Rome, and the death of princes in general, a ruin that forces the Prince to pick up his stones and start laying foundations again—and again and again. Machiavelli's vision of princely action and defeat here must betray his sense of the radical instability of the political world in which he lived, an Italy that, since the French invasion of 1494, seemed always in a state of crisis, its cities conquered one day by one power and then retaken the next day by their original rulers or overrun by someone else. Both the Prince's world and Machiavelli's Italy are ultimately under the sway of Fortune, Machiavelli's symbol of the instability of the world of history. Machiavelli often imagines Fortune as a woman, whom the Prince can beat into submission, although what gets built as a result of that beating remains unclear. When Machiavelli compares Fortune to "one of these destructive [*rovinosi*] rivers," perhaps he does so in order to imagine the Prince as actually *building* something in opposition to it, although what he builds consists of "dikes and embankments" (25.295), not houses, let alone cities. Strikingly, in *The Prince* Machiavelli does not use what was perhaps the most familiar image for Fortune in the Middle Ages and the Renaissance, namely the "wheel of Fortune" (which he had, however, used in his poem "Fortune"). Nevertheless, in the seemingly endless cycle of making foundations, collapsing in ruins, and making foundations again, the Prince does seem caught on some diabolical version of Fortune's wheel.

If one can imagine the Prince as a figure like Amphion, the powerful mythical builder of Thebes, the constant moving of stones as he lays, and lays again, the foundations of his state evokes a very different figure. This figure is not the builder of a city, but a malefactor who has been sentenced to hell where he is condemned to push heavy stones up a steep hill, only to have them roll down to the bottom once he reaches the summit, thus forcing him to repeat the whole process over and over again. This figure is, of course, Sisyphus, and although Machiavelli does not refer to Sisyphus in his writings, he surely knew the story. Homer recounts it in *The Odyssey* (11.593–600), which Machiavelli might have read in Latin translation: Virgil alludes to it in *The Aeneid* (6.616); and Dante in his *Inferno* (7.16–66) makes Sisyphus' punishment the basis for that of the avaricious and the prodigal. Ezio Raimondi has argued that the

Sisyphus myth informs a famous statement Machiavelli makes in the letter of December 10, 1513, to Francesco Vettori, in which he describes the wretchedness of his daily life on his farm, speaks of how he has just written *The Prince,* and reveals how desperate he is to return to Florence, so desperate that he would be willing to serve the Medici "even if they would begin by having me roll a stone around [*voltolare un sasso*]."[5] Raimondi claims that the Roman poet Lucretius, in his *De rerum natura* (3.995–1002), provided Machiavelli with the crucial, political reading of Sisyphus' stone rolling as an allegory of the torments men endure, not in the afterlife, but in this world, in their desperate, futile pursuit of political office. Although Machiavelli's reference to rolling a stone certainly expresses the frustration defined by Lucretius' allegory, Raimondi argues that Machiavelli did not share Lucretius' negative view of political activity, which, however frustrating, was immensely valuable to Machiavelli, indeed his means of self-definition.

Raimondi's argument provides a useful perspective from which to view the Prince's endless laying of foundations, and thus to connect Machiavelli's life with that of the hero he imagines in his book. One may call the Prince's activity Sisyphean, but, as Raimondi suggests, to do so without further qualification would be to see it as hell-on-earth and to make *The Prince* a grim and pessimistic book. To be sure, the Prince's labors will never—can never—cease, but that does not mean he is unhappy as he rolls his stones. In this regard, he is, again, very different from Virgil's Aeneas, for sadness, a melancholy regret over what has been lost, is precisely what the Roman hero feels throughout *The Aeneid,* especially when he goes to war in the second half of the poem, which often turns into an elegy for the loss of youth and beauty. What Aeneas says when he is viewing scenes of the Trojan war carved on the walls of Dido's temple really sums up what Virgil wants his readers to feel about the history of Rome and the burdens its great leaders bear: "Sunt lacrimae rerum," "there are tears in [the very heart of] things" (1.462). While *The Aeneid,* unlike Machiavelli's treatise, can imagine the city of Rome as the end that fulfills and justifies its hero's striving and suffering, Virgil's vision is always tinged with melancholy because of the enormous losses that empire building demands.

Unlike Aeneas, Machiavelli's Prince may never achieve a vision of the house or city whose foundations he is making, but he is certainly not melancholy as he makes them. That does not mean he indulges in the carefree happiness of pastoral as he enjoys the moment and its pleasures. In fact, the verb *godere* (to enjoy) always

5. *Opere,* ed. Martelli, p. 1160; Ezio Raimondi, "Il Sasso del politico," in Raimondi, *Politica e commedia* (Bologna: Il Mulino, 1972), pp. 165–72.

seems slightly suspect to Machiavelli. He rejects, for instance, the supposed wisdom of his fellow Florentines, who sum it up in a favorite proverb: "to enjoy [*godere*] the benefit of time" (3.260). Machiavelli is warning against temporizing here, but his language implicitly pits princely action, the decisive action he admires in the Romans, against the notion that one might stop and *enjoy* anything. One cannot do so simply because time, which "drives all things on" (3.260), will not permit it. In Machiavelli's analysis of Italy's political crisis, he says its rulers have lost their states precisely because they thought they could tarry in the pleasure of the moment; they have failed because they are just like most men: "when they find things good in the present, they enjoy them (*vi si godono*]" (24.294) rather than worrying about future difficulties. The closest Machiavelli comes to endorsing this kind of happiness is what he says about the successors of Alexander the Great: "if they had been united, they might have enjoyed at their leisure [*godere oziosi*]" (4.263) the state that Alexander left them. Here, but only fleetingly, Machiavelli comes close to endorsing the enjoyment of the moment that the adjective "oziosi" links directly to pastoral. Such a moment did not occur, of course, because those rulers did not remain united, nor is it ever a possibility for the Prince, who must always be vigilant, alert, and active.

If the Prince cannot stop and smell the roses of pastoral, that does not mean he is unhappy. On the contrary, happiness essentially defines what he feels. For if princes do what they are supposed to do, if, that is, they succeed—and princes are only Princes if they succeed—then they will be not only "powerful, secure, honored," but also, as Machiavelli adds, "happy [*felici*]" (6.265). Revealingly, although he typically defines princely activity through the opposition of *fondare* and *ruinare,* at one point in chapter 25 he substitutes the verb *felicitare* for *fondare,* remarking on how people are unnecessarily puzzled "when they see this prince happy [*felicitare*] today and in ruins [*ruinare*] tomorrow." Two sentences later, Machiavelli explains that a prince who adapts his actions to suit Fortune will be "felice," whereas he who does not will be "infelice" (25.295). In fact, the entire twenty-fifth chapter resounds with variants on *felice* and *felicitare.* Although editors and translators want to turn *felice* into "prosperous" and *felicitare* into something like "to prosper" or "to succeed," the words have those senses only metaphorically. Basically, *felice* means "happy," although, to do the editors and translators justice, there may also be a trace of the Latin sense of *felix* as "fruitful" or "fortunate" in Machiavelli's *felice.*

To sum up, then: Machiavelli's successful Prince is not filled with a melancholy determination like that of Aeneas, nor does he tarry among the pleasures of pastoral idleness. Forced to move his stones into place over and over again, he resembles Sisyphus, but not the Sisyphus of Homer and Virgil, Dante and Lucretius, the Sisyphus who suffers the pains of hell. Machiavelli's Prince recalls, at least in one important way, another, more modern Sisyphus, the Sisyphus whom Albert Camus describes in his existentialist essay, *The Myth of Sisyphus.* To be sure, Camus's Sisyphus moves his stones around as an act of rebellion, embracing what he does as a way of creating meaning in a meaningless universe in which foundations, not to mention buildings, are unthinkable. By contrast, Machiavelli's Prince thinks he can find meaning in the world as he lays the foundations of the state, even though he may never see the building that would be erected on top of them. Nevertheless, Machiavelli's Prince does join hands with Camus's Sisyphus in that both are committed to action, and in this regard what Camus concludes about his hero's feeling can be said about Machiavelli's hero as well: "One must imagine that Sisyphus is happy."[6]

VICTORIA KAHN

In an earlier article on Agathocles, which Kahn responds to in this essay, she argued that the differences between Cesare Borgia and Agathocles were so slight that Machiavelli must have been ironic in depicting Agathocles as he does. She sees this maneuver on Machiavelli's part as a rhetorical strategy—something that should not be surprising in an author whose prince is a foxlike master of deception, dissimulation, and disguise. According to Kahn, Machiavelli's rhetorical strategy in the chapter featuring Agathocles is to anticipate and complicate readers' hypothetical responses to the prince—namely, their desire to criticize him as evil. Kahn asks: If the reader condemns Cesare Borgia as a model prince, then what is to be made of the fact that Machiavelli presents him mostly in positive terms and then goes out of his way to condemn Agathocles, whose behavior is virtually identical to Borgia's? Kahn's point is that *The Prince* is designed to teach the reader just how hard it is to make simple moral judgments about ruling the way that fifteenth- and sixteenth-century humanists did. On the contrary, because rulers always have to deal with a world that is characterized by the contingent, the unexpected, and the uncertain, the *virtù* they possess will be fundamentally unstable, sometimes, though not always, involving the commission of evil acts as they respond to changing circumstances. In the more recent essay printed here, Kahn does not back away from her earlier view that Machiavelli's work is rhetorical, designed to teach the reader how complicated political judgments are, but now she focuses somewhat less on the ambiguities of *virtù* and more on its complicated relationship to the prince's acquisition of glory.

6. Albert Camus, *Le Mythe de Sisyphe* (Paris: Gallimard, 1942), p. 168.

From Revisiting Agathocles†

Agathocles the Sicilian, who ruled from 316 to 289 BCE, occupies an unusual and symptomatic position in Machiavelli's *The Prince*. Sandwiched between Cesare Borgia in chapter 7 and the discussion of civil principalities in chapter 9, his career illustrates the transition from the exercise of spectacular violence to something verging on republican rule. Born "the son of a potter," Agathocles rose to prominence in Syracuse by betraying his fellow citizens and massacring the nobility. But he lived a long and prosperous life because he understood that cruelties should be done all at once and not prolonged and that a prince who seeks to maintain his power must eventually moderate his violence and attend to the interests of his subjects. In this way, the example of Agathocles implicitly engages the relationship between *The Prince* and the *Discourses:* what is the difference, if any, between the tactics used by the new prince to gain power and those at work in a republic? What is the basis, if any, for Machiavelli's avowed preference for republics? How Machiavellian is Machiavelli anyway?

Agathocles holds an unusual position as well because he is the occasion of Machiavelli's reflection on his own discourse, the occasion, that is, of a metadiscourse about Machiavellianism. In a striking paragraph that follows the description of Agathocles's brutal deeds, Machiavelli tells us that Agathocles rose to power by his own virtù, and yet cautions us that it cannot be called virtù to massacre one's fellow citizens: "a man can get power like this, but not glory." The repetition of *virtù* is clearly designed to prompt the reader to reflect on the meaning of this shifting term, which at times designates the amoral skill of the prince and at other times—as in this passage—seems to designate something more than the skillful acquisition of power. The example of Agathocles thus poses the problem of Machiavellianism in little, asking us to consider not only the relationship between virtù and virtue, but also between virtù and success, and success and glory.

Agathocles appears in at least three ancient sources, all of which worry to a greater or lesser extent about how to interpret his career. Polybius (200–118 BCE) briefly discusses Agathocles in book 9 of *The Histories;* Diodorus Siculus (fl. 30–60 CE) recounts Agathocles's adventures in his *History;* and the Roman historian Justin (second century CE?) describes Agathocles in his *Epitome of Trogus.*[1] * * *

† From *The Review of Politics* 75 (2013): 557–72. © University of Notre Dame. Published by and reproduced with permission of Cambridge University Press. Notes are Kahn's, with full bibliographical information supplied by the editor.

1. In the following pages, I cite *The Prince* from the bilingual edition of Mark Musa (New York: St. Martin's, 1964), and the *Discourses* from the edition of Bernard Crick, trans. Leslie J. Walker, SJ, with revisions by Brian Richardson (Harmondsworth: Penguin Books, 1979). References to *The Prince* and *Discourses* in Italian are to *Il Principe e Discorsi,* ed. Sergio Bertelli (Milan: Feltrinelli, 1977).

Polybius is interesting for our purposes because, like Machiavelli, he sees Agathocles as the occasion for metahistorical or historiographical reflection. He condemns the earlier historian Timaeus for the "excess of rancor" he displays toward Agathocles: "for that Agathocles had great natural advantages is evident from Timaeus's own account of him." "Regarding all this a historian should lay before posterity not only such matters as tend to confirm slanderous accusations, but also what redounds to the credit of this prince; for such is the proper function of history."[2] * * *

* * *

The Roman historian Justin (second century CE?) seems to have followed Polybius's historiographical recommendations, but not his account of Agathocles's death. Justin, too, recounts Agathocles's rise from humble beginnings as "the son of a potter" to his position as tyrant of Syracuse. He describes his cunning murder of the most powerful members of the Syracusan nobility (he invited them to a meeting in a theater and had them massacred) and his skillful handling of the Carthaginian siege of Syracuse by attacking the Carthaginians on their own soil. But, in the end, Agathocles succumbed to "a virulent disease."[3] (In this detail, he seems to anticipate Machiavelli's description of Cesare Borgia.) * * * Justin conspicuously refrains from judging Agathocles's end moralistically; instead, he simply reports the facts. But Agathocles's fall from power and painful death do seem just punishment for a figure whom Justin had earlier described as "a superlative illustration of unprincipled behavior: a king deserting his own army, and a father betraying his sons."[4]

Machiavelli conspicuously omits these details about Agathocles's death. Instead, he describes him as one of those who "live for a long time secure in their country and defend themselves from outside enemies without being conspired against by their own citizens" (73). He was able to do so, Machiavelli tells us, because he performed his violent actions all at once to secure his position and later used such violence only to the advantage of his subjects (73). * * * Nevertheless, Justin's remark about Agathocles's "unprincipled" behavior finds an echo in Machiavelli's pronouncement that Agathocles did not rise to the ranks of the really excellent men. In making this judgment, Machiavelli illustrates his own skill as a reader of history, his own ability—crucial not only to the reader but also the writer of history—to acknowledge Agathocles's achievements without confusing his military success and even his military virtù with glory.

2. Polybius, *The Histories*, trans. W. R. Paton (London: William Heinemann, 1975), 4:347 (12.15).
3. Justin, *Epitome of the Philippic History of Pompeius Trogus*, trans. J. C. Yardley (Atlanta: Scholars Press, 1994), 181.
4. Ibid., 179.

In an earlier essay on Agathocles, I argued that the distinctions in this passage between virtù and virtù were facetious, especially in light of the immediately preceding chapter 7.[5] There Machiavelli described the actions of Cesare Borgia, who also rose to power with the help of bloody massacres and theatrical deception. Borgia famously lured the Orsini family to a pretended peace negotiation and, once they were in his power, slaughtered them. Even more striking was Borgia's murder of his own subordinate Remirro de Orco, who had carried out Borgia's brutal designs to unify the Romagna. * * * After these examples, I argued, the claim that one could not attribute virtù to Agathocles couldn't be taken seriously. It must instead be ironic—a kind of knowing parody of the reader's own moralizing judgment of Machiavelli's examples. Machiavelli's feigned condemnation of Agathocles was, I suggested, analogous to Borgia's condemnation of the brutal actions of Remirro de Orco, and thus a test of the reader's own virtù. Instead of offering moral condemnation, the example was designed to get the reader to understand that virtù is not just equivalent to evil behavior: rather, what counts as virtù will change according to circumstances, as Agathocles himself changed in response to the dictates of his reign.

As clever as I think this interpretation was, I've always been bothered by the fact that it requires Machiavelli to treat military glory ironically. It assumes that, when Machiavelli says a man cannot get glory by acting as Agathocles does, he is only pretending to be concerned about the impossibility of glory while really dismissing such reservations. His mention of glory, according to this interpretation, would then be utterly disingenuous. If I now wish to suggest otherwise, I don't want to imply that Machiavelli is always straightforward. To the contrary, many of the examples in *The Prince* and the *Discourses* are contradictory, and the logic of his texts forces the reader to weigh examples against each other and, often, to read between the lines. * * *

In fact, it's hard to imagine a political theorist with a more acute sense of the ironies of political action. In chapter 7 of *The Prince,* Machiavelli tells us that Borgia did everything he could to consolidate his power but was in the end defeated by "the brevity of [Pope] Alexander's life and his own sickness." Ironically, Borgia failed to anticipate the one thing that was certain—his own mortality. * * * And in the conclusion to chapter 15 of *The Prince,* Machiavelli famously gives the would-be ruler an almost textbook definition of irony when he warns that "something that appears to be a virtue, if pursued, will result in his ruin; while some other thing that appears to be a vice, if pursued, will bring about his security and well-being."

5. Victoria Kahn, "Virtù and the Example of Agathocles in Machiavelli's *The Prince*," *Representations* 13 (1986): 63–85.

In one crucial respect, the Agathocles example is like these other examples, especially the concluding remarks of chapter 15 of *The Prince.* In punning on *virtù,* Machiavelli makes explicit what is implicit throughout his work: the word forces us to think of the relation between the Latin *virtus* (plus its cognate, the Italian *virtù*) and the Italian *le virtù,* that is, between strength and cunning on the one hand and the moral virtues on the other. As we learn in chapters 15 through 18 of *The Prince,* this relationship is neither one of identity nor one of simple difference: there is a relationship between virtù and the virtues, just not the one the moralist wants. Instead of identity, the relationship is one of strategic usefulness: the prince will adopt the conventional virtues when it's politically useful to do so. The virtues, then, are not intrinsically good; their "goodness" depends on how they are used. * * *

But the example of Agathocles is also different from the other examples I have mentioned because, as we've seen, Machiavelli introduces a third term, that of glory. This term, at least when it is understood as military or political glory, is not subject to ironic critique by Machiavelli. In the early chapters of the *Discourses,* Machiavelli praises the Roman Republic for its glorious achievements and the examples he singles out are of leaders who pursued the glory of the republic above any merely individual calculus of self-interest. Later, in book 1, chapter 58, he makes it clear that republics are capable of greater glory than principalities: "And if princes are superior to populaces in drawing up laws, codes of civic life, statutes and new institutions, the populace is so superior in sustaining what has been instituted, that it indubitably adds to the glory [*gloria*] of those who have instituted them" (1.58.256). As Bernard Crick writes about this passage, "The message is plain enough: princes . . . create or restore states, but republics . . . preserve them."[6] * * *

At the same time, Machiavelli makes it clear that it is not always easy to see who deserves a glorious reputation. In book 1, chapter 10, of the *Discourses,* he * * * describes how "almost all men, deceived by the false semblance of good and the false semblance of renown [*gloria*], allow themselves either willfully or ignorantly to slip into the ranks of those who deserve blame rather than praise; and, when they might have founded a republic or a kingdom to their immortal honour, turn their thoughts to tyranny, and fail to see what fame, what glory, security, tranquility, conjoined with peace of mind, they are missing by adopting this course, and what infamy, scorn, abhorrence, danger and disquiet they are incurring" (1.10.135). This is clearly the lesson Agathocles failed to learn, at least at the outset of his reign. Machiavelli then goes on to link this lesson to the reading

6. Introduction to Machiavelli, *Discourses,* ed. Crick, 33.

of history: "Nor is it possible for anybody, whether he be but a private citizen living in some republic, or has been fortunate enough or virtuous enough to have become a prince, to read history and to make use of the records of ancient deeds, without preferring, if he be a private citizen, to conduct himself in his fatherland rather as Scipio did than as Caesar did" * * * (1.10.135).

Caesar is a difficult case, but this difficulty is a key to understanding Machiavelli's interpretation of Agathocles. Machiavelli tells us that Caesar achieved great renown (gloria), but he is then quick to disabuse the reader regarding Caesar's glory: "those who praise him have either been corrupted by his fortune or overawed by the long continuance of the empire which, since it was ruled under that name, did not permit writers to speak freely of him" (1.10.136). An astute reader, Machiavelli tells us, will understand that Roman historians criticized Caesar indirectly by condemning Catiline or praising Brutus. * * * Caesar is guilty of the ultimate infamy in destroying the Roman Republic, while the person who reforms it will win the ultimate glory * * * (1.10.138). In *Discourses* 1.37, Machiavelli calls Caesar "Rome's first tyrant," and he reiterates this view of Caesar in *The Art of War:*

> Pompey and Caesar and almost all the Roman generals after the last Carthaginian war gained fame [*fama*] as brave men but not as good ones, while those who lived before them gained fame [*gloria*] as brave and good. This came about because the latter did not take the waging of war for their profession. And while the republic continued without reproach, no great citizen [*cittadino grande*] ever presumed, by means of such an activity, to retain power in time of peace, so as to break the laws, plunder the provinces, usurp and tyrannize over his native land and in every way gain wealth for himself.[7] * * *

Here Caesar and Pompey, like Agathocles, gained fame but not glory, whereas subsequent Roman generals gained glory because they did not plunder, usurp, and tyrannize over their native land. *Glory,* then, is not simply a product of public relations. It seems instead to be an intrinsic quality of great deeds, although one that can be misrecognized or falsely attributed.

In his thinking about glory, Machiavelli was influenced in particular by the Roman historian Sallust, a favorite of an earlier generation of civic humanists, including Salutati and Bruni. As Patricia Osmond has argued, it was Sallust, "more than any other Roman historian,

7. Niccolò Machiavelli, *The Art of War,* in *The Chief Works and Others,* trans. Allan Gilbert (Durham: Duke University Press, 1989), 2:576–77.

who contributed to the [civic humanist] themes of *libertas, virtus,* and *gloria.*"[8] In the *Bellum Catilinae* 7.1–3, Sallust had linked the establishment of republican government in ancient Rome to the achievement of glorious deeds. * * * In addition, "Sallust's *Catilina* suggested a connection between a popular regime, territorial expansion, and imperial power" that Machiavelli would echo in the *Discourses.* Yet Sallust was also, like Machiavelli, acutely aware that republican rule could in time give way to faction, corruption, and tyranny.[9] It was in this context that he distinguished between true and false glory in *Catilina* 11: describing the rise of the Roman Republic to greatness, Sallust commented, "Ambition drove many men to become false: to have one thought locked in the breast, another ready on the tongue. . . . For the noble and the base alike long for glory [*gloriam*], honour, and power, but the former mount by the true path, whereas the latter, being destitute of noble qualities [*bonae artes*], rely on craft and deception."[1] Machiavelli, of course, did not share Sallust's moral scruples about the use of craft and deception in the realm of politics; but he did subscribe to the distinction between true and false glory.

This distinction between true and false glory inflects Sallust's representation of Caesar and Catiline, but not in the way one might at first think. Machiavelli famously remarks in *Discourses* 3.6 that "everyone has read Sallust's account of the conspiracy of Catiline."[2] His comment in *Discourses* 1.10 that criticizing Catiline might be an indirect way of criticizing Caesar suggests he read Sallust's condemnation of Catiline in this way:

> Lucius Catilina, scion of a noble family, had great vigour both of mind and body, but an evil and depraved nature. From youth up he reveled in civil wars, murder, pillage and political dissension, and amid these he spent his early manhood.[3]

Later, at *Catilina* 54, Sallust compares Caesar and Cato in a way that supports Machiavelli's hunch that the earlier criticism of Catiline could be read as a criticism of Caesar:

> In birth then, in years and in eloquence, they were about equal; in greatness of soul, they were evenly matched, and likewise in renown [*gloria*], although the renown of each was different.

8. Patricia Osmond, "Sallust and Machiavelli: From Civic Humanism to Political Prudence," *Journal of Medieval and Renaissance Studies* 23 (1993): 407–38.
9. Osmond, "Sallust and Machiavelli," 414–15; cf. *Bellum Catilinae* 7–9, in *Sallust,* trans. J. C. Rolfe (Cambridge, MA: Harvard University Press, 1965).
1. *Bellum Catilinae* 11.1, in *Sallust,* 19.
2. *Discourses* 3.6.
3. *Bellum Catilinae* 5.1.

> Caesar was held great [*magnus habebatur*] because of his benefactions and lavish generosity, Cato for the uprightness of his life. The former became famous for his gentleness and compassion, the austerity of the latter brought him prestige. Caesar gained glory [*gloriam*] by giving, helping, and forgiving; Cato by never stooping to bribery. . . . He preferred to be, rather than to seem virtuous; hence the less he sought fame [*gloriam*], the more it pursued him.[4]

Here Sallust indirectly suggests a criticism of Caesar in the guise of praising him. The ironic and asymmetrical contrast between Caesar who gained glory by giving and Cato by never stooping to bribery supports a distinction between true and false glory: Caesar was held great, but Cato achieved true glory. * * *

* * * As Benedetto Fontana has observed, in the *Florentine Histories* Machiavelli analyzed the role of faction and the pursuit of private interest in Florence in much the same way that Sallust did in *Catilina*. In doing so, he implicitly suggested that the Medici were dangerously similar to Catiline. Similarly, Machiavelli's "critique of late republican politics" in the *Discorsi* was "at the same time a critique of Florentine politics and history. The methods used by 'private men' in Rome [were] the very same methods used by the Medici to acquire and maintain their dominion over the Florentine state."[5] * * *

In addition to noting these historical parallels, Machiavelli must also have perceived the similarities between his own rhetorical task and Sallust's. Writing to Caesar at the height of his power, Sallust needed to negotiate a delicate political situation that was in some ways analogous to Machiavelli's own difficult position vis-à-vis the Medici. * * * Although Sallust clearly favored republican rule, he also sought as a client of Caesar to advise his "prince." His tack was to argue that Caesar should seek the glory associated with service to the fatherland, above and beyond the mere acquisition of power. In the "Letter to Caesar," Sallust implicitly cautions Caesar against following the example of the consul Lucius Domitius. In language that echoes his description of Catiline and seems to anticipate Machiavelli's description of Agathocles, he writes, "Has Lucius Domitius great strength? A man whose every member is stained with disgrace or crime, of lying tongue, blood-stained hands, fleeing feet, most dishonourable in those parts which cannot be honourably named."[6] Later, Sallust imagines Caesar being urged by his "patria"

4. *Bellum Catilinae* 54.1–6.
5. Benedetto Fontana, "Sallust and the Politics of Machiavelli," *History of Political Thought* 24 (2003): 106n71.
6. "Ad Caesarem Senem de re publica epistula," in *Sallust,* 479. The authorship of the letter is contested, but it is included in the Loeb edition of Sallust, and was thought to be by Sallust in the Renaissance.

and forefathers to pursue a greater glory than mere military conquest. * * * If Caesar restores Roman freedom, Sallust predicts, he will "tower above all men in glory as the savior of [his] country" (re publica restituta super omnis mortalis gloria agitabis).[7] * * * Although Machiavelli's view of Caesar was more critical than Sallust's, the relevance of this passage to Florentine politics was not lost on Machiavelli, who sought to persuade the Medici to serve their *patria* just as Sallust had sought to persuade Caesar.

For all these reasons, when Machiavelli says that Agathocles did not achieve glory, I am now inclined to accept what he says at face value. Machiavelli wants us to understand that there is a difference between power, which Agathocles incontrovertibly did achieve, and the reputation for glorious deeds, which he did not. And this is important because it helps us understand that Machiavelli sometimes uses "virtù" to refer to political success, while at other times he distinguishes between them. Virtù helps achieve success but does not guarantee success and so is not identical with it. And success in turn is not equivalent to the kind of virtù Machiavelli associates with glory. Agathocles had the virtù to achieve power, understood as success; he did not have the virtù attributed to the really great men, those who achieve glory. Not all kinds of virtù are the same, and some are better than others, not because they preclude "criminal" acts but because they rise to a Roman standard of greatness, the greatness of Roman founders and military commanders.[8]

What then do we make of the distinction, which I earlier argued was ironic, between Cesare Borgia and Agathocles? Machiavelli explicitly tells us that Cesare Borgia is an example of a prince who rose to power with the help of others, while Agathocles is an example of a prince who rose to power by crime (*per scelera*). One way to construe this distinction is that Agathocles was not as skillful as Borgia in managing his reputation. As we've seen, Borgia had his lieutenant Remirro de Orco murdered in the public square for his excessive cruelty to the people of the Romagna, even though (or precisely because) Remirro was only following the directions of Borgia. By contrast, while Agathocles was certainly capable of deception, he erred in not displacing responsibility for his violent acts onto his subordinates. As a result, he was himself blamed for his violent deeds, which others saw as criminal. This might suggest that the "glory" Agathocles failed to achieve is a manufactured glory, brought about by the public management of reputation. Contrary to what I just argued in the preceding paragraph, Machiavelli would then be treating glory ironically, as

7. Ibid., 491.
8. Claude Lefort, *Le travail de l'oeuvre: Machiavel* (Paris: Gallimard, 1972), 380, notes of this passage that virtù is not incompatible with crime but one also can't cover over crime with virtù.

the mere appearance of glory or as the fame that obscures responsibility for criminal acts. And yet I think that this still doesn't quite capture Machiavelli's judgment of Agathocles or, for that matter, Borgia. For Machiavelli also describes Borgia's achievements without attributing glory to them. In this sense, it remains true that the distinction between Borgia and Agathocles is a distinction without a difference. The crucial political difference between Borgia and Agathocles, one might then think, is not that Agathocles was criminal and Borgia was not. The difference is that Borgia came to power with the help of "the arms of others," while Agathocles seized power by himself. But even this difference is less crucial than it seems since, despite relying on the arms of others, Borgia's actions are exemplary for the new prince while Agathocles's manner of rising to power, although without the help of others, is subject to some censure.

Not surprisingly, critics have struggled to understand the example of Agathocles. Claude Lefort and Russell Price have both tried to make sense of Machiavelli's refusal to attribute glory to Agathocles by taking Machiavelli at his word. According to Lefort, Machiavelli first condemns Agathocles's extreme actions. Ultimately, however, Lefort argues, the example of Agathocles is designed to show the prince's reputation is dependent on the people. * * * Russell Price makes a similar argument. According to Price, Agathocles achieves military glory but, judging from Machiavelli's comments in the *Discourses,* he does not achieve political glory.[9]

I now think Lefort and Price are right to take Machiavelli's reservations about Agathocles seriously, but not for the reasons they propose. Contrary to Lefort, Machiavelli nowhere indicates that Agathocles—or any other new prince—needed justification to commit his violent actions. To put this another way, Agathocles's justification is simply his ambition. To crib from chapter 26 of *The Prince,* violence is "justified" when it is necessary and it's necessary to use violence if you want to gain power. * * * Similarly, Price's characterization of Agathocles as one who achieved military glory is refuted by the fact that Machiavelli attributes virtù but not glory to Agathocles. The distinction Machiavelli is making is not between military and political glory, but between military virtù and glory. This is important because it signals that virtù is not the same as glory. * * *

* * * Ultimately, I suggest, Machiavelli's rhetorical task is not only to instruct the prince how to hold on to his power but also how to let go of it. Agathocles illustrates one argument for ceding some power to one's subjects, which we might call the argument from greater longevity: Agathocles retained his position for his entire life

9. Russell Price, "The Theme of 'Gloria' in Machiavelli," *Renaissance Quarterly* 30 (1977): 628.

because he curbed his violent deeds and catered to the interests of his subjects. Machiavelli implicitly suggests the Medici might do so as well. But the more powerful argument is the one concerning glory, a term that is under erasure in chapter 8 but reappears conspicuously in chapter 26.

The choice that Machiavelli presents the Medici is not between Borgia and Agathocles but rather between the two of them and the glory achieved by the really excellent men. This is a choice between merely holding on to one's power or doing something really great for one's principality or one's country. In Sallust's terms, it is a choice between Caesar as he was and as he might have been. * * * Just as Sallust predicted that Caesar will "tower above all men in glory as the savior of [his] country," * * * adding that "it remains to implore the immortal gods that whatever you decide, the result may be propitious to you and to your country"; so Machiavelli urges the Medici not to be tyrants like Caesar and Agathocles but to achieve the greatness and glory which each, in their different ways, failed to do.

I want to return in conclusion to the question of metadiscourse in *The Prince,* to the ways in which Machiavelli reflects on what we might call his own Machiavellianism. In some ways, my revision of my earlier argument has amounted to saying there's a limit to Machiavelli's Machiavellianism, if by this we understand the purely pragmatic pursuit of power. As I've argued, Machiavelli was interested in making distinctions, not only between successful and unsuccessful princes, but between those who achieve glory and those who do not. This last distinction is not purely pragmatic, but it is also not conventionally moral, if by morality we understand either the Ciceronian ideal of *honestas* (the honorable) or a Christian idea of ethical behavior. Machiavelli had no problem with force and fraud, violence and deception, in the realm of politics. He was capable of admiring the great criminal, like Agathocles, who rose from his lowly position to demonstrate extraordinary military and political virtù. Precisely because of this, chapter 8 still constitutes a kind of test of the reader's judgment: on one level it distinguishes between Borgia and Agathocles; on another, it invites us to see that this is a distinction without a difference, at least as far as moral distinctions are concerned. Agathocles is no more criminal than Borgia; the important point is that neither achieved glory. Like his classical antecedents, then, Machiavelli did not confuse Agathocles's virtù or his remarkable career with the glory of the really excellent men. These are men whose glory results from founding, reestablishing, or furthering the greatness of a republic, whether in Rome or Florence. It was the prospect of this glory that Machiavelli held out to the Medici in the concluding chapter of *The Prince.*

ERICA BENNER

From Machiavelli's *Prince:* A New Reading†

* * * Machiavelli's book was first published posthumously in 1532. But Church and other political authorities soon came to view it as a major troublemaker. Its author was denounced to the Inquisition in 1550. When the Church instituted its Index of Prohibited Books in 1559, all Machiavelli's works—not just the *Prince*—were put on the list. * * *

What made this 'little work', the 'whimsy' of a disgraced Florentine civil servant, so threatening—and whom did it threaten most? The *Prince*'s early readers were sharply divided on these questions. Those loyal to the Papacy and Catholic monarchies were the first to denounce it as a godless handbook for tyrants. * * *

Readers with republican and anti-Papal sympathies thought the exact opposite. Behind its morality-subverting mask, they insisted, the *Prince*'s basic purposes were moral: it surreptitiously defended justice, virtue, and civility against the corrupt Popes and monarchs who were the real enemies of human decency. * * *

Five centuries later, many readers might think that these early disputes over the *Prince*'s morality or immorality and its stance toward tyranny missed the book's profounder message: that traditional distinctions between moral and immoral, tyranny and freedom cannot help us to address all the complex issues that arise in political life. On this now widespread view, the *Prince* teaches us—perhaps quite reasonably—that those in power have no choice but to relax their moral standards if they want to stay safe and secure their parties' or countries' interests in the real world. * * *

This book tries to bring some of those conflicts, examples, and categories back to life, so that we can better understand why some of the *Prince*'s most perceptive early readers—including many philosophers who, like Machiavelli, had great literary talents—saw it as a work aimed at restoring high moral standards in politics. Machiavelli's *Prince,* I suggest, is a masterwork of ironic writing with a moral purpose. On the one hand, it warns aspiring princes about the dangers of trying to assert absolute control over people who care about freedom. On the other, it teaches ordinary citizens to recognize early warning signs of control-hungry behaviour in their leaders, and to impress on them the need to establish political and military 'orders' (*ordini*) that can keep tyranny at bay. Machiavelli

† From the introduction to *Machiavelli's* Prince: *A New Reading* (Oxford: Oxford University Press, 2013), pp. xx–xxii, xxviii–xliii. Reprinted by permission of Oxford University Press. Notes are Benner's, with full bibliographical information supplied by the editor.

uses a range of ironic techniques to underscore the problematic character of many princely actions he seems to praise. At the same time, he uses irony to exercise readers' capacities to see through misleading political spin.

At the *Prince*'s core is a biting *critique* of both ruthless *realpolitik* and amoral pragmatism, not a revolutionary new defence of these positions. Far from eroding ancient contrasts between good and evil, just and unjust, or tyranny and freedom, Machiavelli's book shows readers the dire consequences that ensue when our language and practices fail clearly to distinguish them.

[After reviewing Machiavelli's life and placing it in the context of Florentine politics, Benner contends that throughout his life he was animated by a desire to improve his city's defenses and that as early as 1504, in a poem called the *Decennale* (Ten-Year Period), he attacked the self-destructive wars Italian city-states had been waging against one another. Furthermore, in many of his works, such as his great comedy, *La mandragola* (The Mandrake Root), he expressed his scorn for the arrogance of the powerful and criticized the corrupt nature of Florentine politics. Benner argues that the *Prince* was consistent with Machiavelli's other works, but only if we understand it as being profoundly ironic and if we believe that Machiavelli desperately desired to return to Florence and serve the Medici, perhaps motivated by the hope that by working inside the political order he could help to turn Florence into a genuine republic once again.]

* * *

* * * [A]ncient and humanist precepts considered it the duty of good men to help their cities by getting close to rulers—especially unjust or tyrannical ones—and doing whatever they could to influence their conduct for the better. In more oppressive times, they may only be able to restrain a ruler's excesses. But in the best case, they might persuade him to give up the tyranny or principality altogether, and voluntarily establish a republic. Machiavelli took a stab at the second, more radical kind of persuasion in 1520 when, after the death of the *Prince*'s eventual dedicatee Lorenzo II, he was among several known critics of the Medici who were asked to suggest improvements to the government. His response advises the Medici to give up their princely 'state' voluntarily, and suggests reforms that would take the city nearer to the form of a 'true republic'. The arguments are not idealistic. Machiavelli insists that it is in the Medicis' own interests to step down and give power back to 'the whole body of citizens' and their ancient laws. Otherwise their government would never be stable, and must soon turn toward full-blown tyranny or savage partisan warfare. Either way, Machiavelli implores

his addresses to 'imagine how many deaths, how many exiles, how many acts of extortion will result' if matters remain as they are.[1]

In 1513 Machiavelli was in no position to offer similar advice—at least not directly. Despite Vettori's efforts, the Medici cold-shouldered Machiavelli's appeals to give him a chance to prove his good faith and usefulness to his fatherland. But if he was barred from serving it through active politics and unable freely to discuss his ideas for reform, he found indirect ways to express his political views when it was risky to state them outright. In his years of diplomacy and intelligence gathering, Machiavelli had become adept as a writer of coded and semi-cryptic dispatches. In private letters too, he often speaks of being constrained to convey messages by dropping hints or 'signs' (*cenni*) between the lines of innocently chatty text, due to the sensitive content of some exchanges. * * *

What kind of book is the *Prince?* In outward appearance, it resembles other 'mirrors for princes' (*specula principum*), a type of work common in the Middle Ages and Renaissance, with roots in ancient times.[2] These books sought to teach rulers how to do their job in an effective and just manner. They were typically dedicated to younger, less experienced rulers by older men who offered the benefit of their practical or philosophical wisdom. The manner of their teaching could be more or less direct. More direct ones took the form of handbooks that present straightforward rules or maxims, interspersed with examples from ancient history. * * *

Other 'mirrors for princes' were historical and literary works that taught similar lessons indirectly, by presenting images of rulers to be imitated—or avoided. In such works, the author keeps a lower profile than in openly didactic handbooks. Instead of making straightforward judgements about better and worse methods of rule, he offers a complex portrait of a ruler's life and deeds, and invites readers to evaluate them for themselves. Perhaps the greatest work of this type is Xenophon's *Cyropaedia,* meaning 'The Education of Cyrus'. Along with Virgil, Xenophon is one of only two writers whom Machiavelli names in the *Prince,* and the *Cyropaedia* is the only book he names. His manifest interest in that work when writing the *Prince* and later the *Discourses,* where he refers six times to the *Cyropaedia*—more than to any other work except Livy's histories—suggests an essential starting-point, though a challenging one, for

1. Niccolò Machiavelli, *A Discourse on Remodelling the Government of Florence,* in *The Chief Works and Others,* trans. and ed. Allan Gilbert, 3 vols. (Durham, NC: Duke University Press, 1989), 115.
2. For a comparison of the similarities and differences between the *Prince* and other "mirrors for princes" that differs from my interpretation, see Quentin Skinner, *The Foundations of Modern Political Thought,* vol. 1: *The Renaissance* (Cambridge: Cambridge University Press, 1978), 113–38.

readers who seek to understand Machiavelli's message and puzzling methods of writing.

There is one very notable difference between the *Prince* and more conventional 'mirrors for princes' composed nearer to Machiavelli's own times. These sought to teach rulers how to be good monarchs, which meant above all how to avoid doing whatever leads to tyranny. The opposition between good monarchy and bad tyranny lies at their core. Machiavelli's little book seems to dispense with this opposition. The words 'tyrant' and 'tyranny' are altogether absent, an extraordinary omission in a book that appears to have the same educative purposes as other handbooks. Moreover, the *Prince* seems to recommend the most notorious methods and aims that had been associated with tyranny since ancient times. * * *

Does Machiavelli's work thereby break with all traditional political morality, ancient as well as modern? This view gained a wide currency in the twentieth century. But the idea that the *Prince*'s teachings are uniquely 'modern' is a rather recent construction, which appears convincing only if we take the book's morality-subverting assertions at face value. There are very good reasons, however, not to do so.

The word 'irony' comes from the Greek *eirôneia,* meaning dissimulation or feigned ignorance. An ironic statement or work appears to say one thing while conveying another meaning. The presence of irony is signalled by a tension between explicit statements or appearances and quite different, unstated implications of what the ironist presents. * * * Irony is especially suited for political criticism in conditions where it is dangerous for writers to express their views openly. Ironic techniques play down or mask, but seldom completely hide, a writer's critical views of a subject: they use various clues or signals to alert readers to judgements that differ from those made explicitly.

Irony may have constructive as well as critical aims. Ancient writers such as Xenophon, Virgil, Tacitus, and Plutarch used ironic dissimulation as a tool of moral and political education. Its aim was to train readers to distinguish mere appearances of virtue or wisdom from qualities that deserve those names. This philosophical exercise had important practical uses. By reading works that imitate the specious rhetoric and appearances encountered in public life, people learn how these phenomena are generated, and become better equipped to avoid harmful policies or traps set for them by ambitious leaders. * * *

* * *

Why suspect that the *Prince* is a thoroughly ironic work? Discrepancies between the overtly prince-friendly *Prince* and the *Discourses'* clear preference for republics are one ground for this suspicion. The discrepancies are still greater on a careful reading of the *Florentine Histories.* Before and after he wrote the *Prince,* Machiavelli was critical of the methods used by 'new' princes, including the Medici, to make themselves rulers over their own or others' cities. The main theme of his early poems—the *Decennale, Di Fortuna* and *Dell' Ambizione*—is how the unscrupulous methods and ambitions of power-hungry popes, new princes, and *stati* were ruining Italy; while his 1520 *Discursus* directly urges the Medici to restore a *vera repubblica* in Florence or face inevitable disaster. It is hard to believe that the same author whose early and late writings treat the phenomenon of self-aggrandizing, unprincipled new princes as a lethal civil disease would—in a bout of opportunistic job-seeking—purport to teach the same princes how to succeed in their business.

Secondly, the *Prince*'s often shocking content raises the question of whether Machiavelli could reasonably have expected political and Church authorities in his time to welcome his little work. How did he expect the Medici and other ecclesiastical 'princes'—so eager to cast themselves as legitimate champions of order, justice, and religion—to respond to his audacious suggestions that they should assassinate their rivals, break their oaths, and launch offensive wars without any pressing necessity? * * *

The *Prince*'s use of ancient examples raises further suspicions. Most modern readers see nothing problematic in Machiavelli's advice to imitate the Roman Empire's ceaseless struggles for ever-greater 'greatness'; or to pursue grandiose ambitions on the pattern of Theseus, Romulus, or Cyrus; or to use hunting as practice for war. But anyone who consults the *Prince*'s main ancient sources—Xenophon, Sallust, Polybius, Livy, and Plutarch—must be deeply puzzled, since they treat these themes in far more critical ways than Machiavelli appears to do. In some cases, his overt judgements of ancient figures clash so violently with those of his favourite authors that one cannot help but suspect irony. Perhaps not every reader in Machiavelli's times would have read enough Polybius or Livy to realize that the *Prince*'s praise of the despicable and buffoonish Philip V, king of Macedon, was as improbable as its praise of Borgia. But a reader with even a little humanist education would surely have wondered whether, by urging modern princes to imitate the 'criminal' emperor Severus—as Machiavelli calls him in the *Discourses*—the author was being ironic. It is sometimes suggested that he sought to subvert all ancient judgements. A more likely purpose was to expose the corrupt thinking of princes in his 'times', when judgements were so perverted that the actions of devious and violent ancient rulers were widely imitated and admired.

But the best reasons to suspect that the *Prince* is ironic can be found in the style and content of the text itself. * * * Overtones of bold certainty are mingled with doubtful, nervous, or ominous undertones, followed by long discussions of the difficulties—or impossibilities—of ever attaining the goals set out with such confidence. When such problems appear in Machiavelli's masterfully controlled writing, readers who appreciate his logical rigour and literary gifts may reasonably suspect the presence of irony.

As for content, there are serious problems of coherence among the *Prince*'s most general standards. If we try to identify a few basic criteria for evaluating the book's numerous maxims and examples, a text that at first blush seems to present its author's straightforward judgements soon starts to look slippery. Machiavelli, as everyone thinks they know, held that the 'ends justify the means'. But what, in the *Prince,* are the appropriate ends of prudent action? At times the personal greatness, reputation, and survival of the prince himself are all that seem to matter for Machiavelli. At other times, he implies that a prince's desires for power can only be satisfied if he gives priority to the stability, security, and well-being of the 'generality of people' (*universalità*) over his private ambitions. Nor do these two ends always converge in the *Prince.* In chapter 19, for example, one of the two 'happiest' Roman emperors, Severus, achieves great personal power and security by oppressing the people. On the other hand, chapter 12 suggests that princes are strongest who put military commands—including the prince's own command—under strict civilian and legal controls.

In chapters 3 and 4, again, Machiavelli describes—and seems to commend—republican Rome's ambition to dominate the 'free' province of Greece, although he also states that there was no pressing necessity for the conquest. Then in chapter 5 he sets out compelling reasons to respect people's desires to live in freedom from foreign occupation, and warns princes that they must face recurrent violent resistance if they remove that freedom. It is hard to see how Machiavelli, or anyone else, can give equal weight to both these ends—nonnecessary conquest for the sake of maximizing power on the one hand, desires for freedom on the other. And it seems inconsistent that the same book teaches princes and empires how to seize power, even 'absolute' power, over peoples who value self-government. Here and in other instances, the *Prince*'s morally flexible 'Machiavellian' precepts appear to contradict the book's strongest, most consistently developed arguments. * * * But there are, in fact, fiercely critical undertones in Machiavelli's discussions of Rome's imperial ambitions. In the *Discourses* he says that expansion became 'pernicious' to republican Rome during and after the wars with

Carthage and Greece, shows the terrible costs of the city's penchant for constant military expansion, and says point-blank that Rome's imperial overreaching destroyed the republic's cherished liberty and security. * * *

Machiavelli's basic standards become still harder to define when we ask what he considers the most effective means for pursuing princely ends. There is a deep, recurring tension between two 'modes' of action discussed throughout the *Prince*. One is associated with steadiness and trust, the other with changeability and deceptive appearances. * * * Chapter 18 tells princes to break faith when this gives them an edge over rivals, or helps them rise to greatness. Yet in chapter 21 and before, Machiavelli says that it is *always* best to make and keep firm commitments to subjects and allies—even if this sometimes puts the prince on the losing side, and seriously limits what he can do to increase his own power. * * *

There are several easy solutions to the *Prince*'s apparent contradictions. The easiest is to say that they were inadvertent, products of a not very systematic mind or the author's volatile 'passions'. Such accounts will seem implausible to anyone who detects the logical structure, powers of clear judgement, and artistic care that permeate the *Prince*. Another solution sees Machiavelli's inconsistencies as a deliberate expression of scepticism, intended to unsettle readers' received notions of truth and reflect a world where no stable judgements are possible. Sceptical readings are superficially plausible given Machiavelli's highly ambiguous style of discussion. Nonetheless, I find them hard to accept. The *Prince* and all Machiavelli's main writings appeal constantly to stable standards of truth against falsehoods and misleading appearances, and to reasonable judgements against unreasonable opinions. * * *

Among contemporary scholars, perhaps the most favoured solution treats the *Prince*'s inconsistencies as merely apparent: Machiavelli's different political standards are relative to circumstances. * * * At times one should work steadily and cautiously to forestall fortune's downturns, at other times strike and beat her; sometimes break faith, but also know how to glean the benefits of others' trust in your fidelity.

If one looks for a general statement of this circumstance-relative position in the *Prince*, the best candidate is the claim made near the end of chapter 18 that a prince 'needs to have a spirit disposed to change as the winds of fortune and variations [*variazione*] of things command him'. This claim is echoed in chapter 25, where we read that if one 'would change his nature with the times and with affairs, his fortune would not change'. If variability is Machiavelli's overarching criterion of political *virtù,* while careful ordering or stability or freedom are appropriate aims of *virtù* only in some conditions, then many of the *Prince*'s apparent inconsistencies can be explained away.

But if we follow the order of the *Prince*'s text and pay close attention to its language, we find many reasons to doubt that the ability to change one's 'spirit' or one's nature is part of *virtù* at all. Firstly, Machiavelli first commends this ability—or seems to commend it—very late in the book. Before chapter 18, the ability to order and command one's own forces regardless of fortune's 'variations' looked like the height of *virtù* in the *Prince*. The book's main practical proposals call for a *virtù* that builds firm orders to 'govern' (*governare*) fortune. * * *

Secondly, even in chapter 18 and later, Machiavelli does not identify *virtù* with the ability to change at fortune's command. On the contrary, he frequently underscores the deficiencies of those who allow fortune to blow them hither and thither. * * *

Thirdly, just after declaring that men should change their modes with the 'times' in chapter 25, Machiavelli turns around and says that this kind of versatility is well-nigh impossible. * * *

A central argument of this book is that in the basic antithesis between *fortuna* and *virtù,* Machiavelli offers a solution to his own inconsistencies. Early on in the *Prince,* he sets out a general, reflective standard that serves as a touchstone for evaluating the book's particular precepts and examples: namely, that it is better to acquire and hold power by means of one's own *virtù* than by fortune and others' arms. I argue that he uses the antithesis to signal indirect judgements about the prudence and praiseworthiness of actions or maxims. When he stresses the role played by fortune in an agent's actions, however successful, he implies some deficiency in the quality of those actions, even when they are mixed with *virtù*—and even when he lavishes words of praise on them. For fortune and *virtù* are not equally efficacious 'modes' of action, depending on circumstances. Machiavelli maintains that it is *always* better to rely on *virtù* than on fortune, both in principalities or republics, and in corrupt or virtuous political conditions. Some 'modes' of ordering human relations always tend to bring stability and safety, while others always tend toward their opposites. This, I'll suggest, should be our standard for judging the inconsistent policies discussed in the *Prince,* not particular conditions.

Some kinds of *virtù,* moreover, are more conducive to stability and safety than others. What Machiavelli calls '*virtù* of spirit' (*di animo*) is especially effective for acquiring power, winning battles, or making conquests. But his exemplars of exceedingly bold and spirited *virtù* tend to be less skilled at maintaining political power, or at founding a secure legacy for future generations. Since the *virtù* of great captains and conquerors is insufficient for great statesmanship, leaders who fail to develop the political and intellectual virtues needed to maintain what they acquire turn by default to fortune—hoping that something other than their own abilities might prop them up.

Machiavelli's *fortuna-virtù* antithesis is not freestanding. It forms the basis for a patterned, normatively coded language that signals Machiavelli's reflective judgements throughout the *Prince,* and is developed further in his later works. Some words, that is, always have a positive sense associated with *virtù,* while others are always associated with *fortuna* and its destabilizing, *virtù*-corroding effects. * * *

The entire *Prince,* I'll suggest, can be read as a series of confrontations between two kinds of prince, or two 'modes' of princely action: one that depends on *virtù* and 'one's own arms', the other on fortune and 'the arms of others'. If we assume that these 'modes' can be fruitfully combined, or that in some circumstances princes need to rely on fortune more than on *virtù,* we may overlook Machiavelli's subtle criticisms of *any* policy that depends on the advantages he identifies with fortune. * * *

* * *

If the *Prince*'s underlying judgements are decent and moral rather than subversive of traditional moral standards, some might ask, why would Machiavelli have thought he needed to dissimulate through irony? I see three main reasons.

One was defensive: to protect the author of a text that hints very strongly at the hypocrisy of the new Medici authorities—whose dynastic and princely behaviour contradicted their official status as mere 'first citizens' in a free republic, recalling similar hypocrisy in the early Roman *principes*—and at gross corruption in the Church, now headed by a Medici Pope. * * *

A second reason was diplomatic circumspection when seeking to change readers' political judgements. Machiavelli's aim was not just to mock political and religious authorities. The *Prince* also seeks to induce rulers, and their supporters among the people, to recognize their errors and turn toward better forms of government. * * *

A third reason is perhaps the most important, and least often recognized. Like the ancient works it refers to, the *Prince* has an educative and philosophical purpose: to train readers to discriminate between apparent and genuine political prudence. * * * It is essential that they do this decoding for themselves, since it exercises their powers of critical observation. By mimicking the sophistries that abound in political life, the *Prince* induces readers to reflect on what's wrong with these persuasions, and thus arm themselves against their seductions.

Though formally addressed to a prince, the *Prince* speaks to ordinary citizens as well as men aspiring to political greatness. For Machiavelli as for his ancients, the ultimate source of political disorders—including tyranny of one man or empire—is not ambitious individuals *per se,* but the failure of peoples to recognize the signs of danger and causes of disorders before they grow virulent. In his own times, many Italians who had long lived in free republics eagerly embraced new self-styled princes who they hoped would help them win partisan battles or make great conquests for their cities. Having welcomed these men 'in the belief that they will fare better', they found that they were deceived; in fact 'they have done worse', and were now more servile, beaten, and despoiled than before. * * * The best way to teach human beings how to avoid evils is to show how they themselves produce them, often under self-deceptions about their own shrewdness or virtue. While seeming to advise princes to disregard moral principles, the *Prince* uses irony to show peoples how to defend themselves from their own bad judgements.

In stressing the *Prince*'s educative aims, my argument differs from those of several other scholars who have recognized the work's *sotto voce* criticisms of Medici government. In an important 1986 article, for example, Mary Dietz argued that Machiavelli's purposes in the *Prince* were covertly republican, and that he wanted the Medici to give up their pre-eminent power in Florence.[3] I agree with Dietz on these points, and with her view that the *Prince*'s ironies not only mock the Medici but seek to reveal 'certain truths about princely power' that might help republicans to reconstitute a stronger government in future. But I disagree that the *Prince* is 'an act of deception' aimed at luring a gullible prince into following the book's advice, 'and thereby take actions that will jeopardize his power and bring about his demise'. My reading is closer to that of John Langton, who published a thoughtful response to Dietz's article in the same journal, arguing that the *Prince* seeks to teach princes how to convert their quasi-monarchies into republics.[4]

More than either of these arguments, however, I am interested in the *Prince*'s teachings for citizens as well as those for princes; and in its invitation to moral and philosophical reflectiveness, which goes far deeper than espousing a republican message versus princely politics. What are the qualities of a truly praiseworthy statesman? Can amoral means serve good ends? Does security depend on justice?

3. Mary Dietz, "Trapping the Prince: Machiavelli and the Politics of Deception," *American Political Science Review* 80 (1986): 777–99.
4. John Langton, "Machiavelli's Paradox: Trapping or Teaching the Prince," *American Political Science Review* 81 (1987): 1277–88.

Why bother to work hard at building and maintaining free political orders if fortune and fate control much in human affairs? What are the limits of any ruler's, state's, or empire's control over subjects? The *Prince* invites readers to consider these questions from many, often unexpected angles.

Machiavelli's 'little work', then, is not a treatise setting out the author's wisdom to be imbibed second-hand by uncritical readers. It is a series of highly provocative, mind-teasing conversations with the young, the impetuous, and men in power that seeks to improve their powers of political judgement. Machiavelli refers to the discussions in several of the *Prince*'s chapters as 'discourses' (*discorsi*). The word suggests that they are structured as conversations with readers, not as lectures delivered from an authorial pedestal. * * * In the *Prince,* the impression of shifting voices or *personae* is created by a range of devices: shifting pronouns (sometimes 'he', sometimes 'you' for princes), hesitations and doubts following sweepingly assured claims, contrasts between cynical and moderate tones, or between misanthropic and philanthropic assertions in the same chapter.

In content, lectures put forward carefully worked out reasons and conclusions in the voice of a single author who has thought them through. Like a dialogue, a discourse typically offers weakly reasoned but boldly asserted opinions, bringing their flaws to light as discussion progresses. The flawed opinions, however, are not necessarily renounced. The task of assessing them is left to readers, as part of the education in independent judgement that is a basic purpose of dialogical or multi-vocal writing.

What readers take from discourses depends on their own aims and dispositions. Aspiring princes in a hurry to gain power are likely to read quickly, scouring the text for nuggets of second-hand wisdom that they can apply directly to their enterprises. Since their aim is to achieve greatness and glory, they will seize on the most impressive-sounding phrases and examples, not pausing to notice subtle warnings or advice that they might be better off working through more modestly virtuous 'modes'.

As with princes, so with lay readers: those who read the *Prince* in hopes of finding a quick-fix, uncomplicated message may pick out the boldest statements and not trouble themselves too much with the caveats. If they find the amoral advice profound or intriguing, they will be disinclined to notice the subtle ways in which Machiavelli subverts it, and ignore the quietly prudent advice woven into other levels of the text. By contrast, readers who avoid falling into the snares laid by the *Prince*'s web-like writing will recognize puzzles that challenge them to think hard about what they read. If they recognize the superior logical power and practical prudence of the moderate arguments, they will be more inclined to resist the pull of the shocking ones, and work harder to decipher the underlying message. The *Prince* tests readers by moving constantly between the perspective of an impetuous, over-ambitious young man—one seeking the quickest and easiest ways to acquire power, with fortune's help—and judgements more likely to give a state firm foundations.

* * *

GABRIELE PEDULLÀ

In his lengthy introduction to a new Italian edition of *The Prince* with a facing translation in modern Italian, Pedullà sets the scene for the writing of *The Prince* and presents the work as a rhetorical move on Machiavelli's part designed to persuade the Medici to allow him back into Florence and the political life of the city. This fact does not mean that Machiavelli had turned into a Medici partisan or had come to see princely rule as an ideal. Indeed, when Machiavelli criticizes those new princes who obtained their realms by using the arms of others and allied themselves with the local aristocracy rather than the people, he is implicitly criticizing the very tactics employed by the Medici. For Pedullà, Machiavelli was emphasizing the same things in *The Prince* that he did in the *Discourses:* the importance of a citizen army, the mistake involved in making alliances with the nobility, and the creation of an ideal Italian city-state that would drive the "barbarians"—i.e., the French and the Spanish—out of Italy. To understand *The Prince,* Pedullà says we should start with works published by Felix Gilbert and Allan Gilbert in 1938, both of whom saw Machiavelli's treatise as belonging to a specific genre of political writing, the *speculum principis,* the "Mirror for Princes." Widely popular in the Middle Ages and the Renaissance, this genre was cultivated by fifteenth- and sixteenth-century humanists and included books of advice as well as educational manuals for princes, all of which emphasized that to become good rulers princes needed to be taught and to act on the traditional virtues, both pagan and Christian. Faced with the problem that he had not been asked by the Medici to supply them with suggestions about how to rule, Machiavelli solved it, according to Pedullà, by cleverly smuggling his very untraditional advice to them inside a work in this humanist genre, advice that amounted to a warning that the Medici were living through a perpetual state of emergency in the peninsula and that if they were to survive, it was imperative for them to ignore, when necessary, the traditional principles espoused by the humanists.

[Machiavelli's Mirror for Princes and the Art of Tying Knots]†

It is especially in this lack of confidence with regard to a pedagogy based on letters, a pedagogy so typical of the humanists' political thought, that one can perceive what is different about *The Prince*. It is not a matter of the clash between realism and idealism, as people have often said, but of two alternative educational models; or, if you wish, between the ideal of a prince who is completely "humanized" by his daily training in the *studia humanitatis*,[1] and the ideal of a new prince who is an opportunist—in other words, someone who is capable of cultivating the traditional virtues, but also of imitating, in a pinch, the arts of the lion and the fox. * * *

Modern readers spontaneously interpret the opposition between man and animal [in the figure of Chiron] in terms of the alternatives of reason and instinct. Such a reading shows itself to be, at the least, problematic, and not just because in *The Prince* the animalistic arts are as much those of the lion as those of the clever fox. Machiavelli is not telling us that his prince must become a *beast*, but that he must "know how to make use of the beast and the human," learning how to excel in two types of conflicts that are quite different from one another. * * *

Machiavelli is not, in fact, rejecting the teachings of the humanists, but rather limiting himself to pointing out their inadequacy. To have a man reach his full potential as a man by studying literature and philosophy is surely a praiseworthy, useful activity even for a prince, who will be able to learn numerous lessons for the present from the old stories. * * * At the same time, however, such a training regime is not sufficient, and this is the point at which he completely breaks away from the pedagogical program of the fifteenth century. In the eyes of the humanists a man, and even more so, a prince who would be worthy of the name, must be reborn through a life-giving contact with the *humanitates*, but for Machiavelli his virtues as a political being are not exhausted by those he has as a man.

It is futile to deceive oneself: the political field is simply larger. This is what Machiavelli says when he introduces his discussion of Chiron by means of a brilliant, gemlike sentence, essentially a translation of Cicero's *De officiis* (1.11.34), for which his contemporaries did not need any further clarification, but whose subtexts we run the risk of

† From "L'arte fiorentina dei nodi," in Niccolò Machiavelli, *Il principe, Edizione del cinquecentennale, con traduzione a fronte in italiano moderno di Carmine Donzelli, Introduzione e commento di Gabriele Pedullà* (Rome: Donzelli Editore, 2013), pp. xi–civ. Translated and annotated by the editor of this Norton Critical Edition. Reprinted by permission of Verso Books UK. A complete translation of Pedullà's work is forthcoming from Verso Books.

1. I.e., the liberal arts.

not understanding: "You should therefore understand that there are two ways of fighting: one by means of the laws, the other by means of force. The first is proper to man; the second, to animals. But because the first often does not suffice, one must have recourse to the second" (*The Prince,* 18). Interpreters have often ascribed a trivial meaning to these words, as if with that "often does not suffice" Machiavelli was telling us something like "when you cannot win in the proper manner, do not worry about playing dirty, of imposing yourself on others by means of force and, if it is actually necessary, of cheating."

In Cicero the description of these two models of combat serves to reaffirm the principles of *humanitas* and to recommend, for example, clemency toward one's defeated enemies. * * * Starting from the same point, Machiavelli reaches very different conclusions. From his viewpoint, in fact, the second "method of fighting" actually requires that before all else, princes should have qualities that are completely different from, if not actually the opposite of, those recommended by the humanists: cunning, an ability to fake things, ferocity, pitilessness. * * *

Precisely because diplomacy, including the martial diplomacy of fifteenth-century conflicts, does not exhaust all the forms that conflicts could take, humanist pedagogy is deficient when it continually refuses to open itself up to the arts of the lion and the fox. In fact, Machiavelli teaches us that from the moment when we cannot know in advance on what terrain we will be summoned to confront our enemy, it is thus essential to prepare ourselves for both types of conflicts. It is essential, that is, to practice different techniques, and "if we can, not to depart from the good, but if necessary, to know how to adopt that which is evil" (*The Prince,* 18). It is precisely that hard lesson which the great masters of humanism, terrified by the bestial component of politics, refused to impart to their pupils, thus condemning them to ruin. * * *

Along with the disappearance of sections [in *The Prince*] that are specifically pedagogical and humanist, all the first readers of Machiavelli should have noticed another absence, perhaps even more disconcerting from their viewpoint: that of the tyrant. If in classical as well as medieval and humanist political theory the figure of the despot had occupied a central position as the photographic negative of the good ruler, in the pages of *The Prince* the word does not actually appear even once. An absence of that sort could not pass by unnoticed. * * *

[Pedullà writes that from the ancient world up through the Renaissance, jurists worked at establishing a clear definition of the tyrant. One of the greatest medieval legal scholars, Bartolo di Sassoferrato (1313/1314–1357), identified two general principles for defining the tyrant. The first one was that he was recognized as such by a higher authority, such as the Holy Roman Empire or the Church. The second was more complicated: it involved what the tyrant did in order to stay in power, such as murdering distinguished citizens and impoverishing the populace, so that even if he had a secure title, he could still be considered a despot. Bartolo and other jurists thus provided Machiavelli's contemporaries a secure position from which to make judgments about good rulers and tyrants.]

In this context, where the word tyrant does not merely refer generically to a violent and egotistical method of ruling, but possesses a precise, technical meaning (as it did in the *specula* of the humanists), one may account for the dismay experienced by Machiavelli's first readers when they confronted the absence of the word in *The Prince*. Not only does Machiavelli avoid calling some of the most famous Greek despots by the title that ancient sources attributed to them (to be precise, *tyrannus*), but in his treatise he seems to want to take the illegal situation in which every lord lacking some sort of formal recognition found himself and to hide it by using a blatant euphemism, like that of "new prince." * * * Machiavelli's choice thus sounds like a deliberate provocation. What, in fact, were most of the "new princes" which his little work discusses if not manifest tyrants "ex defectu titulo,"[2] always the easiest to condemn using the instruments provided by Bartolo's semiotics? By never pronouncing the decisive word, the only one capable of triggering condemnation and, one would hope, punishment, Machiavelli actually seemed to want to help usurpers erase the traces of the oppression from which their power was originally derived.

What was even more serious is that it must have seemed as though Machiavelli accepted behavior traditionally associated with wicked rulers: a parsimony bordering on avarice (*The Prince*, 16), refusing to exercise clemency (17), having recourse to deceit (18). But there is something still worse. If Machiavelli, in fact, recommends only one of the *cautelae tyrannicae*[3] on Bartolo's list—that of getting rid of eminent figures who could threaten the "state" of the "new prince"—his inviting the prince to rely on fear rather than the gratitude of his subjects could make one suspect that there would be a rapid and uncontrolled proliferation of emergency measures against everyone opposed to him (17). When added together, the disappearance of the term *tyrannus* used to describe Hieron, Agathocles, and Nabith, plus the euphemism of an expression such as "new prince," it was easy to imagine that the taking of such positions would have

2. The phrase means that such a prince lacked any formal recognition from higher authorities of his "title"—that is, his legal right to rule.
3. The precautions of tyrants.

been part of a unique project designed to shelter even the worst rulers from the legal machinery based on evidence that had been designed by the jurists.

This question is particularly important because for something like three centuries Machiavelli's fate was going to be determined almost entirely on this basis: the disappearance of the tyrant. People must have been struck by Machiavelli's stubborn refusal, throughout the entire length of his treatise, to utter that small, but decisive, word, even with regard to princes such as Agathocles and Oliverotto, whom he explicitly pointed out for condemnation by his readers. * * *

Machiavelli's adversaries are in error with regard to the meaning and the limits of the criticism to which *The Prince* subjects previous theorizing. The two problems are obviously interrelated, but we should begin with the second, the question of limits. The anti-Machiavellians criticized *The Prince* for being an indiscriminate defense of tyranny. If it is necessary, however, to review these judgments and to open a grand appeals process, that does not imply at all that Machiavelli does not make a distinction of some type and that all his princes are to be considered the same. * * * Chapter 8 is especially crucial. If the word *tyrant* is never uttered, Machiavelli does introduce another distinction in this chapter, with regard to Oliverotto da Fermo and Agathocles, that between "virtuous" (*virtuosi*) and evil princes. * * * The very singular nature of Chapter 8 within the structure of *The Prince* should persuade us to devote particular attention [to that fact] as we consider it: while the other four types of "new princes" were, in fact, identified by means of the roles that virtue (*virtù*) and fortune played in their acquisition of power, only at this point does Machiavelli introduce a different criterion whose nature is purely moral. The reason for this anomaly is clear: after having reviewed two much-discussed figures such as Hieron and Cesare Borgia, Machiavelli goes out of his way to introduce, using the category of the "wicked," two other condottieri who, considering the times and places in which they were active (as well as some of the things they did), look extraordinarily like the first two, but who, by contrast, do not deserve to be placed among the virtuous (*virtuosi*) or those aided by fortune who sought to redeem themselves from their initial piece of good luck. * * *

The subsequent reception of *The Prince* would show that Machiavelli had had good reason to worry, but that he had not been sufficiently explicit in defining his position, or, more likely, that the scandal involved in having set up Hieron, Nabith, and Borgia among his positive models had by that point so impressed readers that those figures overshadowed all the rest. Still, *The Prince* is certainly not reticent on such matters. On the contrary, precisely because it would be easy to get confused in the case of figures such as Agathocles and Oliverotto, their condemnation leaves no room for uncertainty. * * *

Machiavelli's strategy becomes clearer if we think about the occasion that led him to draft his little work and thus about its recipient. Machiavelli is in the process of persuading Lorenzo to take exceptional measures against the Florentine aristocracy, and to achieve this goal, Machiavelli must first convince him that certain actions traditionally attributed to tyrants are, on the contrary, indispensable for "new princes," but do not transform them into despots when they have recourse to them. And in order to make this point completely clear, Machiavelli really needs Agathocles and Oliverotto, and he also needs to have both of them resemble Hieron and Borgia sufficiently so that he can fully clarify for his readers the enormous difference that exists between them, despite the fact that both groups have done things that in general would have been sufficient to get them branded publicly as manifest tyrants. * * *

Despite his violent deeds, his betrayals, and his reputation for wickedness, the example of Cesare Borgia is so important in *The Prince* precisely because Machiavelli finds himself forced to recognize the unquestionable successes of Borgia's political project and, above all, the enormous benefits that the population of the Romagna had derived from the annihilation of their little local lords. * * * Bartolo would not have had any doubt about the way that a man with Borgia's history would have to have been judged, and the same goes for jurists in the first years of the sixteenth century. Machiavelli seeks, instead, to instill in his own readers a suspicion that things are not so simple. According to Renaissance law, the four characters mentioned in chapters 6, 7, and 8 of *The Prince*—the Sicilian tyrants Agathocles and Hieron as well as the tyrants of the Romagna, Oliverotto da Fermo and Cesare Borgia—all belonged to the same execrable family. But was it really right to consider them equals, or would it not have been more accurate, instead, to conclude, when all is said and done, that the type Agathocles-Oliverotto shares very little with the type Hieron-Borgia?

We know Machiavelli's answer already. To incline toward the second hypothesis, as *The Prince* does, means, however, to call into question Bartolo's entire project. Machiavelli's reasoning is clear: if special political circumstances oblige men to act in ways that, taken individually, can also appear (and often are) rather questionable, the meaning of these actions remains incomprehensible until we place them in a larger context. * * *

It is on the basis of Machiavelli's insistence that we not lose sight of the entire sequence [of the Prince's actions] that nineteenth-century readers attributed to him the maxim that "the end justifies the means," a phrase the Florentine had never uttered. * * * In reality, in *The Prince*, the final result, more than justifying the means, has, if anything, the power to make us understand retrospectively who it is that we have had there before us: whether it is a vulgar tyrant, or a prince who is obliged to have recourse to "strong medicine" for the good of his own subjects; whether it is Agathocles or Hieron, Oliverotto or Borgia. * * *

There are two rules above all that Machiavelli preserves [from the *Speculum* tradition] without any qualification. They are: to imitate princes who pursue the *bonum commune*[4] and not just their private interests (as is amply documented); and to avoid common vices, because such defects, beyond generating feelings of hatred toward them, would render them contemptible and would quickly deprive them of the *maiestas* that is indispensable in a leader. And so, if we go and examine things case by case, we will easily come to the conclusion that yet again Machiavelli's originality translates into a rethinking of boundaries, not their disappearance. Except for liberality, clemency, and fidelity, for which it may be necessary to break the rules at times in exceptional situations, Machiavelli approves of all the other traditional virtues and prescribes them for his "new prince." * * *

So, how to interpret the disappearance of the tyrant? Precisely because Machiavelli never asserted that the end (understood as the outcome) justifies the means, it is an error to attribute to him the idea that what one has done yesterday or today should be excused by the presumed advantages of tomorrow. Rather, Machiavelli displays an extraordinary awareness that the different components that form this figure will only be comprehensible at the end. * * *

With Machiavelli there is an affirmation of a "gray" politics, in which the true identity of the good prince and the bad prince is known only to a handful of wise men capable of going beyond appearances. Even they, however, will always be forced from that moment on to ask themselves repeatedly in which field their own favorites are playing. Are those favorites thinking only of their own interests? Is their invocation of necessity just an alibi? Or are they, instead, actually fighting for the good of the citizenry, and is it with that end in sight that they have lowered themselves to perform acts that they would otherwise find repugnant? In the modern world, politics—if that term still makes sense today—shares this same condition of radical uncertainty. Because of it, every time we fail to understand something hidden behind one of the many masks that power wears—for the great reformer and the bloody despot share the same rules of worldly prudence to such an extent that the two wind up being indistinguishable from one another—we are obliged to see ourselves as Machiavelli's children. Like him, we are forced to place our trust in the unstable signs that speak to us of a future that might never arrive. * * *

4. The common or public good or welfare.

[Pedullà next argues that Machiavelli's rejection of any simple set of rules for separating good princes from bad ones is tied to the temporal dimension of politics that is symbolized by the figure of the wheel of Fortune. Those at the top always face the risk of going to the bottom, and those at the bottom may well rise to the top. Thanks to the continual movement of the wheel, life on earth has no stability, and for Machiavelli that is especially true in politics. Princes may be adaptable, but none of them is so adaptable that sooner or later, he cannot avoid losing. Still, the turning of Fortune's wheel can also open up unforeseen opportunities, such as the one Machiavelli himself is seizing by writing his treatise for a member of the Medici family that ruled Florence and that also included Pope Leo X. Because human affairs, and especially politics, are always changing, Machiavelli, like other writers in the Mirror for Princes tradition, formulates rules but also argues that in certain circumstances, necessity dictates that they must be broken. Because instability is so widespread, however, Machiavelli's prince runs the risk of appealing to *necessitas* to justify "evil" deeds so often as to cast doubt on the value of the norm itself: the less exceptional the exception becomes, the less one can talk of rules being violated because it seems there are nothing but exceptions.]

To reason by way of norms and exceptions means to admit that the *vita activa* is always concerned about exigencies in conflict with one another: to be generous with everyone and not to empty the coffers of the state; to show oneself to be clement and to maintain discipline among one's soldiers; to keep one's word faithfully and to avoid winding up a prisoner of others' deceptions. In short: to respect the precepts traditionally taught to princes without condemning oneself inevitably to defeat because of them. This approach implies that for Machiavelli and his contemporaries (including authors more inclined to allow rulers to violate the principles of justice), political choices present themselves as being profoundly dramatic. This point is particularly important because it clashes with one of the most widespread views with regard to Machiavelli, namely the idea that one must ascribe to the Florentine thinker the notion of a separation between politics and ethics, as Benedetto Croce put it about ninety years ago in an extremely well-known essay, but which has had the effect of generating an infinite number of mistakes about the historical meaning of *The Prince*. To the contrary of what the Neapolitan philosopher believed, morality and politics are not only tightly connected to one another in the political thought of the fifteenth and sixteenth centuries, but they remain that way in Machiavelli's works. Naturally, to speak of a connection does not mean one is talking about an identification. * * *

In place of the equanimity of Croce's distinctions, Machiavelli insists instead on the perennial conflict of different imperatives: a clash that is entirely opposed to the presumption that politics is autonomous. A person who engages in politics, says *The Prince,* accepts the fact that, because of his choice, he will be exposing himself to both material risks (exile, torture, death) and spiritual ones (damnation). For this reason, when recalling with approval the actions of "new princes" such as Hieron and Cesare Borgia, men who did not hesitate in certain situations to violate the principles of justice, but were thus able to secure the well-being of their own citizens, Machiavelli never forgets that the path they tread is very dangerous: as much from a completely worldly perspective as from the viewpoint of a Christian politician, who, while acting in the world, does not stop thinking about the salvation of his soul. If Machiavelli had limited himself to affirming this, there would not be anything particularly scandalous in his pages. The great difference between *The Prince* and the writings of Machiavelli's contemporaries is that he seeks to persuade his readers that it is necessary to go down this path right to the end, no matter what the cost. And to reinforce this very hypothesis—in the unique reference in his entire treatise to the spiritual dangers to which his "new prince" will expose himself—he goes so far as to suggest that men who set aside the imperatives of ethics and religion in order to achieve incredible results may well be able "to find some remedy with men and with God for their condition" (*The Prince*, VIII). * * *

Perhaps it is precisely because Machiavelli is so obsessed with the uncertainties of the sublunary world that an analogous preoccupation with stability and durability runs through his entire work. It is revealed to us in the first place by his constant use of architectural metaphors, starting with the most famous of all: in the twenty-fifth chapter Machiavelli denounces the faults of the fifteenth-century princes who did not know how to defend themselves against the unforeseen and had not constructed in a timely manner the dikes that were indispensable in order to control the destructive force of Fortune's river. * * *

By contrast, what is much more important, because it is widespread in the treatise from one end to the other, is the image of the *foundations* of the political edifice that the "new prince" plans to build. * * * If we set aside a series of more occasional uses of the word, * * * the architectural metaphor of foundations is utilized by Machiavelli almost always only to present the other key thesis of *The Prince:* the absolute need to win the goodwill of the people. If Lorenzo will be in a position to count on that in times of danger, says Machiavelli reassuringly, then he will recognize that he has "laid good foundations" (chapter 9).* * *

It is here, in the struggle against the contingencies of the world, that the architectural metaphor reveals its primary significance. For the most part, in fact, foundations are not visible, and yet they are the only things that count when the storms of Fortune beat down upon fragile human edifices. In a world dominated by the fluidity of both things and desires, the problem of "laying foundations" is tightly bound to that of "standing firm" (*fermare*) with all of its many diverse meanings: to establish (*fermare*) "a government" (*The Prince,* chapter 8), to firm up (*fermare*) "the spirits of its citizens" (chapter 10), to keep in check (*fermare*) its adversaries, as Julius II was able to do, thanks to his impetuosity (chapter 11), or in general to fix in place (*fermare*) one's own state (chapter 24). As one might expect, however, the verb appears, above all, in connection to military matters, where it describes the condition of the prince who possesses his own army. To wit: "if someone bases his state on the arms of mercenaries, it will never be stable [*fermo*] or secure" (chapter 12), whereas "if he has good arms, he will always have good friends, and internal affairs will always be stable [*ferme*] when external affairs are as well" (chapter 19). * * *

The laying of foundations, however, does not refer only to stability, but to autonomy. It is not a matter of Croce's imaginary "autonomy of politics," which we have seen has very little in common with the categories in *The Prince.* Rather, one should talk about the *autonomy of the politician,* that is, of political man. * * * In this regard as well, the connection is established primarily by means of metaphors. Once they have been excavated in the earth, foundations are completely responsible for supporting a building. They are, in other words, sufficient in themselves and have no need of other architectural elements. In this way, the "laying of foundations" is associated precisely with the imperative of "not being dependent," which is another one of the chief points in Machiavelli's pedagogy. * * *

Machiavelli has no doubts: autonomy depends entirely on having one's own arms (or rather, on one's people who are armed). * * * Thus, the behavior of Cesare Borgia is all the more exemplary, since, initially lacking his own army, he directed all his efforts to obtain one for himself, until—as Machiavelli puts it in one of his magnificent expressions—"he had nothing but his own soldiers and depended only on himself," having "full possession of his own arms" (13). * * *

For Machiavelli, only military autonomy * * * is capable of offering the desired "security," a security—it seems superfluous to recall here—that was so much more important in a time when, thanks to the French and Spanish armies, no one seemed to be able to find shelter from the storm. It is not accidental that the verb with which Machiavelli describes the process through which princes make themselves independent is "to make oneself secure" (*assicurarsi*). In the economy of the treatise, this term alludes to operations that are also quite different from one another, but all of them, finally, have the same objective: to render the prince's condition more stable. * * * The need to make oneself secure thus constitutes one of the strongest arguments in favor of choosing to establish one's foundations on the people rather than on the nobility: in fact, "with the people as his enemy, a prince can never make himself secure because there are too many of them; one can secure oneself against the nobility because they are few," according to the teaching of the Spartan Nabith (9).

As always in Machiavelli, however, the same action can also be seen from the opposite viewpoint. Corresponding to the prince's desire for security there are in fact the analogous aspirations of the other political actors—the people, the nobility, the other princes. * * * In all of his works Machiavelli never stops insisting on their interdependence. * * * We have already seen this in the rejection of Bartolo's semiotics of power, constructed on the basis of abstract principles that hardly ever took the general context into account. In the constantly changing world of politics, no one is ever completely free, that is, has complete control over his own choices, because a majority of his decisions * * * will be constrained ahead of time by the choices made by others. Every abstract precept thus runs the risk of turning out to be futile. Directly out of this reflection on the necessary connections that link individuals to one another and all of them to a time and place, however, there arises the opposing desire in Machiavelli: to teach the prince not to place in others his own hopes for survival in the pitiless struggle for dominance. * * *

For any reader whatsoever in the early years of the sixteenth century, Machiavelli's insistence on the necessity that people "depend on themselves alone" had a very precise meaning: it meant, in other words, that once provided with arms, any prince could easily ignore the legal obligations on which, at least in formal terms, the entire European state-system was based. * * * The "new princes" of the fifteenth century had all pursued, using every means available, the coveted title that would have made them into a little intermediate step along the great political stairway that connected the smallest local existences to the pope and the emperor. For them, the primary objective was to tie themselves to a superior power, or, in other words, to become "dependent": to insert themselves into the system of reciprocal rights and duties that feudal legitimacy entailed. The more a little ruler abandoned the condition of independence in order to get himself recognized as a "liege lord" by one of the great, universal powers, the more—as Machiavelli's contemporaries perceived it—he could go to sleep and enjoy peaceful dreams. * * *

The Prince can also be read as a conscious reaction against this world. By affirming that what we get from others is not really our own and that the only thing we possess is a title, Machiavelli could not have shown himself more skeptical with regard to the system of feudal legitimations into which his contemporaries had already lowered themselves. In fact, it is precisely for this reason that the Florentine ex-Secretary had no interest in creating a constitutional framework for "new princes." In and of themselves, as we have seen, titles are only empty words and in the best case scenario, have only a secondary importance: as in the case of Cesare [Borgia], titles will arrive afterwards, legitimizing a supremacy inscribed directly in the order of things. Why, then, invest so much energy and so much wealth in them? And especially, why "place oneself under obligation," if "the arms of others," to which a state entrusts itself and which ties it to a more powerful ruler, deprive it of power in the very moment that it seems to provide it? * * *

In *The Prince,* the process of achieving autonomy does not concern only the great political powers toward which the new prince could find himself "obligated" (such as the Papacy, the Empire, France, and Spain) or the few Italian states that in 1513 were still in a position to conduct an independent foreign policy (virtually only Genoa, Siena, Ferrara, and Venice). By insisting on "not being dependent on others," Machiavelli actually formulates a more general principle that is valid for the high as well as the low, and for men and institutions as well as the material world. Only by using this master key can one interpret the significance of the chapters on fortresses (*The Prince*, 20) and on the secretary (22–23), which are generally presented as a sort of unexpected descent between the chapters concerned with the scandal involving the princely virtues (15–19) and the three concluding chapters that lead the reader to the final exhortation to free Italy from the barbarians (24–26). Fortresses and secretaries have, in fact, one characteristic in common with the "arms of others": all three give the prince the illusion of being more "secure" about things than he is in reality. * * *

One of the great lessons of *The Prince,* as we have seen, is that without a doubt, a politician must make his own foundation by himself: a large part of Machiavelli's treatise, in fact, does nothing but teach us the ways in which this process of dissolving the ties binding the prince [to others] can be carried to its successful conclusion. Yet, at the same time, independence cannot be the point of departure that is required for political action. Whoever looks to found a "state" will have to concern himself just as much with tying a growing number of supporters to his own project. In other words, in place of the links that bound the "new prince" to his benefactors and allies, new knots must be tied that put him, this time, in a position of dominance after having inverted, though not dissolved, the preceding asymmetrical relationship. * * *

Following in the wake of Cicero (*De officiis* 2.7.23), a long tradition had unanimously confirmed the necessity of pursuing the love of one's fellow-citizens and of remaining wary of using threats as an instrument, but quite frequently, those [writers] who had praised the solidity of the bonds founded on past favors were the same who elsewhere lamented the tendency of men, and especially that of the [common] people, to show themselves to be ungrateful. Machiavelli's clear embracing of a position in favor of fear can be read, then, as an attempt to resolve once and for all this contradiction. If the frequent displays of ingratitude should teach anything, *The Prince* seems to say, it is that love constitutes a link connecting people that is less strong than what its admirers keep repeating about it. * * *

To affirm that "men will always turn out to be wicked for you if they are not forced by some necessity to be good" (*The Prince*, 20) signifies that one is placing one's bet on the threat of pain, but above all, that one is rethinking the question of the bonds [among people, institutions, etc.]. To create a sense of necessity can mean many different things, and Machiavelli, who knows well how much the people appreciate their own "security," would never have been capable of suggesting to the prince that he should transform his own realm into a police state. * * *

Fear is thus only part of the solution to the great problem of the ingratitude and instability of men. As long as love coincides with gratitude pure and simple, it constitutes too weak a foundation to be trusted, in that the person who loves can, at the first series of difficulties, withdraw his own love without suffering any damage. For his own tranquility, the prince must instead place his subjects in the position of wanting him to "preserve himself"; he must act, in other words, so that the interests of all of them come together and that the first ones to hope for his success should be the people. * * *

However strange it may seem, this love that coincides with a solid, confident interest in the future is something that can be imposed on others: in fact, one can place one's trust only in a love that has been imposed on others, or so Machiavelli gives us to understand. The model of this relationship of mutual advantage is presented to us at the end of chapter 9 of *The Prince*: "a wise prince should think of a way by means of which his citizens, always and in every kind of situation, would have need of the state and of him; and then they will always be faithful." * * *

The first readers [of *The Prince*] must have experienced a certain discomfort when confronting affirmations of this sort. On the one side, to be sure, Machiavelli seemed to hold firmly one of the implicit principles of the political thought of the humanists, to wit, that the bond of "mutua caritas,"[5] which, when it ties together the ruler and the ruled, constitutes the best guarantee of stability that one could

5. A mutual love for one another.

desire. *** *The Prince,* however, marks a violent swerving away with respect to fifteenth-century treatises when it transforms love into a matter of "need" which must be artfully inculcated in one's subjects, and especially when, in an explicitly utilitarian manner, there is a decline in a bond that up until that moment political thinkers had preferred to describe using the lexicon of spontaneous affection. Naturally, the humanists were also aware of the good effects of "mutua caritas," and they derived from it a powerful argument to convince princes that they had the opportunity to care for the good of their subjects, but in comparison with them, in Machiavelli the utilitarian goals involved in devoting attention to the people are stated with a harshness that is downright embarrassing. To sum it all up, *The Prince* confirms what Hannibal said in a speech that Livy had him deliver: the "communis utilitas," that is, the welfare of the people, is "societatis maximum vinculum," is the strongest bond in the community (*Ab urbe condita* 36.7). ***

The traditional attitude aimed at constructing as many different ties as there were people *** who wished to bind themselves together. For each one of them, it was supposed, the prince or the republic had to nourish a different connection based on a contractual relationship that imitated the one between lord and vassal. *** For this model, Machiavelli substitutes another one that is completely different, in which citizens recognize one another through their prince, not so much because they are tied to him by his granting them special benefits on an individual basis, but because the entire community experiences—indirectly, but concretely—the positive effects of a government that respects the laws and is capable of guaranteeing the safety of everyone from threats both internal and external. ***

In reality, with his obsession about ties [among people], Machiavelli takes great care to avoid proposing a prince who is completely free with respect to the rights of and his duties toward the collectivity. *** On the contrary, even in the case of monarchies and aristocratic institutions there are actually limits that guarantee the beneficence and continuing survival of the government, as Machiavelli will say explicitly in the *Discourses:* "a prince who can do whatever he wants is insane," and "there is no one who can speak to a wicked prince, nor is there any remedy for that but the sword" (*Discourses* 1.58). *** The birth of a new "state" (even in the more limited sense of achieving supreme power in one), with its new laws and its new institutions, does in fact require the aspiring prince to act "alone if he wants to create a new republic from scratch, or to reform it entirely, going beyond its ancient institutions," as reads the title of *Discourses* 1.9 (composed in defense of Romulus to justify his killing of his brother). As Machiavelli says later on: when confronting a profound crisis, "staying within normal limits is inadequate if ordinary methods are bad; instead, it is necessary to take extraordinary measures, as in the case of resorting to violence and arms, and before all else, to become the prince of that city and to be able to arrange things according to one's own methods" (*Discourses* 1.18). It is uniquely in such difficult situations that the aspiring prince must be free to create and dissolve bonds without finding that, in what concerns him personally, he is forced to answer to anyone at all for his deeds throughout the entire period during which this radical work of refounding the state is required. Only once the parenthesis involving this refounding of the state (with its inevitable episodes of violence) is closed, the question of ties also presents itself anew to him, although at that point exiting from the state of emergency and returning to life as it was before could not be that easy. * * *

Weak ties and strong ties. Ties that restrain and ties that make collective action possible. Ties between individuals and between institutions. A great forest of knots through which the politician must learn how to move prudently: Machiavelli's world is fashioned that way. In short, for these same concepts to show themselves in all their malleability, it will be necessary for Machiavelli to abandon his reflections on principalities in favor of those on republics. * * * The fundamental theory of the *Discourses on the First Decade of Titus Livy*—the theory of the mixed constitution—is nothing other than a grand meditation on the ties that are necessary so that no citizen should take possession of all the power, while avoiding at the same time that the nets and laces securing civic life end up by paralyzing the state inside a system of interlocking vetoes. * * *

For at least thirty years, the most influential interpretations of Machiavelli developed in the Anglophone world—those of John G. A. Pocock and Quentin Skinner—depict the ex-Secretary as a theorist of republican liberty. * * * And yet, should anyone look for an abstract reflection on the sense and the definition of the word *liberty* in *The Prince* or the *Discourses,* he would inevitably wind up disappointed: although Machiavelli surely nourished throughout his life a special affection for "civic life," he does not dwell on this problem, taking for granted that his readers would know what he was talking about. * * *

This silence means a great deal. Without doubt, the "civic life" of Rome always stood as the great model for Machiavelli. And yet, his thought is described rather better if we take it from the other side—seemingly the opposite one—that of the ties on which, for good or for ill, the success or ruin of republics or principalities depend. In short, with no offense intended toward any of his most qualified interpreters, in Machiavelli there is no theory of liberty (at least in the terms of contemporary political philosophy); instead, in his writings we can find an extremely detailed set of reflections on the interconnections [among people and institutions] that make liberty possible. * * *

Much more than with poisonings and knifings, as the anti-Machiavellian tradition has repeated for centuries, *The Prince* thus has to do with the loosening and strengthening of knots more than with anything else. In terms of ties it will even be possible to explain as well the particular situation in which Machiavelli found himself with respect to the two great anthropological paradigms by means of which the summoning of men to social life has been explained. The ancient fable (Aristotle) would have individuals moved to unite themselves as a group by an irrepressible drive towards sociability which has its origin in nature itself, * * * evolving little by little from the family toward ever more complex communities. The modern fable (Hobbes) describes, by contrast, how the first men, scattered in the forests like wild animals and engaged in a difficult competition for a survival that is destined to last only until the point is reached when, in the name of peace and security, single individuals give up their own liberty through a social contract involving their subjection that ratifies the beginning of communal living by means of a tie that is no longer natural, but artificial.

For Machiavelli, a third model has equal weight. In his pages there is nothing or almost nothing said about any originary moment, but the fact that there is no State to be reached as a definitive landing place means that neither is there a starting point from which we are destined to take our leave once and for all. The ties to be strengthened and loosened represent precisely the nature of politics, where no achievement is spontaneous and, above all, is going to last forever (because there is no natural foundation of sociability to guarantee it), but where everything proceeds by mean of corrections, adjustments, hypotheses, new initiatives, and false starts. And this happens because, when all is said and done, all positions are reversible, and for every tie that fails, one can always substitute another one, unforeseeable and unforeseen, but perhaps less unforeseeable and less unforeseen by those who had dedicated themselves to an attentive reading of stories from antiquity.

Niccolò Machiavelli: A Chronology of His Life and Times

1469	Niccolò di Bernardo dei Machiavelli is born on May 3, the third of four children and the first son of Bernardo Machiavelli and Bartolomea di Stefano Nelli. The Machiavelli family, believed to have been descended from the marquesses of Tuscany, had been one of the more prominent ones in Florence since the thirteenth century, but Bernardo, a doctor of laws, is professionally unsuccessful and is barred from holding public office as an insolvent debtor.
1475	Bernardo receives a copy of Livy's *History of Rome* from the printer for whom he created the index.
1470s–90s	Niccolò is given something like a typical humanist education, learning Latin and perhaps some Greek, but who educated him and how he was educated remain unknown.
1478	The Pazzi Conspiracy: an attempt by members of the Pazzi family to kill Lorenzo the Magnificent and his brother Giuliano de' Medici. Lorenzo is wounded, but survives; his brother does not. The Pazzi family is banished from Florence, and Lorenzo further consolidates his rule over the city.
1486	Bernardo assigns Niccolò the task of binding his books, including Livy's *History*.
1492	Christopher Columbus, sailing under the banner of Ferdinand of Aragon and Isabella of Castile, "discovers" the New World. Ferdinand succeeds in expelling the Moors from their last stronghold in Granada in southern Spain.

In Florence, Lorenzo the Magnificent de' Medici dies on April 8.

Rodrigo Borgia (de Borja) is elected pope on August 11, taking the name of Alexander VI. He has four children: Giovanni, a condottiere (mercenary captain) who is murdered in 1497; Cesare, who is a condottiere and replaces his brother in 1497 as the head of the papal army and is presented as an ideal prince in *The Prince;* Lucrezia, who is rumored (none of the rumors has been substantiated) to have slept with her father and her brother Cesare and to have murdered people with poison she kept in a ring; and Gioffre, who rules the tiny state of Squillace in Calabria as a feudal vassal of Naples.

1494 The French king, Charles VIII, invades the peninsula in order to claim the Kingdom of Naples, which he captures the next year and partitions with the Spanish king, Ferdinand of Aragon.

Lorenzo de' Medici's son Piero meets with Charles when he invades Tuscany, accepts all of Charles's demands, surrendering several castles as well as Pisa and Livorno to him, is branded a traitor when he returns to Florence in November, and is forced to flee the city with the rest of the Medici family.

Florence is proclaimed a "popular" republic under the leadership of the charismatic Dominican preacher Girolamo Savonarola, the head of the Convent of San Marco, who saw Charles as God's instrument to punish the Church for its corruption and seeks to turn Florence into an ideal Christian state.

About this time, Niccolò begins working as a clerk in the Second Chancery, the bureaucratic office in the Florentine government that was concerned with diplomatic and military matters.

1495 Charles VIII is driven out of Italy after a number of city-states as well as Spain and the Holy Roman Empire, frightened by Charles's successes, form the League of Venice against him on March 31.

1497 Five Florentines, Medici sympathizers, are put to death by Savonarola without being granted the right to appeal. Public opinion begins to turn against him.

Savonarola is excommunicated by Pope Alexander VI on May 12.

1498 Savonarola is brought to trial in March by the Signoria, the governing body of Florence, and after being tortured, is condemned to death, then hanged and burned at the stake together with two of his disciples on May 23.

On June 19, Niccolò is made the Secretary (essentially the head) of the Second Chancery. As such, he is also the secretary to The Ten of Peace and Liberty, the committee overseeing military and foreign affairs.

1499 The French king, Louis XII, who succeeded Charles VIII in 1498, invades Italy and occupies Milan on October 6, which the French would hold, almost without interruption, for the next twelve years.

1500 Louis XII takes Naples, but, worried about seeing France invaded by Spain, signs the Treaty of Granada on November 11, dividing Naples with the Spanish.

Bernardo dies in May.

In July Niccolò is sent on his first foreign mission to the court of Louis XII in France.

1501 Niccolò marries Marietta Corsini. He will have four surviving sons and a daughter with her.

1502 Niccolò is sent on diplomatic missions to Cesare Borgia in June and October.

Piero Soderini is made the *Gonfaloniere a vita* (Chief Magistrate for Life) of the Florentine Republic in September.

1503 Pope Alexander VI dies on August 18 and is succeeded on September 22 by Francesco Todeschini Piccolomini as Pius III, who dies on October 18.

Pius III is succeeded by Giuliano della Rovere on November 1, who takes the name of Julius II and rules until his death on February 21, 1513.

Without the support of his father as pope, Cesare Borgia is imprisoned in Naples and is later transferred to Spain, where he is eventually freed and serves as a condottiere for the king of Navarre. He dies in an ambush in March 1507.

1504 Niccolò writes his *Decennale primo* (*The First Decade*), a history in verse of the first ten years of the Florentine Republic (i.e., 1494–1504).

Niccolò is sent on a diplomatic mission to the court of Louis XII in January.

1506 Louis XII signs the Treaty of Blois on September 22, by which he retains Milan and Genoa, while the Spanish get Naples.

Niccolò persuades Soderini to let him create a citizen militia, including men from the *contrada,* the countryside around Florence.

1507 Niccolò is sent on a diplomatic mission in December to the Holy Roman Emperor Maximilian I, passing through the German-speaking areas of Switzerland on his way there.

1508 Pope Julius II, joining France, Spain, and the Holy Roman Empire, forms the League of Cambrai on December 10 against Venice.

Niccolò writes his *Rapporto delle cose della Magna* (*Report on German Affairs*) based on what he had observed in Switzerland and Austria.

1509 The League of Cambrai (mainly the French) defeats the Venetians at the battle of Agnadello (Vailà) on May 14.

The Florentine citizen militia, led by Niccolò, takes the city of Pisa on June 8.

Niccolò writes the *Decennale secondo* (*The Second Decade*) on the history of the Florentine Republic (1504–14), but work on it is interrupted, and he never completes it.

1510 Worried about France's growing power, Pope Julius II forms the Holy League against France with Spain, the Holy Roman Empire, Venice, and England.

In June, Niccolò is sent on a diplomatic mission to France in a futile attempt to persuade the French to allow Florence to remain neutral in its struggle with the papacy and Spain.

1512 The French win the battle of Ravenna on April 11 but lose their best captain, Gaston de Foix, and are driven from Milan in August by Swiss mercenaries working for the Holy League.

Charles V's army invades Italy in the late summer and marches on Florence, defeating Florentine troops, which include many members of Niccolò's citizen militia, at Prato, after which partisans of the Medici, led by Cardinal Giovanni de' Medici, force the Signoria to restore the Medici, led by Giuliano de' Medici, to power on September 16.

Niccolò loses his position as the Secretary of the Second Chancery on November 7 and three days later is exiled from Florence but refused permission to leave Florentine territory. He begins an eight-year exile from the city on his little farm at Sant'Andrea in Percussina near the town of San Casciano, south of Florence.

1513 Niccolò's name is found on a list of conspirators against the Medici; he is arrested on February 12 and tortured, but released on March 13 after a general amnesty for political prisoners is proclaimed to celebrate the election on March 11 of Giovanni de' Medici as Pope Leo X.

The French are routed by the Swiss at the battle of Novara on June 6 and withdraw from the peninsula.

Niccolò begins the writing of the *Discorsi* (*Discourses*), probably finishing it in 1517.

Niccolò interrupts his work on the *Discourses* to write *Il principe* (*The Prince*), probably finishing it in 1515 when manuscript copies of it begin circulating.

1515 The French king, Francis I, invades Italy and with his Venetian allies defeats the Swiss at the battle of Marignano on September 13–14.

1516 The Dutch Humanist Desiderius Erasmus publishes *The Education of a Christian Prince,* an example of a typical work in the *Speculum principis* (Mirror for Princes) tradition.

The English Humanist and statesman Thomas More publishes *Utopia*, the idealistic vision of a perfect state, the kind of vision Machiavelli denounces at the start of Chapter 15 in *The Prince.*

Giuliano de' Medici dies on March 17, and Niccolò dedicates *The Prince* to Lorenzo de' Medici instead.

On September 13, the Treaty of Noyon splits northern Italy between France and Venice.

1517 The German theologian Martin Luther posts his Ninety-Five Theses on the door of the castle church in Wittenberg, Germany, on October 31; this marks the beginning of the Protestant Reformation.

1518 Niccolò most likely writes his original comedy *La mandragola* (*The Mandrake Root*), satirizing Florence and its rulers. He also writes his one novella, *Belfagor arcidiavolo* (*The Arch-Devil Belfagor*), sometime between 1518 and 1527.

1519 The Spanish king, Charles V, is elected Holy Roman Emperor on June 28.

1520 In March a meeting is arranged between Niccolò and Cardinal Giulio de' Medici in Lucca, thus beginning Niccolò's rapprochement with the family. Niccolò is invited to advise the Medici on the best form of government for Florence and produces the *Discursus florentinarum rerum* (*Discourse on Florentine Affairs*) for Giulio in late 1520 or early 1521.

Niccolò is sent to Lucca in July by Giulio de' Medici to deal with a case of bankruptcy; he writes *La vita di Castruccio Castracani da Lucca* (*The Life of Castruccio Castracani of Lucca*), finishing it by August 25.

On November 8 Giulio has the *Studio fiorentino* (University of Florence) appoint Niccolò the official historiographer of the city and commissions him to write a history of the city.

1521 Niccolò publishes his *Arte della guerra* (*The Art of War*), a dialogue set in the gardens of the Rucellai family, referred to as the Orti Oricellari.

Niccolò is sent to the town of Carpi by the Florentine government on May 21 to negotiate the separation of the Franciscans' monasteries in Florentine territory from the rest of their monasteries in Tuscany. In a letter of May 14, he was also asked by the Masters of the Wool Merchants Guild to arrange for a preacher to come and preach in Florence during Lent.

1523 On November 19, Giulio de' Medici is elected pope and takes the name Clement VII.

1524 Niccolò writes *Clizia,* a free reworking of the Roman playwright Plautus's *Casina;* it is put on the following January.

1525 Francis I invades Italy and is decisively beaten at Pavia on February 2; he is captured, taken to Spain, and the next year forced to sign the Treaty of Madrid by which he renounces his claims to Italy and Flanders and cedes Burgundy to Charles V.

Niccolò writes the *Discorso o dialogo intorno a la nostra lingua* (*Discourse or Dialogue on Our Language*).

In June Niccolò presents his *Istorie fiorentine* (*History of Florence*) to Giulio de' Medici, now Pope Clement VII, in Rome.

1526 On March 22, Francis I repudiates the Treaty of Madrid and forms the League of Cognac with Clement VII, Florence, the Sforza of Milan, and Venice against Spain and the Holy Roman Empire.

In April Niccolò is made secretary to the commission in charge of the fortification of the walls of Florence.

1527 Charles V sends an army into Italy under Charles de Bourbon to attack Rome, which falls on May 6 and is brutally sacked for a week.

In May Florence throws out the Medici and reestablishes the Republic.

Still refused an office in the new government, Niccolò dies on June 27.

1528 In April Francis I sends an army by way of Genoa to besiege Naples, but the Genoese rebel and join Charles V, and the French army besieging Naples is decimated by the plague.

1529 On June 21, French forces coming to assist Francis are decisively defeated by the army of Charles V at the Battle of Landriano.

France signs the Treaty of Cambrai on August 5, renouncing all claims in Italy; the French will, however, invade Italy several more times in the next two decades.

1531 The *Discourses* is published by Antonio Blado d'Asola in Rome.

1532 *The Prince* and *The Life of Castruccio Castracani* are published together by Antonio Blado d'Asola in Rome.

1559 The Treaty of Cateau-Cambrésis is signed on April 3 between France and Spain. France yields

Milan and the Kingdom of the Two Sicilies to Spain, thus marking its definitive expulsion from Italy and completing Spain's domination of the peninsula.

1564 Niccolò's works are put on the Index of Forbidden Books by the Church.

1569 On August 21 the Grand Duchy of Tuscany is created. Cosimo I de' Medici (1519–1574), who was the duke of Florence from 1537, now becomes the Grand Duke of Tuscany.

Selected Bibliography

• indicates items included or excerpted in this Norton Critical Edition.

Because this book is aimed at an Anglophone reading audience, the suggestions for further reading are largely limited to books and articles in English; a few key works in Italian have also been included. This bibliography is not exhaustive but merely indicates materials that are historically important for Machiavelli studies and that I have found personally rewarding.

Ascoli, Albert R., and Victoria Kahn, editors. *Machiavelli and the Discourse of Literature.* Ithaca, NY: Cornell UP, 1993.

Bàrberi-Squarotti, Giorgio. *La forma tragica del "Principe" e altri saggi sul Machiavelli.* Florence: Olschki, 1963.

Benner, Erica. *Machiavelli's Ethics.* Princeton, NJ: Princeton UP, 2009.

• ———. *Machiavelli's "Prince": A New Reading.* Oxford: Oxford UP, 2013.

• Berlin, Isaiah. "The Originality of Machiavelli." In *Against the Current: Essays in the History of Ideas,* edited by Henry Hardy, 2nd ed. Princeton, NJ: Princeton UP, 2013, pp. 33–100. (This essay is an expanded version of "The Question of Machiavelli," first published in *The New York Review of Books,* November 4, 1971.)

Biow, Douglas. "Open Secrets: The Place of the Renaissance Secretary." In *Doctors, Ambassadors, Secretaries: Humanism and Professions in Renaissance Italy.* Chicago: U of Chicago P, 2002, pp. 155–80.

Black, Robert. *Machiavelli.* Abington-on-Thames, UK: Routledge, 2013.

Bock, Gisela, Quentin Skinner, and Maurizio Viroli, editors. *Machiavelli and Republicanism.* Cambridge: Cambridge UP, 1990.

Chabod, Federico. *Machiavelli and the Renaissance,* translated by David Moore. New York: Harper & Row, 1958.

Cox, Virginia. "Machiavelli and the *Rhetorica ad Herennium:* Deliberative Rhetoric in *The Prince.*" *The Sixteenth Century Journal* 28 (1997): 1109–41.

Fido, Franco. "Machiavelli in His Time and Ours." *Italian Quarterly* 13 (1970): 3–21.

Fleisher, Martin, editor. *Machiavelli and the Nature of Political Thought.* New York: Atheneum, 1972.

Frazier, Alison K. "Machiavelli, Trauma, and the Scandal of *The Prince*: An Essay in Speculative History." In *History in the Comic Mode: Medieval Communities and the Matter of Person,* edited by Rachel Fulton and Bruce W. Holsinger. New York: Columbia UP, 2007, pp. 192–202, 348–52.

Garver, Eugene. *Machiavelli and the History of Prudence.* Madison: U of Wisconsin P, 1987.

Geerken, John N. "Machiavelli's Moses and Renaissance Politics." *Journal of the History of Ideas* 60 (1999): 579–95.

Gilbert, Allan H. *Machiavelli's "Prince" and Its Forerunners: "The Prince" as a Typical Book "de Regimine Principum."* Durham, NC: Duke UP, 1938.

Gilbert, Felix. *Machiavelli and Guicciardini: Politics and History in Sixteenth-Century Florence*. Princeton, NJ: Princeton UP, 1965.

Greene, Thomas M. "The End of Discourse in Machiavelli's *Prince*." *Yale French Studies* 67 (1984): 57–71.

Hale, John R. *Machiavelli and Renaissance Italy*. New York: Collier, 1963.

Hexter, J. H. "*Il Principe* and *lo stato*." *Studies in the Renaissance* 4 (1956): 113–38.

• Hörnqvist, Mikael. *Machiavelli and Empire*. Cambridge: Cambridge UP, 2004.

• Hulliung, Mark. *Citizen Machiavelli*. Princeton, NJ: Princeton UP, 1983. Rpt. New Brunswick, NJ: Transaction Publishers, 2015.

Kahn, Victoria. *Machiavellian Rhetoric: From the Counter-Reformation to Milton*. Princeton, NJ: Princeton UP, 1994.

• ———. "Revisiting Agathocles." *The Review of Politics* 75 (2013): 557–72.

———. "*Virtù* and the Example of Agathocles in Machiavelli's *Prince*." *Representations* 13 (1986): 63–83.

Lukes, Timothy J. "Lionizing Machiavelli." *The American Political Science Review* 95 (2001): 561–75.

Mansfield, Harvey. *Machiavelli's Virtue*. Chicago: U of Chicago P, 1996.

McCanles, Michael. *The Discourse of "Il Principe."* Malibu: Undena Publications, 1983.

McCormick, John P. *Machiavellian Democracy*. Cambridge: Cambridge UP, 2011.

Najemy, John M. *Between Friends: Discourses of Power and Desire in the Machiavelli-Vettori Letters of 1513–1515*. Princeton, NJ: Princeton UP, 1993.

• ———. "Language and *The Prince*." In *Texts in Culture: Niccolò Machiavelli's "Prince": New Interdisciplinary Essays*, edited by Martin Coyle. Manchester: Manchester UP, 1995, pp. 89–114.

———. "Machiavelli and Cesare Borgia: A Reconsideration of Chapter 7 of *The Prince*." *The Review of Politics* 75 (2013): 539–55.

———. "Papirius and the Chickens, or Machiavelli on the Necessity of Interpreting Religion." *Journal of the History of Ideas* 60 (1999): 659–81.

Parel, Anthony. *The Machiavellian Cosmos*. New Haven, CT: Yale UP, 1992.

• Pedullà, Gabriele. "Introduzione." Niccolò Machiavelli, *Il Principe, edizione del cinquecentennale, con traduzione moderna di Carmine Donzelli, Introduzione e commento di Gabriele Pedullà*. Rome: Donzelli, 2013, pp. xi–civ.

• Pitkin, Hanna F. *Fortune Is a Woman: Gender and Politics in the Thought of Niccolò Machiavelli*. Berkeley: U of California P, 1984.

• Pocock, J. G. A. *The Machiavellian Moment: Florentine Political Thought and the Atlantic Republican Tradition*. Princeton, NJ: Princeton UP, 1975.

Price, Russell. "The Senses of *Virtù* in Machiavelli." *European Studies Review* 3 (1973): 315–45.

———. "The Theme of *Gloria* in Machiavelli." *Renaissance Quarterly* 30 (1977): 588–631.

Raimondi, Ezio. "Machiavelli and the Rhetoric of the Warrior." *Modern Language Notes* 92 (1977): 1–16.

———. *Politica e commedia: Dal Beroaldo al Machiavelli*. Bologna: Il Mulino, 1972.

Rebhorn, Wayne A. *Foxes and Lions: Machiavelli's Confidence Men*. Ithaca, NY: Cornell UP, 1988.

• ———. "Machiavelli's *Prince* in the Epic Tradition." In *The Cambridge Companion to Machiavelli*, edited by John M. Najemy. Cambridge: Cambridge UP, 2010, pp. 80–93.

———. "Machiavelli's *Vita di Castruccio Castracani*: Charismatic Spectacles and the Irony of History." In *Opening the Borders: Inclusivity and Early Modern Studies, Essays in Honor of James V. Mirollo*, edited by Peter Herman. Newark: U of Delaware P, 1999, pp. 54–82.

Ridolfi, Robert. *The Life of Niccolò Machiavelli*, translated by Cecil Grayson. Chicago: U of Chicago P, 1963.

Sasso, Gennaro. *Machiavelli e Cesare Borgia: Storia di un giudizio.* Rome: Ateneo, 1966.

———. *Niccolò Machiavelli: Storia del suo pensiero politico.* Naples: Istituto italiano per gli studi storici, 1958.

• Skinner, Quentin. *The Foundations of Political Thought.* Volume 1: *The Renaissance*. Cambridge: Cambridge UP, 1998. Originally published 1978.

———. *Machiavelli.* New York: Hill & Wang, 1981.

Strauss, Leo. *Thoughts on Machiavelli.* Glencoe, IL: Free Press, 1959.

• Viroli, Maurizio. *From Politics to Reason of State: The Acquisition and Transformation of the Language of Politics 1250–1600.* Cambridge: Cambridge UP, 1992.

———. *Machiavelli.* Oxford: Oxford UP, 1998.

———. *Redeeming "The Prince": The Meaning of Machiavelli's Masterpiece.* Princeton, NJ: Princeton UP, 2014.

Whitfield, John Humphreys. *Discourses on Machiavelli.* Cambridge: Cambridge UP, 1969.

Index

Note: Rome and Florence (the Roman empire, the Roman Senate, the Roman armies; the Florentine people, the Florentine government, the city of Florence, the army and allies of Florence) constitute allusions too frequent and too ill-defined to be included in this index. Also omitted are passing references to large national unities, such as Spain, France, Germany, and England. For individual works by Machiavelli, see entries under his name.